P9-APE-078

CHICAGO REVIEW PRESS

Library of Congress Cataloging-in-Publication Data

Kent, Sherry.
    Sweet home Chicago: the real city guide / Sherry Kent, Mary
Szpur, Tem Horwitz—3rd ed.
        p. cm.
    Rev. ed. of: Sweet home Chicago2. 2nd ed., expanded & rev.
c1977.
    Includes index.
    ISBN 1-556-52006-9 : $8.95
    1. Chicago (Ill.)—Description—1981—Guide-books. I. Szpur,
Mary. II. Horwitz, Tem. III. Sweet home Chicago2. IV. Title.
F548.18.K46 1987
917.73'110433—dc19   87-15633
                                                                 CIP

Cover painting: "Chicago Fire," by Joe Hindley, watercolor, 1981.
J. Hindley Studio, Chicago.

CONTENTS

INTRODUCTION

Chicago is on the rise. With people moving back into the city, buildings going up all over, a reform government firmly in place, community groups spearheading efforts to improve run-down neighborhoods, and our actors and musicians getting the national attention they deserve, this country is sitting up and taking notice of Chicago. Not too long ago, some people were writing this city off as a rust belt has-been. But Chicago has come back—strong, roaring, and robust.

Chicago is, above all, an easy place to live in. You can get around without a car, you can live close to the center of the city, and you don't need to spend a lot of money to have a good time. This is a city unburdened by pretensions—celebrity just isn't a big deal here. Chicago is not a place where old money or good bloodlines mean much. Yet for all its down-to-earth qualities, Chicago is also a first-rate, world-class center for art, music, theater, business, and education.

The book was put together by us and the contributing authors, most of them friends or acquaintances, longtime residents of this city, who, like us, know Chicago, flaws and all, and love it. (All unsigned chapters were written by us.) We've gone to great lengths to make this book as accurate as possible, but things change quickly here, and information becomes obsolete before you know it—we realize there are bound to be errors.

In those chapters—such as restaurants—where other guidebooks list everything available, we have been selective, mentioning only personal favorites or places offering good values for the money. In those areas where a combination of broad overview and detailed analysis seemed appropriate—such as theater, art, and literary life—we have been more comprehensive.

We have tried to be personal and honest, each of us writing from our own viewpoint. We have also tried to write about the south side and west side as well as the north side, since the trendier parts of the city seem to get the lion's share of media coverage. The book is written for visitors and residents alike, for everyone who wants to know all sides of the city.

Chicago is an old city, a beautiful city, a quintessentially American city, with a gorgeous lakeshore, an impressive downtown, and logically planned boulevards and streets. The sense of community is very strong. Our politicians make national news. Our incredible mix of Slavs, blacks, and Hispanics, Asians, Indians, and Irish, Germans, Italians, and many other groups are taken for granted by Chicagoans, but have surprised many an out-of-towner. Above all, Chicago is an open city, ripe for exploring. Go check it out!

—Sherry Kent and Mary Szpur

P.S.   This guidebook is the third edition of *Sweet Home Chicago*. The first two editions (which came out in 1974 and 1977) were written with a countercultural slant. But times have changed, we have changed, and our edition

1

reflects these changes. Although we've moved the book closer to the main-stream, our edition contains some of the best qualities of the first two: practical information you won't get in glossy guidebooks, written in a friendly, casual style by people who know it from the inside.

THE
REAL CITY

Schoenhofen Memorial at Graceland Cemetery.

THE OTHER
TOP TEN SIGHTS

Maybe you've already seen all the standard tourist sights—the museums, the skyscrapers, the Water Tower, the lakeshore. Or maybe you find traditional sightseeing a bit sterile. In either case, we've come up with a few alternate sights and activities that we think are closer to the real Chicago.

LOWER WACKER DRIVE

Down in the bowels of the city, under Michigan Avenue and Wacker Drive, lives Chicago's underground world. The bright lights of Michigan and Wacker have their dark, lower-level counterparts: streets that run along the same routes, but at the level of the river, where the dark, dank basements of the big buildings are. A secret world unto itself, lit only by green and yellow fluorescent light, the city's lower depths follow the winding streets curving to follow the river. There's no commercial activity here—except for Billy Goat Tavern, a real basement kind of place. Most of the action takes place on the loading docks: this is where the big buildings above, such as the Tribune Tower, get their daily necessities. The thrill of Lower Wacker and Michigan is in the journey through this eerie, curving world under the turmoil above.

For pedestrians, the underground is a sheltered path for walking north or south under Michigan Avenue, safe from the rain, wind, and snow. For motorists, Lower Wacker and Lower Michigan are short-cuts for avoiding the congested traffic above. The short-cut runs from 500 North (Grand Avenue) to 500 South (Congress Parkway and the interchanges for the Eisenhower, Dan Ryan, and Kennedy Expressways). Both pedestrians and motorists who use these routes get unusual views of the city from the bottom up, and of the river at its shores.

Lower Michigan and Lower Wacker were built according to the Burnham Plan of 1909 for Chicago, primarily to alleviate the terrible traffic jams that were making driving downtown chaotic. The double-decked Michigan Avenue bridge was built to take some of the burden off the Wabash Avenue bridge further west. Commercial vehicles were to use the lower level, leaving the upper level for car traffic. This double-tiered design for a bridge was a first, and was later adopted the world over. The Burnham Plan also called for a double-decked circular road to ring the Loop; Wacker Drive was the only part of this plan that was finished. The other two parts were to have been underground levels of the Eisenhower Expressway and Lake Shore Drive.

By car, getting onto Lower Wacker Drive is easier said than done, and a complete mystery to the uninitiated. Only certain streets go all the way through to descend onto Lower Wacker Drive; a few of them are: Grand Avenue, Kinzie Street, Illinois Street, Randolph Street, and the Wacker

Drive exit off the Eisenhower Expressway. To see Lower Wacker for the first time, try entering from Grand Avenue, and don't forget to turn your lights on as you descend into the depths.

You are driving directly underneath Michigan Avenue. If you were on foot, you could enter some of the buildings above—note how their addresses are posted. About one block before you reach the Michigan Avenue bridge, you'll see **Billy Goat Tavern,** a great place for cheeseburgers and late night conversations. Mike Royko and John Belushi made Billy Goat's famous. John Belushi also made a star out of Lower Wacker Drive by featuring a car chase scene through these streets in *Blues Brothers*.

Turn right just after you cross the river. You are now directly underneath Wacker Drive. Lower Wacker follows the curve of the river for a long, long way. All along the road, you'll see views of the big river buildings from the belly up—**Marina Towers, Merchandise Mart, Union Station**—and boats at your level on the river. It's dark as night except for the glowing green lights.

You can exit at several places or travel all the way to the end—where the Eisenhower Expressway starts (just before it runs under the Post Office Building) and where you can catch the interchanges onto the Dan Ryan and Kennedy Expressways. Don't forget to turn your lights off as you leave (if it's daylight).

By foot, Lower Wacker Drive can be experienced by walking along the river for a bird's eye view of the waterway, the barges that flow down it, and the buildings that flank it.

THE RAVENSWOOD EL

The Ravenswood elevated train is the best combination roller coaster/sightseeing car ride in the city. If you have guests in town, don't drive them to the Loop, take the Ravenswood. The best views can be seen going south from the north side. Try to sit in the front car, facing front (south). You'll probably have to beat someone else to the seat.

What's so great about an el? Think of it as a ride, not as public transportation. The el takes plenty of sharp turns and jogs, and speeds up and slows down to add drama to the ride. It passes through urban canyons and a lot of nice scenery. Even Hollywood has recognized the thrills of the Ravenswood and paid it tribute recently by filming a chase scene in the 1985 movie *Running Scared* on the tracks of the Ravenswood el when it crosses the Chicago River. That panoramic scene was the best one in the movie.

The best part of the Ravenswood is between Armitage, when the Ravenswood diverges from the route it has been sharing with the Howard el, and the stop at Clark and Lake. From that point, when it circles the Loop, the sights are still good but less spectacular.

Going south from Armitage at a good clip, the Ravenswood slows up to make an S-shaped series of sharp turns over North Avenue. As you sway to the left, then right, look down to see how what used to be a bombed-out area is changing hands to become gentrified and expensive. Like it or not, this is how Chicago is changing. You can see the Loop from its backside at this point. It's a great view that gets better as you come closer.

You'll travel east for a few blocks, edging close to the lake. Then, after the Sedgwick stop, you'll make a 90 degree turn south, heading straight for the River North area. Look on either side of you at the first of several canyons of buildings. Indulge your voyeuristic self by staring boldly into the private residences and businesses that line either side of the el tracks. Along this part of the Ravenswood line, you'll see cubicles and work spaces of new-money offices, as well as floors filled to overflowing with machinery that does who-knows-what.

You'll make a few more gentle turns at the Chicago stop. The billboards and graphics posted here for el riders are usually visually arresting. Look out the window just past the Chicago stop at the streets below to see the brilliant banners of the galleries in the River North art gallery district, as well as the neon signs of some of the trendiest new restaurants in Chicago.

Now you enter another canyon of buildings on your way into the Loop. It gets darker in the car as the structures block the sun. As you feel the el car curve to the east, look west. What the train is curving around is the huge, massive Merchandise Mart building, an enormous hulking presence (owned by the Kennedy family) flanking the Chicago River. The Mart houses, among other businesses and offices, thousands of showrooms for furnishings.

After the train rounds the bend created by the Merchandise Mart, you come to the best part of the ride—out into the light to cross the Chicago River. This is the certainly the most flattering view of the river and one of the best of the city. To your west, you'll see the gentle green curve of the 333 N. Wacker Drive building, reflecting the river on the sweep of its sides. It's a lovely sight. Even the cement bridges look good here. To your east, you'll see the corncobs of Marina Towers, and further down, the white of the buildings near Michigan Avenue. This view never fails to take our breath away. Once again, Hollywood must have seen eye to eye with us, because one of the climactic scenes from the film *Code of Silence* was filmed here: Chuck Norris's fall off of a Ravenswood el car into the Chicago River.

At this point, the el turns sharply east to wend its way through more city canyons. As the Ravenswood circles the Loop (the area it circles is the official Loop, and the loop made by the train is how our downtown got its nickname), you'll see the blue and red panels of the State of Illinois Center, the remodeled Chicago Theater on State Street, the stores and offices on the second floor of buildings on Wabash Avenue (good places to observe people working), the crowds walking towards Michigan Avenue, and the Board of Trade and Board of Options Exchange on Van Buren. The cycle starts again after the train finishes the loop at Wells Street.

All this, for only a dollar.

CITY COUNCIL

City Hall, 121 N. LaSalle, second floor

Chicago politics are by turn exciting, infuriating, embarrassing, hilarious. Our local politics make national news. Our politicians are so outrageous, they make our city famous. They are our Rocky Mountains, our Eiffel Tower, our Love Canal, all rolled into one. Our politicians are a unique breed, to say the least. Even if politics make you glassy eyed with boredom, attend a city council meeting, where the mayor and the aldermen decide how to run the city. Especially when a controversial issue is slated for review, the visit will awaken your sense of wonder at the silliness of human beings when egos and power collide.

A lot of bad blood has flowed freely at city council meetings in the past. Aldermen have shoved each other and called each other nasty names. They have mutinied and stormed out of meetings, calling the mayor a liar and a cheat. They have been heckled by the audience and have yelled insults back. This is all run of the mill to anyone who watches the TV news in Chicago. There have also been some amusing moments. Aldermen have slept soundly, ignoring their constituents in the viewing areas. They have shamelessly played to the press packed into the "press pen" along one wall, directing their speeches to the cameras instead of to the audience. It looks ridiculous.

A local comedian, Aaron Freeman, made his initial career based on a clever satire of the city council when meetings were at their most acrimonious in recent years—when Harold Washington was first elected mayor and was fighting for control of the council. Freeman's routine, which he called "Council Wars" after the *Star Wars* movies about good and evil forces warring in space, featured Harold Skytalker and villain Darth Vrdolyak in starring roles.

City council meetings are held on the second floor of City Hall, at 121 N. LaSalle (LaSalle and Washington). The council chamber is a big green room whose style recalls the chamber at the United Nations. (The similarities stop there, though—the U.N. General Assembly agrees far more often than our city council.) All meetings are open to the public, and people do show up. The public can sit on the main floor behind the aldermen or in the balcony. The meetings are held about once a week, on an ad-hoc basis. There is no set day for council meetings—call 744-3081 to find out when and at what time the next meeting is. Tack on about an hour to the time they tell you, because city council meetings never start on time.

Certain issues bring out big crowds. The audience is not supposed to offer their opinions, but sometimes they do anyway. Come and join the show. The whole world may not be watching, but if the show is good enough, all of greater Chicago and northern Illinois will be watching at 5, 6, and 10.

NAVY PIER

Grand Avenue at the Lake

The city recently ran a campaign called "Come Back to Navy Pier," encouraging people to take advantage of the lovely 5/8 mile-long pier at Grand Avenue. Undecided about what to do with Navy Pier (no longer used as a pier), the city's campaign was another in a long line of ideas for how to use this unusual structure. We hope this campaign is a success, but not so much so that Navy Pier becomes overrun with people. Navy Pier's charms are simple: on a warm summer day it's very pleasant walk along the promenade that runs along the Pier (about a mile long), watching the sailboats on the lake, catching Lake Michigan fish, enjoying the unique view of the skyline. Your view of the city from the end of the Pier is just as nice as what those people can see from their sailboats, and you won't get wet. From here you also get a good view of the locks that control the Chicago River and make it flow backwards, an engineering feat that was quite a marvel in the early part of this century.

At the end of the pier is a gorgeous horseshoe-shaped auditorium, East End Ballroom, that was remodeled a few years back at considerable expense. (You may have seen this auditorium in the film *The Color of Money*, filmed here in 1986.) The curves along the dome-shaped ceiling are outlined with small lights. The wall facing the lake at the promenade's end is covered with curving windows that flood the room with natural light and allow a beautiful sight of sun, water and sky. Concerts and exhibitions (like the annual International ArtExpo held in May) are held in the auditorium, and the view is spectacular. Singer Bonnie Koloc told her audience at a folk music concert held in the auditorium that she had never sung in a place where the view was so magnificent—all she could see out the windows as she sang were sky, lake, and boats.

Navy Pier is probably the nicest, quietest place to enjoy Lake Michigan close to the Loop. One reason for its tranquility is the restriction on traffic (no cars are allowed). You have to walk, bike, or jog over a mile out and back along the promenade, a physical effort not everyone is willing to make. Let's hope that the city keeps the no-car rule. And on hot summer days, some people swear that it's 10 degrees cooler at the end of the Pier, because of the strong breezes coming off the lake. In the days before air conditioning, this made the Pier a popular place in the summer.

Many Chicagoans only know the Pier as the site of the old Chicagofests, which were music festivals held in the past under the Bilandic and Byrne administrations. But the Pier has been used for many purposes besides its original function as a dock for commercial steamships. It has been used as the site for college classes, as a navy training school, and as an exposition center. The pier's heyday was in the 1920s, when it was a popular place to stroll and cool off at the lakeshore during the warm months. But beginning in the 1930s recreational activity fell off, as did commercial shipping activity because of the increasing use of trucks for transporting goods. The final blow to the pier was the opening of more modern port facilities at Calumet Harbor south of the city in the early 1970s.

Navy Pier housed the first campus of the undergraduate division of the University of Illinois at Chicago (1946-1966). After the UIC campus opened on Halsted Street in 1966, the Pier was only used sporadically, and it rapidly deteriorated. Little money has been spent on basic facilities like sewers for many years (the roof leaked even when U of I held classes there), which means that before any redevelopment can occur, a large investment must be made in basic improvements.

The city has been juggling many ideas for the use of Navy Pier, including poorly designed, impractical ones. There is agreement that the Pier will be used primarily as a recreational and cultural facility, but the specifics haven't been ironed out yet. Among the special activities the city scheduled at the Pier recently were art classes, concerts, and a flea market; jogging, biking, picnicing, and fishing are possible whenever the Pier is open. In fact, not long ago we met a guy fishing at the Pier who spends every summer weekend there. He had several buckets of carp to prove that the fishing's good.

In 1985 Mayor Harold Washington appointed a Navy Pier Task Force to recommend a development concept for the Pier. The Task Force's recommendations centered around the idea of developing the Pier primarily as a recreational and cultural center, with limited commercial use. The final report's plan included an enclosed botanical garden, cafes, farmers markets, and many arts-oriented activities: small museums, theaters, performance spaces, exhibition spaces, and artists' studios. Development will be expensive, and probably will be phased in as funds become available.

For the time being, Navy Pier is open from Memorial Day through Labor Day. As it becomes more popular and more activities are offered, the city may extend the season. Just go and enjoy.

RIVER NORTH ART GALLERIES

West Erie, Huron, and Superior Streets between Wells and Sedgwick

On certain Friday evenings, usually the first or second Friday of each month, a number of galleries in the booming River North area just north of the Chicago River hold openings of new exhibitions. Home to over 40 art galleries and perfect for gallery-hopping, River North, bounded by Wells, Sedgwick, Erie, and Chicago, is the heart of the city's art scene. Openings for new shows, listed in the newspapers' weekend editions, attract many members of Chicago's creative community; artists and art cognoscenti gather to schmooze, sip gratis (watered-down) wine, and generally make the art scene. It's a good place to check out the latest artsy looks in hairstyles and clothing—everyone seems to be trying to outhip everyone else. The first Friday opening night of the season in September is usually the liveliest, as people renew acquaintances after the month-long hiatus in August. On this Friday night, Huron and Superior Streets look almost like Mardi Gras, as gallery-hoppers crowd the sidewalks between gallery visits, enjoying the late-summer weather.

The art galleries moved to this area of rehabbed factories in the early 1980s to escape the escalating rents on East Ontario and Erie Streets and West Hubbard and Illinois Streets. Besides cheaper rents, another attraction was the large, informal openness of the newer galleries, which many owners feel better shows off the art. Some of the spaces have been especially well rehabbed, like those in the former candy factory at 212 W. Superior, which retains much of the original brick-and-beam interiors. The Northern Illinois University Art Gallery has a well-designed space in this building.

River North's galleries have a wide range of specialties: ceramics, naive paintings and sculpture, Slavic painting, native American art, works by black American artists, decorative furniture, and works made of paper. Some members of the city's art community dismiss the River North gallery district, calling it an art mall. In River North's defense, the high concentration of galleries at such close proximity allows you to see an incredible amount of art in a short period of time. If you don't like what you see in one gallery, chances are that something in the next loft will appeal to you. Furthermore, the concentration of galleries and the chic restaurants nearby have brought out a lot of people who might not otherwise have made an effort to see new art.

Of course, you don't have to visit on an opening night. The galleries are generally open from 10 or 11 am until 5 pm Tuesdays through Saturdays, but check the Friday newspapers to make sure. Once you get to River North, pick up a copy of Art Now's **Chicago Gallery Guide,** available free at almost any gallery. The guide lists the current exhibits and hours of all galleries throughout the city (even in the suburbs and other midwestern cities—in case you want to know what's going on in Sioux City). If you enjoy what you've seen, branch out and view some art in other areas of the city. And don't neglect the **Museum of Contemporary Art,** about a mile east of the River North area. MCA shows the newest, most cutting edge art in this part of the country.

MAXWELL STREET

Maxwell Street and neighboring streets, near Halsted Street

Every Sunday morning, Maxwell Street (1300 South, at Halsted Street) and the streets around it become Chicago's sprawling, barely organized, open air flea market. Operating continuously since the turn of the century, when Eastern European Jewish peddlers set up their stalls here to sell junk and produce, Maxwell Street is a place of hurly-burly, hawkers and hustlers, where the selling's never done, and where petty fences and half-honest merchants sell their stolen TVs, used clothing, old automobile tools, and even a few new items to the crowds that come. The market has seen ethnic groups come and go. Originally Jewish immigrants manned the tables; they were succeeded by blacks, who in turn were gradually joined by Hispanic merchants; today you see more and more Asian immigrants selling goods here. The street hawkers seem to pick up the trade from their predecessors: some of the black guys have been heard to utter a word or two of Yiddish.

When you go to Maxwell Street, expect to find everything on sale: socks, VCRs, produce, tapes and records (often by artists you've never heard of), doorknobs, grapefruit knives, ginzu knives, switchblade combs, chandeliers. Once I found hard disk computer drives for sale, something never sold in stores. Where did they come from? Don't ask.

"What's this?" you may ask, and the seller will tell you, "It's one of those things, uh, for uh, you know. . ." You don't, so you ask, "What do you call this?" "Uh. . .it's a. . .it's a. . .I don't think it has a name." Or you may ask, "Is this real?" tugging at a fake fur cap. "Yeah. Yeah. Sure." the man behind the table lies, "It's from Alaska. They grow a lot of them there."

On Maxwell Street you'll find 43 pairs of your favorite tangerine-colored knee socks for sale for 50 cents a pair or 4 electric typewriters and 6 adding machines for 5 dollars apiece if you take them all now. Of course, the knee socks slip down to your ankles, and the typewriters are in Hebrew, but how can you pass up such bargains? Maybe you'd like a set of encyclopedias. They've got the 1965 edition of Encyclopaedia Britannica with only a couple of volumes missing, and it's a steal at $15. You may find the TV someone took from your apartment last month, but don't try to claim ownership. Just buy it back. You can probably get it for a song. There is so much merchandise on the Street you are certain to find something you want, maybe even—hope against hope—something you need.

Maxwell Street is a rare amalgam of the ethnic groups and social classes that make up Chicago. Get there early, the closer to dawn the better. Most of the best buys are gone by the time the stragglers arrive at 10 am. By noon the merchants are closing down their tables. Go with some friends and don't be afraid to waste some small change on oddities you won't find anywhere else. Even if you don't buy anything, what you're really there for is the Maxwell Street experience.

GRACELAND CEMETERY

> In Graceland Cemetery, where the Midwest holds hands with
> history, the soft-spoken headstones, the dignified shafts, the serene
> tombs are footnotes to the saga of an inland city. Here in 119 acres
> of a rolling parklike haven of peace, lie the pioneers, leaders, build-
> ers and dreamers who wrote the story of the Midwest with their
> lives and left a skyline where they found a sand dune.
> —"Historical Sketch of Graceland Cemetery Chicago"
> (booklet sold at the cemetery office)

4001 N. Clark St., 525-1105
While some people may shudder at the idea of touring a cemetery, Graceland Cemetery with its splendid examples of Victorian-era burial monuments
is an excellent place for sightseeing for those with an eye for architecture
and an appreciation of history. The graveyard, located a few blocks north
of **Wrigley Field** (a shrine in itself), is both an architectural showcase and
the burial ground of Chicago's movers and shakers from the big boom years
following the Great Fire. John Kinzie, first permanent white settler in the
city, George Pullman, inventor of the Pullman railroad car, Potter Palmer,
who developed State Street and built the Palmer Houses, his wife Bertha,
a major figure in Chicago's art community, Jack Johnson, first black to win
the world heavyweight championship, Cyrus McCormick, inventor of the
reaper, Marshall Field, of retail fame, Alan Pinkerton, founder of the Pinkerton Detective Agency, architects Louis Sullivan, Daniel Burnham, and
Mies van der Rohe, who created Chicago's great architectural legacy, meat-
packer Philip Armour, and William Hulbert, co-founder of the National
League and first president of the baseball franchise now called the Cubs,
are all buried in Graceland.

The grounds are landscaped and beautiful, complete with swans on a small
lake. But what is truly startling about this cemetery is the number of grandiose monuments built by Chicago's Gilded Age barons with huge fortunes
and even bigger egos. Many monuments are beautiful, but just as many are
fantastical and garish. It wasn't unusual for the late Victorian elite to build
large monuments with obelisks, pyramids, and angels to decorate the grave-
sites of their dead, but the scale of the monuments at Graceland is frequently
overwhelming.

Graceland's monuments provide amazing historical insight into the fantasies of the politicians, tycoons, architects, and inventors buried underneath.
The Palmers take their eternal nap beneath a pretentious, pseudo-Greek
temple overlooking Lake Willowmere. The brewing baron Peter Schoenhofen sleeps the sleep of ages below an impressive pyramid decorated with
both a Christian and a pre-Christian symbol (an angel and a sphinx). And
a majestic Corinthian column and curving, Greek-style benches adorn the
gravesite of George Pullman. His family so feared repercussions from former
employees who had participated in the infamous Pullman strike that they
encased his coffin in tons of steel and concrete.

Daniel Burnham, the Father of the Chicago Plan, took over a small island
in the middle of Lake Willowmere and marked his grave, and those of the
rest of his family, with rough-cut glacial boulders. Appropriate for a city

planner. Burnham's boulder sits in the center, dominating those marking the rest of his family.

Another granite boulder, studded with art deco architectural and decorative motifs, indicates Louis Sullivan's grave. Sullivan's marker, erected years after his death by friends and associates, is quite different from the elaborate Getty Tomb Sullivan designed for George Getty, the lumber merchant. The classically elegant Getty memorial is considered by some to be his finest work and has been designated a city landmark. Yet another beautiful monument is the large Celtic cross atop the grave of architect John Wellborn Root.

Other treasures in Graceland include sculptures by Daniel Chester French—a wistful woman called "Memory" at the Field family plot; and turn-of-the-century sculptor Loredo Taft—don't miss his haunting figure of death, "Eternal Silence," at the Graves family site and his marvelous figure of "The Crusader" at the grave of Victor Lawson, the founder of the *Chicago Daily News*. On a more whimsical note is the large granite baseball atop the grave of National League founder William Hulbert.

The **Chicago Architecture Foundation** (326-1393) offers tours of Graceland on several weekends during the fall. At other times of the year, you can purchase a map or guidebook at the cemetery office and take a self-guided tour.

HYDE PARK AND THE POINT

55th Street and Lake Michigan

Want to relax on the lake in an uncrowded, untrendy spot, and feel like you're getting away from the oppressive city? No place beats Promontory Point, known as "The Point," at 55th Street and Lake Michigan, in Hyde Park. The Point is a triangle of grassy land—a promontory—that juts out into the lake. It's also a breezy, relaxed place where people go to barbecue, talk, play softball, and let their dogs run loose.

The water is fairly deep here, and swimming is forbidden. Nevertheless, the Point attracts windsurfers and long-distance swimmers. The reason: this is one of the few places along the city's lakeshore where you can swim long distances without getting hassled. Many people regularly swim from the Point south a half-mile to another promontory, then back. Ted Erikson, a former world record holder for swimming the English Channel, and his son, who holds a current record for swimming the Channel, used to train off the Point.

The Point has no beach, only grass and rocks, so there are no hordes of noisy beach people around to contend with. Bring your cooler and grill, set a blanket down facing the lake, take out a good book, and take it easy. Contemplate the vast expanse of water, and drink in the beautiful view of the skyline. Take a walk around—the beach just to the south is lovely in the early morning, before anyone gets there. You get one of the best views of the city skyline from the Point.

The area around the Point is as laid back as the Point itself, and Hyde Park is a liberal, unpretentious community. By Chicago standards at least, Hyde Park is fairly well integrated, and its very nonchalance toward that issue is refreshing. Some points of interest in Hyde Park are:

The parrots in Eastview Park, 53rd and the lake. That's right. Parrots. A colony of parrots—they're big and vivid green and loud—native to the Andes Mountains in South America (where they are considered a pest) somehow ended up living free in Chicago, and have become a fixture in this park in Hyde Park. The colony has as many as 20 members that live in one big nest in the trees in the south edge of the park, near the tennis courts.

Valois Cafeteria and Coffee Shop, 1500 E. 53rd, which serves excellent, cheap home cooking. You can sit as long as you want and stare at passersby and no one will mind. A lot of other patrons are doing the same thing.

The David and Alfred Smart Gallery, 5550 S. Greenwood, which houses a small, interesting collection that contains a little bit of everything, including European and Oriental art, twentieth century painting and sculpture, and traveling exhibitions. Admission is free.

The Oriental Institute, a first-rate museum of ancient Near Eastern archaeology, religion, and art. The Institute, which helped date the Dead Sea scrolls and still conducts expeditions as ongoing research, houses Egyptian mummies and a 40-ton winged bull, among other things. Admission is free.

Frank Lloyd Wright's Robie House, 5757 S. Woodlawn. The Robie House has been labeled a masterpiece of American housing, yet was almost destroyed in 1957. It now houses University of Chicago offices.

Gill's Liquors at 1238 E. 47th St. may be the only place in the world that sells gallon jugs of beer that they claim never goes flat and doesn't need refrigeration. They have two drive-up windows through which they'll hoist you the jugs. Worth the experience.

Promontory Point is the only section of the lakeshore between Grant and Jackson Parks that was developed according to the plans outlined by the 1919 Lake Front Ordinance. Had all the plans for the area called Burnham Park by the ordinance been carried out, more of the southern lakeshore might have been landscaped as nicely as the Point. During the winter, you can cross-country ski up and down the lake here—it's a nice trail. The view of the lake when a storm is whipping up clouds and waves is spectacular. Simply put, the Point is probably the nicest place in the city to enjoy the lake, far from the crowds and the maddening cars.

TOUR OF FRANK LLOYD WRIGHT ARCHITECTURE IN OAK PARK

Due west of Chicago lies Oak Park, a beautiful older suburb with a progressive, educated population (lots of university faculty live here) very involved in their community. Oak Park shares some characteristics with Chicago: a highly developed identity, a strong sense of history, and some Chicago-type problems due to its contiguous border with Chicago at the high-crime Austin area. Oak Park also shares another characteristic with its neighbor to the east—some beautiful architecture. Oak Park's collection of single family houses designed by Frank Lloyd Wright, together with **Unity Temple** (a nondenominational church done by Wright) and Wright's own home and studio, comprise the largest collection—25 buildings—of Wright buildings in the world. The Wright homes are lovely and real crowd pleasers. The neighborhoods they are set in are quiet, pleasant, and sedate. Taking a tour of Wright architecture is a great way to spend a Sunday afternoon. Take your parents, your friend Ann from France, or drop by yourself.

The houses were built over a period of 20 years in Wright's career, and they show how he developed in style and maturity over that time. Very early on, Wright exhibited what was then a radical approach to architecture in the homes he built for certain committed clients who allowed him fuller expression of his ideas. Compared to other homes being built at that time (the early part of this century), Wright's architecture looked very different and new, and still looks fresh today.

If you just want to wander around this area without a guidebook, you can see most of the homes between Lake Street on the south, Iowa Street on the north, Marion Street on the west, and Scoville Street on the east. Most of Wright's houses are easily recognized and quite distinctive by virtue of their horizontal lines, their flat planes, and their tell-tale ornamentation— stained glass windows and the Wright style of grillwork. Some of his earlier homes are a little harder to recognize without a map. If you would like a map, the "Architectural Guide Map of Oak Park and River Forest" available for $1.50 from the Visitors Center (see below) is an excellent guide. House locations are marked with tiny photographs.

If you prefer a more formal start for your tour, or if you want to walk through the area with a guide, visit one of two centers for tourists: the **Visitors Center** and the **Frank Lloyd Wright Home and Studio**. Both centers (they are affiliated) offer maps and guidebooks and sell tickets for the excellent tours given by the Wright Home and Studio. The Visitors Center, located at 158 Forest Avenue, is open 10 am-5 pm every day from March through November. The Frank Lloyd Wright Home and Studio, located at 951 Chicago Avenue, which houses the Ginko Tree Bookshop, is open daily from 10 am-5 pm. Weekend afternoon tours cost $7 for the complete tour, or $4 for one of any three parts of the tour. Tours start at Unity Temple, at the corner of Lake Street and Wentworth. You can buy tour tickets at Unity. Call 848-1978 for tour times and more information.

Oak Park is easy to get to by public transportation or by car. By public transit take the Lake/Dan Ryan el from any of its stations in the Loop; Wabash Avenue has several of these stations. Get off at the Oak Park Avenue or Harlem Avenue stops, and walk north to the Visitors Center at 158 Forest Avenue. By car, take the Eisenhower Expressway (I-290) west from the Loop to Harlem Avenue (IL 43), then exit north and follow the brown and white signs to the Visitors Center. Parking is available at the Center.

SULZER LIBRARY/RAVENSWOOD AREA

4455 N. Lincoln Ave., 728-8652

Conrad Sulzer Regional Library in Ravenswood is so popular with area residents that the librarians have a difficult time getting people to go home at closing time. For those of us who love libraries and are frustrated with the lack of a central library in Chicago, Sulzer is our mecca.

Sulzer Library, only a couple of years old, was built to replace the old Hild Library, which the community had outgrown. The old library had been especially dear to the Ravenswood neighborhood, and the architects wisely solicited input from library patrons in designing the new building. Some of their favorite features from the old building were its plentiful windows, a large skylight, and fanciful murals in the children's area. These ideas were incorporated into the design of the new building, and the result is a very successful public building: one that is both practical and well-received by its users.

The magnificent entryway is probably the most striking feature of the library. A beautiful wagon-wheel skylight floods the entrance with natural light. Behind the circulation desk, a wide, grand staircase leads to the second floor and the large, airy adult reading room. The colorful wooden tables and chairs you see here and throughout the building are decorated with scenes from literary and fantasy themes. It's not surprising that a nicely designed home for books makes you feel like reading. You can thank architects Hammond Beeby and Babka for the Sulzer library.

After you've checked out several books from the library's collection, you'll be ready to explore some of the sights in the surrounding neighborhood. A couple of blocks up the street from Sulzer is the former **Krause Music Store** at 4611 N. Lincoln (now the Arntzen-Coleman Funeral Home). The building's facade was the last executed commission of the great architect Louis Sullivan. Notice the intricate ornamentation on the entryway. The decorations are typical of Sullivan's finely detailed work. While this is not Sullivan's finest work, even lesser examples of his beautiful, intricate ornamentation are a treat.

You've feasted on books and art; now you may be ready to enjoy a delicious snack. Backtrack a couple of blocks south to Montrose, then head west 3 blocks to **Lutz's** bakery and cafe at 2454 W. Montrose. Confections from Lutz's will tempt even the strongest-willed dieter. This wonderful authentic German bakery has been a Chicago favorite for generations. We always take hard-to-please guests from out of town here early in their stay—it gives them a great first impression of the city. The quaint, elegant European-style cafe adjoining the bakery takes us back to our trip to Vienna. Coffee is graciously served on a silver platter with both whipped and unwhipped cream. Choosing a torte or pastry from the rotating showcase of delicacies is difficult, since everything is delectable, and we've tried them all—Hazelnut, Grand Marnier, Black Forest Cherry, and more.

This concludes our tour of the Ravenswood area. If you're feeling adventurous, you can catch the Ravenswood el at Montrose and Damen and take a thrilling ride to the Loop (see above).

NEIGHBORHOODS

When you ask confirmed Chicagoans where they live, chances are they won't give you a street address. Logan Square, they'll say—or Lakeview, or South Loop, or Beverly, or any one of the 77 identifiable neighborhoods that tranform the monotonous grid of Chicago's streets into a crazy quilt of local history and traditions, ethnic pride and prejudice, small-town friendliness and xenophobia. Neighborhoods make the city liveable, and their variety make it fascinating.

Chicago's neighborhoods have undergone major changes in the last fifteen years. Many of the tightly knit ethnic enclaves broke apart when residents fled incoming blacks and Latinos, continuing the trend of "white flight" established in the 50s and 60s. But the past fifteen years have seen another trend—the return of the Baby Boomers to the neighborhoods their parents had fled years before. Raised in the Wonder Bread suburbs, they were attracted by the city's gritty urbanity, and the complex visual tapestry of its buildings. The inexpensiveness of the buildings didn't hurt either. Others, interested in living in the city but preferring something newer and more elegant, moved into the highrises that sprang up around the Loop.

Everyone knows of someone who made a killing in real estate when a neighborhood "turned around." This potential to make money attracts people to redeveloping areas that were once ethnic enclaves or hopeless slums. In writing this chapter we quickly realized how often the word "rehabbed" kept coming up. It couldn't be helped. A good deal of Chicago has been "rehabbed" since the early 70's, and much more of it is being or about to be "rehabbed." Such rehabbing has been a boon for the city, revitalizing housing, increasing tax revenues, and attracting new residents.

This rebirth of the city is all the more reason to cherish those qualities that make each neighborhood unique. In the neighborhood descriptions that follow, we've concentrated on the lakefront communities because they're still where most people who have a choice prefer to live. The lakefront has a near-monopoly on the city's amenities: nightlife, specialty shops, sophisticated restaurants, live entertainment, first-run movies. But it's also possible to live the good life west of Ashland Avenue, and we've included those untrendy areas that offer interesting alternatives to the lakefront, or a taste of old Chicago.

SOUTH LOOP

(From Congress Parkway south to Roosevelt Road, between Canal Street and Grant Park)

Ten years ago the only residents of the South Loop—sometimes known as Burnham Park—were sleeping on subway grates. Today this area boasts many attractive restaurants, bars, and shops, and offers the widest variety of housing ever crowded into a single neighborhood. In a one-square-mile area you find rehabbed lofts, luxury condominiums, rental units and town-

17

houses. Only a short walk from the Loop, this area is a natural for professionals tired of long commutes and bumper-to-bumper rush hours.

Dearborn Park

Built in the early 80s, Dearborn Park occupies what used to be the railyards behind the old Dearborn Street Station. Made up of several high-rises and a development of one- and two-story townhouses, Dearborn Park looks like a little suburb in the city. Dearborn Station itself is being converted to an elegant indoor shopping arcade along the lines of Faneuil Hall in Boston. When the renovation is complete, Dearborn Station will be a centerpiece to the South Loop.

Printer's Row

North of Dearborn Park is Printer's Row, once the center of Chicago's commercial printing industry. The former warehouses have been converted into rental units and luxury lofts/condominiums, and the business strip along Dearborn contains a number of upscale shops and restaurants, as well as what must be the first warehouse ever converted to an Episcopal Church—Grace Place.

River City

To the west of Dearborn Park, built along the Chicago River, is River City. Designed by Bertrand Goldberg, the architect of Marina City, this self-proclaimed prototype for future urban communities looks like a modern version of a medieval castle. Completely self-contained, River City has its own health club, market, and medical center. Future plans call for a marina and a Tivoli-like park of islands, putting River City at the forefront of efforts to beautify the Chicago River.

NEAR WEST SIDE

West Loop

(West of the river from Canal Street west to Racine, from the Eisenhower expressway north to Ohio)

Consisting of scattered loft apartments and the imposing **Presidential Towers**—four identical skyscrapers just west of the Loop—the Near West Side is another example of a neighborhood redeemed from near skid-row status. Partially funded by the Federal Government, Presidential Towers can take a lot of credit for reviving the area—the conversion of nearby warehouses into rentals and condos would have occurred much slower without them. The Presidential Towers are a self-contained city of steel and glass, not a bad place to hole up during our long, cold winters, but the Towers are isolated from the life of the city. Except for the Greek restaurant district along Halsted, the area has, as yet, no nightlife to speak of.

Taylor St.

(From the Eisenhower expressway south to Roosevelt Road, between the Dan Ryan expressway and Ashland)

What happens when you take one of the oldest Italian neighborhoods in the city and tear a large part of it down to build a sprawling campus for a new university? You get a mixed neighborhood like **University of Illinois at Chicago/Taylor Street**. To the north is the original, and still lively, **Greektown**. (Greektown, though, consists mostly of commercial Greek restaurants, not Greek residents.) To the east and south is **Maxwell Street,** home every Sunday morning to the largest open-air marketplace in the city. And then there's Taylor Street, which has never been as prosperous or as vibrant as it is now. Good Italian restaurants abound, along with Italian beef and sausage joints, Italian ice stands, and old women sitting on their stoops. You'll see more people out on the streets and sidewalks here than in almost any other part of the city.

In the 60s, Mayor Daley dropped the university into this area because he wanted a major institution to anchor the Loop from the west side ghettos. Although at first the Italian residents resented the university students because the bulldozers had caused the relocation of so many of their friends and relatives, they've come to accept the students. The area has now stabilized, and is finally getting recognition for its interesting ethnicity and its convenience—the Loop is only a couple of stops away on the el. The Taylor Street area has one of the lowest crime rates in the city. Today English majors rent apartments from guys who drive garbage trucks for the city. Until recently, few U of I students had any interaction with neighborhood residents because they couldn't live on campus—there were no dorms. That may change soon, however, with the opening of a new dorm at Harrison and Halsted. The rents and real estate are getting pricey because the neighborhood has been discovered, but families that have lived here for generations won't ever leave. Be forewarned, though: apartment vacancies are commonly advertised by word of mouth only.

RIVER NORTH

(Between Clark Street and the River on the west, from Kinzie north to Chicago Avenue)

Many call River North Chicago's hottest neighborhood. With more than its share of popular restaurants, a booming gallery district, and an ample and attractive supply of lofts, apartments, and office space, River North attracts a diverse cross-section of Chicago's population. The bohemians, artists, and art collectors come for the gallery openings in the Superior-Huron area (see The Other Top Ten). The after work crowds come for the trendy restaurants like **Scoozi,** the **Dixie Bar and Grill,** and the **Hard Rock Cafe.** And lovers of the truly kitsch come for **Ed Debevic's** and the **Rock-and-Roll McDonald's** (on Clark St.).

Until the early 80s River North was a seedy, half-populated warehouse district whose uneven sidewalks were littered with broken glass and the occasional wino sleeping it off. The only businesses were adult bookstores, greasy spoons, and unsavory bars. Today, the area boasts an incredible diversity: **Ditka's** (a restaurant owned by the Bears' head coach), the **Baton** (host to Chicago's finest drag show, a *La Cage aux Folles*), the **Peace Museum** (the world's first), **City** (an ultra-hip furniture and design store), and the **Raccoon Club** (a nightclub). And there are still a few adult bookstores in the area, if that's what appeals to you.

New highrises and continued conversion of warehouses into loft-space are likely to turn this primarily commercial area into quite a residential community in the next few years.

NORTH LAKEFRONT

Gold Coast/Near North
(From the lake west to LaSalle Street, between Chicago and North Avenues)
Probably the most exclusive neighborhood in Chicago. Ever since the cream
of Chicago society followed Potter Palmer north from South Prairie Avenue,
Chicago's old-money elite has lived here. Most of the mansions that once
graced the area have been replaced by high-rises, and the neighborhood has
the highest population density in the city. Cardinal Bernardin lives in one
of the few remaining mansions on Astor Street, facing the south end of
Lincoln Park at North Avenue.

The first high-rise apartments built in Chicago were the elegant 9- and 10-
story structures along Lake Shore Drive south of the Oak Street Beach. The
newer high-rises—such as the **John Hancock Building** and the **Newberry
Plaza**—may be taller and come with more amenities, but they don't come
close to the beauty and charm of these older buildings. Parking on the street is
nearly impossible, but most of the residents can afford inside parking.

The **Rush Street** nightclub district is home to some of the glitziest singles
bars in the country. Conventioneers hang out here. Mammoth **Sandburg
Village** lies north of the Rush Street area. Six thousand young professionals
live in this huge apartment and condo complex that was built with funds
supposedly allocated for urban renewal in the 1960s. Still, housing in Sandburg is more reasonably priced than in the apartments nearer to the lake.
The Gold Coast may be expensive, but it's convenient—you're only a minute
from the lake, the Magnificent Mile, and Lincoln Park.

Just south of the Gold Coast and east of Michigan Avenue lies the neighborhood of **Streeterville.** For many years a purely commercial district,
Streeterville became a residential area in the 70s when high-rises were built
along Ontario, Erie, and Fairbanks, and the area gained popularity as a safe
neighborhood, convenient to the Loop, and not too expensive—studio apartments can be found for under $500.

Old Town
(From Division north to Armitage, between LaSalle and Sheffield)
Anyone who lived in Chicago during the Psychedelic Sixties has fond memories of Old Town, then the countercultural mecca of the city. Most of what
you remember is gone. The Earl, Big John's, the Sneak Joint. All gone.
Even the Old Town School of Folk Music has moved out. And the streetlife
has all but disappeared.

Luckily the **Old Town Ale House** is still in business, as are **Barbara's
Bookstore,** the **Bowl and Roll,** and **O'Rourke's,** arguably the best Irish bar
in town. The famous **Second City Theater** still makes its home here, as does
the newer **Zanies'** comedy club. And, of course, the **Old Town Art Fair** is
still held every June, attracting artisans from throughout the midwest to
display their wares: jewelry, pottery, weaving, clothing, paintings, and photography.

In contrast to Old Town's bohemian days, today's residents are serious,
older professionals, some with small children. Housing is expensive. Even
Old St. Michael's Church has turned its former school into luxury condominiums. The area north of North Avenue looks a lot like Old Town's
northern neighbor, Lincoln Park. And like Lincoln Park, the western bound-

ary of Old Town has been creeping steadily westward for the last few years as developers build new middle- and upper-middle class housing all the way to Halsted Street.

Lincoln Park
(From the lakefront west to Ashland, between Armitage and Diversey)
Fat City. Flashy, fashionable, perhaps a bit bored by its own success, Lincoln Park is the Valhalla of conspicuous consumption. It's where you go to impress and be impressed, to check out the latest styles, to hustle or just to watch.

Lincoln Park is really a collection of neighborhoods, bordered on the south by North Avenue, on the east by the lake, and on the north by Diversey. The western boundary is harder to fix, because instead of creeping blight, Lincoln Park has been experiencing creeping renewal. The "hot" real estate area used to be strictly east of Halsted; then the western border jumped to Larrabee; and from there the border jumped to Ashland.

Within this general area are huge highrises overlooking the lake; modern townhouses and mid-rise developments; two-flats, three-flats and walk-up apartment buildings of various ages and sizes; tastefully restored 19th-century row houses on quiet, leafy side streets—a marvelous housing mix that somehow manages to coexist with glitzy commercial strips like Clark, Armitage, Halsted, and Lincoln Avenue. Rents and property values are constantly on the rise, and you have to have money (or be willing to live in a shoebox-sized apartment) to afford to live here.

What you get for your money, though, is impressive: Plenty of good restaurants. Lots of nightlife: blues bars, rock clubs, movies, off-Loop theaters, singles bars. Chic specialty shops. Great bookstores. The park. The lakefront. The zoo.

Lincoln Park bars used to be more low-key than those on Rush Street and attracted a different crowd, but the corners of Lincoln and Armitage and Halsted and Armitage now resemble Rush Street or Fort Lauderdale on Friday and Saturday nights.

Lakeview
(From the lakefront west to Ashland, between Diversey and Irving Park Road)
Well on its way to becoming another Lincoln Park, Lakeview is home to some of Chicago's more established dance and theater companies (**Steppenwolf, The Organic, MoMing, The Remains Theatre**), many fine restaurants, plenty of watering holes, and the hottest new dance clubs in Chicago: **Medusa's, Clubland, Cabaret Metro.** Also not be missed in Lakeview: **Leona's** (for great Italian food) and **Ann Sather's** (famous for Swedish home-style cooking).

Like Lincoln Park, housing in Lakeview varies greatly, from highrises near the lake, to single family houses and two- and three-flats west of Halsted. Some parts of Lakeview are as expensive as Lincoln Park, while others are reasonable but creeping up.

Lakeview has a few rough spots, especially near the el stops, but most of the area is safe, attractive, or quickly becoming so. Belmont and Sheffield, in the heart of the community, was once one of the sleaziest corners in the city. People going to the Quiet Knight to hear Sonny Rollins, Bob Marley or Tom Waits had to step over a sidewalk carpeted with winos and junkies. That's changed. The Quiet Knight is long gone and now you're more likely to be trampled by new wave teenie boppers on their way to Clubland or Medusa's.

Again like Lincoln Park, Lakeview is made up of a number of smaller neighborhoods including **Lakeview East,** still more commonly known as New Town, and **Wrigleyville** (named after Wrigley Field, called "Cubs Park" by the uninformed). Residents of Wrigleyville have their own special neighborhood problem: The Cubs. After baseball games, hundreds of drunken Cubs fans converge on this usually quiet neighborhood and generally cause all sorts of mayhem. The Tribune Company, which owns the Cubs, are sincerely trying to cut down on the amount of beer sold to fans, restricting sales of beer to the first seven innings of the game only. Unless these efforts succeed in quieting the residents' fears, Wrigley Field's hopes of getting night baseball are dim.

Besides sports fans and trendies, Lakeview is also home to a large gay community. Some of Chicago's most popular gay bars are located on Halsted Street in New Town, and many of the businesses in Lakeview are gay-owned or gay-run. Multiracial, multiethnic, liberal-minded, the Lakeview neighborhood is a funkier version of Lincoln Park. It remains to be seen whether Lakeview will go the same upscale route as Lincoln Park, as rehabbing efforts continue and new luxury townhouses are built.

Uptown
(From the lakefront west to Ashland, between Irving Park Road and Foster)
Until very recently, Uptown was an area to avoid, but now its run-down but once elegant housing stock has made this area a prime target for gentrification; rehabbing efforts are already taming the southernmost parts of Uptown. Some Uptown residents are less than enthusiastic about the influx of rehabbers and speculators, and wonder where the low-income residents will go: many ended up in Uptown after being pushed out by gentrification efforts in other parts of the city.

Uptown is, for the time being, the most ethnically diverse neighborhood in the city, a true melting pot of blacks, American Indians, Hispanics, Filipinos, Vietnamese, and Appalachians. A Little Vietnam has sprung up on Argyle Street between Broadway and Sheridan, where there are many Vietnamese restaurants and businesses. On Argyle you can see a Vietnamese travel agent, a Vietnamese CPA, and a Vietnamese barber shop, all in a single store front. You can also find a Vietnamese pharmacy that sells close to a thousand kinds of folk remedies—and no aspirin.

Three grand movie palaces and dance halls—the **Riviera,** the **Aragon Ballroom,** and the **Uptown Theater**—once made the intersection of Broadway and Lawrence a major entertainment center. The Riviera, now restored to its former glory, is a lively dance club. The Uptown hosts occasional concerts but is badly in need of renovation. The Aragon, surviving several reincarnations as a roller rink and a disco, is now a Latin dance club, and a sometime rock concert hall. Also worth catching: the **Green Mill Lounge,** home of the Uptown Poetry Slam.

At a time when every other neighborhood claims to be the next Lincoln Park or the next Lakeview, Uptown has the best shot at the coveted title of next up-and-coming neighborhood in Chicago.

Edgewater
(Between Foster and Devon, from the lakefront to Ravenswood)
Another community on the rise is Edgewater, a desirable, moderately priced neighborhood to the north of Uptown. Like Uptown, Edgewater has

proved to be irresistible to refugees from Lakeview and Lincoln Park looking for good, inexpensive housing. With its many fine apartment buildings and single family homes on tree lined streets, this is certainly prime real estate for rehabbing, and residents of Edgewater have access to the beach between Balmoral and Foster.

Again like Uptown, Edgewater has a diverse population of American Indians, Hispanics, Greeks, blacks, Cubans, Japanese, Cambodians, Koreans, and Chinese. Senn High School boasts of teaching English as a second language to students from almost 50 different countries.

A major force for improving the quality of life in this area is the **Edgewater Community Council.** The ECC was instrumental, for example, in getting the city and state to purchase the former Edgewater Golf Club at Ridge and Pratt and develop it into **Warren State Park.** More recently, the group's recreation committee helped the Park District acquire and renovate the former **Armory** on Broadway, now the largest indoor park facility in the city. The ECC has also opened a **North Side Cultural Center** on Sheridan Road in one of the two remaining mansions there—saving the last open lakefront properties in Edgewater from high-rise developers. ECC's broad focus also includes Operation Lakewatch to combat lake pollution; education initiatives to improve public education; and current efforts to deal with lakefront erosion. Edgewater also contains dozens of block clubs working to improve and stabilize the neighborhood.

In the southwest corner of Edgewater is **Andersonville,** between Foster and Bryn Mawr along Clark Street. This old Swedish enclave still has a number of interesting Swedish restaurants and bakeries, and the **Swedish American Museum.** The **Reflections Theater Company,** a relative new-comer to the area, makes their home in an old vaudeville house turned moviehouse turned off-off-Loop Theatre. This gutsy group was the first theater in the U.S. to perform all three plays in Lanford Wilson's *Talley Trilogy* in repertory.

East Rogers Park

(From the lakefront west to Ridge, between Devon and the Evanston border)
Located on the northern end of the city, this neighborhood features some excellent, uncrowded beaches, and an amazing ethnic mix. Once predominantly Jewish and middle class, integration occurred quietly, almost unnoticed, over the last decade or so as Rogers Park welcomed immigrants from every corner of the globe: Asians, Hispanics, Soviet Jews, Jamaicans and other Caribbean peoples in the city. Kilmer Grade School enrolls students who speak more than 70 native languages—it claims to have the most diverse student body in the country. Adding to the area's diversity, **Loyola University** and **Mundelein College** are located at the southeast corner of Rogers Park.

Two earthy Rogers Park institutions well worth a visit are the **No Exit Cafe** and the **Heartland** restaurant, both located close to the Morse Street el stop. For three decades, the No Exit coffeehouse has offered folk music (mixed with a little jazz and classical) in a relaxed, low-key atmosphere. Here you can spend a lazy afternoon playing Go or Scrabble and sipping herbal tea. The Heartland, known for nutritious vegetarian meals so good you forget that it's health food, looks like it was transplanted, lock, stock, building and all, from Berkeley, California circa 1967.

West Rogers Park
(From Devon north to the Evanston border, between Ridge and the Chicago River)
West Rogers, also known as **Northtown** or **West Ridge,** formerly a Jewish enclave, is now experiencing an influx of Asian immigrants. Devon near Western, where once Jewish merchants dominated unchallenged, is the midwest's longest stretch of sari shops. There are still several wonderful Jewish bakeries on Devon (most open on Sundays, some closed on Saturdays), but every year there are fewer delis and more Indian restaurants and groceries on the street that was once synonymous with ethnic Jewish Chicago.

Indian Boundary Park is West Rogers Park's best kept secret. This safe, well kept park boasts a small zoo, a duck pond, tennis courts, and a community theater. West Rogers Park is also home to the city's newest park, **Warren State Park,** with a 9-hole golf course, tennis courts, and a bike path.

SOUTH LAKEFRONT

Hyde Park
(Between 51st and 59th Streets, from the lake west to Washington Park)
Mayor Washington's home, Hyde Park, is cosmopolitan, tolerant of eccentricity, very liberal, active politically, and free of the commercial congestion that plagues most lakefront neighborhoods. Thanks to the **University of Chicago,** which has one of the largest private police forces in the country, Hyde Park has a remarkably low crime rate. Especially when you consider that it is an island of prosperity surrounded on three sides by poverty. Both Hyde Park and **Kenwood,** its northern neighbor, have some beautiful old mansions from the days when the area was home to some of Chicago's wealthiest families.

In the 20s and 30s, Hyde Park was a bohemian enclave, with a flourishing artists' and writers' colony. In the 50s, 55th Street was famous for its bars, where the jazz greats of the bebop era played. But there's nothing bohemian about Hyde Park today. A university-backed urban renewal project has replaced most of the seedy, low-rent apartment buildings and storefronts with townhouses and shopping centers.

Stable it certainly is—so much so that the rental apartment vacancy rate is one of the city's lowest. Racial tension is minimal. But integrated? Though the area has long had a reputation as an integrated, liberal community, this is not entirely accurate. The neighborhood is sharply divided, economically and socially: blacks, students, and faculty each live in neatly delineated sections of the community.

The presence of the University of Chicago with its world-class faculty and its ultra serious students guarantees that Hyde Park will always be a cultural oasis of sorts. Where else can you find five excellent bookstores within a four-block radius?

(Note: A walking tour of Hyde Park is described in the Other Top Ten chapter.)

South Shore
(From Jackson Park south to 79th Street, between the Lake and Stony Island)
South Shore still retains much of its gracious past. It has a large, beautiful beachfront park (**Rainbow Park** at 79th and the Lake), and due to the efforts

of determined residents, it still has the **South Shore Community Center,** once a country club, now a park and cultural center open to the public. Once predominantly Jewish, South Shore is now mostly black, with some solidly middle-class areas, and others that are poor and deteriorating. Loyal residents and a very supportive business community, especially the **South Shore Bank,** may succeed in revitalizing the area. Through a network of profit and not-for-profit agencies that work to improve housing and employment opportunities for neighborhood residents, South Shore Bank is rebuilding confidence in the community. As one community activist told us, every neighborhood would love to have a South Shore Bank.

WEST SIDE

West Town
(Between Grand and Division, from the Kennedy expressway west to Western Ave.)
The delights of West Town, Nelson Algren's old stomping grounds, are diverse and discombobulating. This area once boasted the largest Polish population outside of Warsaw; there is still a large though aging Polish community here and a trickle of new Polish immigrants. The new residents are mostly Puerto Rican and Mexican. Milwaukee Avenue has to be one of the most amazing shopping thoroughfares in the city. Every block is crammed with shops and every shop is crammed with merchandise (mostly cheap): shoes, radios, digital watches, knickknacks. All your clothing needs can be supplied several times over in a single block. Most housing in West Town is poor and deteriorating, and although a few homeowners are trying to fix their houses, many absentee landlords just don't care.

One exception is the **Ukrainian Village,** a pleasant ethnic enclave located on both sides of Chicago Avenue from Damen to beyond Western. Here the streets are immaculate with no graffiti in sight. Housing is inexpensive, which makes the neighborhood attractive to younger people who can't afford Lincoln Park or Lakeview. Besides two exceptionally beautiful Ukrainian Catholic churches, **St. Nicholas** and **Sts. Volodymyr and Olha,** the neighborhood boasts the fine **Ukrainian National Museum** and the **Ukrainian Institute of Modern Art.** If you want to sample some authentic Ukrainian cooking, try **Galans** on Chicago Avenue. One warning: don't make the mistake of referring to the residents as Russians; Ukrainians have their own language and culture and bristle at being lumped together with Russians.

There is a burgeoning new wave scene in West Town, in places like the **Rainbo Club,** the **Artful Dodger,** the **Lizard Lounge** and the **Get Me High Lounge.** This area also contains the only Russian Orthodox church ever designed by Louis Sullivan (**Holy Trinity Orthodox Cathedral,** on Leavitt near Division).

Wicker Park
(From Division to Armitage, between the Kennedy expressway and Western Avenue)
Wicker Park contains many magnificent homes—some are so large they can only be called mansions—yet rents are low so the area is popular with artists. The area is just beginning to undergo gentrification, and pockets of prosperity exist among the poverty. There is still time to buy into this neighborhood

Sts. Volodymyr and Olha Ukrainian Catholic Church.

before prices go through the roof. You'll be sharing space with a large community of Hispanics and a growing community of creative types. Neighborhood artists can often be seen elbow to elbow with older Polish residents in the popular **Busy Bee** restaurant (Damen near North Avenue).

Wicker Park also contains several remarkable churches, legacies left by the Polish immigrants who settled here a century ago. Facing the Kennedy expressway is a landmark church, the magnificent, copper-domed **St. Mary of the Angels**, at Wood and Cortland. This church has been called one of the finest examples of Roman Renaissance churches (in the style of St. Peter's in Rome) in this country. A few blocks away are **St. Stanislaus Kostka** and **Holy Trinity Roman Catholic**, both on Noble Street near Division, built late in the nineteenth century. These beautiful churches can be seen from the Kennedy expressway, but it's worth a little effort to get a closer look. For awhile it looked as though Holy Trinity might be closed by the Church, but it was given a reprieve by the Archdiocese, which recently designated it a "mission church" for new Polish immigrants.

NORTHWEST SIDE

Logan Square
(*From the Kennedy expressway west to Kimball, between Armitage and Diversey*)
The heart of Logan Square has always been Milwaukee Avenue. Once this strip was dominated by Polish merchants, but now the businesses cater to the area's Mexican, Puerto Rican, and Cuban residents. A few remnants of

the original Polish community remain in Logan Square, although the real Polish community thrives further north on Milwaukee.

Along Logan, Humboldt, and Kedzie Boulevards and Palmer Square are some beautiful homes that have already attracted rehabbers. Away from the boulevards, this neighborhood has solid but less attractive housing stock. **Logan Square** itself (the intersection of Milwaukee, Logan and Kedzie) with its striking monument commemorating Illinois' 100th birthday, may be the most beautiful intersection in the city and suggests what Daniel Burnham had in mind in his Chicago Plan. Also worth noting: the **Axe Street Arena,** Logan Square's alternative art gallery and performance space (2778 N. Milwaukee).

Logan Square has two strong community organizations: the **Logan Square Neighborhood Association** and the **Hispanic Housing Development Corporation.** LSNA works to remove blighted buildings and combat crime in the neighborhood, while HHDC concentrates on rehabilitating deteriorated buildings. LSNA has been particularly successful at eliminating gang strongholds. With these powerful groups working to improve Logan Square, the area's future looks bright.

Just to the east of Logan Square is **Bucktown,** another former Polish community that is now largely Hispanic. Quiet, safe, and inexpensive, Bucktown is attracting rehabbers and other residents eager for a good buy.

Lincoln Square/Ravenswood
(From Ravenswood Avenue west to the Chicago River, between Montrose and Bryn Mawr)
Once home to a large German population, Lincoln Square, also called **Ravenswood,** still has some German residents as well as German restaurants and delis. Part of Ravenswood is also known as the new Greektown, created when the Dan Ryan expressway and the University of Illinois cut out most of old Greektown (near Halsted and Jackson). The Greektown nickname is a misnomer, however, since many other ethnic groups, including Asians, have moved into this area. This is now a crowded and exciting place to be; the restaurants are great and the atmosphere is very continental. **Miomir's Serbian Club,** an authentic Eastern European-style nightclub, is a slice of the old country on Lawrence Avenue. Within just a few blocks of Miomir's can be found a lively Mexican dance club, **Casanova's, King's Manor** (a bawdy, Middle Ages-style dining hall), many good Thai restaurants, some Greek places, and a couple of German restaurants from the old days. Lincoln Square rents are not as high as in the lakefront neighborhoods and you're close to the Ravenswood el line.

SOUTH AND SOUTHWEST SIDES

Chinatown
(Between Canal St. and Lake Shore Drive, from the Stevenson expressway north to the Sante Fe railroad yards)
The big news in Chinatown is the neighborhood's planned expansion into the abandoned railroad yards immediately to the north. For years, Chinatown has been one of the most densely populated area of the city and eager to expand its borders—especially with a large number of immigrants expected from Hong Kong in 1997, the year ownership of that former English colony reverts to the People's Republic of China.

The Chinatown annex will include retail space, residential townhouses, and an apartment building for the elderly. The housing units have been specially designed to accommodate Chinese family values, and most townhouses will include detached in-law quarters as part of the townhouse.

Chinatown's main attraction, however, remains the many great restaurants and interesting grocery stores around Wentworth Avenue near Cermak Road. With active, involved residents and a strong local business community, Chinatown has a bright future.

Pilsen
(Between Halsted and Western, from 16th Street on the north to Cermak and Blue Island on the south)
Once the center of Chicago's sizeable Bohemian community, today only a few elderly Bohemians are left, and the neighborhood is now solidly Mexican and Puerto Rican. For years students and faculty of the School of the Art Institute have found inexpensive loft space in Pilsen, and, as often happens, real estate developers have come close on the heels of the artists. Pilsen may go the way of Soho in New York.

However, before that happens rehabbers will have the Pilsen community to contend with. Pilsen residents have complained to the *Tribune* on at least one occasion about the interloping "yuppies" trying to break apart the Hispanic community. Strong and well-organized, Pilsen's residents have in the past waged a successful campaign for a branch public library and resisted the School Board's attempts to bus their children out of the neighborhood.

The heart of Pilsen is 18th Street, where you'll find some of the best and least expensive Mexican restaurants in the city. So much the better if you speak Spanish.

Also worth noting in Pilsen: **The Mexican Fine Arts Center and Museum,** showcasing Mexican art and culture; and the **Blue Rider Theater,** run by performance artist Donna Blue Lachman; a recent performance was a piece about Frida Kahlo, wife of Mexican muralist Diego Rivera.

Marquette Park/Chicago Lawn
(From 59th Street south to 75th, between Western Avenue and Central Park)
If you don't know anything else about Marquette Park, you know that as recently as five years ago this white working class neighborhood was plagued by racial tension that received a lot of media coverage. Marquette Park has a lot to live down—for a while they were headquarters for the tiny but vocal American Nazi Party. But like Chicago's other working class areas, Marquette Park is adjusting to the new realities of Harold Washington's Chicago.

In fact, 63rd Street, the heart of Marquette Park, has undergone quite a metamorphosis in recent years, with the area's new Hispanic and Middle Eastern residents opening many restaurants, ethnic food stores, social clubs, and bars, and sharing the street with more established Polish and Lithuanian businesses.

Along 69th street from Western to California you'll find Chicago's Lithuanian community, where you can find Lithuanian food, buy Lithuanian books, and even catch a Lithuanian theater group. Worth noting on 69th Street: **Tulpe** and **Neringa,** two of the great Lithuanian restaurants in the area.

Marquette Park is the largest park on the southwest side, and includes a lagoon, a 9-hole golf course, and a beautiful rose garden. The park is heavily used for soccer, softball, and football games on weekends.

Marquette holds many treasures for sweet tooths: **Gertie's Own Ice Cream,** an old-fashioned ice cream parlor serving rich homemade ice cream; **Hoeffken's**—some call it the best bakery in the city; **Dove Candies,** the home of the famous Dove ice cream bar.

Little Village (La Villita)
(From Kedzie to Pulaski, between Cermak and the Stevenson expressway)
A large, new, and prosperous Mexican enclave. 26th Street was once heavily Eastern European, but these days, you can close your eyes on a Saturday night and think you're in Guadalajara. Some of the finest Mexican restaurants in the city are located here, many providing strolling Mariachis and authentic ambience. How authentic? So authentic that Mexican-Americans from all over Chicago crowd into this little neighborhood for a nostalgic taste of their homeland.

Beverly
(From 88th Street south to 107th, between Western Avenue on the west and Ashland, Beverly, and Vincennes Avenues on the east)
Beverly is a gem. There was a brief scare during the 70s when some home-owners were afraid that white flight would cause a panic, but, largely due to the efforts of the **Beverly Area Planning Association** (BAPA), it didn't. BAPA put in a rumor hotline and sued a local realtor accused of block-busting tactics. The area is now stable and integrated. Beverly includes some of the finest housing stock on the south side. The schools in Beverly are good, and the parks, though small, are well kept. Beverly also has its own active art center, **Beverly Art Center.** If you didn't know better, you would think this was a suburb. Beverly is a middle and upper class neighborhood, with mostly Irish Catholic and black residents.

Longwood Drive from 87th Street south is one of the most beautiful residential streets in the city. Longwood straddles an ancient geological ridge and the surrounding area is rolling and even has—believe it or not—hills. In fact, the highest point in the city is the hill at the intersection of 111th and Lothair. If you drive or walk down Longwood, don't miss the replica of an Irish castle (now a Unitarian church) at 103rd St.

For an in-depth history of Chicago's neighborhoods, see *Chicago, City of Neighborhoods* by Dominic A. Pacyga and Ellen Skerrett (Loyola University Press, 1986). For current news about Chicago neighborhoods, check out the Neighborhood News column that appears in the *Reader.*

—Philip Charles, Jack Helbig, and the Editors

CHICAGO POLITICS

The 1980s will go down in Chicago history as the years when the well-oiled Democratic machine crafted by mayor Richard Daley gradually rusted and, finally, ground to a halt. It was a machine fueled by the theory that making the trains run on time, picking up the garbage and keeping the street lights repaired were all keys to a politician's most important job: getting out the vote. It was a theory that worked as well as Daley's Chicago.

RICHARD J. DALEY
Mayor, 1955-1976

Greatest Contribution: Building the Democratic machine for the "City that works."

Memorable Quotes: "The policeman isn't there to create disorder, the policeman is there to preserve disorder" (after the so-called "police riots" at the 1968 Democratic convention). "What kind of a father would I be if I didn't help my sons?" (Answering critics of a city insurance contract handed to his son's company), followed by, "If they don't like it, they can kiss my mistletoe!" (That was the public quote. In a private meeting with union bosses, Daley reportedly said, "They can kiss my ass!")

Daley and the Media: By post-Watergate investigative journalism's standards, reporters were soft on Daley. While he and the City Hall press corps were usually chums, Daley was angered by any criticism of his machine politics, and responded with gems like these: "(reporters) get a few drinks and they get a little high and they write a lot of things that are not true," and, "We have had a lot of dishonest reporters in this city; we still have. I can spit on some from here."

Biggest Mistake While in Office: Running the city for the present. Daley left a legacy of expensive union contracts, bloated payrolls, and finagled budgets; all were used to keep his constituents happy while he was in office, but created deficits and strikes for his successors.

Daley's machine began with a neighbor, the guy at the end of the block. He was named precinct captain, and anyone who needed a garbage can replaced, a ticket fixed, or a new job just knocked on his door. He would work his way through the Democratic chain of command to fill the needs of the neighborhood. When election time rolled around, the chain of command worked its way down to the precinct captain, who rarely even needed to remind his neighbors how the party had served them so well over the years.

As Daley was fond of saying, "Good government is good politics, and good politics is good government." Following that credo, Daley often blurred the line between politics and government, but few voters seemed to mind, at least not those who played Daley's game. After all, as Alderman Vito Marzullo reflected, on completing his ninth term in office, "I help my people that wanna be helped." They showed their willingness to be helped by working for the party, and were rewarded with the best of city services. Those who "didn't want to be helped" might, however, have trouble getting a missing stop sign replaced or might find an unusual number of city inspectors combing their place of business.

While everyone likes prompt garbage services, new curbs and paved streets, the most effective vote-getting tool in Chicago has always been the patronage job. Daley created a virtual army of patronage workers, padding the payroll citywide with party loyalists (also known in some quarters as "political hacks"). This, of course, made getting out the vote even easier. As the *Chicago Sun-Times* once estimated, a patronage job is worth an average of 25 votes, including the new employee, his or her relatives, friends, and neighbors. An extremely grateful employee (or, one with a big family) could drum up as many as 100 votes.

During the Daley years, patronage hiring (and the accompanying firings of party enemies) were completely legal. However, they were not deemed enough to swing any given election. So, the Daley machine perfected illegal means of getting out the vote, as well. Hence, the Chicago slogan, "Vote early, and vote often" and the proliferation of "ghost voters," party members so loyal they continued to vote Democratic long after going to their graves.

How did Daley get away with all of that? Who was to stop him? Not the cronies he helped elect to the State's Attorney's office (county prosecutors) or to the Board of Elections. Not the patronage workers in the Police Department, who had letters of recommendation from party sponsors in their personnel files.

Even if some disgruntled soul did press charges of election fraud, the case would most likely be heard by a judge who was elected by Daley's machine. At one point, a survey by columnist Mike Royko showed that all but 12 of Cook County's 120 judges had, at one time or another, held either a city or county patronage job.

Daley's power over county elections also gave him power over the state legislature. Home rule power let the Mayor set most policies without input from Springfield. However, when Daley was restricted or when he needed a bigger chunk of state or federal funds, he needed only to line up his ducks in the General Assembly.

Needless to say, that created a rift between Chicago and downstate communities (adding insult to injury, the term "downstate" is used to refer to just about any Illinois city outside of Chicago). That rift extends to the present, when suburban and small-town Illinois carefully guards its tax contributions, lest they end up in Chicago, and a vote for Chicago-backed legislation can backfire against a downstater at election time.

The machine, and the city, ran smoothly during Daley's 21 years in office. At least, in the white wards. In black wards, where votes were either not needed to carry elections or were easy enough to buy for a few bucks on election day, services lagged and jobs were tough to come by. There was a growing resentment of the Democratic machine, a resentment that bubbled to the surface when Martin Luther King was assassinated in April, 1968.

Angry blacks took to the streets of Chicago, as they did in most big cities, in a wave of destruction. Daley ordered his police chief to tell his troops to "shoot to kill any arsonists because they're potential murderers, and to shoot to maim or cripple anyone looting." Both blacks and whites were shocked by that order, and the mayor backed down, but not before 11 blacks were killed, 500 injured, and 3,000 arrested. Daley claimed he had been misunderstood; his press secretary blamed the media, saying, "They should have printed what he meant, not what he said."

Few had forgotten what the Mayor had said, however, when the police again faced off with an angry mob later that year. In August of '68, the Democratic National Convention was the scene of what the President's Commission on Violence later termed a "police riot." Some 5,000 antiwar activists from across the country were drummed out of their Lincoln Park camp after curfew by police using mace, clubs, and any handy blunt object. The national media followed the action (though reporters were, themselves, police targets) and when the smoke cleared, Daley insisted the coverage ignored an important point: "No one lost their lives in Chicago," he bragged. However, Daley's machine had lost some of its momentum, as blacks and reformists capitalized on the mayor's mistakes. Luckily for Daley, they then lacked the most basic weapon to fight back: an army of registered voters. It would be more than a decade before they figured out how to effectively use that weapon to topple the machine. More on that later.

Daley's reign ended with his fatal heart attack December 20, 1976. Though he had suffered a stroke two years earlier, Da Mare had seemed so invincible that no plans had been made for a successor. Party bosses were shocked to find, next in line, City Council President Pro Tem Wilson Frost: a (gasp!) black man. Rather than let him take over as mayor, even temporarily, fellow aldermen (city council members) literally locked Frost out of the city council chambers. When the doors opened, Alderman Michael Bilandic (a white) had been duly named Interim Mayor by fellow aldermen. Chicago's black community never forgot that slap to black party loyalist Frost: it was another step in the inevitable black retreat from Daley's machine.

MICHAEL BILANDIC
Mayor, 1977-1979

Greatest Contribution: A caretaker in most legislative and financial areas, Bilandic did show Chicago how to have a good time with Chicagofest, an annual lakefront party of food, music, and entertainment that continued until 1985, when it was cancelled for lack of funding.

Memorable Quotes: None. With his softspoken, monotone delivery, Bilandic never mastered the art of the quotable quote.

Bilandic and the Media: Like Daley, Bilandic was not a media sophisticate. Unlike Daley, he could not even strike a casual, friendly tone with the press. His one attempt at image-building failed miserably: reporters laughed out loud when a campaign film was unveiled, set to the macho "Rocky" theme music.

Biggest Mistake in Office: Serving only as caretaker. With no plans for the future, Bilandic made even Jane Byrne's wacky schemes seem attractive.

Despite the trickery that put him in the mayor's seat, Bilandic won election the following year and expected little trouble staying in office. When he was up for re-election in 1979, his record as an adequate caretaker of the City That Works was deemed all he would need to keep his job. Neither Bilandic nor party bosses could forsee the force of the upcoming blizzard of '79—a storm with enough power to shut down Chicago, and to blow its mayor out of office.

Bilandic's opponent was Jane Byrne. Daley's token female cabinet member as head of the city's consumer sales office, Byrne also served as co-chairman of the Cook County Democratic Party while Daley was alive. She was dumped soon after he died, by party leaders who would later discover this is a woman who keeps a grudge with a capital G.

Byrne rode into the campaign with a stack of departmental memos that she claimed proved Bilandic "greased" a taxi fare increase for his buddies at the local cab companies. For most of the campaign, however, she was something of an insider's joke, with a goofy wig and an even goofier string of gimmicky press conferences. Few took Byrne, or the grass roots coalition she claimed to be building, seriously. Until the Blizzard of '79.

When the snow fell, the city stood still. Office workers packed a change of clothing each morning, unsure whether they would be able to make it home in the evening. Snow clogged the bus and train routes and filled so many parking spaces that Bilandic ordered a long list of school and municipal lots cleared for neighborhood use. Unfortunately for Bilandic, the order was lost in a bureaucratic shuffle, and a newspaper photo of one of the still-buried lots, captioned, "Mayor Bilandic says park here," was permanently etched in beleaguered voters' minds. That was Bilandic's first mistake.

Big mistake number two: When the trains that always ran on time broke down under the weight of the storm, Bilandic opted for express routes to make the most of the equipment that was left. Those express trains breezed right through the inner city's black neighborhoods to get the white folks home on time. It was the last straw for black voters, who joined Byrne's grass roots coalition and propelled her into office. With her own, hand-lettered "Bill of Rights," Byrne was touted as the city's first reform mayor.

JANE M. BYRNE
Mayor, 1979-1983

Greatest Contribution: Putting the first crack in the Democratic machine. Though she had party roots, and returned there after the election, Byrne got into office without machine help, proving to others (like Harold Washington) it could be done.

Memorable Quotes: "I never said that!" (Often used to explain away her erroneous statements.) "Let me tell you something. . . ." (Another common phrase, signaling a protracted explanation, usually a jumble of half-sentences and minor details that would prove more confusing than enlightening.)

Byrne and the Media: Though she would often wink at and joke with reporters, Byrne's sense of humor does not include an ability to laugh at herself, making her a prime target for an often cruel press corps. One City Hall reporter regularly referred to Byrne as "the Bitch" and most on the beat did a vicious, if not somewhat accurate imitation of Lady Jane.

Biggest Mistake While in Office: Failing to deliver the reforms she promised. Mayor Byrne was too quick to make deals with the "evil cabal" of party bosses denounced by Candidate Byrne. Though off to a strong start in satisfying the minority voters who elected her, Byrne had forsaken them by the end of her term.

It was only a matter of weeks before Byrne discovered how different City Hall can look from the Mayor's perch, and she quickly cut a deal with the men she had, as a candidate, labeled the "evil cabal." These were the party bosses who controlled the city council and most city departments. Byrne quickly became an expert at running the system she once despised. She handed plum contracts to friends who, in turn, filled her re-election war chest. She boosted existing taxes and created new ones (some were later declared unconstitutional by the courts) so that she could conveniently give taxpayers a big break at election time.

Like mayors before her, Byrne ignored the needs of the black community. City services continued to be concentrated in white wards (remember, this is what the Urban League has called the most segregated city in the country). Byrne did promote blacks in her cabinet and on city boards, but when some appointees became too independent, she bounced them in favor of whites.

A near-riot erupted at City Hall when Byrne dumped two school board members and then two public housing board members, letting those two institutions that serve a majority of blacks be controlled by a majority of whites. That boisterous protest failed to signal to Byrne her growing problem with black voters. It did, however, attract the attention of Congressman Harold Washington, a black who had run unsuccessfully for mayor against Bilandic in '77.

Washington was a reluctant candidate, insisting that thousands of new black voters be registered as a sign of their enthusiasm for his campaign. It was done, and Washington threw his hat into the Democratic primary ring alongside that of Byrne and Richard M. Daley. As son of the late mayor, this Daley was considered by many to be the heir apparent to the Chicago throne. Never mind that he was inarticulate and something of a bumbler (a local theatre production of the time portrayed Richie as always wearing his pajamas, signifying his youth and inexperience as well as his generally awkward manner).

Daley does have a knack for surrounding himself with the right people, and that talent helped him win election two years earlier as Cook County State's Attorney, where he had done an effective job. So, he was embraced by many as the Great White Hope: strong enough to beat the Dark Horse Washington and more reliable than Byrne, who was flighty and (to party bosses who had crossed her years before) vindictive.

Daley was endorsed by both the *Chicago Tribune* and *Chicago Sun-Times*, but his stock plummeted in the final days of the campaign as the polls showed that, instead of winning, Daley would only split the white vote, acting as the spoiler who would make Harold Washington a shoo-in. Democrats pulled out all the stops for Byrne. County party chairman Ed Vrdolyak, in typically blunt Chicago style, told a party rally, "Don't kid yourself: we're fighting to keep the city the way it is." It was a fight Vrdolyak would lose.

"We won!," screamed the headline of the black newspaper, the *Chicago Daily Defender*, on the morning after Washington's victory. Even more grating to whites was the Reverend Jesse Jackson's cry, "It's our turn!," picked up by chanting throngs at Washington's election-night headquarters.*

As if being black was not enough to make Washington an enemy of party leaders, he was (as he himself might put it) a double anathema, since he also spurned the party game, rejecting the traditional post-election deal-making that usually solidified the candidate's base of power.

These two facts meant that, for the first time since the machine was rolling, the winner of the Democratic mayoral primary was not assured victory in the general election. Democrats immediately began jumping ship to, either ertly or covertly, support Republican candidate Bernard Epton. Epton promised to save the city from financial ruin, but his double-entendre slogan, "Before it's too late," served as a rallying cry for panicking whites. It was an answer to Jackson's election-night boast.

Even without active party support, Washington proved unbeatable. His strong base of support in the black wards combined with the swing vote of so-called "lakefront liberals," the white, yuppie bloc, to make Washington the city's first black mayor.

HAROLD WASHINGTON
Mayor, 1983-??

Greatest Contribution: Integrating City Hall. Not only did Washington bring in many blacks, he gave Chicago its first Hispanic school board president, first handicapped member of the transit authority board, first female budget chief, and, overall, put more blacks, Hispanics, and women in authority than did any previous mayor.

Memorable Quotes: Washington made "burgeoning," "potpourri" and "obfuscation" household words in Chicago. The show-stopper: Washington's assertion that he would not "lay supine before the juggernaut," testimony to his determination to win Council Wars.

Washington and the Meida: Like most politicians, Washington often claimed the media blew his failures out of proportion and down-played his successes. In reality, he got along well with reporters, and earned the respect of most.

Biggest Mistake While in Office: Not working hard enough to woo white voters. Washington shares the blame for stirring up racial confrontation, whether by accident or design.

Washington may have been a reluctant candidate but, once he won the election, he tackled his new job "with gusto," as he was fond of saying. He startled reporters who questioned his commitment to the job by insisting he'd be mayor "for 20 years," and that joke became a standard crowd pleaser for the remainder of Washington's first term.

As Mayor, Washington continued to spurn party regulars, refusing to huddle with "the evil cabal." The few Byrne loyalists who groveled for

---

*Jackson embarrassed Washington with that blatant appeal, but it propelled the Reverend into the national spotlight, where he solidified his role as National Black Spokesman by becoming the first black presidential candidate in 1980. Locally, however, Jackson is but one of many black leaders, and perhaps less of a black power broker than on the national scene.

Washington's support were told, "no deals," and they quickly formed an alliance with the aldermen who were too proud to beg.

Washington may have thought that, as mayor, he held all of the important cards, but that alliance proved him wrong. Twenty-nine aldermen against him formed a voting majority in the City Council, stopping most of Washington's promised reforms and launching Chicago's own Civil War.

"Council Wars," a term coined by local comedian Aaron Freeman, was fought on two fronts: in the courts and in the council chambers. In the council, Washington was a loser. Alderman and County Party Chairman Ed Vrdolyak controlled the majority of votes, and his bloc buried, by rewriting council rules, nearly every piece of new legislation and most appointments Washington offered.

Washington lost those battles, but he won the war with the help of the courts. First, the machine practice of hiring friends and firing enemies was declared unconstitutional. That took the carrot off the machine's operational stick, since patronage jobs were the machine's power base.

Second, and even more devastating, the courts declared Chicago's gerrymandered ward map illegal. Wards that strengthened the party's base were found to weaken the voice of minority voters, carving up their neighborhoods until they were no longer a threat to machine candidates. New elections were ordered, and when they were over, Washington had his council majority.

In control at last, after nearly three years in office, Washington pushed through one reform after another. He dumped the unnecessary fourth man on every garbage crew (jobs that had long been used to pad the party's patronage army, at taxpayers' expense), gave tenants the power to fight neglectful landlords, and pushed through a sweeping ethics law that limited campaign contributions elected officials could accept from city contractors. Washington even wrested control of the last machine stronghold: the park system. Washington also breathed life into a gay civil rights ordinance, but was handed his first big defeat when the Catholic church lobbied successfully against the bill. Washington was forced to put the matter on hold while his aides negotiated with church leaders, looking for a way to improve the status of the city's gays without appearing to condone their sexual preferences.

"Mayor Washington is like Chicago's skyline: he has his ups and downs," noted the *Chicago Sun-Times* in a 13-part series analyzing the mayor's progress. "Mayor Washington's Chicago: A Critical Examination," published through the summer and fall of 1986, concluded that, "for the first time, some of the have-nots feel as though they belong."

"Washington has broken new ground," the *Sun-Times* continued. "As the city's first black mayor, he has given more power to neighborhoods and has spread money and services more evenly."

Is this true reform or, as Vrydolyak claims, just groundwork for a new machine? Many long-time observers of Chicago's political scene doubt true reform is possible here. For too long, reform has meant a chance for outsiders to become insiders. However, Washington's brand of reform seems to satisfy voters. He beat back a tough challenge from former Mayor Jane Byrne in the March, 1987 one-on-one primary contest. In that race, which Byrne had insisted was a more accurate referendum on Washington than was the three-way race of 1983, Washington finished nearly 80,000 votes ahead of Byrne.

In the April, 1987 general election, anti-Washington voters were split three ways, between candidates Ed Vrdolyak (running on the Solidarity Party ticket), Cook County assessor Thomas Hynes (Chicago First Party), and Byrne's former budget chief Donald Haider (Republican Party). Three weeks before the election, Washington appeared unbeatable and aldermen who had spent four years fighting the mayor began slinking into his office to curry favor. Two days before the election Hynes dropped out, urging one or the other of Washington's challengers to do the same. Neither followed Hynes' lead.

Two hours after the polls closed, both Vrdolyak and Haider were forced to admit Washington's machine had grown stronger than theirs. The first mayor to be elected to a second term since Richard J. Daley, Washington now has more than wishful thinking or bluster to help fulfill his promise of being Chicago's mayor "for 20 years."

Postscript: So you want to get involved in Chicago's exciting political scene.

To find out where you can register to vote in the city, call 269-7900 or write the **Board of Election Commissioners,** 121 N. LaSalle, Chicago, IL 60602. They can also tell you the name of your alderman and how to contact him or her. For voter registration in suburban Cook County, call 443-5150 or write the **County Clerk** at 118 N. LaSalle, Chicago, IL 60602.

And to get even more involved in politics, try one of these:

Democratic Party of Cook County, 134 N. LaSalle, Chicago, IL 60602, 263-0575.

Independent Voters of Illinois, 220 S. State, Chicago, IL 60604, 663-4203.

League of Women Voters, 67 E. Madison, Chicago, IL 60603, 236-0315.

Republican Headquarters, 221 N. LaSalle, Chicago, IL 60601, 642-6400.

—Marj Halperin

ENTERTAINMENT

Poet Paul Carroll and his wife Maryrose in O'Rourke's.

EATING

Here's our insider's guide to our favorite Chicago eateries and food shops. The following information, like all information in our high-tech world, ages all too quickly—so it's a good idea to call ahead to double-check hours, menu, and prices before you make plans.

RESTAURANTS

Army & Lou's
422 E. 75th   483-6550
Mon, Wed & Thur 11 am-11 pm, Fri & Sat 11 am-12 pm,
Sun 9 am-11 pm, closed Tues
Soul Food, Mid South, Inexpensive
Soul food and Creole cooking with a wide following. Out of town visitors have been known to charter limos to A & L's so they can savor some greens, beans, chicken, or ribs—not to mention the tasty peach cobbler. Army & Lou's makes a dynamite Cajun seafood gumbo, and they've been making it since long before those folks on the north side discovered Creole food. Both fried and smothered chicken (with cornbread dressing) are done up well here.

Avanzare
161 E. Huron   337-8056
Lunch Mon-Fri 11:30 am-2 pm, Dinner Sun-Thur 5:30 pm-9:30 pm,
Fri & Sat until 10:30 pm
Italian, Near North, Expensive
Sophisticated, pleasant dining spot serving imaginatively prepared Northern Italian food. The chef's award-winning pasta and seafood creations are superb, and the grand cafe-style atmosphere adds to the restaurant's attraction. One of the best places in town to go when someone else is treating, or when you're on an expense account. Reservations are a must.

The Bagel
3000 W. Devon   764-3377
Sun-Thur 6:30 am-10 pm, Fri & Sat until 11 pm
Deli, Far North, Inexpensive
The best Jewish food this side of the Hudson. All of your favorite specialties prepared better than Bubbie used to make. The blintzes, whitefish stuffed with gefilte fish, French toast made with challah bread, and the complimentary bialys and onion rolls are to die for. A popular place for breakfast.

Bangkok Star
1443 W. Fullerton   348-8868
Thur-Tues 4:30 pm-10 pm, Fri & Sat until 10:30 pm, closed Wed
Thai, Mid North, Inexpensive
Great Thai food, particularly the curry dishes. You can fry your tongue here, if you like that sort of thing. Also serves milder versions for those

41

with more delicate palates. They'll make your food just as hot or as mild as you like it.

Belden Deli
2315 N. Clark   935-2752
Open 24 hours
Deli, Near North, Inexpensive
Untrendy Lincoln Park delicatessen with corned beef sandwiches, matzo ball soup and home-baked goods. The free dill pickles alone make this place worth a visit, but we come here for deli food and late night people watching. Also a location in Rogers Park at 7572 N. Western, but this one is better.

The Berghoff
17 W. Adams   427-3170
Mon-Thur 11 am-9:30 pm, Fri & Sat until 10 pm, closed Sun
German, Loop, Moderate
A longtime Chicago favorite, the Berghoff serves hearty, well-prepared German fare at respectable prices. Also serves an excellent whitefish. Legendary rye bread comes with every meal. Tasty house light and dark beer, also a good house root beer. Large, elegant bustling rooms with an old world atmosphere. Old habits die hard here—parties of women may receive less than the Berghoff's usually attentive service. The stand-up bar (men-only until the 1970s) is a great place to enjoy a draft of Berghoff's own with a fresh-carved corned or roast beef sandwich.

Busy Bee
1546 N. Damen   772-4433
Mon-Sat 6 am-8 pm, Sun 7 am-7:30 pm
Polish, Near Northwest, Inexpensive
Small, unpretentious neighborhood restaurant in Wicker Park serving good, cheap, traditional Polish food. A complete dinner runs around $5. The pierogi are out of this world. Try the combination plate of Polish specialties. Note the hours—this place closes EARLY. If you sit in the first dining room (the one with the counter in the middle) you may be able to see the Polish women in the kitchen, rolling out pierogi dough and giggling among themselves.

La Capannina
7353 W. Grand, Elmwood Park   452-0900
Mon-Sat 4 pm-11:30 pm, Sun 2:30-10:30 pm
Italian, Far West, Inexpensive
Good, reliable, moderately priced Italian food. Servings are not stingy. Arrabbiata sauce is a mouth-burner but delicious if you like a spicy tomato sauce on your pasta. Satisfying veal, fish, and chicken dishes, too. Huge desserts, a little on the sweet side.

Cape Cod Room
140 E. Walton   787-2200
Mon-Sun 12 pm-11 pm
Seafood, Near North, Expensive
A terrific, old-fashioned seafood place for times when cost is no object. Fresh fish, always well-prepared. Simply wonderful. New England clam chowder and bookbinder red-snapper soup are exceptional. A good place for an expense-account lunch or dinner. Reservations are necessary.

Catfish Digby's
68 E. Cermak   842-7142
Sun-Thur 11 am-10 pm, Fri & Sat until 2 am
Seafood, Near South, Inexpensive
Friendly carryout place/restaurant located east of Chinatown, near Mc-
Cormick Place. Interesting combination of seafood and soul food items. You
can get cooked greens with your fried catfish or red beans and rice with
Digby's seafood gumbo. The seafood ranks among the best in the city, and
their fried chicken isn't bad, either. Finish off with the marvelous sweet
potato pie. Another location at 81st and Stony Island.

La Choza
7630 N. Paulina   465-9401
Tues-Sun Noon-11:30 pm, until midnight on Sat, closed Mon
Mexican, Far North, Inexpensive
Sprawling Mexican restaurant in a somewhat shabby section of Rogers Park
just north of the Howard Street el stop. Serves the usual Mexican food plus
a variety of steak entrees. Try a kamoosh appetizer! Outdoor patios in
summer. Bring your own liquor. A favorite of many area restaurant employees.

Cooking and Hospitality Institute of Chicago
858 N. Orleans   944-0882
Mon-Fri noon seating only
Gourmet, Near North, Moderate
Let the budding chefs of CHIC try out their creations on your palate. Menu
changes daily, offerings are always original and delectable both to the eye
and to the tongue. The chefs enjoy making beautiful and amusing garnishes,
for example, the sliced potato that turns out to be a pear slice, and what
looks like a pear, but is really twice-baked potatoes molded into a pear form.
Luncheon is a multi-course feast, and includes appetizer, salad, entree, and
vegetables.

Courtyards of Plaka
340 S. Halsted   263-0767
Sun-Thur 11 am-midnight, Fri & Sat until 1 am
Greek. Near West, Moderate
More daring than the old Greektown standbys, a little fancier than its neighbors, yet not at all pretentious. Plaka offers more than just saganaki, moussaka and spinach-cheese pie. The red snapper and garlicky codfish are excellent.
Among the standard Greek dishes, moussaka is a standout. And if you want
to gorge, order the Athenian feast—12 items for about $14.

Daruma
2901 Central, Evanston   864-6633
Tues-Sat 11:30 am-2:15 pm, Tues-Thur 4:30 pm-9:45 pm,
Fri & Sat until 10:45 pm, Sun until 8:45 pm
Japanese, North Suburban, Moderate
Popular North Evanston spot for great Japanese food at moderate prices.
Serves outstanding noodle soups. We especially like the nabeyaki udon
(noodle soup with shrimp, vegetables and fish cakes). Sushi and sashimi are
also available, of course.

Dave's Italian Kitchen
906 Church, Evanston   864-6000
Sun-Thur 4:30 pm-10:30 pm, Fri & Sat until 12:30 am
Lunch Mon-Fri 11 am-2 pm
Italian, North Suburban, Inexpensive
Delicious, cheap Italian food and a good wine list. You can't go wrong with
the minestrone or the eggplant parmigiana. But then we've enjoyed every-
thing we've ever had here. Popular with Northwestern students.

Ed Debevic's
640 N. Wells   664-1707
Mon-Thur 11 am-midnight; Fri & Sat until 1 am, Sun until 11 pm
American, Near North, Inexpensive
Trendy but fun tongue-in-cheek tribute to the diners of the fifties, complete
with meatloaf and mashed potatoes, Green River and chili dogs. And it's
inexpensive. The chocolate shakes are great and the New England clam
chowder is surprisingly good. Ed's own beer (made at the Augsburger brew-
ery) is served in paper cups. Excellent jukebox selections (late 50's/early
60's) and kitschy signs on the walls. Interesting vending machines in the
johns. Long waits for tables during peak hours.

Doll San
4520 N. Lincoln   271-2881
11 am-11 pm daily
Japanese/Korean, Mid North, Inexpensive
This Japanese-Korean restaurant makes a great sushi, along with their other
Oriental specialties. Try the California roll sushi made with crabmeat. The
tempura and Korean bulkoghi are also good.

Edwardo's
1321 E. 57th (Mid South)   241-7960
1937 W. Howard (Far North)   761-7040
1212 N. Dearborn (Near North)   337-4490
521 S. Dearborn (Near South)   939-3366
Sun-Thur 11 am-12:30 am, Fri & Sat 12 pm-12 am
Pizza, Inexpensive
Some of the best pizza in a great pizza town. Edwardo's invented souffle
stuffed pizza, a new twist on Chicago-style pizza. It's twice as thick as a pan
pizza, and they say it's even good for you. Mozzarella cheese and spinach
or broccoli are mixed together for a souffle effect. We like the spinach souffle
version.

Florence
1030 W. Taylor   829-1857
Tues-Fri 11:30 am-2 pm, 5:30-9 pm; Sat 5:30-9 pm, closed Sun & Mon
Italian, Near West, Moderate
This small, charming, beautifully decorated restaurant (see the lovely mural
painted by one of the owners) in the old Italian neighborhood near the
University of Illinois campus serves wonderful Northern Italian food. We're
partial to the linguini gorgonzola and the whipped ricotta dessert. Reservations are advised, especially on weekends. Parking around Florence can
be difficult.

La Fontanella
2414 S. Oakley   927-5249
Lunch Tues-Fri 11:30 am-3 pm; Dinner Tues, Wed-Sun
4:30 pm-9:30 pm, Thur until 10:30 pm, Fri & Sat until 11:30 pm
Italian, Near Southwest, Moderate
La Fontanella's homemade pasta and unsurpassed meatballs are two reasons
why this is a longtime favorite Italian spot. It's located in the small Italian
enclave near 24th & Western.

Frances' Food Shop
2453 N. Clark   248-4580
Tues-Sun 7 am-10 pm, closed Mon
Deli, Near North, Inexpensive
Famous for steam tables full of good, home-style food. Frances' forte is
breakfast—you can choose from dozens of omelette combinations, or mix
and match your favorite fillings. Also known for their great cheese blintzes.

French Kitchen
3437 W. 63rd   776-6715
Tues-Sat 5 pm-10 pm, Sun 3 pm-8 pm, closed Mon
French, Mid Southwest, Moderate
Tiny, elegant storefront restaurant in Marquette Park serving a limited menu
of moderately priced French food. Among the choices are some appealing
seafood entrees, including a delicious shrimp and scallops dish and a moist,
flavorful sole en sac (cooked in a bag). Many tempting desserts are available,
including a fantastic chocolate mousse. Reservations are necessary.

Galans
2210 W. Chicago   292-1000
Tues-Fri 11:30 am-9 pm, Sat 5 pm-10 pm,
Sun 11:30 am-9 pm, closed Mon
Ukrainian, Near Northwest, Moderate
Ukrainian Village restaurant featuring authentic ethnic cooking. The typical
Ukrainian dishes—holubtsi (stuffed cabbage rolls), kielbasa, and pierohy
(stuffed dumplings)—are consistently good and not super filling. Worth
noting are the borscht and the kartoplyanyk (potato pancake stuffed with
beef). If you can't decide, try the Kozak feast—10 courses for about $14.
For dessert, try the nalysnyky—exquisite, thin baked pancakes filled with
cheese or fruit. Ukrainian musicians, which have included singers and ban-
dura players, perform on weekends.

Gandhi India
2601 W. Devon   761-8714
Sun-Thur 5 pm-10 pm, Fri & Sat 5 pm-11 pm;
Lunch 11:30 am-3:30 pm Mon-Sun
East Indian, Far North, Inexpensive
Nestled among sari shops in Chicago's Little India, this spot is a favorite
among Indians. Tasty, unusually seasoned dishes—and each is uniquely
flavorful. The tandoori chicken and lamb shishkebabs are highly recommended; you might also try the deliciously different Indian crepes. All-you-
can-eat lunch buffet every day.

Gino's East
160 E. Superior   943-1124
Mon-Thur 11 am-11 pm, Fri & Sat until midnight, Sun 2 pm-10 pm
Pizza, Near North, Inexpensive
The archetypical Chicago pizza place. Every Chicagoan has a favorite pizza,
but Gino's name pops up most often when we survey our pizza-loving
friends. Long lines outside, even in subzero weather, attest to Gino's popularity. Great, great pan pizza. If you don't want to wait in line, Gino's
carryout location one door east (988-4200) sells slices until 6 pm every day
but Sunday.

Gladys' Luncheonette
4527 S. Indiana   548-6848
Mon-Sat 6 am-12 am, closed Sun
Soul Food, Mid South, Inexpensive
The enticing aromas will pull you in from outside. Gladys makes delicious
breakfasts, served any time of day. Great biscuits, ham, grits, and eggs.
Also famous for fried chicken, smothered chicken, smothered steak, and
soul food.

Golden Shell
10063 S. Avenue N   221-9876
Daily 6 am-midnight
Yugoslavian, Far South, Inexpensive
Not just a seafood joint as you might think from the name, but a Yugoslavian eatery. Located in the far southeast side's steel mill district, this
large restaurant offers many Serbian-Croatian specialties: a gypsy platter
and many lamb and eggplant dishes. Good seafood, too. Generous portions and low prices. Breakfast special available all day includes eggs, ba-
con, sausage, crepes, French bread, fried potatoes and coffee for about
$3.50. Music and belly dancers on weekends; lingerie shows at lunch every
weekday.

Gradley's Bar and Grill
3119 W. 111th   233-4004
Mon-Fri 11 am-9 pm, Sat 11 am-4 pm, closed Sun
American, Far Southwest, Inexpensive
Located in the Mount Greenwood neighborhood, Gradley's is known for
great home cooking in a particularly friendly atmosphere at low prices.
They're especially famous for juicy burgers and a huge assortment of deli
sandwiches. Seafood, steaks, Italian dishes, too. Walk through the liquor
store to get to the restaurant.

Un Grand Cafe
2300 N. Lincoln Park West   348-8886
Mon-Thur 6 pm-11 pm, Fri & Sat until midnight, closed Sun
French, Near North, Expensive
Simple but elegant bistro. Everything that comes out of the kitchen is just
about perfect—both in appearance and taste. The simplest ingredients—
like steak and potatoes—are routinely turned into a standout dinner. Very
classy, and the prices aren't exorbitant.

Greek Islands
200 S. Halsted   782-9855
Sun-Thur 11 am-12 am, Fri & Sat until 1 am
Greek, Near West, Inexpensive to moderate
Festive, almost orgiastic atmosphere makes this one of the most enjoyable
spots in Greektown. The food is not spectacular, but it's reliable, and after
a few glasses of roditys you won't care. Have a drink in the bar before or
after dinner. The beautiful, polished wood bar is decorated with pictures
of the Islands and is a fine place for philosophizing. Make sure you take a
cab home if you drink too much Greek wine.

Hatsuhana
160 E. Ontario   280-8287
Lunch Mon-Fri noon-2 pm, Dinner Mon-Sat 5:45 pm-10 pm, closed Sun
Japanese, Near North, Moderate to expensive
The main attraction: a staggeringly large variety of exquisitely prepared fish.
Superb sushi and sashimi, definitely the best in the city. A bustling sushi
emporium.

Healthy Food Restaurant
3236 S. Halsted   326-2724
Mon-Sat 6:30 am-8 pm, Sun 8 am-8 pm
Lithuanian, Mid South, Inexpensive
A Bridgeport favorite for good, hearty, Lithuanian food. You can have a
wholesome, filling meal for very little money here. The soups are good,
apple strudel is great, and blynas (fruit-filled pancakes) are memorable.

Heartland Cafe
7000 N. Glenwood   465-8005
Mon-Fri 8 am-10 pm, Sat until 12 am, Sun 9 am-10 pm
Health Food/American, Far North, Inexpensive
A Rogers Park institution, this place has the feel of Berkeley in the late 60s.
While many vegetarian items are on the menu, plenty of fish is available as
well. The house salad is a lush mountain of various veggies. Scrumptious
cornbread is among the best in the city. Warm, relaxed atmosphere. You
can take your time here, but the staff will, too. There's now a bar where
you can hear live music (often jazz) on the weekends.

Jerome's
2450 N. Clark   327-2207
Sat 8 am-4 pm, 5 pm to 12 am; Sun 10 am-3 pm, 5 pm-10 pm;
Mon 5 pm-11 pm, Tue-Fri 11:30 am-4 pm, 5 pm-11 pm;
Fri 11:30 am-4 pm, 5 pm-12 am
Gourmet, Near North, Moderate
Imagine Alice's Restaurant after Alice gets her MBA and discovers bal-
samic vinegar and shitakii mushrooms, and you have an idea of what Jer-
ome's is like. Fresh fruits and vegetables and whole grain breads share the
menu with elegant nouvelle dishes prepared for an upscale clientele. Brunch
is great. Art pieces (for sale) by the starving artist waitstaff adorn the
walls.

Kavkaz
6405 N. Claremont   338-1316
Mon-Thur 12 am-10 pm, Fri until 1 am, Sat until 2 am
Georgian-Russian, Far North, Moderate
Specialties from the Soviet Republic of Georgia and neighboring countries.
Georgian cuisine is a mixture of Eastern European and Middle Eastern
influences; many dishes are reminiscent of Greek or Turkish cooking. Don't
overlook the appetizers, it's their forte here. If you come with a group of
four or more, try the combination appetizer plate, which allows you to sample
a number of items. Liquor prices are high.

Kotobuki
5547 N. Clark   275-6588
Mon-Thur 5 pm-10 pm, Fri & Sat until 10:30 pm, Sun 4 pm-9 pm,
Lunch Mon-Fri 11 am-2 pm
(closed Wed)
Japanese, Far North, Moderate
Japanese restaurant featuring excellent teriyaki and tempura. Many inter-
esting varieties of sushi, always very fresh. Also offers some exotic appetizers.
Good-sized portions.

Leona's
3215 N. Sheffield   327-8861
Sun-Thur 11 am-1 am, Fri & Sat until 2 am
Italian, Mid North, Inexpensive to moderate
Enormous, spread-out restaurant that just happens to have some pretty
decent pizza; other Italian meals and snacks, too. A good place to go after
seeing a play at one of several off-Loop theaters in the area—and Leona's
stays open late.

Lindo Mexico
2642 N. Lincoln   871-4832
Sun-Thur 11 am-2 am, Fri & Sat until 5 am
Mexican, Mid North, Inexpensive
The usual Mexican fare served in colorful, festive rooms. Like many Mexican places, the portions are large and the Margaritas are decent. Burritos
are especially good. Attractive indoor and outdoor gardens. The decor here
is truly lindo (beautiful). A second location is at 1934 N. Maple, Evanston.

Little Bucharest
3001 N. Ashland   929-8640
Lunch Mon-Sat 11 am-2 pm, Dinner Mon-Thur 5 pm-10 pm,
Fri & Sat 4 pm-11 pm
closed Sun
Romanian, Mid North, Moderate
Very pleasant Romanian restaurant. The portions are enormous. One good
entree is veal tournedo, an enormous ball of stuffed veal. Romanian food is
richer than it looks, so eat accordingly. Many tempting desserts, like fudgy
Bavarian chocolate cake and many varieties of rich pastries and tortes, so
try to save room.

Little Joe's Pizzeria and Restaurant
2921 W. 63rd   476-5233
Mon-Thur 11 am-midnight; Fri-Sat 11 am-1 am; Sun 2 pm-midnight
Italian, Mid Southwest, Inexpensive
Southwest side favorite serving inexpensive, fabulous food. Crispy thin crust
pizza and lots of good Italian dishes. Try the chicken vesuvio or parmigiana
or any of the tasty veal dinners, made with large, thick steaks.

La Llama
3811 N. Ashland   327-7756
Tues-Sun 5 pm-10 pm, closed Mon
Peruvian, Mid North, Expensive
Superb Peruvian food. The menu, no longer prix fixe as it used to be, is
strictly a la carte. Go to La Llama to nosh on appetizers—all 17 varieties
are mouth-watering. The appetizers are so good, you may never get around
to ordering a main course. The owners feel that their restaurant inspired
the current "grazing" craze. Expensive, but worth it.

Peter Lo's
6144 N. Lincoln   267-0436
Mon & Wed 5 pm-10 pm, Thur 11:30 am-10pm, Fri until 11 pm;
Sat 4 pm-11 pm, Sun 4 pm-10 pm, closed Tues
Chinese, Far North, Moderate
You could spend all night at Peter's reading the menu—there are well over
a hundred items. But don't—the Mandarin/Szechuan/Hunan cooking is too
good to miss. Just writing this gives us cravings for Peter's moo shu. It's
available in chicken, pork, beef and vegetable versions. In the summer
months, Peter serves his sensational cold summer noodles. Cold, that is, to
the touch. To the tongue the noodles are hot and spicy.

Lutz's
2454 W. Montrose   478-7785
Tues-Thur 7 am-10 pm, Fri & Sat 7 am-11 pm, Sun 7 am-10 pm,
closed Mon
German, Mid North, Inexpensive
A wonderful place to have German-style pastries and European coffee ele-
gantly served mit schlag (with cream) on a silver platter. Sandwiches and
ice cream desserts are also on the menu, but at Lutz's you must try the
pastries. Hazelnut, Grand Marnier, and Black Forest cherry tortes are among
the chef's superb creations. A nice place to bring your parents.

Maller Building Coffee Shop
5 S. Wabash, 3rd floor   263-7696
Mon-Fri 6 am-4:30 pm, Sat 6 am-2 pm
Deli, Loop, Inexpensive
A reliable Loop institution serving traditional delicatessen fare: lox and
bagels, chopped liver, corned beef, blintzes. They make a terrific egg salad
sandwich. It's usually packed during the lunch hour.

Mama Desta's Red Sea
3216 N. Clark   935-7561
Tues-Sun noon to midnight, Mon 4 pm-midnight
Ethiopian, Mid North, Inexpensive
Lakewood's own Ethiopian restaurant. Interestingly flavored stews and sau-
tees served with soft, tortilla-like injera bread for dipping. The wat dishes

are hot and spicy, alitcha dishes are well seasoned but not hot. Come with a group of four or so; that way you can sample a variety of items from the menu. Not always consistent (one week's somewhat hot dish is another's HOT HOT one), but for its uniqueness Mama Desta's should not be missed.

Manny's Coffee Shop
1141 S. Jefferson   939-2855
Mon-Sat 5 am-5 pm, closed Sun
Deli, Near South, Inexpensive
For serious lovers of deli food. It's all here: knishes, potato pancakes, blintzes, liver and onions, and of course a great corned beef sandwich. If you order soup, be ready to tell the guys behind the steam tables whether you want it with a matzo ball, kreplach, noodles, or rice—the servers work fast and won't tolerate people holding up the line. We always overeat here because everything looks and tastes so good. A fun, bustling place.

Maple Tree Inn
10730 S. Western   239-3688
Mon-Thur 5 pm-9:30 pm, Fri-Sat until 10:30 pm
Cajun, Far Southwest, Moderate
Great Louisiana-style cooking on the far southwest side. Try a Boat (Po' Boy sandwiches stuffed with your choice of seafood) or the flavorful jambalaya. Dixie beer from New Orleans is available, but if you're bolder, order a Cajun martini or a Hurricane. Save room for the superb pecan pie.

Matsuya
3469 N. Clark   248-2677
Wed-Mon noon-midnight, closed Tues
Japanese, Mid North, Moderate
A warm atmosphere and consistently good food have earned Matsuya a fine reputation. Lots of fresh fish charbroiled to perfection. The combination plates are a bargain and the way to go if you're unfamiliar with Japanese cuisine. Excellent sushi.

Medici on 57th
1450 E. 57th   667-7394
Mon-Thur 11:30 am-12:30 am, Fri & Sat until 1:30 am,
Sun 9 am-Midnight
American, Mid South, Inexpensive
Real college-y atmosphere. Constant classical music. Four-seater booths with 20 years' worth of graffiti scratched into the woodwork. Great place for coffee, burgers, and pizza. No liquor, but you can bring your own wine or beer.

Mekong
4953 N. Broadway (Far North)   271-0206
400 N. State (Near North)   222-9191
Mon, Tue, Thur 10 am-10 pm, Fri 10 am-11 pm,
Sat & Sun 9 am-11 pm, closed Wed
Vietnamese, Moderate
A huge selection of Vietnamese and Chinese foods are offered at this popular, distinctive restaurant in the new Little Vietnam section of the city, along

Argyle Street in Uptown. Reasonable prices, friendly service. Tasty appetizers, including thin, spicy pork egg rolls and stuffed chicken wings. Lemon grass chicken is exceptional.

Metropolis
163 W. North Ave.   642-2130
11 am-9 pm Mon-Thur, until 10:30 pm Fri & Sat
Gourmet, Near North, Moderate
Imaginatively prepared nouvelle cuisine. The menu changes daily, but everything from Metropolis' kitchen is delicious. The flavorful cold curry chicken is a standout, as are the luscious, rich desserts.

Mi Pueblo
2908 W. 59th   737-2700
Daily 11 am-11 pm
Mexican, Mid Southwest, Inexpensive
Some friends visiting from Mexico City were favorably impressed with Mi Pueblo. Superior Mexican food, particularly the guacamole. Sombreros—hat-shaped tortillas filled with a chorizo sauce—are unusual and not to be missed. Good margaritas. A wide variety of Mexican beers are available.

Lou Mitchell's
565 W. Jackson   939-3111
Mon-Fri 5:30 am-4 pm, Sat 5:30 am-2:30 pm, closed Sun
American/Breakfast, West Loop, Inexpensive
All fresh ingredients. Hand-baked goods and double-yolk eggs. Delicious omelettes and eggs done your way are delivered to your table in a skillet. Deep-fried French toast made with thick Greek bread. GREAT coffee. Long elbow-to-elbow tables in the middle of the dining room. Long lines for breakfast, especially on Saturday. Definitely our favorite breakfast place. Lou greets customers and hands out Milk Duds to the ladies to sweeten the wait. Located near Union Station.

Monique's Cafe
213 W. Institute Place   642-2210
Tues-Thur 5:30-9:30 pm, Fri-Sat 5:30-10:30 pm;
also Mon-Sun 11:30 am-3 pm
Gourmet, Near North, Moderate to expensive
Classy French cafe in the booming River North area. Good prepared food and superb fresh goods. If seafood sausage is on the menu, don't pass it up. Notoriously decadent desserts—forget your diet and indulge in the raspberry-and-chocolate Marquis torte. A good place to bring your parents or out-of-town guests. Moderately expensive, but worth every penny.

Neringa
2632 W. 71st   476-9026
8 am-8 pm daily
Lithuanian, Mid Southwest, Inexpensive
Ample portions of hearty, home-cooked Lithuanian food, and it's hard to spend a lot of money. Specialties include dumplings, kugale, roast pork, and many good soups.

Nuevo Leon
1515 W. 18th   421-1517
Sun 8 am-1 am, Mon-Thur until 3 am, Fri & Sat until 5 am
Mexican, Near South, Inexpensive
We're tried a lot of Mexican spots over the years, but we keep coming back to Nuevo Leon. It has never disappointed us. The people are friendly, the food is delicious and cheap. The old reliable tacos, burritos, and enchiladas are good here, but many Mexican customers prefer the steak entrees.

On the Tao
1218 W. Morse   743-5955
Tues-Sun 5 pm-11 pm
Chinese, Far North, Moderate
Excellent Cantonese food prepared with an original flourish. Dishes are prepared simply but creatively. No MSG or salt is used in cooking, and fresh vegetables are in abundance. On the Tao is probably the best Chinese restaurant in Chicago.

La Paella
2920 N. Clark   528-0757
Tues-Sat 5:30 pm-11 pm, Sun 5:30 pm-10 pm, closed Mon
Spanish, Mid North, Expensive
Seductive, dimly lit Spanish restaurant serving mostly seafood items. Paella, the restaurant's namesake dish, is superb. You might want to try something more unusual, like fish cheeks or lamb sweetbreads. Expensive, but romance doesn't come cheap. A great place for seduction.

Pars Cove
4353 N. Central   725-3177
Mon-Thur 4 pm-10 pm, Fri & Sat 12 pm-11 pm, Sun 12 pm-10 pm
Persian, Far Northwest, Moderate
Exotic Persian food at reasonable prices. Pars Cove serves both delicious seafood and fine Persian cuisine, plus many vegetarian items. Among many good dishes are the charbroiled salmon, chicken, beef, and lamb versions of kabobs, gormah sabzi (a spicy stew), and fried chicken. Tasty Persian flatbread comes with every meal. The yogurt-like dessert is delicious and not too sweet. They offer several package deals, like the dinner for two, which includes any two entrees, a bottle of wine, appetizers, bread, salad bar, soup, and dessert at an incredibly low price (about $24). A second restaurant is at 435 W. Diversey, 549-1515.

Pilsner
6725 W. Cermak, Berwyn   484-2294
Sun 11 am-8:30 pm, Tues-Sat until 9 pm, closed Mon
Czech, West Suburban, Inexpensive
Authentic Czech restaurant, a real family-type place. Some typical Czech dishes to try are kachna knedliky a zeli (duck dumplings and sauerkraut), or polizka a jatrove knedlicky (liver dumpling soup). Prices are very reasonable.

Pizzeria Uno
29 E. Ohio   321-1000
Mon 5 pm-1 am, Tues-Fri 11:30 am-1 am,
Sat until 2 am, Sun 1 pm-8 pm

Pizzeria Due
619 N. Wabash   943-2400
Mon-Fri 11:30 am-3 am, Sat 5 pm-4 am, Sun 4 pm-midnight
Pizza, Near North, Inexpensive
Still a deep-dish pizza favorite after all these years. There's a lot more
competition now, but Uno and Due continue to draw crowds of pizza lovers.
The crust is delightful.

Playa Azul
1514 W. 18th   421-2252
Mon-Thur 8 am-Midnight; Fri & Sat until 4 am, Sun until 2 am
Mexican, Near South, Inexpensive to moderate
Popular Pilsen restaurant features some of the best Mexican seafood anywhere. Generous portions. For a good appetizer, try the vuelva la vita seafood
cocktail (it means "come back to life"). Also makes a good ceviche. Look
for the restaurant with the blue shark painted on the picture window. A
second restaurant is at 4005 N. Broadway, 472-8924.

Resi's Bierstube
2034 W. Irving Park   472-1749
Mon-Thur 5 pm-10 pm, Fri & Sat until 11pm
German, Mid North, Inexpensive
Informal German restaurant serving great brats and over 50 different kinds
of beer, including a very authentic Weissbier. Welcoming atmosphere. Outdoor beer garden in summer.

Ann Sather's
929 W. Belmont   348-2378
Sun-Thur 7 am-Midnight, Fri & Sat until 2 am
Swedish, Mid North, Inexpensive
Homestyle Swedish cooking in the funky Belmont neighborhood. Simple,
good food at reasonable prices. A basket of fresh baked breads comes with
your meal and includes an unusual offering of breads: Swedish limpa, onion
rolls, and Ann's famous cinnamon rolls. Delicious Swedish veal-and-potato
sausages are mild but flavorful. Breakfast is a specialty; the omelettes (all
kinds) and pancakes with lingonberries will knock you out. A second Ann
Sather's is located in Andersonville at 5207 N. Clark, 271-6677.

Shaw's Crab House
21 E. Hubbard   527-2722
Mon-Thur 11:30 am-10:00 pm, Fri until 11 pm,
Sat 5 pm-11 pm, Sun 4 pm-9 pm
Seafood, Near North, Expensive
Some of the best seafood available anywhere, but you'll pay for it. Shaw's
is best known for their outstanding crab cakes, great clam chowder, and
fine key lime pie. Even dyed-in-the-wool New Englanders will concede that
Shaw's New England clam chowder is first-rate.

Phil Smidt & Son
1205 N. Calumet Ave., Hammond, Ind.   (219) 659-0025
Mon-Thur 11:15 am-9:30 pm, Fri & Sat until 10:30 pm
Seafood, South Suburban, Moderate
It may not be in our area code, but it's just over the Skyway bridge, a hair across the state line, and it's great. Phil's great lake perch drowned in butter has no rivals. Smidt's is synonymous with frog legs—there just isn't any other place to go if you like them. Dinners are all-you-can-eat feasts.

Szechuan House
600 N. Michigan   642-3900
Mon-Fri 11:30 am-10:30 pm, Sat 11 pm, Sun 11:30 am-10:30 pm
Chinese, Near North, Moderate to expensive
Spicy Chinese food served in an elegant, refined atmosphere. Many unusual dishes are prepared, including Szechuan snails and ground shrimp wrapped in seaweed and deep-fried. You can get Chinese food as hot as you like it here. One of the more expensive Chinese restaurants in the city.

Three Happiness
2130 S. Wentworth   791-1228
Dim sum daily 10 am–2 pm
Chinese, Near South, Inexpensive
A Chinatown favorite for dim sum. Try to arrive early on weekends to avoid a long wait.

Three Happiness
209 W. Cermak   842-1964
Mon, Tue, Wed, Fri, & Sat 8 am-4 am,
Sun 8 am-2 am, Thur 8 am-8 pm
Chinese, Near South, Inexpensive
It's very confusing—two restaurants with the same name within one block of each other. We like this one for good, simple Chinese food. The place is very popular with Chinese patrons—a good sign.

Tipsuda I & II
1639-49 E. 55th   324-9296
Mon-Sat 11 am-10 pm, Sun 11 am-9 pm
Thai, Mid South, Inexpensive
One of the few Thai restaurants in Chicago without "Thai" or "Bangkok" in their name, and among the best. Two restaurants, two separate kitchens, operated only one storefront apart in Hyde Park. The menu is the same for both. In cold weather, go to 1639 E. 55th—the space is larger and warmer.

Valois
1518 E. 53rd   667-0647
Mon-Sun 6 am-10 pm
American, Mid South, Inexpensive
If you live in or visit Hyde Park, you must, simply must, go to Valois. The food is great and inexpensive and the place is so tacky it's hip. Here, locals rub elbows with professors and graduate students and police and everyone lingers over their coffee. (The manager doesn't ever mind.) Hearty biscuits come with dinners. Also serves a fantastic breakfast.

Vernon Park Tap (also known as **Tufano's**)
1073 W. Vernon Park Place
Tues-Sat 5 pm-9:30 pm, Sun 4 pm-9 pm, closed Mon
Italian, Near West, Inexpensive
There's no sign here—just look for a bustling bar visible through a large picture window. You'll find good, cheap Italian food here in the old Italian neighborhood next to the University of Illinois. Unbelievably low prices—none of the entrees costs more than $5. Don't bother asking about any meatless dinners—they don't have any. Many long-time customers. But expect gruff service if you look like a student. The owners schedule their annual vacation during the university's new student week in September, hoping to discourage student business.

Yugo Inn
2824 N. Ashland   348-6444
Wed-Sun 5 pm-Midnight, closed Mon & Tues
Yugoslavian, Mid North, Moderate
The food served here is authentic, mostly Serbian cuisine. Large rostilj (grilled meats) menu—beef, pork, and veal. Some good native dishes, such as cevapcici (kabobs of spicy, ground meat sausages with diced onions) and raznjici (beef or pork grilled on a skewer and served like American shish-kebobs). Other good dishes include paprikash, moussaka, and sarma (cabbage rolls). Cozy dining room, decorated with beautiful folk crafts.

CARRY-OUTS AND QUICK FOOD

BURGERS

Billy Goat
430 N. Michigan (lower level)
222-1525
Unmatched anywhere for great, greasy, cheap cheeseburgers, excellent pickles, and the coldest beer around. There's a second location at 309 W. Washington, but nothing beats the original.

Goldyburgers
7316 Circle Ave., Forest Park
366-0750
Royalburgers are great with a cold beer.

Moody's Pub
5910 N. Broadway
275-2696
Moody's juicy burgers are famous all over the city.

Muskie's Hamburgers
2870 N. Lincoln
883-1633
50s-style hamburger joint serving authentic burgers, fries, and shakes.

Pig Outs
3591 N. Milwaukee
282-1200
Good burgers as well as tasty chili, sausages, and hot dogs.

Redamak's
2263 N. Lincoln
787-9866
Unfancy but great burgers in an upscale setting.

Top-Notch Beefburgers
2116 W. 95th
445-7218
This place looked like a 50s diner before that was in. The burgers have been great for over 40 years.

CHICKEN

Harold's Chicken Shack
1364 E. 53rd
667-9835
Look for a neon sign showing a
picture of a man trying to ax a
chicken. Ask for your chicken and
fries with hot sauce. This is just
one of more than two dozen
outlets; check the phone book for
others.

Jerry's Kitchen
449 W. North
280-9340
Tasty fried chicken. The dinners
are a good deal.

CHILI

Bishop's
1958 W. 18th
829-6345
A Chicago favorite for 50-some
years. Bishop's chili is made the
old-fashioned way, without
tomatoes.

Lindy's
3685 S. Archer
927-7807
Another Chicago chili institution.

HOT DOGS

Byron's
1017 W. Irving Park
281-7474
Great dogs served with green
peppers and cucumbers, as well as
the usual trimmings. A second
location is at 1701 W. Lawrence.

Fluky's
6821 N. Western
274-3652
A favorite of many Chicagoans.
Many hot dog variations are
available. Also serves a good
breakfast.

Gold Coast Dogs
418 N. State
527-1222
Besides tasty red hots, they also
have good burgers and sandwiches,
all made with the freshest
ingredients. Cheese fries are made
with real cheese—imagine that!
Also a location at 2100 N. Clark
St.

JR's Hot Dogs
4441 S. Kedzie
890-3944
also at 4426 S. Pulaski, 4205 W.
63rd, and 8346 S. Pulaski

Snyder's
9900 S. Western
No phone
Open March to October
Long a Beverly area favorite.

Superdawg
6363 N. Milwaukee
763-0660
Look for the huge dancing male
and female hot dogs on the roof of
this drive-in.

Wolfy's
2734 W. Peterson
743-0207
A Rogers Park favorite for dogs
and fries.

ITALIAN BEEF

Al's Bar B Q
1079 W. Taylor
226-4017
The original and the best. Other
locations at 2231 N. Lincoln and
169 W. Ontario.

Mr. Beef
666 N. Orleans
337-8500
Another great Italian beef
sandwich.

MEXICAN FOOD

Cuernavaca Restaurant
1158 W. 18th
829-1147
Delicioso burritos.

Lalo
4126 W. 26th
762-1505
3515 W. 26th
522-0345
Simply good, cheap, authentic
Mexican food. Try the rice water,
a popular Mexican substitute for
soda pop.

PASTA

Mama Mia Pasta
711 N. State
787-5606
116 S. Michigan
580-0788
Mama Mia can't be beat for a
delicious, quick, and cheap meal
when you're downtown or on the
near north side.

PIZZA

Bacino's
2204 N. Lincoln
472-7400
75 E. Wacker
263-0070
A favorite place for pan pizza.

Carmen's
6568 N. Sheridan
465-1700
1600 Orrington, Evanston
328-6131
Tasty thin-crust and pan pizza.

Connie's
2373 S. Archer
326-3443
You can either go to the
restaurant, have one delivered if
you live nearby, or flag down a
Connie's delivery truck in the
Loop and buy a ready-made pizza
off the truck.

Edwardo's
1321 E. 57th
241-7960
1937 W. Howard
761-7040
521 S. Dearborn
939-3366
Famous for their stuffed and
souffle pizzas. Many other
locations in the city and suburbs;
check the phone book for the
location nearest you.

Father & Son Pizza
2475 N. Milwaukee
252-2620
A longtime Chicago favorite for
thin-crust pizza.

Geppetto's
113 N. Oak Park, Oak Park
386-9200
Great pan pizza.

Giordano's
747 N. Rush
951-0747
1840 N. Clark
944-6100
3214 W. 63rd
436-2969
A favorite for pan pizza; good thin
crust, too. Again, many outlets;
check the phone book for the
location nearest you.

Home Run Inn
4254 W. 31st
247-9696
Southwest side favorite for
thincrust pizza.

Leona's
3215 N. Sheffield
327-8861
Great, crispy thin crust pizza;
delicious pan and stuffed versions
also. Open late every night.

O'Fame
750 W. Webster
929-5111
Word is spreading about their
terrific thin crust pizza. Check it
out.

RIBS

Edith's Bar-BQ
1863 N. Clybourn
327-5160

Lem's Bar-B-Q House
311 E. 75th
994-2428

Leon's Bar-B-Q
8251 S. Cottage Grove
488-4556
Generally acknowledged as the
best, most authentic barbecued
ribs. Served on real white bread,
and they're open quite late. Check
out the bullet-proof glass decor.
Two other south side locations, at
1640 E. 79th and 1158 W. 59th,
and one on the north side, at 2411
N. Clark.

Twin Anchors
1655 N. Sedgwick
266-1616
The ribs at this neighborhood bar
in Old Town have many devoted
fans. The barbecue sauce is what
makes the ribs special.

SEAFOOD

Ben's Shrimp House
1049 W. North Ave.
337-0263
Tasty fried shrimp served with a
wonderful hot sauce.

Calumet Fisheries
3259 E. 95th
933-9855
Famous for their fried shrimp,
perch, and catfish, and smoked
fish. Located near Calumet
Harbor.

The Fish House
530 N. Wells
642-4158
Good catfish, fish chips, chowder,
and fried shrimp by the pound.

SUBMARINES AND SANDWICHES

Brett's Kitchen
233 W. Superior
664-6354
Huge sandwich menu. Try the
vegetarian special or a Reuben.

Capt'n Nemo's
7367 N. Clark
CAP-NEMO
Dozens of hearty, delicious subs.
Also has good homemade soups,
which they'll give you a free taste
of. Another location is at 3311 N.
Marshfield.

Fontano's
1058 W. Polk
226-8815
Super sub place in the back of a
grocery store. Their giardinera is
one of the best. People will follow
you down the street and ask where
you got that great-smelling
sandwich!

Chicago Sweets

BAKERIES

Ann's
2158 W. Chicago
384-5562
Ukrainian baked goods. Great
chewy rye bread. Their poppyseed
and apple strudels, honeybread,

and cheesecake are excellent too.
Open until 8 or 9 pm every day.

Augusta
901 N. Ashland
486-1017
Polish bakery. Outstanding
kolachky and rye bread.

Bennison's
1000 Davis St., Evanston
328-9434
An Evanston favorite for
Continental pastries and baked
goods.

The Bread Shop
3400 N. Halsted
528-8108
Natural-grain breads and delicious,
healthy baked goods.

Dinkel's
3329 N. Lincoln
281-7300
German bakery with good pastries,
and loads of varieties of top-notch
strudel.

Eli's Cheesecake Outlet Store
6510 W. Dakin
736-3417
Eli's cheesecake is available all over
the area, but you can get a
cheaper, slightly bruised one here.
Chocolate chip flavor is fabulous.

Gitel's Kosher Bakery
2701 W. Devon
262-3701
Wonderful Jewish bakery. Good
poppy seed rolls and cinnamon
stick cookies.

Hoeffken's
3044 W. 63rd
737-0390
A Marquette Park favorite with a
huge variety of baked goods—you
name it, they bake it here. Coffee
cakes, sweet rolls, and party cakes
are superb.

Lutz's
2458 W. Montrose
478-7785
Well-known for their delectable
German pastries and tortes. It's
mobbed just before holidays.

New York Bagels & Bialys
4714 W. Touhy, Lincolnwood
677-9388
Everyone we surveyed said this is
the best place to get bagels in the
entire area, and we agree. Open 24
hours.

Nuti Bakery
6017 W. Grand
237-0181
A terrific Italian bakery. Dreamy
cakes and tortes, and their cannoli
can't be beat.

Original Ferrara
2210 W. Taylor
666-2200
Delicious Italian cookies and
pastries, a longtime favorite in the
Taylor Street neighborhood.

Roeser's
3216 W. North Ave.
489-6900
A Humboldt Park institution for
over 70 years. Superb whipped-
cream cakes.

Swedish Bakery (Bjuhr's)
5348 N. Clark
561-8919
Authentic Swedish baked goods in
the Andersonville neighborhood.
Limpa bread, cardamom coffee
cake, anise bread, and tortes are
popular.

Tuzik's Kedzie Bakery
5311 S. Kedzie
776-4283
Polish bakery. Warsaw logs in 12
flavors are the biggest seller. Good
kolachky and rye breads.

Weber's Bakery
7055 W. Archer
586-1234
Great breads are baked here,
including every variety of rye you
can think of. Good rolls, kolachky,
and cinnamon bread.

CANDY & ICE CREAM

Many (but not all) ice cream parlors close during the winter months. It's a good idea to call ahead to make sure they're open.

Affy Tapple
7110 N. Clark
338-1100
Freshly made caramel apples sold right at the factory. You can buy ones with broken sticks at a reduced price.

Al Gelato
7434 W. North Ave., Elmwood Park
453-9737
814 Church, Evanston
869-9133
Lots of exotic flavors. Delicious, but expensive.

Cupid Candies
4709 W. 95th
423-2729
3230 W. 95th, Evergreen Park
636-4433
They make their own chocolate and candies. Good ice cream is available, too.

Dove Candies & Ice Cream
6000 S. Pulaski
582-3119
5172 W. 95th
857-9676
Home of the Dove Ice Cream bar.

Garrett Popcorn Shops
10 W. Madison, 263-8466
26 E. Randolph, 443-9430
670 N. Michigan, 944-4730
It's not uncommon to see a line of people that goes out the door at these places. Cheese and caramel are the most popular flavors—buy a bag of each or ask for one bag that mixes the two.

Gertie's Ice Creams
5858 S. Kedzie
737-7634
7600 S. Pulaski
582-2510
Wonderful ice cream served by friendly staff in old-fashioned ice cream parlors.

Kid Millions
2808 N. Halsted
348-5865
Homemade ice cream made on the premises. A variety of mix-ins are available: crushed Oreos, bits of Heath bars, etc. Good, authentic egg creams.

Margie's Candies
1960 N. Western
384-1035
Homemade candy and good ice cream. Known for their fabulously rich hot fudge sundaes. Open until midnight 365 days a year.

Mario's Italian Lemonade
1070 W. Taylor
No phone
Delicious Italian ices in many flavors; most made with fresh fruit.

Petersen's
1100 Chicago Ave., Oak Park
386-6131
Wonderful, rich ice cream with many flavor concoctions.

Rainbow Cone
9233 S. Western
No phone
Open May to October
The lines sometimes go around the corner for the famous rainbow cone, which is stacked with orange sherbet and pistachio, vanilla, strawberry, and chocolate ice cream.

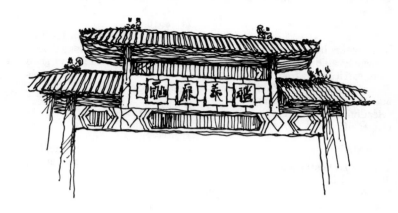

GROCERIES AND MARKETS
Coffee and Tea

Coffee & Tea Exchange
3300 N. Broadway
528-2241
An enormous selection of coffees
and teas from all over the world.

Color Me Coffee
3000 N. Sheffield
935-7669
Coffees and teas by the pound,
fresh pastries and fresh brewed
coffee.

Java Express
10701 S. Hale
Fresh coffee, tea, pastries, and
sandwiches are served. Also coffees
by the pound to take home.

Markland Hubbard
1931 W. 95th
239-5757
Coffee, tea, herbs, and spices. Also
sells gourmet cookware.

Nuts on Clark
3830 N. Clark
871-8777
Coffees are sold by the pound,
along with nuts, candy, and pasta.

Ethnic Foods

CHINESE

New Quan Wah
2217 S. Wentworth
225-8285
Full line of Chinese products is
available, as well as tasty cooked
foods.

Wah May Company
2410 S. Wentworth
225-9119
A pleasantly jumbled store packed
with produce, jars, noodles, and
chinaware.

Oriental Food Market & Cooking School
2801 W. Howard
274-2826
The owners here are knowledgeable and helpful. The store carries food from China, Japan, Thailand, the Philippines, and Korea, as well as a big selection of cookware. Cooking classes offered.

GERMAN

Kuhn's Delicatessen
3053 N. Lincoln
525-9019
The window displays here are always enticing. Lots of excellent sausages and salads. Also breads, coffees and teas, and tortes.

GREEK

Athens Grocery
324 S. Halsted
332-6737
Feta and other cheese, Greek olives, grape leaves, salads, and other Greek staples.

INDIAN

Patel Brothers
2610 W. Devon
262-7777
Exotic spices and seasonings, and a wide assortment of beans, rice, pickles, and chutneys.

ITALIAN

Conte di Savoia
555 W. Roosevelt
666-3471
Over 50 years old. Virgin olive oils, imported pastas, espresso beans, as well as goods from other countries besides Italy.

Convito Italiano
11 E. Chestnut
943-2983
Gourmet Italian prepared foods, wines, breads, and cheeses.

Gino's Italian Imports
3420-22 N. Harlem Ave.
745-8310
In the city's far western Italian enclave. Excellent sausages, along with pastas, oils, and other goods.

JAPANESE

Star Market
3349 N. Clark
472-0599
Excellent selection of fish and seafood. Seaweed, greens, and canned goods.

KOREAN

Oriental Market
5131 N. Western Ave.
989-7811
Produce, fresh seaweed, tofu, and frozen fish in a converted gas station.

MEXICAN

La Guadalupana
3215 W. 26th St.
847-3191
Mexican produce, meats, and other products.

Trujillo Carniceria
3300 W. 26th St.
277-0686
Small supermarket and butcher shop.

MIDDLE EASTERN

Middle Eastern Bakery & Grocery
1512 W. Foster Ave.
561-2224
Good selection of dried beans, lentils, and grains. Bulk item prices are very good.

Middle East Trading
2636 W. Devon
262-2848

POLISH

Caesar's Polish Deli
901 N. Damen Ave.
486-6190
Grocery store and deli with
pierogi, homemade soups, and
other Polish specialties.

THAI and VIETNAMESE

Hoa-An Co.
1131 W. Argyle
275-4643
Chinese, Thai, Philippine, and
Vietnamese foods.

Hai Grocery
5014 N. Broadway
561-5345
Fresh produce and seafood, as well
as herbs, noodles, and canned
goods.

Fish

Burhop's
745 N. LaSalle
642-8600
3025 N. Clark
327-6750
Fresh fish and seafish and
cookware too. A Chicago standby.

Chicago Fish House
1250 W. Division
227-7000
Largest wholesale fish market in
the region.

Dicola's Seafood
10754 S. Western
238-7071
Great breaded and fried shrimp,
catfish, and smelt, as well as a
good selection of fresh fish. Good
prices.

Pick Fisheries
702 W. Fulton Market
226-4700
Fresh and frozen fish at discount
prices.

Fruits and Vegetables

North Water Market
2858 W. Devon, 764-1455
2626 W. Devon, 764-3557
1430 W. Morse, 973-1300
These markets have a great
selection of very fresh and
beautiful-looking produce.

Randolph Street Market
Various proprietors in the 800-900
blocks of West Randolph (north
side of the street)
Go early in the morning for the
choicest fresh produce.

Van Laten's
10057 S. Western
881-9307

Gourmet

Charlotte Charles
2501 N. Elston
772-8310
Distributor of gourmet foods, open
to the public one Friday and
Saturday a month. Good bargains
on gourmet foodstuffs, but the
selection is different on each visit.
Adventurous cooks will be
pleasantly surprised.

**Kenessey's Gourmets
Internationale**
403 W. Belmont
929-7500
Gourmet foods, pastry shop, and
restaurant.

Treasure Island
75 W. Elm, 440-1144
1639 N. Wells, 642-1105
3460 N. Broadway, 327-3880
666 N. Lake Shore Dr. (mini
store), 664-0400
Clybourn and Webster

A delightful chain of gourmet
grocery stores, with five locations
in the city. Carries hard-to-find
herbs, imported canned and other
goods, fantastic salads in its
delicatessen, and other surprises.

Zambrana's
2346 N. Clark
935-0200
Wide variety of attractive-looking
prepared foods, baked goods,
wines, cheeses, coffees, and pastas.
Fresh-cut flowers, too.

Health Food

Foodworks
935 W. Armitage, 935-6800
1002 W. Diversey, 348-7800
1527 W. Morse, 465-6200
Combination grocery and health
food stores. Stores on Armitage
and Diversey have small meat
departments. All three feature
beautiful-looking, high quality
produce. Prices are a little high.

Rainbow Grocery
946 W. Wellington
929-1400
This may be the last co-op health
food grocery left in the city. Some
organically grown produce. Run by
the Foodworks chain.

Meats

Gepperth's Market
1970 N. Halsted
549-3883
An reliable meat purveyor that has
been around for a long time.

Paulina Market
3501 N. Lincoln
248-6272
Homemade German-style sausages,
whole hams, prime meats and
dressed poultry.

**Romanian Kosher Sausage
Company**
7200 N. Clark
561-4141
Quality sausages, smoked meat,
poultry, and prime meats. Try
their garlic franks!

Nuts

Georgia Nut Co.
3325 N. California
539-0240

Save by buying in bulk. Many
varieties of nuts, candy, and dried
fruit are sold.

Nuts on Clark
3830 N. Clark
871-8777
Not only lots of nuts sold by the pound, but also a huge selection of candies and spices, coffees, and some pasta. Pick up some nuts on the way to a Cubs game.

Ricci Nuts
162 W. Superior
787-7660
Nut lovers can stock up here. Raw, roasted and salt-free nuts of many types are available.

NIGHTLIFE

We've decided that a lively nightlife means three things: laughing, dancing, and drinking. Here are some ideas of where to do all three.

COMEDY CLUBS

Chicago comedy is hot, hot, hot. Not since the late 1950s, when places such as Mr. Kelly's on Rush Street featured young rising comics like Bob Newhart and Shelley Berman, has Chicago had a comedy scene as hot as it is today. Local comics such as Emo Phillips and Judy Tenuta are making it nationally; national acts like Jay Leno and Steve Wright are making a point of coming to Chicago. And comedy clubs are popping up everywhere like mushrooms. So if you like comedy, you've come to the right place.

The thing to remember is that there are two kinds of comedy in Chicago—improv and standup—and the two are very different. Standup is the faster and raunchier style of the two. Improv takes longer to develop but can be more poignant than standup—think of those great sketches on Saturday Night Live. The original cast, that is. Chicago has an incredible number of improv groups, most of them bad or at least half-bad. But a few stand out: **Second City, Friends of the Zoo, Practical Theatre, Duck Logic, Avant Garfielde, Baron's Barracudas,** and the **Belmento Players.**

Improvisation

Here are the best places for improv in Chicago.

CrossCurrents
3206 N. Wilton   472-7778
Easily the hippest and most active cabaret for cutting edge improv in the city. At times no less than 4 shows will be running concurrently. Check the *Reader* to find out who's playing when.

Improvisation Institute
2939 W. Belmont   588-2668
Not only the home to a great improv group—the Belmento Players—but also a great place to learn improvisation, if that is your wont.

The Roxy
1505 W. Fullerton   472-8100
A good mix of Second City-like comedy and great singers. Great performing area. Sometimes great comedy.

Second City and **Second City ETC**
1616 N. Wells   337-3992
The home of Chicago-style improv, for many years Second City was the undisputed king of improv. Lately that hasn't been true. Recent shows have been tired and trite, full of the same bits and pitched to an audience that only guffaws at sex jokes. Hardly the place it was even ten years ago when Del Close still directed there. Still, tickets are hard to come by, even with two stages and long-running shows. Make reservations at least a week ahead of time.

Stand-up Comedy

Boston, New York, and San Francisco may have livelier stand up scenes, but Chicago is quickly catching up. The following are the best clubs in a rapidly growing club scene.

Comedy Cottage
9751 W. Higgins Rd., Rosemont   696-4077
Once upon a time the Comedy Womb and the Comedy Cottage were the only places for comedy in Chicago, and many big comedians like Emo Phillips owe their careers to these clubs. The clubs remain, and they continue their policy of featuring both established and new comedians. The shows are always good. The Comedy Cottage suffers from having too large a room. Most seats are good, but a few are terrible.

Comedy Womb
The Pines Restaurant, 8030 W. Ogden, Lyons   442-5755
A nice mix of new and established comedians with a famous comic every once in a while.

Zanies
1548 N. Wells   337-4027
Certainly the best stand up club in the city and not a bad performing space for comedy. But avoid the first two rows unless you like being insulted by the stand ups when they run out of material. Attracts some of the best comedians in the country.

DANCE CLUBS

Most dance clubs usually play taped music and occasionally schedule live music. Some of the clubs listed below have live music; otherwise, turn to the Music chapters to find some places where you can dance to live music. Clubs may change music format depending on the night, so it's usually a good idea to call ahead to find out what's playing.

DOWNTOWN

Charlie Club
112 S. Michigan   726-0510
Dance on four floors of this flashy downtown club. The deejay plays a variety of disco and house music. People flock to Charlie's to work up a sweat after work. Space on the dance floor gets pretty tight, especially on the nights ladies get in free. You don't have to be a member to go to the disco.

NORTH SIDE

Artful Dodger
1734 N. Wabansia   227-6859
A Wicker Park institution, the Dodger offers a good alternative to mainstream dance music. The deejays, music aficionados with far-flung tastes, are allowed to pursue their particular interests on the house sound sytem, with varied, often danceable results. The artsy clientele is disdainful of outsiders, but don't let that bother you.

Avalon
959 W. Belmont   472-3020
Once Tuts, and earlier known as the Quiet Knight, the revamped, spacious
Avalon is booking lots of local rock bands.

Berlin
954 W. Belmont   348-4975
A very hip video dance bar with an unusual, often bizarre crowd. Both gays
and straights hang out here. Interesting theme nights, like male dancers on
Tuesdays, or the Psychotronic Film Festival held every once in a while.
One of the wilder places to be on Halloween.

Cabaret Metro and Smart Bar
3730 N. Clark   549-0203
The city's premier place to see outre and underground rock acts. Set in a
bizarre, labyrinthine, decaying rococo building. Cabaret Metro's dance floor
often gets jammed with sweaty bodies displaying the latest post-new wave
fashions, dancing with decadent abandon. When no bands are scheduled,
Video Metro takes over, showing interesting, locally produced videos. In
the basement of the complex, the Smart Bar offers hot dance mixes.

Casanova's
2421 W. Lawrence   271-3661
Sizzling late-night Latin dance club. Dress code; steep cover on weekends.

Clubland at the Vic
3145 N. Sheffield   472-0366
Clubland's stock-in-trade is the video dance party, featuring more picture
tubes than you can shake a stick at. Patrons are of the youngish, suburban,
affluent type.

Erik the Red
6255 N. McCormick   267-0090
Far north side version of the longtime south side favorite dance club. The
crowd tends to be rather young.

Exit
1653 N. Wells   440-0535
The highest mohawk-per-capita ratio in the city. Regularly features local,
and occasionally national and international live acts. Cavelike ambience,
sunken pit dance floor, and ghoulish barmaids are fitting accompaniment
for the punk and dirge music spun here on dance nights.

Jukebox Saturday Night
2251 N. Lincoln   525-5000
No punkers here, just affluent young professional types and lots of oldies
(records) from the 50s and 60s. You can't miss the building; there's half of
a '56 Chevy jutting out of the brick wall. If your idea of fun is a night of
hula hoop and twist contests, this is the place for you.

Limelight
632 N. Dearborn   337-2985
Franchised New York chic comes to Chicago. Set in a lovely downtown
mansion, the Limelight illustrates what happens when wealth is permitted
to dictate taste. The trappings are distracting, the music predictable, and

the staff pretentious. Some people like it, nonetheless. Sometimes offers interesting live entertainment.

Medusa's
3257 N. Sheffield

No-alcohol, after-hours dance club. Mostly teens in the early evening. The place closes from 11 pm-midnight; from midnight on you have to be at least 18 to get in. Worth a visit if only to see the wild setup on the dance floor and the ever-changing multimedia barrages and, of course, the clientele.

Neo
2350 N. Clark   528-2622

The first successful new wave dance club in the city and the Lincoln Park home of Chicago's upscale post-punk fashion victims. High-profile enough to attract a contingent of mildly voyeuristic business people. Good music and atmosphere.

950-Lucky Number
950 W. Wrightwood   929-8955

Comfortable and unpretentious dance club. Things get a little tight space-wise, especially when the occasional band is set up, but if you get there early enough to get a spot on the dance floor it can be worthwhile.

Octagon
2483 N. Clark   549-1132

If you like dancing to the latest dance tunes but feel a little out of place among people with mohawks and purple hair, this may be the place for you. It does get punkier late at night, though. Roomy dance floor and an outstanding sound system. No cover or minimum.

Orbit Room
3708 N. Broadway   348-0301

If Judy Jetson were in art school right now, this is probably where she would hang out. The decor is wonderfully reminiscent of 1950s futurism and every table has its own TV screen. Dance music is fairly standard.

Riviera Night Club
4746 N. Broadway   769-6300

A beautiful old building with a great dance floor and good sound system. The owners have created a space-age night club environment, replete with lasers and fog machines, in a former movie palace. Excellent selection of live and taped music and a nice seating arrangement. Cover charges and drinks are stiff, but when there's a concert these are a relative bargain.

SOUTH SIDE

Erik the Red
11050 S. Spaulding   779-3033

Ever-popular dance spot, always packed with young south siders. The bar has a slide for the patrons' amusement. Mostly deejay music.

Fantasy Nite Club
1638 W. 79th   994-4797

Elegant, beautifully decorated disco on the far south side. Deejays from WGCI often host hot mix shows here. Sometimes features live music, but the cover charge gets pretty high for live shows. When this place gets jammin', it really moves.

P. J. Flaherty's
2535 W. 95th St., Evergreen Park   423-3046
Big dance floor in this south side room that features rock, blues, and R & B groups, often of national caliber.

Powerhouse
2210 S. Michigan   225-7877
Open Wed, Fri & Sat only
Serious partying here: the place doesn't open until midnight, closes at 8 am. House music, a Chicago original, is what this place is about. Body-jack until your duller friends are getting up for breakfast.

Taste
6331 S. Lowe   873-6700
High-tech disco that plays a paradoxical mix of R & B and classical jazz. The jazz is played for the after-work crowd; later, the more contemporary music takes over. Sophisticated light show adds drama to the dance floor.

BARS

The main activity at the places listed below is drinking or eating. Other bars that also feature live music are listed in the Music chapters. There are thousands of bars in Chicago, so don't get miffed if you don't find your favorite place listed below.

LOOP AND ENVIRONS

Bar RR (The Ranch), 56 W. Randolph
About as un-downtown as you can get, the Bar RR is a country and western bar featuring live music by the house band, the Sundowners. Really, we're not kidding. Attracts a wide variety of people. Decorated in basic wild west, the bar opens at 7 am, in time for a few bloody marys before work. One of a handful of places in the Loop open late at night—4 am Wednesday through Friday and 5 am on Saturday.

Berghoff, 17 W. Adams
For many years Berghoff was a stand-up bar for men only, but during the 70s they finally relented and opened it to women. The wonderful wood paneled room appears little changed since the restaurant's opening early in the 20th century. House-brand draft beer is excellent and perfect for washing down the delicious sandwiches available here.

Binyon's, 327 S. Plymouth
Famous for its turtle soup, Binyon's is a comfortable south Loop bar popular with Federal Center employees and LaSalle street traders and attorneys.

Greek Islands, 200 S. Halsted
A legendary drinking place with bartenders who are always quick with the ouzo and roditys. Best described by a friend of ours who wrote: "I have heard the Greek Islands described in terms of orgiastic emotion. I've seen well-dressed men stumble out of that place at all hours of the day and night

with tears in their eyes. I've seen women in gowns doubled up with laughter in the gutter in front of the place." Do they put something in the roditys?

Miller's Pub, 23 E. Adams
One of the few places in the Loop open after 9 pm. Serving food until around midnight, drinks until 4 am every night. The ribs are great.

Moosehead Bar & Grill, 163 W. Harrison
Located in the developing Printer's Row area just south of the Loop, Moosehead attracts a diverse crowd—traders from the nearby exchanges, people in business suits, students, and some artsy types—all of whom appreciate the owners' fine taste in music. Live music is featured nightly—jazz, swing, blues, and even mambo.

NEAR SOUTH

Blackie's, 755 S. Clark
A great place for lunch, Blackie's becomes your average neighborhood bar in the evening. Located in the Printer's Row area.

Moonraker's, 733 S. Dearborn
Upscale restaurant and bar with 50s futurist cocktail bar decor. Nice place for long conversations over dinner or late drinks.

NEAR NORTH

Bijan Restaurant and Lounge, 663 N. State
Dark and elegant but low-keyed. A favorite place to unwind after work.

Billy Goat, 430 N. Michigan
Located just north of the river on the lower level of Michigan Avenue, this Chicago institution attracts an earthier crowd than most near north side places. Frequented by newspaper staffers, working-class people, and curious drop-ins who've read about Billy Goat's in Royko's column. Great greasy cheeseburgers are meant to be consumed with an Old Style or two. The waiters are a bit gruff but amazingly efficient. The bar is the perfect metaphor for the old, hard working-class town of Sandburg's day.

Brehon's, 731 N. Wells
Unpretentious, authentic Irish tavern with a remarkably sane atmosphere.

City Lights, 223 W. Ontario
Glitzy, noisy, crowded club owned by Bears coach Mike Ditka. A place to be seen. Casual but not too casual (no jeans). Lots of celebrity hounds here.

Green Door Tavern, 678 N. Orleans
Formerly a dive, recently spruced up for the River North gentry, the Green Door still retains some of its former charm and certainly is more comfortable than any other River North bar. Good burgers.

Images, 875 N. Michigan
Located on the 96th floor of the John Hancock building. The spectacular view is the only reason to check this place out.

Ireland's, 500 N. LaSalle
An older, traditional bar in a building reputedly once owned by Al Capone. Not too crowded after work, and the happy hour munchies aren't bad.

O'Sullivan's Public House, 495 N. Milwaukee
Off the beaten path, but worth going out of your way for. A beautiful old Irish saloon with dark wood and a comfortable spilled-beer atmosphere. Live music most nights, a small dance floor, and late closing make this an unusual place to take your sweetie.

Out Takes, 14 W. Ontario
Recent addition to the hot Ontario St. entertainment district. The bar is an enormous fish tank.

Pippins Tavern, 806 N. Rush
A college hangout for the students from the downtown campus of Loyola University. Ignore the Rush Street address; this really is a college bar, with pinball machines, video games, and drunk youngsters.

Raccoon Club, 812 N. Franklin
Elegant Art Deco bar and cabaret features owner Jan Hobson and her Bad Review on Saturday nights; other top acts perform at other times. Ralph Cramden and Ed Norton are nowhere to be found.

RUSH STREET

If you're out to look at or meet members of the opposite sex, then Rush Street is the place you're looking for. Singles bars abound, servicing the trendy under-40 crowd. You're likely to encounter many tourists here, especially when there's a big convention in town. Some of the bars are classy and some are casual, but I would recommend leaving the jeans and sneakers at home if you plan on bar hopping. It's also wise to leave your car at home, because parking is hard to come by (and not cheap when you can find it). If you drink a little too much, you'll be safer in a cab anyway.

Butch McGuire's
20 W. Division
The original singles bar.

Eddie Rockets
9 W. Division
A very hot singles disco.

Eliot's Nesst
20 E. Bellevue
A favorite with people in the advertising business, I hear.

Harry's Cafe
1035 N. Rush
Singles, singles, everywhere. An upscale meet market.

Mother's
26 W. Division
Here's where they filmed parts of "About Last Night"—and the movie captured it perfectly.

She-nannigans
16 W. Division
A typical meet market.

Snuggery
15 W. Division
The second story dance floor affords an interesting view for voyeurs on the street below.

OLD TOWN/LINCOLN PARK

There isn't much of a bar scene in Old Town any more. What's left are a few old favorites with loyal followings. In Lincoln Park, most of the bohemian bars have been replaced by trendy singles and sports bars. You have to look pretty hard to find a decent neighborhood bar here. But taverns are plentiful on Clark Street and Lincoln Avenue; you're bound to find something to your liking.

Beaumont, 2020 N. Halsted
One of the hottest singles bars in the city. Don't go unless you know what you're getting into.

Burwood, 724 W. Wrightwood
Casual, friendly place that mostly attracts people from the neighborhood. Free popcorn and the TV's always on.

Deja Vu (also known as **Vu Bar**), 2624 N. Lincoln
A real find, this place is slightly off the beaten track. The owners feature a variety of entertainment: jazz, swing, blues, country & western, live comedy, and dance parties. It's easier to park and not quite as crowded as spots further south on Lincoln.

Four Farthings, 2060 N. Cleveland
One of the better (and smaller) singles bars. Excellent jukebox. Packed most days, but at its homey best on Sundays.

Grant's, 2138 N. Halsted
Comfy watering hole on the Halsted Street strip. Pool table in the back room. Good happy hour munchies.

Hunt Club, 1983 N. Clybourn
Hot singles bar that attracts many sports fans, because Yale grad Gary Fencik, one of the Bears, is part-owner. Almost always packed to the gills. Outdoor beer garden is nice.

Irish Eyes, 2519 N. Lincoln
Inviting neighborhood bar featuring Irish folk music. Guinness on draft.

John Barleycorn, 658 W. Belden
Longtime favorite from Lincoln Park's bohemian days. Art slides flash continuously on a screen and classical music plays in the background. Relaxed, inviting atmosphere and decent food. Especially good are their homemade potato chips.

Kelly's Pub, 949 W. Webster
Irish bar frequented by DePaul students and neighborhood people. Not a bad place to hang out.

Lilly's, 2513 N. Lincoln
Small, intimate place that features old-time bluesmen playing non-electrified blues. One of the few places in this part of town that still has the original stucco walls and brick floor. Check it out.

Marge's, 1758 N. Sedgwick
Old Town favorite serving the basics—burgers, chili, and brews. Homey atmosphere.

Nick's, 1973 N. Halsted
One of the more laid back spots in this part of town. Everyone likes the jukebox and almost everyone likes the shower heads set surrealistically twelve feet above the ground. So crowded on Saturday nights you need a shoe horn to get in the door.

Old Town Ale House, 219 W. North Ave.
Comfortable place for a few brews across North Avenue from Second City.
Second City actors have been known to drink here from time to time. If
you examine the mural painted on the wall you may recognize one or two
Second City alumni.

O'Rourke's Public House, 319 W. North Ave.
An Old Town institution, this Irish pub cultivates a somewhat intellectual
clientele that's serious about their drinking. Poster-photos of the great Irish
authors—Shaw, O'Casey, Joyce—watch you while you drink.

Red Lion, 2446 N. Lincoln
Across the street from the Biograph, this cozy British pub is a good choice
for an after-movie drink. Good English-style food—actually, it's better than
British food.

Ultimate Sports Bar, 356 W. Armitage
The name says it all. A young, fit clientele hangs out here. A boxing ring
serves as a dance floor, and you can shoot hoops in the basketball shooting
cage. Stay away if the Bears ever win another Super Bowl. For die-hard
sports fans only.

LAKEVIEW/NEW TOWN

This is the current capital of hipness and where you're most likely to encounter people in post-punk attire. The dance scene is big here; if you're
looking for a dance club, see the section on Dance Clubs in this chapter.
Gay bars are concentrated on Halsted and Broadway streets.

CrossCurrents, 3206 N. Wilton
An eclectic bar and cabaret with a comfortable, elegant-looking bar, a large
cabaret room, and several rooms upstairs. There's always a show in the
cabaret and often live jazz music in the bar as well. Bookings are wonderfully
unpredictable, from comedy to salsa to deejay parties to performance art.
The owner rents out the upstairs space at a low fee to organizations running
charitable benefits or to political groups.

Gaslight Corner, 2858 N. Halsted
Your normal neighborhood bar. Good homestyle cooking, a wide screen
TV, and a rathskeller in the basement. Funkier theater types hang out here—
Steppenwolf is right across the street.

Ginger Man, 3740 N. Clark
Relaxed club that is a favorite among Lakeview residents. A good place for
conversation.

Joel's, 3133 N. Clark
Decorated in neo-industrial chic, this is the theater hangout in town. Located
around the corner from the Organic Theater.

Maxtavern, 2856 N. Racine
Both comfortable and hip, and known for their excellent musical selections.
They boast of having no TV in the bar.

Oz, 2917 N. Sheffield
One of those high-tech, neo-art nouveau, neon-all-over-the-place kind of places. Live jazz most nights. A large selection of wines sold by the glass. The garden out back is wonderful on quiet, cool summer evenings.

Sheffield's, 3258 N. Sheffield
Despite all the gentrification going on around it, this place still has the feel of a neighborhood tavern. A small bar, yet they still manage to find room for a stage where a few musicians or actors put on a shoestring show.

FURTHER OUT

Rainbo Club, 1150 N. Damen
Wicker Park bar features good album selections on the house stereo and interesting exhibitions by neighborhood artists (many of whom hang out there).

Resi's Bierstube, 2034 W. Irving Park
Warm, authentic German atmosphere, over 50 different kinds of beer, and great German cooking. Noted for their Weissbier.

FAR NORTH

There aren't as many bars in the Rogers Park area as there used to be. Two reasons are the higher drinking age (many Rogers Park residents are students at Loyola or Mundelein and under the legal drinking age) and the fact that Evanston has gone wet—its residents no longer have to cross Howard Street to get a drink.

Hamilton's, 6341 N. Broadway
Rambling tavern caters mostly to Loyola and Mundelein students, but the place is so spacious that anyone can find a comfortable spot. TVs and video games are all over the place.

Moody's Pub, 5910 N. Broadway
One of the cozier bars around. Fireplace in winter, an inviting outdoor patio in summer. Famous for their burgers.

EVANSTON

Leslee's, Sherman and Grove, Evanston
A classy and comfortable place for jazz, drinks, and conversation. A favorite among Evanstonians and Rogers Parkers since Evanston went wet.

NEAR SOUTH SIDE

Chickrick's, 2512 S. Michigan
An enormous nightclub with a disco, a show room, and a two-level bar. During the week it's a popular after-work place for people who work downtown or at the nearby Michael Reese Medical Center. On weekends the place is mobbed and the crowd is much younger. Lots of south siders come here on Saturday night to show off their finery. A hot place late at night.

Cotton Club, 1710 S. Michigan
Classy meeting place for professional types, a "buppy" (black urban professional) hangout. Management is fussy about who gets in: they like to fill

the club with stylishly dressed, successful looking people. Separate rooms for jazz and disco music, plus the main bar.

HYDE PARK

The Cove, 1730 E. 55th
A great jazz jukebox (one of the best in the city) sets the mood in this art deco conversation pit. The subdued atmosphere lends itself to heavy duty talking. A baby grand piano in the adjoining room lends itself to impromptu practice sessions with patrons.

House of Tiki, 1612 E. 53rd St.
The House of Tiki (House of Tacky to U of C students), open until 4 am, is where Hyde Parkers go after every place else is closed. And the night brings out the eccentric types for sure. Good fish and chips, but avoid the other food items on the menu. Do try the polynesian drinks; the prices are right.

Woodlawn Tap (Jimmy's), 1172 E. 55th
Cheap food, imported beers, and highbrow conversation are the hallmark of this icon in Hyde Park. Three rooms, dark, well used, and a bit worse for wear, make this a comfortable place. The only bar in the midwest with a complete 11th edition (1911) Encyclopedia Britannica behind the bar.

FAR SOUTH

End of the Rainbow, 3126 E. 79th
Comfortable, southeast side club that stays open late into the night.

Godfather, 1545 E. 87th
Relaxing atmosphere. A nice place to sit down and talk, because the music isn't turned up too loud.

Sweet Georgia Brown, 9335 S. Stony Island
A civilized place for drinks, music, and maybe a little dancing.

SOUTHWEST SIDE

Dubliner, 10910 S. Western
Crowded, friendly, filled with people who know each other: your typical southwest side neighborhood bar. Patrons are a good mix: local Irish and other folk who grew up together, professional and working types of all ages. This place is a big supporter of Vietnam Vets—the idea for the big veterans' parade in 1986 started over beers at the Dubliner. Ask Rita, Chicago's finest bartender, about the outings she plans for patrons.

Frank's Speakeasy, 63rd & California
This neighborhood bar in the heart of Marquette Park appeals to a younger crowd. It's another typical southwest side joint: everyone knows everyone else, and your friends' brothers and sisters know your brothers and sisters.

Maple Tree Inn, 10730 S. Western
Intimate, cave-like bar below the street-level Cajun restaurant. There's also a jazz club on the 3rd floor and in the summer, a large, pleasant beer garden outside with live jazz.

Reilly's Daughter, 4010 W. 111th St., Oak Lawn
Just 40 feet west of the city limits, a big sports bar for young, wild jocks
and their ilk. A mostly college-age crowd. Biggest day of the year is the day
of the south side Irish St. Pat's day parade.

WEST

Tuddi Toots', 6500 W. North Ave.
One of the hottest night spots on the far west side. Excellent restaurant and
bar with sports theme. Three 9-foot TV screens so you won't miss a minute
of that big game. State-of-the-art dance floor includes lasers, fog machine,
and video equipment.

LATE NIGHT
AND ALL NIGHT

Slowly, Chicago businesses are waking up to the fact that many locals like to stay up late and do all sorts of things after midnight—eat, dance, drink, shop, even get haircuts and car washes. Late night activities, after all, are one reason we live in the city and not the north shore suburbs.

Opening and closing hours for these places may change; it's always a good idea to phone ahead about hours and show times.

LOOP AT LATE NIGHT

The Loop takes on a completely different quality at night, when it is quiet, uncrowded, safe (the crime rate is low and the pickpockets have all gone home), and parking is easy. Michigan Avenue is dreamily beautiful at night. The areas just south (Printer's Row) and west (around Presidential Towers) of downtown are becoming busier and livelier; we hope this trend will spill over into the Loop.

Finding food in the Loop late at night is still a challenge, although rumors are always circulating that more late-night restaurants will open soon. Try the **Italian Village,** located on the top floor of 71 W. Monroe. Open every day until midnight during the week, and 1 am Friday and Saturday. The food is excellent, the lighting romantic, and the selection of wines is good. Moderately priced. 332-7005.

Another long-time stand-by in the Loop is **Miller's Pub,** located at 23 E. Adams. Miller's is open every day until 4 am. Probably best known for their ribs and the photos of sports and other celebrities all over the place. The bar is friendly and the prices are moderate. 922-7446.

You can eat 24 hours a day at the **Pavilion Restaurant** on the ground floor of the plush, glittery (in a tasteful way) Chicago Hilton and Towers located at 720 S. Michigan. The food is decent, the place is quiet and pleasant, and the prices are moderate considering the setting. 922-4400.

Kitty O'Shea's tavern in the same Chicago Hilton and Towers building (ground level) serves Irish food and features Irish music every night (except Sunday). Times for music are 5 pm-7 pm and 9 pm-1 am Monday through Friday, and 8 pm-1 am Saturday. Open until midnight Sunday (no music). 922-4400.

Catch some of the best jazz acts in the country at **Joe Segal's Jazz Showcase** in the Blackstone Hotel at 636 S. Michigan. Fridays and Saturdays, shows are usually scheduled at 9 pm, 11 pm, and 1 am. Tuesdays through Fridays and on Sundays, show times are usually at 8 pm and 10 pm. Call to confirm times. The club has been known to close for weeks at a time during winter so call ahead. Cover charge. No drink minimum. 427-4300.

For a truly remarkable downtown experience, take the stairs down to the **Bar RR Ranch** at 56 W. Randolph. The Bar RR is an anomaly for the

Loop—live country western music in a dive-y atmosphere. Open until 4 am Wednesday through Friday, until 5 am on Saturday, and until 2 am Sunday through Tuesday. The house band, the Sundowners (they've been playing there forever) plays decent country music and gets the crowd dancing every Wednesday through Saturday night. Their chili, available in numerous variations, is really good. Prices are fairly low for a Loop establishment. 263-8207.

You can grab a good cup of coffee or sticky sweet donuts all night long at the **Dunkin Donuts** at 39 W. Jackson.

A quick cab ride or walk for the more adventurous is a good 24-hour gyros and sandwich place just southwest of the Loop at **Greek Town Gyros** at 239 S. Halsted. They also serve beer. Moderate prices. 236-9310.

Or you can cab it in the other direction to **Billy Goat Tavern** at 430 N. Michigan, lower level. Located in the depths of the city's underground streets about one block north of the river on the west side of lower Michigan Avenue, Billy Goat's is for many people the quintessential Chicago hangout. They have great, greasy cheeseburgers and exceptional pickles (for those of us who notice pickles). Open until 2 am every day except Saturday, when it closes at 3 am. 222-1525.

A little further north is the **Rock n' roll McDonald's** restaurant at 600 N. Clark. It's open 24 hours a day and is, I kid you not, more interesting than most McDonald's. Rock paraphernalia decorate the walls, all the booths have mini-jukeboxes with a good oldies selection that you can play for free, and if you're lucky, you'll run into Macman, who wears red leotards and refills your Cokes and makes deliveries (daytime only) in his Macmobile, a red 50s Chevy. They've even had rock n' roll concerts in the parking lot in the summer. 664-7940.

Pizzeria Due at 619 N. Wabash serves arguably the best deep-dish pizza in the city. Crowded and fun. They also serve other Italian dishes. Open Fridays and Saturdays until 2:30 am, Monday through Thursday until 1:30 am, and closes early on Sunday at 4 pm. 943-2400.

LATE NIGHT FOOD

Many Chicago neighborhoods have corner coffee shops that open early and close late. Sometimes they even stay open 24 hours on the weekends. For example, the **Diner Grill** at 1635 W. Irving Park Rd. on the north side serves typical diner food (on the greasy side but the shakes are OK and I like the old-time diner look of the place) 24 hours a day every day; on the other side of the city, **Fielo's Restaurant** at 10352 S. Western serves a Greek-flavored menu 24 hours on the weekends. Keep your eyes peeled for these places in your area; they come in handy.

SOUTH OF THE LOOP

Just south of the Loop are clusters of restaurants in **Greektown** and **Chinatown**. In general, you can be served excellent dinners at a number of restaurants in both areas until midnight on weekdays, and 1 am on Fridays and Saturdays.

Another group of low-priced restaurants serving consistently good Mexican food in an interesting Hispanic neighborhood is in Pilsen, southwest of the Loop. Try **Nuevo Leon** at 1515 W. 18th St., open nightly until 2 am or sometimes later (it seems to vary). 421-1517. Or walk down about one block east to **Parrillita Restaurant** at 1409 W. 18th St., open 24 hours on Fridays through Sundays, and until 10 pm the rest of the week. 421-9779.

Close to Pilsen is another great night spot, **Lawrence's Fisheries,** at 2120 S. Canal. Open 24 hours, Lawrence's is a big fish shop that carries all sorts of prepared fish, ready to carry out: terrific smoked shrimp and trout, and just about every other kind of seafood, from frogs legs to fried clams. Don't worry about the deserted look of the neighborhood—I've never had any trouble there. 225-2113.

The **White Palace Grill** at 1159 S. Canal is like a cross between a White Castle's and a Steak and Shake. Open 24 hours a day for burgers, fries, and the like. 939-7167.

There's always a line, day or night, at **Jim's Original** hot dog stand on Halsted at Maxwell Streets (just north of Pilsen and southwest of the Loop). What those people are waiting for are great sandwiches: polish and pork chop sandwiches, hot dogs, hamburgers, and fries. They smother everything with grilled onions unless you say different. Great hot peppers. Cheap. You'll know the place by the grilled onion aroma. I feel comfortable here at night (the area looks worse than it really is) but some people don't, so use your judgment.

NEAR NORTH SIDE

During the summer, the people-watching is unexcelled from the outdoor tables at **Melvin's Cafe,** 1116 N. State. You'll probably have to wait to get a table, and once you're sitting, you'll have to order a minimum dollar amount of drink or food, but watching and discussing the off-Rush Street crowd is worth it. Open till 2 am every day except Saturday, when it closes at 3 am. 664-0356.

In Lincoln Park is a dependable stand-by that's always a good time—the **Belden Deli** at 2315 N. Clark. Open 24 hours. Portions are filling, there's plenty of seating, always lots of people to watch, and big desserts. 935-2752.

If it's late and you're in the mood for a nicer restaurant, try **Mel Markon's** at 2150 N. Lincoln Park West. Open until 4 am every day except Friday and Saturday, when it's open until 5 am. Traditional deli specialties and more. The food is good and the place looks nice. 525-5550.

Leon's Bar-B-Q started on the south side, was a huge success and expanded to more south side locations, then finally added one up north. The sauce is delicious and the ribs tender. The Lincoln Park location, at 2411 N. Clark, is open until 3 am on weekdays, and until 4 am on Fridays and Saturdays. Carry-out service only. 281-7427.

Another Lincoln Park restaurant with late hours is **Lindo Mexico** at 2642 N. Lincoln. Open until 2 am on weekdays and until 5 am on weekends. Good fare at moderate prices. 871-4832.

Believe it or not, you can get good, home-cooked food like fried chicken, stuffed peppers, or broasted chicken at very reasonable prices in Lincoln Park—at **Peter's Broasted Chicken,** just a block east of the Biograph Theater at 742 W. Fullerton. Peter's changes their special dinner menu every night. The room is small and cozy, like a good diner. Open 24 hours Friday and Saturday, until midnight the rest of the week. 327-4134.

The two **El Presidente** restaurants at 2531 N. Lincoln (528-8121; open until 5 am every day) and 2558 N. Ashland (525-7938; open 24 hours every day) offer good Mexican food in the late hours.

Ann Sather's at 929 W. Belmont is open nightly till 11 pm except Friday and Saturday, when it closes at 2 am. Down-home Swedish food is served at very reasonable prices. Great cinnamon rolls and lots of unusual folks to watch if you can get a good seat on the street side. 348-2378.

The **Melrose** at 3233 N. Broadway is open 24 hours and offers good breakfasts and coffee shop food all night long at fair prices. Sidewalk tables are set up during warm weather. 327-2060.

FURTHER NORTH AND NORTHWEST

You can get good Pakistani food until 2 am every day at **Tasty Eat** on 1618 W. Montrose. Try the cooked lentils in a creamy sauce or the karahi gosht— lamb stewed in a spicy tomato sauce. 784-5973.

Good Korean food day or night can be found at the **Poong Mi House** at 3752 W. Lawrence. 478-0217.

Kofield's on the far northwest side serves a wide selection of Greek and deli food 24 hours a day at 5035 N. Lincoln. 334-2182.

The **Belmont Snack Shop,** located at 3407 W. Belmont and open 24 hours, serves great steak and eggs, chili, and cheeseburgers. 463-7878.

The **Bowmanville Cafe** at 5159 N. Lincoln has burgers, chicken, and sandwiches, as well as breakfast anytime, 24 hours a day. 561-2233.

A lot of people say **New York Bagels and Bialys** has the best bagels and bialys in the city. Open 24 hours; located at 4714 W. Touhy in Lincolnwood. Also serves sandwiches. 677-9388.

SOUTH SIDE

In Hyde Park, the **House of Tiki** (dubbed House of Tacky by U of C students) at 1612 E. 53rd St. exudes Polynesian kitsch and serves really good fish and chips and chicken wings, but stay away from the other dishes. Open until 4 am every day, and 5 am on Saturdays. Keep your eyes open for the plastic blowfish lamps. 684-1221.

Leon's Bar-B-Q at 8249 S. Cottage Grove is open until 5 am on weekdays, and until 6 am on Fridays and Saturdays. Delicious ribs. You can eat inside at this location. 488-4556.

Down south on 9031 S. Stony Island, the famed **Soul Queen Restaurant** serves soul food until 11:30 pm weekdays, 2 am Fridays and Saturdays. 731-3366.

The **New Queen of the Sea Restaurant** also down south at 8701 S. Stony Island serves excellent soul food—a smorgasbord of short ribs, blackeyed peas, greens, and other dishes—24 hours a day, every day. 221-3711.

CHAIN RESTAURANTS

The next three listings are chains open all night long. Look in the white or yellow page phone books for their locations in the city.

Most **Wag's** restaurants (owned by Walgreen's) are open 24 hours. The food is nothing to rave about, but the chili's not bad, there's lots of coffee, and the prices are right.

All **Dunkin Donuts** are open 24 hours. Their coffee is actually pretty good.

White Castle restaurants—39 locations throughout the Chicago area—are also open 24 hours. The food is, well, food. People in the know call their burgers "sliders"—there's a reason for that.

EARLY MORNING FOOD

Near the University of Illinois at Chicago, **Manny's Coffee Shop** at 1139 S. Jefferson opens at 5 am to serve great deli food, cafeteria style. It's a huge place with lots of dishes to choose from. We get a kick from the guys who serve the food. This is a place with character. Closed Sundays. 939-2855.

Everyone should visit **Lou Mitchell's** in the Loop at least once. Lou is what you call a character. Women get Milk Duds while they wait for a table to open up. The omelettes are delicious (try the Greek) and so are the baked goods. Great coffee. 565 W. Jackson. Closed Sundays. 939-3111.

The **Cozy Cafe** restaurants at 1846 W. Belmont (528-1155; open 6 am-10 pm every day except Sunday, 6 am-3 pm) and 2819 N. Lincoln (549-9374, open 7 am-3 pm every day) have rabid fans. Excellent cheap breakfasts in a homey setting. The ham hash, biscuits and gravy, and home fries are especially good. You'll be served coffee while you wait, which you may have to do on weekends. Terrific jukebox.

SHOWS

If you like your female impersonators professional, funny, and ravishing, then visit the **Baton Lounge** at 436 N. Clark. Audiences for the early shows consist mostly of suburbanites who come in packs for a wild night in the city; later shows draw a more eclectic crowd. Shows are at 10 pm, midnight, and 2 am Wednesdays, Thursdays, and Sundays; 10 pm, 12:30 am, and 3 am Fridays and Saturdays. Closed Mondays and Tuesdays. Reservations are a must (call 644-5269). Cover charge and two-drink minimum. Chili Pepper and Leslie are local legends.

Deni's Den at 2941 N. Clark offers Greek food, terrific Greek music, and dancing in a bright, airy room. Music on Wednesday through Sunday, starting at 8:30 pm and lasting until 4 am, and 5 am on Saturday. The place is hopping at midnight. It gets really crowded on weekends. 348-8888.

CrossCurrents Cafe and Cabaret at 3206 N. Wilton offers an eclectic schedule of late-night "cabaret" shows. The bar is open until 2 am; show times vary, so call ahead. In the past, shows have ranged from comedy to all sorts of music to one-person dramas. A relaxed bar with an excellent beer selection adjoins the cabaret. 472-7883.

You might find it hard to believe that the north side—especially Halsted Street—is a mecca of great Chicago blues, but **Kingston Mines,** at 2548 N. Halsted, really gets cooking in the wee hours. Open until 4 am, 5 am on Saturdays. 477-4646.

O'Sullivan's, at 495 N. Milwaukee, is an easygoing place with a nice mix of people and live music five days a week (Wednesday through Sunday). Open until 4 am Tuesday through Friday, 5 am on Saturday, and 2 am on

Sunday. Music varies: big band, rock, R & B, eclectic. They answer the phone: "World famous O'Sullivan's!" Every Saturday night, Gerry Grossman, "The Human Jukebox"—ask him any pop song, he'll play it—is featured. 733-2927.

BARS
It's not hard to find bars in the city that stay open till 2 am on Fridays and 3 am on Saturdays. To find bars that are open later, you generally have to be in one of the entertainment zones. Turn to the Nightlife chapter for bar listings.

DANCE CLUBS
Most dance clubs are open until 4 am, and 5 am on Saturdays. See the Nightlife and Music chapters for listings of dance places. Some restaurants feature dancing into the very late hours—usually these are ethnic places. You might try the **Baby Doll Polka Club** at 6102 S. Central for some enthusiastic polkas to a good house band, or **Asi Es Colombia** at 3910 N. Lincoln for hot salsa. See the Rock and Country chapter for more ideas.

BOWLING

When it's 3 am and you're still restless, consider bowling as an outlet for those roving blues. The following alleys are open 24 hours.

Miami Bowl
5023 S. Archer (at Pulaski)
585-8787

Starlite Bowl
734 E. 87th St.
483-8500

Riviera Lanes
1515 North Ave.
Melrose Park
345-9393

Waveland Bowl
3700 N. Western
472-5900
Bowling at its finest. The adjoining restaurant serves a combination American-Philippino menu.

POST OFFICES

You won't find a live person to wait on you in the middle of the night at the main post office at 433 W. Van Buren, but at least you can find stamps, a change machine (so you can buy the stamps), a scale for weighing, and 24-hour mail pick-up. Open 24 hours. 765-3210.

There's a full-service, 24-hour post office just west of the city at 6801 W. 73rd St. in Bedford Park. Open 24 hours every day except on weekends; it closes at 6 pm on Saturday and reopens Monday morning. 563-5760.

NEWSSTANDS AND CURRENCY EXCHANGES

Open 24 hours are newsstands at: Clark and Diversey and the intersection of Lincoln, Halsted, and Fullerton. Both carry the *New York Times*.

If your license plates expire at midnight, or if you have a middle-of-the-night urge to pay your utility bills (it happens) or cash a check, there are 24-hour currency exchanges at:

780 N. Milwaukee (at Chicago/Ogden/Milwaukee intersection)   666-0988
Open 24 hours every day except Saturday, when it closes at midnight, and Sunday, when it closes at 5 pm.

1938 W. North   227-6656
6858 S. Ashland Ave.   436-7300

PHARMACIES

Northwestern Pharmacy
1576 N. Milwaukee Ave.   486-0987
Open 8 am-midnight every day.

Perry Drugs
990 W. Fullerton Ave.   975-0339
Non-prescription drugs only available 24 hours; the pharmacy isn't open all night.

Walgreen's stores have a number of pharmacies open 24 hours in the area. The whole store is open as well, so you can do your little-bit-of-everything shopping at slightly higher prices at the same time. The 24-hour stores are located at:

757 N. Michigan
664-8686

3302 W. Belmont Ave.
267-2328

Howard St. and Western Ave.
764-1765

6310 N. Nagle
774-2225

7501 S. State St.
224-1211

1554 E. 55th St.
667-1177

95th St. and Cicero Ave.
Oak Lawn
425-6960

7175 W. Cermak Rd.
Cermak Plaza, Berwyn
795-9030

GROCERIES

The **Dominick's** chain has about 40 24-hour stores in the city. You can also cash checks here. Good produce and a wider selection of items than most big chain groceries.

The **Jewel** chain also has about 40 24-hour stores scattered throughout the city. You can cash checks here too.

Almost all the **7-Eleven** and **White Hen Pantry** stores in the city are open through the night. Prices are a little higher, but at least they're open. You can also buy lottery tickets whenever your heart desires. Some 7-Elevens are also renting videos.

VIDEO RENTALS AND RECORD STORES

Downtown Records & Video
34 E. Oak St.   649-0922
Open 10 am-midnight nightly except Sunday, when it closes at 10 pm. Buy albums or rent videos right off the Rush Street carnival.

Peaches
1162 N. State St.   943-2893
10 am-midnight every day (except Sunday, when it closes at 10 pm) for buying records and renting videos.

The Late Late Show
5338 N. Lincoln Ave.   275-6711
Open for renting videos until 4 am Monday through Friday; 2 am Saturday and Sunday. After you get your video, you can get a drink at the Hidden Cove Lounge, which is attached to the video store.

HAIRCUTS

These **Cut & Dry** salons are open 10 am-midnight Monday through Friday, and 10 am-6 pm Saturday.

5533 W. Montrose Ave.
685-7755

2702 N. Central Ave.
637-0047

4721 N. Harlem Ave., Norridge
457-2223

COPIES

Kinko's Copies   There's been many a time that the 24-hour copying service Kinko provides (at low prices) has saved a terribly urgent project of mine. Locations open 24 hours are at:

2451 N. Lincoln Ave.
327-7770

444 N. Wells St.
670-4460

CAR WASHES

Hand car washes 24 hours a day? This is what makes this city great. **Ivy Brothers Car Wash** at 1729 N. Clybourn Ave. washes your car by hand in about 10 minutes for about $6. The sign out front says 24 hours, but they play it by ear. Better call ahead to make sure. 337-7764.

Or, you can do it yourself for $1 (you get four minutes of soap) at **National Pride Car Wash** at 5970 N. Clark St. 764-1451.

HEALTH CLUBS

The **Charlie Club** at 112 S. Michigan Avenue is open 24 hours a day. The building it's in is gorgeous, and the club has a swimming pool, Nautilus machines, saunas, racquetball courts, classes, exercise machines, and other attractions. There are other locations in the northern suburbs. Call about the initiation fee and monthly charges. 726-0510.

The **Lakeshore Athletic Center** at 1320 W. Fullerton Avenue is open 5:30 am-midnight Monday through Friday and 6 am-11 pm Saturday and Sunday. A beautiful, huge facility with nice tennis courts, swimming pool, Nautilus machines, running track, and classes, among other things. Call about the initiation fee and monthly charges. 477-9888.

LOCKSMITHS

It's not fun to be locked out at any time, much less at 4 am. These places will serve you 24 hours.

Amazing Lock Service
739 W. Belmont
935-8900

The Lock Works
3789 S. Archer
523-7338

MUSEUMS

Chicago is a city of museums: art museums, science museums, ethnic museums, children's museums, even a peace museum. The following is a quick review of Chicago's major museums.

Prices listed are for adult admission. Call the museums for information on discounts for children, students, and seniors. If you're interested in museums with ongoing special exhibits and programs for children, please turn to the Kids chapter.

Adler Planetarium
1300 S. Lake Shore Drive   322-0300
Mon-Thur 9:30am-4:30pm; Fri 9:30am-9pm; Sat, Sun & Hol 9:30-5pm
Free admission
The first planetarium built in the Western Hemisphere, Adler doesn't show its age. Emphasizing astronomy and general exploration, the planetarium features realistic sky shows, exhibits depicting the history of exploration, an extensive collection of antique astronomical instruments, and courses in astronomy and navigation. Doane Observatory is open to the public following the evening sky shows. And the view of the city skyline from Adler is magnificent.

Art Institute of Chicago
Michigan at Adams   443-3600
Mon, Wed Thur & Fri 10:30am-4:30pm, Tues until 8pm, Sat 10am-5pm, Sun & Holidays 12pm-5pm
Suggested admission $4.50, free on Tues
World-class art museum with a renowned collection of Impressionist and post-Impressionist paintings. Also has a good collection of works by the Modernists (Chagall, Picasso, Matisse), some outstanding Renaissance paintings, extensive exhibits on Oriental and primitive art, a fine photographic collection, and much more. Mounts many large-scale special exhibitions, and offers lectures by well-known art historians and artists open to the general public. Student art gallery in the art school (east) wing is often worth checking out. Well-stocked bookstore has a comprehensive selection of books on art and architecture.

Balzekas Museum of Lithuanian Culture
6500 S. Pulaski   582-6500
Daily 10am-4pm, Thur until 8pm
$2 admission
Balzekas focuses on the history, art, and culture of Lithuania, one of three Baltic nations absorbed by the Soviet Union in 1940. The newly expanded museum features exhibits on antique armor and weapons, folk art, native costumes, amber, and decorative objects. Displays rotating shows of contemporary and seasonal Lithuanian art. Special children's exhibit.

Chicago Academy of Sciences
2001 N. Clark   549-0606
Daily 10am-5pm
$1 admission
Natural history museum focuses on the ecology and geology of Chicago and the Great Lakes region. Find out how Blue Island got its name. The Academy also has one of the first observatories built.

Chicago Historical Society
Clark St. at North Ave.   642-4600
Mon-Sat 9:30am-4:30pm, Sun 12-5pm
$1.50 admission
Located in an elegant building at the south end of Lincoln Park, the Chicago Historical Society's museum and library is devoted to reminding visitors of past events that shaped the city. Exhibits, slides, and dioramas depict the Chicago Fire, pioneer life, the Civil War, and the life of Abraham Lincoln. The Society also publishes a well-written magazine, *Chicago History*.

Chicago Public Library Cultural Center
Michigan and Randolph   346-3278 (or dial F-I-N-E-A-R-T)
Mon-Thur 9am-7pm, Fri 9am-6pm, Sat 9am-5pm, closed Sun
Free admission
The building itself is a showcase, with lots of marble throughout and a lovely Tiffany-domed rotunda and grand staircase restored to their original beauty. The Cultural Center usually has several art shows on display. Past exhibits

have included paintings, photos, textiles, and sculpture. Often the Center's displays are Chicago-related—focusing on the city, its people, and their cultures.

DuSable Museum of African American History
740 E. 56th Pl.   947-0600
Mon-Fri 9am-5pm, Sat & Sun 12pm-5pm
$2 admission
Museum and research library highlight the cultural and historical significance of black Americans and their African ancestors. The museum displays paintings, sculpture, and African artifacts. The research end of the museum is unstuffy, community-oriented, and very helpful in assisting teachers. The library's collection includes tapes, slides, films, and sound recordings by and about black Americans.

Field Museum of Natural History
Roosevelt Rd. and S. Lake Shore Dr.   922-9410
Daily 9am-5pm
$2 admission, free on Thur
Housed in a spectacular neo-classical marble building on the lakefront, the Field Museum focuses on zoology, geology, botany, and anthropology. The museum recently shifted its focus to a greater emphasis on anthropology, which has resulted in major exhibitions on Asian and Pacific art and culture. Don't miss the Egyptian mummies, breathtaking jewels, the African watering hole, and the free-standing dinosaur skeletons.

Fine Arts Research and Holographic Center Museum
1134 W. Washington   226-1007
Wed-Sun 12:30pm-5pm
$2.50 admission
The most complete museum of holography (three-dimensional, laser-produced images) in the country. The Center promotes holography as an art form. Films and drawings demonstrate holographic technique. Interesting gift items.

Museum of Broadcast Communications
800 S. Wells   987-1500
Wed 12pm-9pm, Thur-Sun 12pm-5pm, Sat 10am-5pm
During Chicago's glory days of broadcasting, many national radio and television shows originated here. Among them, *Little Orphan Annie*, *Studs' Place*, and *Kukla, Fran, and Ollie*. These shows and many others are preserved at the Museum of Broadcast Communications. With a library of over 400 radio shows and 900 TV shows (and still growing), this museum will satisfy both casual browsers and dedicated students of the broadcast arts. The MBC also contains a collection of classic radios and vintage TV sets, and a working radio station. Call ahead to find out what's playing at the Kraft Television Museum Theatre.

Museum of Contemporary Art
237 E. Ontario   280-2660
Tues-Sat 10am-5pm, Sun 12pm-5pm, closed Mon
$3.00 admission, free on Tues
More a large gallery than a museum, MCA intentionally doesn't have much of a permanent collection, and instead concentrates on showing the very

newest, cutting edge art. Contemporary art in every medium is shown here: installations, performance, video, sculpture, computer graphics, crafts, photography, painting. Unusual arty knickknacks are sold in the museum store. The artist Christo once "wrapped" the building in tarps.

Museum of Science and Industry
57th and S. Lake Shore Dr.
684-1414 (information 24 hours a day from touch-tone phones)
Museum: Mon-Fri 9:30am-4pm, Sat & Sun 9:30am-5:30pm
free admission (supplemental fee for some exhibits)
Space Center & Omnimax Theater: Tues-Sat 9:30am-8pm, Sun 9:30-5:30,
    Mon 9:30am-4pm, $4 admission for Omnimax
2,000 displays, with lots of buttons to push, demonstrate the impact of science and technology on modern life. The museum has wide appeal for adults and children alike because of the participatory nature of its exhibits. No wonder it's the most popular tourist attraction in the city. See the coal mine, the German sub, the Apollo 8 command module, chicks hatching, a walk-through heart, and much more. The new **Crown Space Center and Omnimax Theater,** opened in 1986, features spectacular films on a 5-story domed screen and extensive displays on air and space travel, including artifacts from space missions. It's a good idea to call ahead to check on Omnimax ticket availability.

Oriental Institute
University of Chicago   1155 E. 58th
702-9520
Tues-Sat 10am-4pm, Sun 12pm-4pm, closed Mon
Free admission
A first-rate museum of ancient Near Eastern (Egypt, Mesopotamia, Iran, and the Holy Land) archaeology, religion, art, and history, but the primary focus is archaeology. The Institute conducts ongoing research in the Near East, so its collection is up to date and you can be sure that they've got their facts right. The collection dates from around 9000 B.C. through the 10th century A.D. Treasures include Egyptian mummies, fragments from the Dead Sea scrolls, and a 40-ton winged bull from the throne room of King Sargon II of Assyria.

Peace Museum
430 W. Erie   440-1860
Tues-Sun 12pm-5pm, Thur until 8pm, closed Mon
$2 admission
The first and only museum of its kind in the country, the Peace Museum promotes the art of peace through exhibits and educational programs on issues related to war and peace. The museum's collection includes artwork, manuscripts, and some more unusual items, such as John Lennon's guitar and sections of the 18-mile peace ribbon made of embroidered and appliqued fabric that was once wrapped around the Pentagon, White House, and the national monuments in Washington, D.C., illustrating what people stand to lose in a nuclear war. The museum acts as a clearinghouse for information on peace-related organizations and activities.

Polish Museum of America
984 N. Milwaukee 384-3352
Daily 1pm-4pm
Free admission
Largest ethnic museum in the country. The core of the collection was brought to New York for the 1939 World's Fair and ended up in Chicago, home of the largest Polish community outside of Warsaw, after the outbreak of World War II. The museum features an exquisite stained glass window depicting "Poland Reborn," exhibits of Polish costumes, military memorabilia, and folk art. Also on display are exhibits on Polish pioneers in science and the arts.

Shedd Aquarium
1200 S. Lake Shore Dr. 939-2438
Daily 10am-5pm
$2 admission, free on Thur
The largest indoor aquarium in the world, with more than 700 species of aquatic life from every climate. See the tropical fish in day-glow colors swim in salt-water tanks. Don't miss the enormous, realistic 90,000-gallon Coral Reef, where you can watch divers hand-feeding the fish. The aquarium is a peaceful respite from the city on most weekdays.

David and Alfred Smart Gallery
University of Chicago
5550 S. Greenwood 702-0200
Tues-Sat 10am-4pm, Sun 12pm-4pm, closed Mon
Free admission
A small, interesting and often overlooked art collection. Collection includes representative examples of European and Oriental art, 20th century painting and sculpture, and the dining room set from Frank Lloyd Wright's Robie House. The museum hosts many traveling exhibitions, and recently was the only Chicago museum to participate in a rare showing of 19th century Soviet painting in the U.S.—one of the first since the Russian Revolution.

Maurice Spertus Museum of Judaica
618 S. Michigan 922-9012
Sun-Thur 10am-5pm, Tues until 8pm, Fri 10am-3pm, closed Sat
$2 admission, free on Fri
The permanent collection includes Jewish decorative arts and religious objects, and the unforgettable Holocaust Memorial. Often schedules impressive special exhibitions of works by Jewish artists.

Terra Museum of American Art
664 N. Michigan 664-3939
Mon, Wed-Sat 10am-5pm, Sun 12pm-5pm, Tues 12pm-8pm
$4 admission
2600 Central Park Ave., Evanston 328-3400
$3 admission
One of a handful of museums in the U.S. devoted exclusively to American art. Strong on American Impressionists, naive art, and contemporary painters. Due to the popularity of the Terra collection, the museum moved to new, larger quarters on Michigan Avenue in 1987; the Evanston location

will be used as a satellite museum. (The Evanston gallery was closed for remodeling at press time.)

Ukrainian Institute of Modern Art
2320 W. Chicago   227-5522
Tues-Sun 12pm-4pm, closed Mon
Suggested admission $2
A small but well-run museum with a fine collection of modern paintings and sculpture housed in a building beautifully remodeled by Stanley Tigerman. UIMA has an excellent permanent collection and features changing exhibitions of modern art. Most works are by artists of Ukrainian descent, but the museum also shows works by non-Ukrainians. The Institute functions as a cultural center for the Ukrainian community in which it is located. The staff is friendly and knowledgeable and will happily answer questions about Ukrainian art, history, or culture.

ARTS
&
CULTURE

Montrose Harbor. Photo by Glenn Kaupert.

CLASSICAL MUSIC

Any Chicagoan will tell you that we have the best singers (the Lyric Opera) and the best players (the Chicago Symphony Orchestra) in the world. But that's only a grandiose starting point: we have five colleges and conservatories with complete music programs, a second professional opera company, and several more professional orchestras. We also boast dozens of community orchestras, chamber orchestras, and choral groups. And many other locales routinely offer classical music: restaurants, subway stations, public parks, and churches (for those who worship music). The best source for classical event listings is *Chicago* magazine, especially if you're planning to see a group that sells out well in advance, because the other sources list only events for the coming week. Another source is the Chicago *Reader*, the free weekly. Both the *Sun-Times* and the *Tribune* publish Friday pull-out sections that list the entertainment events for the upcoming week. Opportunities to hear classical music abound in Chicago—the listing below should give you an idea of how much is going on here.

ORCHESTRAS

Yes, the **Chicago Symphony** is the "greatest symphony orchestra in the world" (ask any armchair, first chair, or second chair aficionado). The orchestra is eager to please its subscription audience with warhorses, but it manages to forcefeed modern music by combining the likes of Beethoven and Berg on the same program. There are two other fully professional orchestras in Chicago: the **Orchestra of Illinois** and the **Grant Park Symphony**. The Orchestra of Illinois is primarily made up of members of the Lyric Opera, and in addition to their own concerts, they act as a "pit band" for touring companies ranging from the American Ballet Theatre to pop singers entertaining the conventioneers at McCormick Place. The Grant Park Symphony provides a free summer concert series at the Petrillo Band Shell (just south of the Art Institute), June through August. The Grant Park Symphony's programming is always interesting—a recent reason included both a Beethoven series and the premiere of a new composer that combined a 200-piece orchestra with a rock band.

Also during the summer, the Chicago Symphony leaves downtown for the Ravinia Festival in north suburban Highland Park. Ravinia and Grant Park both provide preconcert picnic grounds: Ravinia caters to the white wine, romantic candles on checkered tablecloth crowd; Grant Park sports more bologna sandwiches and Sprite.

A note to students: CSO tickets aren't cheap, but they offer a special series just for you, and those tickets are cheap. The student ticket series goes on sale each year in mid-September. Call 435-8111 for information.

Chicago proper and virtually every suburb has a nearby community orchestra, and many of them are conducted by members of the CSO (equivalent to Hollywood superstars finally getting their chance to direct a minor motion picture). The better sounding orchestras cheat: they hire professionals or "ringers" to round out the orchestra. (String players are always the weakest part of these orchestras—you need so many of them, and it only takes one or two to wreck the melody.) Three of the best community orchestras are the **Northbrook Symphony,** the **Evanston Symphony,** and the **Lake Forest Symphony.** If you're interested in joining an orchestra, call the one nearest you: they often accept new members with a perfunctory audition, or none at all (unless you're a wind, horn, or percussion player—then you may be competing with frustrated professionals).

Chicago Symphony Orchestra
220 S. Michigan Ave.
Chicago, IL 60604
435-8111 (tickets)
435-8122 (schedule)

Ravinia Festival
Green Bay and Lake Cook Rds
Highland Park, IL 60035
728-4642 (R-A-V-I-N-I-A)

Orchestra of Illinois
506 S. Wabash, Suite 534
Chicago, IL 60605
341-1975

Grant Park Symphony Orchestra
Performances: Petrillo Music Shell, Grant Park
Schedules: 425 E. McFetridge
Chicago, IL 60605
294-2493

Evanston Symphony Orchestra
P.O. Box 778
Evanston, IL 60204
965-2440

Northbrook Symphony Orchestra
P.O. Box 308
Northbrook, IL 60062
272-0755

Lake Forest Symphony
700 E. Westleigh Rd.
Lake Forest, IL 60045
295-2135

OPERA

The **Lyric Opera** claims as much worldwide attention as the CSO, and like the Symphony, they stage crowdpleasers all the time (their subscribers are even less tolerant of "experimentation"—a good main floor seat at the Lyric is $50 and up). A recent innovation was the installation of an English subtitle screen that projects above the action: it can be ignored if you want to listen and watch without being too aware of the awful plot developments that characterize grand opera.

   Chicago Opera Theatre balances the Lyric with modest productions of generally lighter, shorter works; COT has also enlisted the aid of local playwrights and directors of straight theatre to help stage their productions. **Light Opera Works** at Northwestern's Evanston campus (not affiliated with the University) is another alternative to the Lyric: they specialize in Gilbert and Sullivan, and American musicals that may or may not be opera, depending on who's pontificating (Bernstein had to conduct *West Side Story* on Deutsche-Grammophone with Kiri Te Kanawa to prove to everybody that his opera is an opera).

   Finally, a method for combining opera with gastronomy is to contact **Monastero's Restaurant** (3935 W. Devon, 588-2515): every spring the owners sponsor a contest for all the opera students in the area. The finalists sing to you, just as you're polishing off a full course Italian meal.

Chicago Opera Theater
410 S. Michigan, Room 540
Chicago, IL 60605
663-0555

Lyric Opera of Chicago
20 N. Wacker Dr.
Chicago, IL 60606
332-2244

Light Opera Works
927 Noyes
Evanston, IL 60201
869-6300

CHORAL GROUPS

The most likely location for a choral concert in Chicago is a church: the acoustics are not good, but the surroundings compensate. For Renaissance music, you might try the **Chicago Monteverdi Singers**; the **Oriana Singers** range from baroque to contemporary. The **William Ferris Chorale** emphasizes Renaissance and a capella contemporary music. And if you want to get in on the action yourself, there are about a dozen opportunities to sing the

Do-It-Yourself-Messiah over the Christmas holidays. The big one is conducted by CSO choral director Margaret Hillis, and has taken place at various
concert halls downtown. Tickets are free, but usually all are given out on
the first day they're available. Watch the newspapers in early- to mid-
November for an announcement about Hillis' DIYM; you have to mail in
a self-addressed, stamped envelope to the address given. The concert is
sponsored by Talman Home Federal; call 434-3322 for more information.
    Call for performance locations.

Apollo Chorus of Chicago–960-2251
Chicago Chamber Choir–935-3800
Chicago Monteverdi Singers–663-6434
Glen Ellyn Children's Chorus–858-2471
North Shore Choral Society–864-6944
Oriana Singers–465-5656
William Ferris Chorale–922-2070
Windy City Gay Chorus–871-SING

CHAMBER ENSEMBLES

Chicago has three great string quartet series: **Chamber Music Chicago** is
downtown, the **University of Chicago** sponsors concerts at Mandel Hall,
and **Chamber Music of the North Shore** has a three-concert season in north
suburban Winnetka. (The best buy is the U of C series.) Other notable
groups: the **Chicago Ensemble** is made up of about a dozen musicians, and
three to five of them may perform at any given concert. Their repertoire is
refreshingly varied (many of the small string chamber groups stick to baroque). Speaking of Baroque, **Music of the Baroque** performs (surprise)
mainly seventeenth century pieces, and like many of the other ensembles,
they repeat their programs in different parts of the city.
    Again, call the numbers listed for performance locations.

Chamber Music Chicago–663-1628
Chamber Music of the North Shore–835-5084
Chicago Brass Quintet–663-4730
Chicago Chamber Brass–869-6310
Chicago Chamber Orchestra–922-5570
Chicago Ensemble–549-7010
Chicago String Ensemble–332-0567
The City Musick–642-1766
Contemporary Chamber Players–702-8484
Harwood Early Music Ensemble–719-2468
Highland Park Strings–831-3622
Music of the Baroque–461-9541
University of Chicago Chamber Series–702-8484

SCHOOLS

We have five great music schools: **Northwestern, DePaul, University of
Chicago,** the **American Conservatory of Music,** and **Chicago Musical
College of Roosevelt University.** All of these institutions are filled with

students and faculty that have to perform in public (either to graduate, or to keep their jobs). If you call them, they will usually send you an activity schedule for their entire school year.

American Conservatory of Music
Stevens Building
116 S. Michigan Ave.
Chicago, IL 60603
263-4161

Chicago Musical College of Roosevelt University
430 S. Michigan Ave.
Chicago, IL 60605
341-3780

DePaul University
804 W. Belden Ave.
Chicago, IL 60614
341-8373

Northwestern University
711 Elgin Rd.
Evanston, IL 60201
491-7575

University of Chicago
5845 S. Ellis
Chicago, IL 60637
702-8484

RECORDS AND RADIO

Two FM stations play classical music full time: **WFMT** (98.7) and **WNIB** (97.1). In addition to music, WFMT features talk shows and in-depth news reports. WNIB has a smaller audience and is more experimental in its programming.

We finally have a record store in the Chicago area devoted exclusively to classical music. **Ravinia Classical Music** (493 Roger Williams, Highland Park, 433-8505) carries classical records, tapes, CD's, videos, books, and magazines.

Rose Records (214 S. Wabash, 987-9044) claims to be the largest record store in the country. They stock all the classics and have an entire floor of cut-outs, including boxed sets of operas and symphonies. Rose recently acquired Laury's Records, so there are now numerous city and suburban outlets for this great retailer. If you're looking for good used classical records, try the **Record Exchange** in Rogers Park (1505 W. Morse, 973-0452). They don't splurge on niceties such as carpeting or fixtures, but the stock is extensive.

FREE!

The **Chicago Public Library Cultural Center**, located at 78 E. Washington, hosts several free classical music concert series. All the concerts are held in the Preston Bradley Hall, a spacious room ornamented with beautiful mosaics. The **Chicago Chamber Orchestra**, conducted by Dieter Kober, performs at the Center on occasion, usually on selected Sunday afternoons, from fall to spring. The **Chicago Symphony String Quartet** also plays at the Center on occasional weekend afternoons. A very popular series, the **Talman Dame Myra Hess Memorial Concerts**, held at 12:15 pm every Wednesday, features a varied program of classical music played by individuals or small ensembles. For young people, the Center offers the **Young People's Concert Series**, held every third Thursday of every month during the school year. The concerts, at 10:30 am and noon, serve to introduce young people to classical music in various forms. For information about any of these programs, call 744-6630.

Check out any of the Loop subway stations; Chicago has finally gotten around to loosening restrictions on street musicians—they used to get arrested for begging if they played with an open case in front of them. And if you're downtown on a weekday, you might hear a free lunchtime concert at the Daley Plaza.

The **Grant Park Symphony** plays for free at the Petrillo Music Shell in Grant Park from June through August on Wednesday nights and weekend nights.

Finally, it's not exactly free, but if you're planning to go out for a fine dinner, you might consider the fondue restaurants: **Geja's** (340 W. Armitage, 281-9101) offers classical guitar; **Fondue Stube** (2717 W. Peterson; 784-2200) provides a string trio. Also, a string trio plays during Sunday brunch at **Monique's Cafe** (213 W. Institute Pl., 642-2210).

If you don't find what you want in the above listings, try calling this umbrella organization for classical music:

Chicago Music Alliance, 410 S. Michigan, Room 819, Chicago, IL 60605, 987-9296

—Steve Spiegel

BLUES AND JAZZ

Come on, baby don't you want to go,
Back to that same old place—
Sweet Home Chicago.
    —Robert Johnson, Mississippi blues guitarist

BLUES

An odd combination of politics, culture, and circumstance brought blacks to the city and gave rise to the distinctive style of music known as the **Chicago Blues**. No other part of the country had such an unusual sound, and few could boast such an abundance of talent. Even today, though its popularity has waned and the audience has changed, Chicago blues is being kept alive by long-time practitioners and a whole new set of younger players who have recently emerged. On any given night in Chicago, there is more fine blues being played than is available in the rest of the country combined. What was it about the city that made this all happen?

The two World Wars were the biggest impetus to black migration. While the boll weevil and floods decimated southern agriculture, northern wartime industries were actively recruiting black workers for wages as much as five times what could be earned in the south.

Chicago became a major destination; first, because it was easy to get to. The Illinois Central Railroad ran from New Orleans—a trip that took 24 hours and about $17 in 1940. For blacks in Tennessee, Louisiana, Arkansas, and especially Mississippi, Chicago was simply the most convenient stop. People from the Delta already felt a connection to Chicago through the local black newspaper, the *Chicago Daily Defender*, and the well-known mail order houses, Sears Roebuck and Company and Montgomery Ward and Company.

Changing conditions in these people's lives—the move from north to south, farm to factory, kerosene to electricity—made for a changed music. Chicago blues was a louder, faster, electrified version of the country blues Delta blacks heard in their youth. From the 1920s on, Chicago clubs such as the Rhumboogie, El Grotto, Club Trianon, Du Drop In, Club Zanzibar, and others hired bands. Amateurs, up-and-comers, and newcomers livened the scene on Maxwell Street. The late forties and fifties were the heyday of Chicago blues. Several new factors played a role in this development: the wartime ban on recording ended, shellac to make records was no longer rationed, and small labels were looking for new talent because the major labels had already gobbled up the established, more traditional artists.

Probably the best-known new label was run by two brothers named Leonard and Philip. They started in 1947 with their Aristocrat label, but in 1950 they changed the name to their own—Chess Records.

Chess, J.O.B., Chance, Parrott, Vee-Jay, United, and other labels released a string of records that, for a brief period, captured the imagination of the

101

public. The roster of musicians who came to Chicago and shaped the sound of its blues is phenomenal: Sonny Boy Williamson (I and II), Little Walter, Elmore James, Sunnyland Slim, Muddy Waters, Johnny Shines, Roosevelt Sykes, Homesick James, J.B. Hutto, Big Walter Horton, Howlin' Wolf, Willie Dixon, Otis Spann, Jimmy Reed, and later Otis Rush, Magic Sam, Buddy Guy, Junior Wells, Hound Dog Taylor, James Cotton, Magic Slim, Koko Taylor, Jimmy Dawkins, Luther Allison, Mighty Joe Young, and Jimmy Johnson.

Through the early fifties, Chicago blues artists and labels enjoyed national success, but the party ended before it had barely started. Ironically, it was rock and roll, the offspring of blues, that was a major factor in its demise. Increasing prosperity, a decline in radio play, and blues' link with the pre-civil rights past all made it less appealing to black audiences. Soul music took the place of the blues. The small labels folded and the blues players retired.

In the sixties, British rockers introduced blues to their young, white audience. And a small but steady stream of new performers kept the tradition alive. Today, the blues is enjoying a revival in Chicago. Several new clubs have opened. Young performers are making the scene, while old ones draw larger audiences. The free annual **Blues Fest** held in Grant Park in June attracts larger and more enthusiastic crowds with every passing year.

Blues recording has also revived. One of the country's premier blues labels, **Alligator Records**, is based in Chicago and releases excellent albums from the city's and the nation's finest players. **Delmark/Pearl** has started up its reissue series again. And local labels like **Rooster Blues**, **Red Beans**, and **Blind Pig** provide an outlet for younger players.

Radio offers a limited amount of blues programming, mostly confined to specialty shows. Pervis Spann, "The Blues Man," still reigns during the early morning hours on WVON (1450 AM). WBEZ's (91.5 FM) "Blues Before Sunrise" has expanded to two nights, Saturday and Sunday, 12 am-5 am. "Bluesbreakers" with Tom Marker continues its several-year run on Monday nights on WXRT (93.1 FM). College stations WHPK (88.3 FM), WNUR (89.3 FM), and WZRD (88.3 FM) usually have some blues shows, but the schedule may vary from quarter to quarter.

A good place to look for blues recordings is **Jazz Record Mart**, 11 W. Grand, 222-1467.

The current club scene is very exciting. You can hear live blues seven nights a week in Chicago. Talent from all over the country plays here, but just as, or even more, exciting are the new and old Chicago musicians that perform nightly. The clubs listed below specialize in blues, but several other congenial, eclectic nightspots—such as **FitzGerald's** in Berwyn, **P.J. Flaherty's** on the southwest side, and **Stagger Lee's**—include blues in the interesting mix of acts they book. So do many of the places listed under the Jazz section.

Biddy Mulligan's
7644 N. Sheridan   761-6532
Though their bookings have expanded to include young up-and-coming bands, rock has-beens, and assorted other oddities, Biddy's is still first and foremost a blues club, and still features some of the best blues in the city. There's a friendly corner bar feeling here, enhanced by the nice mix of

neighborhood folks, students, and diehard blues fans that generally inhabit the place. There's no flash, and frequently not enough seats, but the music and mood are usually so good you won't even notice. Biddy's is open Wednesday through Sunday. Covers are reasonable and there's no drink minimum.

Blue Chicago
937 N. State   642-6261
Probably the only blues club in the city, past or present, with mauve walls. But the comfortable, ample room showcasing some of the best local talent is beginning to catch on with tourists and natives alike. In any case, it's a step up from the usually bland Rush Street entertainment scene.

B.L.U.E.S.
2519 N. Halsted   528-1012
Almost any night of the week this narrow, smoky room is jam-packed with blues fans, musicians, and adventurous tourists, and for good reason. The music is excellent and brings out a lot of good-spirited audience involvement. Bookings lean toward the cream of the local crop and there's a feeling that the place is committed to Chicago history and tradition. One of the city's premier blues clubs.

East of the Ryan
914 E. 79th St.   874-1500
Strong programming features blues greats, soul, R&B, and jazz in this south side club located in a Spanish-style motel.

Kingston Mines
2548 N. Halsted   477-4646
They advertise themselves (somewhat tongue-in-cheek) as "The Playground of the Stars" because of the many rock types that continue to drop by for their late night shows. The real action, however, remains on the Mines' two stages, and it happens every night of the week. Weeknights, newer bands are featured. The continuous shows on weekends boast the best Chicago and national blues players. One of the main reasons the Chicago blues scene is so exciting.

Lees Unleaded Blues
7401 S. South Chicago   493-3477
South side blues live three nights a week.

Lilly's
2513 N. Lincoln   525-2422
A tasteful but friendly near north hangout on weekdays that turns blue on Thursdays through Saturdays. It works because the talent is excellent, the space is small but welcoming, and between sets you can explore one of the city's best jukeboxes.

New Checkerboard Lounge
423 E. 43rd St.   624-3240
One of the last of the legendary south side blues bars. The New Checkerboard features big-name blues acts, south side favorites seldom seen at the other end of town, and Monday night open jams. The live music begins most nights at 9:30 pm.

Rosa's
3420 W. Armitage   342-0452
One of the most promising newer additions to the scene and located near West Town, Rosa's attracts one of the most comfortably mixed crowds in an already diverse scene. The bar is small and funky (just like you always imagined blues bars to be). The small stage in back is not much bigger than the pool table in front. You won't see big-name blues stars here, but the musicians you do hear at Rosa's are solid and enthusiastic. There's no pretense to the place, just good music for a good price seven nights a week.

Wise Fools
2270 N. Lincoln   929-1510
Last but not least by a long shot. Wise Fools has been a long-standing focal point for the Chicago blues scene. Scrunch yourself into the main room and you'll hear some of the finest sounds around. Weekdays, an occasional jazz or other musical ensemble will play, but on weekends it's the best in blues all the way. Wise Fools is also one of the friendliest places around. Live music seven nights a week.

JAZZ

Mention Chicago and the Roaring Twenties, and you conjure up images of gangsters and tommy guns, speakeasies and bathtub gin. Perhaps this imaginary scene includes the tinkling of a piano or the sound of a Dixieland band. In fact, the nightspots and high life of the twenties gave jobs to many musicians and gave birth to a thing called jazz.

The same factors that helped shape Chicago blues played a part in putting Chicago at the center of jazz history. New Orleans musicians, influenced by the marching bands of the 1800s, were the main innovators of the early "pre-jazz" style of music. When the legendary Storyville district in New Orleans shut down, these musicians joined the northward migration to Chicago.

One of these migrants was King Oliver. By the early twenties, Oliver and the Creole Jazz Band with Louis Armstrong reached their peak. These transplanted Chicagoans defined the New Orleans style, considered to be the first "true" jazz. At the same time in Chicago, Bix Beiderbecke and the Wolverines and the Austin High Gang were also making their mark on early jazz.

By the end of the decade, Chicago's star dimmed. Many musicians relocated to New York as the end of Prohibition and the start of the Depression destroyed the club scene. The big bands were ushering in a new era of jazz—the age of swing. Only the band of master jazz pianist Earl Hines would make a mark during this time.

From the mid-forties into the early fifties, the local scene picked up again. The south side, Hyde Park, the Loop, and Old Town had scores of clubs and musicians digging the new sounds of bop and cool. Artists such as Von Freeman, Ira Sullivan, Johnny Griffin, Wilbur Ware, and Gene Ammons got their start at that time. But again, the scene declined during the Eisenhower years.

It wasn't until the sixties that the city's jazz scene substantially improved. Ahmad Jamal and Ramsey Lewis scored commercial hits, but the exciting developments were coming from another direction. A south side "rehearsal band" led by Richard Abrams became the focal point for a loose aggregate of young, avant-garde musicians. Influenced by the earlier experiments in Chicago of Sun Ra and "free jazz" ideas from all over the country, this group of musicians, called the Experimental Band, eventually evolved into one of the major forces in modernist jazz—the Association for the Advancement of Creative Musicians, or AACM. Ironically, AACM musicians such as Joseph Jarman, Anthony Braxton, George Lewis, Roscoe Mitchell, and Lester Bowie would be hailed around the world, but ignored in their hometown.

More recently, Chicago has reflected the changes and evolutions of jazz. Chicago native Herbie Hancock joined Miles Davis in the sixties. His early-seventies albums helped define fusion, and his more recent electro-funk and rap experiments have been enormously successful.

Another Miles alum and Chicago artist, sax player Bill Evans, has come into the spotlight as a solo artist. Jerry Goodman, formerly of the Flock, and fusion pioneers, the Mahavishnu Orchestra, recently returned to recording. Local musicians Paul Wertico and Steve Rodby have turned up in a number of settings, including the Pat Metheny Group. And the band Shadowfax, who got started here, became leaders in the "new age" style of jazz.

Chicago may not be in the forefront of jazz innovation or home to many jazz stars these days, but the local scene is remarkably healthy and diverse. In the last several years, the number and variety of jazz clubs have grown. Many young players are also beginning to develop solid reputations and gain local recognition. Chicago is also a regular stop for jazz greats from all over the world. On any given night, you can hear just about any style of jazz: Dixieland, big band, Latin, fusion, avant-garde, new age, or new traditionalist.

The city's annual **Jazz Festival**, held the Wednesday through Sunday before Labor Day, has become a world-class event. Drawing on local, national, and international talent, it presents the music and the city at its very best.

The low point of the Chicago jazz scene is radio. That a city of this size and with a continually growing audience does not have a 24-hour jazz station is appalling. WBEE (1570 AM) is waiting for FCC approval to remain on the air 24 hours a day, but its signal does not penetrate into the northern half of the metropolitan area. WBEZ (91.5 FM) only offers its excellent "Jazz Forum" in the evening and on Sunday afternoons, with some syndicated jazz shows on weekends. "Jazz Transfusion" on WXRT (93.1 FM) continues Sunday nights from 9 pm-1 am. Daddy O'Daylie spins on Sunday noon-5 pm on WJPC (950 AM). Rock station WLUP (97.9 FM) runs a syndicated show with sax/fusion artist Bob James Sunday mornings 8 am-10 am. College stations WZRD (88.3 FM), WNUR (89.3 FM), and WHPK (88.3 FM) generally have some jazz programming, though schedules may change on quarter-to-quarter basis.

A good place to look for jazz recordings is **Jazz Record Mart**, 11 W. Grand, 222-1467.

In addition to the clubs listed here, dozens of other city and suburban lounges, restaurants, cocktail bars, hotels, and other nightspots feature some jazz on occasion. Local clubs such as **Orphans** on Lincoln Avenue, **FitzGerald's** in Berwyn, **P.J. Flaherty's** on the southwest side, the **Vu, No**

Exit in Rogers Park, **Links Hall** on Sheffield Avenue, the **Wise Fools** and **Holstein's** on Lincoln Avenue all book jazz acts regularly, but not exclusively. Larger venues such as the **Auditorium**, the **Holiday Star**, the **Vic**, the **Park West**, and **Ravinia** occasionally host national acts.

Andy's
11 E. Hubbard   642-6805

Lots of three-piece suits and yellow-dotted ties at this place just north of the Loop, yet somehow Andy's radiates a relaxed warmth. Sit at the huge oval bar that dominates the front half of the room, or one of the many tables back by the stage for lunchtime, after work, or weekend jazz. Jazz lunches are on Wednesdays, Thursdays, and Fridays noon-2:30 pm. Weeknights, some of the finest local talents play 5 pm-8 pm or 8:30 pm. Saturdays, Andy's is open 6 pm-1 am for music or food. Their Saturday night bookings generally feature the best local talent.

The Bulls
1916 N. Lincoln Park West   337-3000

A long-time Lincoln Park favorite. Step down into a cozy, intimate jazz cave for music seven nights a week. The music tends toward the contemporary and entertaining and the late-night warm ambiance makes the Bulls a steady attraction for Chicago club-goers.

Dixie Bar and Grill
227 W. Chicago   642-3336

Some of the best Chicago jazz talent is lost in the clatter of dishes and the chatter of bar and dinner patrons at this hip Cajun eatery in one of the fastest developing areas of the city. There's no cover charge to hear some excellent players every night except Sunday, but it's hard not to be distracted when the rest of the place is busy.

George's
230 W. Kinzie   644-2290

Cool classiness fairly accurately defines this place. There's good food, good sound, and good sight lines. One of the few places in town that books national acts, George's performers are never less than first class.

The Get Me High Lounge
1758 N. Honore   278-8154

Don't be surprised if you feel a sudden urge to spout Ginsberg's "Howl" or debate the metaphysical implications of abstract expressionism in this Wicker Park joint. Then again, don't be surprised if you just get the urge to giggle. It's just that kind of place. Bucktown's secret no more, the Get Me High is still one of the most unique and truly cool spots in town. This cubby hole of a space is bursting with posters, pictures, weird "art" objects, wind-up toys, fishing poles, and who knows what else. A raised stage in back features good local jazz players every night of the week. And the loopy friendliness of the place is instantly infectious. Unless you're terminally square, there's no way you can help but dig it, daddy-o.

Green Mill
4802 N. Broadway   878-5552

First opened in 1907, this Chicago institution has hosted polo games, gangsters, even the film *Thief*. The recent elaborate renovation has returned the

Mill to its former glory, making it one of the most striking rooms in the city. The Mill's long-time connection with Chicago jazz has been restored as well. Excellent local players can be heard every night but Sunday, when the unique "Uptown Poetry Slam" is held. The crowd is a great mix of neighborhood types, tourists looking for the ghost of Al Capone, and avid jazz fans of all kinds. The staff greet you with a nice blend of respectful friendliness. Prices are dirt cheap.

Joe Segal's Jazz Showcase
636 S. Michigan Ave. (in the Blackstone Hotel)   427-4300
Stories about old man Segal, not all of them flattering, are practically part of Chicago musical folklore by now. But Segal has undeniably, and almost single-handedly, provided Chicago with world-class jazz for several decades. Ensconced in the fading glory of the Blackstone Hotel, the Showcase presents a muted atmosphere that's neither elegant nor funky. The space slips from view when any of the top-rate acts that are always booked there take the stage. Few places in the city book out-of-town jazz acts and none can match the uncompromised reputation for quality that the Showcase has. There's music every Tuesday through Sunday, with most artists playing for the whole week's run. Every August, Segal celebrates Charlie Parker Month. During the annual Jazz Festival, the showcase becomes the scene for after-fest jams. No drink minimum. Segal's a quirky, but unequaled jazz legend. Don't forget to ask him about the two-for-one discounts. Call ahead in the winter months—they take a long vacation.

KiKus
754 W. Wellington   281-7878
Strong jazz programming at this New Town club.

Leslee's
Sherman and Grove, Evanston   328-8304
This restaurant and bar in Chicago's most immediate northern neighbor is slowly beginning to be recognized for the fine jazz spot it is. A pleasant, if somewhat muted space, Leslee's offers music with no cover seven nights a week. A diverse set of talented local players regularly performs here.

Moosehead Bar and Grill
163 W. Harrison   922-3640
This large, cheery room, located on the southern edge of the Loop, looks like some crazy Canadian's attic gone berserk. Old posters, pictures, plane and ship models, flags, snowshoes, and hundreds of other odd bits of antiques and weird junk fill up almost every square inch of wall space. Mooosehead attracts the crowds from the Loop after work, River City, and the near south side—a lively and congenial mix. The staff are friendly and seem to be having a good time. Blues, salsa, and first-rate jazz groups play 5:30 pm weekdays, 9 pm Saturdays, and 7 pm Sundays. There's also a jazz brunch Sunday afternoons.

New Apartment Lounge
504 E. 75th St.   483-7728
Bookings are erratic, but some great national acts occasionally pop up here. Chicago jazz great Von Freeman, in residence every Tuesday night, is a must-see—and hear.

The Other Place
377 E. 75th St.   874-5476
Excellent jazz consistently. Comfortable, well-run establishment where Sarah
Vaughan and Sammy Davis Jr. have been known to stop by when they're
in town. The crowd is well dressed and the place gets crowded on the
weekends. Some of the best jazz in town.

Oz
2917 N. Sheffield   975-8100
A yupster hangout weekdays, Oz welcomes fine Chicago performers Thursdays through Saturdays to its glass-block-and-pink-flamingo-cool elegance.

—Chris Heim

FOLK MUSIC

Although it's difficult for folk music enthusiasts not to mourn the halcyon days of the '60s and '70s, take heart: "Folk music is inevitable," according to Jim Hirsch, director of the Old Town School of Folk Music. The Chicago folk music scene, while not burgeoning, is healthy enough to be surviving the 1980s, which is more than can be said of most cities. In fact, folk music is being performed seven nights a week in the Chicago area—by contemporary singer-songwriters, interpreters of traditional American folk songs, bluegrass and ethnic groups, and many others. Chicago is also the home of an excellent record label, **Flying Fish,** that distributes national as well as local folk acts.

Listed here are clubs, coffeehouses, schools, groups, festivals, and radio programs whose mainstay is folk music. Several other places in the city and suburbs sometimes feature folk artists (e.g., Orphan's on Lincoln Ave., FitzGerald's in Berwyn), and there are lots of ethnic clubs and restaurants that present live music. *Chicago* magazine and the *Reader* are good places to check for these.

IN THE CITY

Old Town School of Folk Music
909 W. Armitage Ave.   525-7793
The Old Town School is one of Chicago's cultural treasures. Established in 1957, the school was the nation's first permanent home for folk music. Today, after weathering some severe financial storms in the early '80s, the institution is healthy, and is currently renovating its turn-of-the-century building; the school also plans to expand its operations nationwide.

The school presents 16 to 18 concerts a year. Performances by singer-songwriters (like Tom Paxton) are less common these days, as bookings more and more reflect director Jim Hirsch's preference for traditional and ethnic music. Admission prices vary, and you should buy tickets in advance, especially if you want to get into the early show on the weekend.

The Old Town School also offers a fascinating array of private and group music lessons; instruments taught range from autoharp to zither but include more mainstream pursuits as well (e.g. piano, guitar, banjo). You can take folk or clog dancing, voice, or "Wiggleworms," a popular music class for parents and toddlers. Again, fees are reasonable, and if you register for two classes, the second is half-price.

With branches in the suburbs of Mt. Prospect and LaGrange and in Madison, Wisconsin, the school plans to open even more outposts across the country. And the almost 100-year-old building the school calls home is due to be completely renovated in 1987, including the addition of a folk music museum.

Annual membership, which costs $20 for individuals and $35 for families, entitles you to discounts and preferred seating for selected concerts, plus an Old Town School T-shirt.

Holstein's

2464 N. Lincoln Ave.   327-3331

(Editor's note: as we went to press, the Holsteins announced plans to close their club at the end of 1987. The club will be greatly missed.)

Holstein's isn't quite old enough to be a Chicago folk music tradition yet, but its owners, the Holstein brothers, have been involved in the folk scene here for many years. Remember the Earl of Old Town? Somebody Else's Troubles? Stages? Ed and Fred Holstein took what they learned while booking, operating, and performing at those now sadly missed clubs and opened their own in 1981.

Holstein's is the premier folk night club in the city, if not the country. Ed books nationally and internationally known performers on the weekends and local acts during the week. Sellout crowds usually turn out for Tom Paxton, John Hartford, Doc Watson, Claudia Schmidt, and Livingston Taylor. Fred Holstein, "Chicago's troubador," is a regular performer.

The listening room is separate from the bar, which is a friendly place to have a drink, listen to the jukebox (which has some great folk classics), or talk to the performers after the set.

The listening room is fairly intimate, and if you get there very early, you can get seated at one of the front tables, which are practically on top of the stage. (Sitting that close to the musicians can make the difference between an enjoyable evening and an extraordinary one!) Music is taken seriously here, and Ed asks patrons to refrain from talking during the sets.

No Exit

6970 N. Glenwood Ave.   743-3355

The No Exit Cafe and Gallery, like the Old Town School of Folk Music, was born in the late 1950s. And although the coffeehouse has moved a few times during the last 25 years or so, the laid-back, comfortable, funky-eclectic atmosphere doesn't seem to have changed much; when you go there for the first time, you may feel that you have entered a time warp.

Most of the folk musicians who perform at No Exit are less well known than those who play at Holstein's, but owners Brian and Sue Kozin believe in giving talented musicians—even the ones who don't have a large following—the chance to perform. In the same vein, the cover charges (Thursday through Sunday only) and food prices are very low by big-city standards—to enable more people to hear and appreciate folk music, according to Sue.

Among the regular performers at No Exit is Art Thieme, a nationally known singer of American traditional folk songs who plays many instruments (including the saw) and tells great stories and groan-worthy puns. Jazz nights and open stage are also popular.

There is an extensive menu of coffees (including espresso and cappuccino), teas, salads, sandwiches, and pastries, but never a minimum food charge.

Even when there's no live music, the No Exit is a gentle, relaxing place to spend a few minutes or a few hours; there are lots of board games and books around, and nobody will bother you if you want to be alone.

Earl's Pub

2470 N. Lincoln   929-0660

Newer folk club run by Earl Pionke of Earl of Old Town fame. Folk, country, and blues music are featured. Emphasis is on local acts. Low or no cover most nights.

University of Chicago Folk Festival

Mandel and Ida Noyes Halls, 5801 S. Ellis   702-7300

This annual three-day winter festival (usually held in January) celebrated its 25th anniversary in 1985. The emphasis is on traditional (and sometimes obscure) folk music from all over the country and beyond. The festival is known for presenting a good mix of styles, including blues, bluegrass, and zydeco. There are many free events, including workshops, and of course, jam sessions. Get concert tickets early, though; many performances are sellouts.

WFMT-City of Chicago Folk Festival

Petrillo Music Shell, Grant Park   744-3315

A free, day-long folk music festival than began in 1985, this annual event has featured such notable performers as Pete Seeger, Bob Gibson, Tom Paxton, John Hartford, Trapezoid, and Liam Clancy and Tommy Makem. It usually takes place around July 4, during Taste of Chicago, so watch the local media for listings.

IN THE SUBURBS

David Adler Cultural Center

School of Folk and Old Time Music

1700 N. Milwaukee Ave., Libertyville   367-0707

This is a very active center for folk music, with programs including concerts, workshops, private lessons, children's concerts, open stages, and barn dances. Director Doug Miller is a leader in preserving and promoting the traditional folk music of Illinois.

Hogeye Music and Hogeye Folk Arts

1920 Central St., Evanston   475-0260

Hogeye Music is a folk musician's heaven—a store full of folk instruments, records, books, and music. Recently, some of the Hogeye people branched out to form Hogeye Folk Arts, a nonprofit organization that presents concerts and workshops at the Noyes Cultural Arts Center, also in Evanston. Tickets for the monthly concerts, with artists such as Bill Staines, Rosalie Sorrels, and Bob Franke, cost about $5. Membership in Hogeye Folk Arts costs $10 for individuals, $15 for families, and entitles you to discounts, a newsletter, and rental of instruction and concert videotapes.

Plank Road Folk Music Society

P.O. Box 283, Brookfield, IL 60513   387-9312 or 450-9152

This nonprofit organization sponsors concerts, barn dances, and other activities in conjunction with Two Way Street coffeehouse. A yearly membership fee of $3 entitles you to a newsletter and discounts on concerts.

Two-Way Street Coffeehouse

1047 Curtiss, Downers Grove   969-9720

Established in the 1960s, this nonprofit coffeehouse in a church basement presents local folk performers on Friday nights for a suggested $1 donation. Snacks and nonalcoholic beverages are available. (See also "Plank Road Folk Music Society.")

Another option for folk music is the **Blind Faith Cafe** (525 Dempster, Evanston, 328-6875). The restaurant features live music nightly, along with its all-vegetarian menu.

ON THE RADIO

WNUR 89.3 FM
The Folk Show
Sunday, 8am to 12pm

WBEZ 91.5 FM
Flea Market
Sunday, 5 to 7 pm
Folk music showcase playing an eclectic mix—from Zulu songs to bluegrass tunes, from Celtic ballads to Venetian lute music. Sometimes broadcasts live—look for them at Navy Pier during the summer.

The Folk Sampler
Saturday, 7 to 8 pm

A Mixed Bag
Saturday, 8 to 9 pm

Bluegrass '87
Sunday, 7 to 8 pm

The Thistle and Shamrock
Sunday, 8 to 9 pm

Our Front Porch
Sunday, 9 to 10 pm

WFMT 98.7 FM
The Midnight Special (originates in Chicago)
Saturday, 10:15 pm (approx.) to 12:15 am
Repeated Wednesday, 1 to 3 pm
Broadcast via cable in some locations around the United States.

Folkstage (originates in Chicago)
Sunday, 12:15 to 12:45 am
(immediately following the Midnight Special)

—Nancy Liskar

ROCK, COUNTRY, ETHNIC AND MORE

ROCK/NEW WAVE

The faces, places, and names change constantly. Bands form, make music, and dissolve. Clubs open, thrive briefly, and fold. Records are cut, listened to, then forgotten. But the rock scene itself is remarkably constant.

From juke joints to major concert halls, Chicago has many places where music is played nightly by recent garage graduates and international superstars. You can also dance to the selections of deejays and veejays or make your own selections on juke boxes stocked with old favorites and hot new tunes. Whatever style of music or atmosphere you prefer, you can find a spot in the city to your tastes.

However, this hot rock scene rarely rewards the local bands. Despite being one of the nation's largest music markets, Chicago rarely produces successful rock recording artists. Groups with big-time potential often have to go to New York or Los Angeles before they can attract the attention of a major record label. They're forced to do so because so there is a scarcity of medium-sized independent labels that can launch groups toward success via local FM and college radio stations. Bars and clubs are continuing to replace live entertainment with videos and records.

Chicago can be a great place to listen to rock music, but it's less than an ideal place to make a living at it.

Clubs

Few clubs book only rock acts. You're most likely to hear live rock and new wave music at dance clubs and bars. Bars that showcase rock as well as other acts include **Gaspar's** at 1539 W. Belmont (871-6680), **FitzGerald's** at 6615 W. Roosevelt Rd. in Berwyn (788-2118), **Danny's** at 1951 W. Dickens Ave. (489-6457), **Avalon Niteclub** at 959 W. Belmont (472-3020), **Batteries Not Included**, featuring mostly hard core bands at 2201 N. Clybourn (348-9529), **Club Stodola**, a heavy punk bar that books local bands, at 5553 W. Belmont (343-7430), **Cubby Bear**, across from Wrigley Field at 1059 W. Addison (327-1662), **P.J. Flaherty's** on the south side at 2535 W. 95th (423-3046), and **Park West Playlot** at 2554 N. Halsted (472-7157).

Dance clubs that often book good rock and new music include: **Cabaret Metro** at 3730 N. Clark (549-0203), **Exit** at 1653 N. Wells (440-0535), **Limelight** at 632 N. Dearborn (337-2985), **Neo** at 2350 N. Clark (528-2622), **950-Lucky Number** at 950 W. Wrightwood (929-8955), **Orbit Room** at 3708 N. Broadway (348-0301), and the **Riviera Night Club** at 4746 N. Racine (769-6300).

And finally, some places that don't have live music but consistently play good music courtesy of quality DJs are the **Artful Dodger** at 1734 W. Wabansia (227-6859), **Maxtavern** at 2856 N. Racine (348-5055), **Berlin** at 954 W. Belmont (348-4975), **Medusa's** at 3257 N. Sheffield, and **Rainbo Club** at 1150 N. Damen (489-5999).

See more about these and other bars in the Nightlife chapter.

Making Music

With the numerous bars and clubs in Chicago, the city would seem like an ideal place to become a professional musician. Yet few Chicago area bands attain any significant level of success. The scarcity of Chicago-based recording stars points to some obvious gaps in the support network that fosters successful acts.

The most glaring of these is that no major recording labels are based in the midwest. The failure of the local scene to produce stars, however, can't be blamed solely on geography. Chicago hasn't had a major breakthrough act in recent years to draw attention to the scene here, and the city's medium-sized labels haven't developed the clout to distribute locally recorded products. The scene has thus far failed to develop a coherent, identifiable Chicago sound that could make for more effective marketing and wider public acceptance of local music.

Several Chicago groups have recently drawn limited national attention and made noteworthy records, but none has produced an actual hit.

Ministry, an electronic dance band, has recorded a string of 12-inch singles that were local floor fillers and received club play nationwide. But a rumored major label contract never materialized, and the group's greater success has been hampered by the limited distribution and backing that their local label was able to provide.

Another promising act, the **Way Moves**, has drawn a strong following in its appearances at the big Chicago dance clubs. They also have made at least one national TV appearance (on the "Today Show," strangely enough), but have so far failed to land a major record deal.

Finally, **Nicholas Tremulis** has been working for years at fusing elements of rock, rhythm and blues, and soul into his own unique sound. His efforts appear to be beginning to bear fruit. His debut album has drawn substantial airplay on local FM stations and he has made several successful appearances at the big local clubs. Whether greater success awaits him remains to be seen.

If you happen to be in a band and want to start recording, there are plenty of facilities in Chicago. Even with a well-produced demo tape, however, getting your music heard by the right people can be a problem. Unsolicited tapes submitted by bands are seldom paid much attention by scouts at the big record companies. Hiring an agent or attorney to help you get listened to is expensive and carries no guarantee of success. You can also go it alone if you like—the services of pressing plants are available at a cost—but the chances of cutting a truly independent record that also cuts a profit are (as someone once said) less than zero.

This is where the services of a strong, local independent label are sorely missed. Distribution and marketing are the critical needs. One local label, **WaxTrax Records,** has a partial solution to it in that its owners run record stores (of the same name) here and in other cities. But effective national distribution is beyond the scope of any of the local labels currently in existence.

The absence of an authentic local rock sound in particularly disappointing when you consider the potential here. The city's role as a seminal center in the growth of rock n' roll (the local **Chess** label recorded many classic rock and blues sides) would lead you to expect a strong roots sound to exist here. The presence of the world's most fertile blues scene would also seem to provide the grounding necessary for such a sound. But while groups such as the Blasters from Los Angeles and the Fabulous Thunderbirds from Austin have broken through with a traditional rock sound, no similar roots of rock movement has developed here.

But keep your ears open—the one thing sure about the situation is that it's subject to change.

—Chris Carr

COUNTRY

There's not a whole lot of country in Chicago, but there is some. Here are a few places that often feature country music. Remember that some of the eclectic clubs (listed below) schedule country acts as well.

The Bar RR Ranch
56 W. Randolph
263-8207
Live country music in the Loop played by the Sundowners.

Iron Rail Pub
5843 W. Irving Park Rd.
736-4670

Nashville North
101 E. Irving Park, Bensenville
595-0170

J.N.P. Lounge
4754 W. Fullerton
772-3020

Main Street's Pub
1572 N. Milwaukee
489-3160

ECLECTIC CLUBS

Eclectic is used freely nowadays to describe many entertainment spots in Chicago: dance clubs that alternate live acts with taped music, restaurants that turn into dance halls late at night, and music clubs that don't limit their bookings to performers of one type of music. **Orphan's**, for example, on 2462 N. Lincoln (929-2677), books jazz, rock, blues, and folk acts. **FitzGerald's** on 6615 W. Roosevelt Road (788-2118) in Berwyn, is a favorite for the pleasant room and the excellent programming that includes blues, R & B, rockabilly, country, Cajun, and rock. **Gaspar's** at 1359 W. Belmont (871-6680) features mostly rock and occasionally Latin and salsa music. **Boombala**, 2950 N. Lincoln (871-2686) books jazz, rock, and folk acts in a room with tablecloths and candlelight. The **Raccoon Club**, at 812 N. Franklin (943-1928), is a bit more formal and classy and offers cool jazz, cabaret singers, and blues. And finally, **CrossCurrents** at 3206 N. Wilton (472-7884) doesn't only book all sorts of dance music, including salsa, but also theatrical acts, comedy, and improvisational groups.

CONCERT HALLS

Chicago is home to several excellent large-scale and mid-sized showplaces, as well as some that are not as nice. Additional options to the ones listed below include concert halls at area colleges: Northwestern University's **Pick-Staiger** and the University of Chicago's **Mandel Hall** are good facilities, for example. Concerts at these settings are often less publicized than standard concert events, so you can see some great bands in more intimate, less crowded surroundings. During the summer, the city's extensive programs of free or very cheap outdoor neighborhood festivals showcase high-quality local talent.

Aragon Entertainment Center
1106 W. Lawrence Ave.   561-9500
Once Chicago's glitziest swing-era dance spot (it still has a beautiful hardwood floor), the Aragon's decline into a frowzy rock n' roll music hall may present a perfect index of the decay of social mores. The Uptown neighborhood around the Aragon is sleazy but slowly gentrifying. Acoustics are bad and the room gets unbearably hot during the summer. Yet, for some reason, the place offers just the right chemistry for certain concerts, and some of our fondest concert-going memories are from the Aragon. The ornate Arabian Nights decor alone is worth the price of admission.

Arie Crown Theatre, McCormick Place
23rd St. and Lake Shore Drive   791-6000
A huge theatre notorious for its terrible acoustics. The sound bounces all over the place. For hearing music, this place should be your last choice. Ticket prices are high to boot.

Auditorium Theatre
70 E. Congress Parkway   922-2110
Architect Louis Sullivan's landmark concert hall, owned by Roosevelt University, often features rock's more elegant stars. A large room with excellent acoustics and sight lines. Easily the most opulent setting for pop concerts in the city. Seating extends a considerable distance from the stage.

Bismark Theatre
171 W. Randolph, adjoining the Bismark Hotel   236-0123
Formerly the meeting place of the Democratic Party of Chicago, the Bismark has good acoustics and sometimes sets up a dance floor in front of the stage, depending on the group performing. Plan on parking in paid parking lots. The structural deficiencies of the theater were rather dramatically exposed recently when the area around the stage sunk several feet during a crowded concert (no one was injured). Structural repairs were quickly made. Prices are generally on the high side.

Centre East
7701-A Lincoln Ave., Skokie   673-6300
Housed in the auditorium of what used to be a high school, Centre East's main strength is its programming. They show an interesting mix of shows,

ranging from comedians and blues singers to special interest movies and lectures.

Chicago Theater
175 N. State   236-4300
An old theater that has been beautifully restored. It's worth taking a tour throughout all the levels to see the murals, chandeliers, and winding hallways. Programming is diverse—from musicals and cabaret singers to pop groups. Prices are high.

Holiday Star Theater
I-65 and US 30, Merrillville, Indiana   734-7266
A little over an hour's drive from the city. Big room with good acoustics and sight lines. A good place for a concert.

Links Hall
3435 N. Sheffield Ave.   281-0824
Easily the most anti-commercial venue around, Links Hall gives new meaning to the phrase "variety entertainment." The fare offered includes poetry and performance art as well music ranging from hardcore punk to ethnic varieties. Occasionally features an adventuresome nationally known act. The performance space is comparatively small, but the admission price is reasonable and the place has a positive spirit.

Park West
322 W. Armitage Ave.   929-5959
One of the finest medium-sized showcases in the country with excellent acoustics and sight lines. The Park West has a slick veneer, and usually presents acts with well-established appeal. Steep ticket prices and a drink minimum can make the evening expensive; still this is often the perfect setting to see an old favorite. The management has experimented lately in showcasing the most promising area bands in its "Local Heroes" concert series. Saturday nights, Park West hosts a crowded video dance party where crowds tend to be nattier than at most venues, so wear your best.

Poplar Creek
4777 W. Higgins Rd., Hoffman Estates   426-1222
An outdoor concert arena, Poplar Creek's physical layout is reasonable and you can see and hear well, but it is poorly run and promoted, and the dictatorial ushers seem bent on removing any chance of spontaneity in the concert. You'll be searched for bottles and cans upon entering the grounds. Despite acres of parking lots, if you arrive late, you'll never find a place to park.

Ravinia Festival
Ravinia Park Rd., Highland Park   728-4642 (R-A-V-I-N-I-A)
Open during the summer. An outdoor concert area offering plenty of seating on the grass and featuring the Chicago Symphony, pop singers, jazz performers, ballet and modern dance. See more below under "Summer Music."

Rosemont Horizon
6920 N. Mannheim Rd., Rosemont   635-6600
Every big city seems to have a huge concert hall like the Rosemont. The sound is fair to poor. The seats on the side near the stage are the best. If you get seats on the main floor, you will often have to stand.

University of Illinois at Chicago Pavilion
1150 W. Harrison   413-5700
A well-run, solid, large concert hall on the campus of the University of
Illinois at Chicago. The sound system is good. Easy access by public transportation or expressway, and hassle-free parking.

The Vic
3145 N. Sheffield Ave.   472-0366
A refurbished old theater, the Vic is the perfect size for more intimate
concerts. Recent live entertainment booked by the Vic has been excellent.
The floor slopes down to the stage, making for good sight lines. You'll
probably be seated next to strangers at your table.

Ticketron: T-I-C-K-E-T-S

Ticketmaster: 559-1212 or 902-1500

—Chris Carr

GOSPEL

Chicago is a mecca for soulful gospel music. The exuberance and emotion
of gospel music has long attracted fans, both churchgoers and nonchurch-
goers alike. You don't have to be a Baptist to enjoy it.

Chicago now hosts a **gospel fest** in the summer, at the Petrillo Music
shell in Grant Park. An independent gospel label—**I Am Records**—is based
in Chicago and boasts many local artists on its roster. There are many
excellent church choirs in the city. A few are listed below; call to confirm
times and dates of concerts. Record stores that carry gospel music include
the **Pentecostal Word Explosion** at 7900 S. Prairie and **New Sound Records
& Tapes** at 5958 W. Lake. A number of local radio stations air gospel
shows, among them: **WBMX-FM's** "Inspirational Stroll" on Sundays, 4:30-
8:00 am, and **WGCI-FM's** "The Music of Love and Inspiration," on Sundays, 8:00 am-noon. Some smaller stations, including **WCRM-FM, WMBI-
FM**, and **WVON-AM**, play gospel all the time. You can catch local and
national stars on the weekly syndicated television program "**Saturday Night
Sing**," airing at 10:30 pm Saturdays on UHF channel 38.

Chicago Gospel Music Assembly   745-3797
Non-profit organization that helps choirs record their music and sponsors
concerts.

First Corinthians Baptist Church
11359 S. State   821-5558
Reverend Claude Tears, Choir director: Sharon Tears
The excellent choir performs at the 11 am Sunday service. Those interested
in the choir only should attend the 12:15 pm Sunday performances. Special
choir performances are also held every third Sunday of each month at 7:30
pm.

Fellowship Missionary Baptist Church
45th Pl. and Princeton Ave.   924-3232
Reverend Clay Evans
Services featuring the well-known Fellowship Baptist Choir are held at 10:30
am on Sundays. The choir is also broadcast Sundays at 9 pm on WCFL
AM radio.

ETHNIC

You can hear music of most nationalities somewhere in Chicago. Folk music and dance troupes from all over the world swing through here regularly. Often, these groups will perform at local high schools (Lane Tech is a big one for ethnic concerts) or at the Auditorium Theater. Did you know there is a fine Lithuanian opera company here? Look for notices about ethnic music performances in the papers or take a stroll through the appropriate neighborhood and look for posters. Many ethnic groups have private clubs with music (private in the sense they are not advertised and you may have to be in-the-know somehow to know where they are).

The clubs listed below are very accessible to anyone and should give you a taste of the music of other cultures. Most, not all, are restaurants. You may or may not have to order food, depending on the place. In any case, call ahead to find out. In most of these places, the later you go, the better. Most encourage patrons to dance, often until 4 and 5 am (it can get pretty wild, in a Zorba type of way).

Deni's Den
2941 N. Clark   348-8888
The owners have even flown bands in from Greece to perform in this bright, airy restaurant whose whitewashed walls make you think you're on the islands. The music is terrific; the band plays a lot of music by Mikis Theodorakis (composer for the movie "Z"). Great late hours for music: music starts Wednesday through Sunday at 8:30; closes at 4 am every day but Saturday, when it closes at 5 am. Dancing strongly encouraged. Gets crowded on the weekends. No cover.

Baby Doll Polka Club
6102 S. Central   582-9706
The owners, Eddie ("the Prince of Polka") and Irene Korosa are local polka legends. Eddie wrote "The Baby Doll Polka" and other polka hits, and his band, Eddie Korosa and the Merrymakers, pound out the tunes from 9:30 pm-3 am Friday and Saturday, and 5 pm-midnight on Sunday. Gets wild on Saturday nights with enthusiastic dancers crowding the dance floor. Irene knows everyone. No cover.

Desanka's Place
4343 N. Lincoln   525-8171
Nice family-run Serbian restaurant and lounge featuring performers from Yugoslavia as well as local Serbian pop singers. Music starts at 8 pm on Tuesday, and Friday through Sunday. Closes 2 am. Moderate prices, no cover.

Kitty O'Shea's
Chicago Hilton and Towers, ground floor
720 S. Michigan   922-4400
An Irish pub with Irish food and Irish music. Music every night but Sunday. Monday through Friday, shows are scheduled at 5 pm-7 pm and 9 pm-1 am. On Saturday at 8 pm-1 am. No cover. Stop by if you're out late in the Loop.

Maryla Night Club Polonaise
3196 N. Milwaukee   545-4152
Polish restaurant with dancing to eastern European bands. Go late for dancing
on the roomy dance floor. Moderate cover charge, cheap prices.

Miomir's Serbian Cafe
2255 W. Lawrence   784-2111
Serbian restaurant with great music. The star is Jovan, who plays eastern
European folk and popular music on myriad instruments, often playing two
trumpets and saxophones at a time—it's his special trick. Music nightly.
No cover.

Moscow at Night
3058 W. Peterson   338-6600
Friendly Russian and European restaurant with bands playing a mixture of
Russian, Polish, other eastern and middle European, and American music
on Friday from 8 pm-1 am, on Saturday from 8 pm-3 am, and Sunday 7
pm-12 am. Dancing encouraged.

The Rafters
9757 S. Commercial   731-0288
East-side bar featuring Serbian and Croatian music on Saturday nights at
10 pm. No cover.

Sinbad's Lounge
2201 W. Montrose   463-0044
Restaurant and nightclub featuring Assyrian and middle eastern music on
Wednesday through Sunday night. Music starts at 10 pm. Also have belly
dancers.

6511 Club
6511 S. Kedzie   778-9434
A real Irish pub where you're likely to hear authentic brogues at the table
next to you. Music starts on Friday nights at 10:30 pm, and you can catch
informal jams other nights. No cover.

Skorpios
2811 N. Central   736-8488
Fantastic Greek music and big crowds to hear it on the weekends. Go late,
when it gets swinging. Music on Wednesday through Sunday; starts at 9:30
pm.

Zum Lieben Augustin
4600 N. Lincoln   334-2919
German restaurant and night club with a band and dancing on weekends.
The dance floor is small but that doesn't stop patrons from doing the waltz
and polka. Music starts at 9 pm.

REGGAE

Chicago has a large population of Jamaican emigres and a lively reggae scene.

Wild Hare and Singing Armadillo Frog Sanctuary
3530 N. Clark   327-0800
Chicago's oldest reggae club and the center for reggae in the midwest. You can see the best local and imported bands at the Wild Hare. A real mix of people. Shows generally start at 10:30.

Cubby Bear
1059 W. Addison   327-1662
Another big spot for reggae. Fairly large room featuring local and national acts. Shows are usually at 10 pm. Cover charge.

Negril
6232 N. Broadway   761-4133
Friendly, smaller room featuring local and other reggae acts. Dancing.

Hummingbird Supper Club
8620 S. Ashland Ave.   445-0500
Reggae on the south side.

SALSA

Asi Es Colombia
3910 N. Lincoln   348-7444
Large salsa dance club featuring excellent bands and some terrific dancers to watch if you don't salsa yourself. Call ahead to find out what music is playing. Come before 9 pm if you want a table. The snacks are very good. Men are requested to wear jackets. Cover charge, no drink minimum.

Latin Village
2528 N. Lincoln   472-6166
Big dance floor and great salsa bands that start playing at 10 pm. Come early to get a table. Dress nicely—jeans are not allowed. Cover charge and two-drink minimum. Open late.

Moosehead Bar and Grill
163 W. Harrison   922-3640
Every Monday night is Latin Jazz night in this big, pleasant room on the southern edge of the Loop. Victor Parra is a regular act. The music is good and lots of people come regularly to dance. Cover charge.

Tania's
2659 N. Milwaukee   235-7120
Cuban night club and restaurant in Logan Square featuring salsa music on the weekends. Dress nicely. Lots of fun. No cover charge or minimum.

SUMMER MUSIC

Summer is the season for some special music experiences in Chicago.
   Ravinia is an outdoor park located in the northern suburb of Highland Park, which features all kinds of music and dance acts and is open only during the summer. You sit on the grass (bring your own chairs, food, and wine—some picnics get fairly elaborate) or in seats under the covered pavilion (more money and harder to get). The Chicago Symphony Orchestra plays

here in the summer, as do jazz performers, pop singers and groups, concert singers, ballet companies, and modern dance troupes. It can get crowded but it's nice and relaxing on a warm summer night. You can get there on the Chicago and Northwestern commuter train (get off at the Ravinia stop); buses also run to Ravinia from various locations in the city. Call 728-4642 for more information.

Grant Park's Petrillo Music Shell at Columbus Drive and Jackson Boulevard is the location for outdoor summer concerts featuring the fine Grant Park Symphony and Chorus. Concerts often have guest conductors and showcase young soloists. Recent programming has been more experimental and has included more vocalists. It gets crowded, but pleasantly so.

Two Loop plazas have short lunchtime concerts during the summer: The **Daley Center Plaza** surrounding the Picasso at Washington and Clark Streets features a real mixed bag of music during the noon hour—ethnic folk music and dancers, blues singers, school orchestras, children's choirs, gospel, and much more. The crowd is also more of a mix than the almost exclusively business person crowd you'll find at concerts at the **First National Plaza** at Madison and Clark Streets. The music here leans more to pop, jazz, rock, and even funk played by more established performers.

Street musicians and beach musicians play all over the city when the weather gets hot. In the subway stations downtown, you can hear everything from a classical quartet to heartfelt blues. On the streets in the Loop, crowds form around some of the more popular street musicians: the woman drummer, the bluegrass fiddler who brings out his pet ferret, and the big bongo groups.

SPECIAL EVENTS

Chicago regularly hosts some high-quality musical events that are worth checking out. There's something for most tastes.

The University of Chicago Folk Festival, usually held in January, is one of the best traditional music festivals in the country, attracting fans from all over the midwest and beyond. The programming is eclectic and always interesting: Appalachian music, Cajun, bluegrass, traditional Irish, lusty blues, gospel, Western swing, and Chicago ethnic, to name a few. The performers teach and perform at all-day workshops as well. Look for details in the paper or the *Reader*, or call the University for information.

The Blues Fest, held in June in Grant Park, attracts the best national and local acts to the Petrillo stage. More crowded and noisy every year, but a great chance to hear top acts. Stake out a place to sit early in the evening.

The Jazz Festival, held the Wednesday through Sunday before Labor Day, also in Grant Park, also draws local, national, and international talent. Also noisy and crowded, but worth it to hear the music.

Every August is **Charlie Parker Month** at Joe Segal's Jazz Showcase (see Jazz heading earlier in this chapter). Joe brings together a series of shows featuring musicians who worked with or were heavily influenced by this jazz legend.

Neighborhood festivals held all over city neighborhoods during the summer can occasionally draw some excellent bands and performers. Note especially the fests in the Lincoln Park and Lakeview areas—they usually get some good local blues and rock groups. Ethnic neighborhoods draw fine musicians and sometimes import nationally known performers for their festivals.

MUSICAL INSTRUMENT SHOPS

If you want to buy or rent all sorts of musical instruments, you have hundreds of places to choose from—from pawn shops to craftsmens' studios to big shops. Ask musician friends and other people in the know for suggestions. Here are just a few places.

STRING

Bein & Fushi
410 S. Michigan Ave.
663-1005
The best for strings—Chicago Symphony performers buy here—but very expensive.

Fritz Reuter & Sons
1565 W. Howard
764-2766
A good place with an excellent reputation. Owners are violin makers trained in Europe.

Kenneth Warren & Son
407 S. Dearborn, 7th floor
427-7475
Strings downtown.

GUITAR

Hogeye Music
1920 Central, Evanston
475-0260
Guitars, banjos, etc. Lessons too.

Snukst Music
6611 S. Pulaski
585-7923

Sound Post
1239 Chicago, Evanston
866-6866
Folk and electric guitar, drums.

PIANO

Kurt Saphir Pianos
310 W. Chicago
440-1164
Good reputation.

Hendricks Music Company
755 N. Wells
664-5522
Steinway dealer.

RECORD AND CD STORES

Rose Records
214 S. Wabash   987-9044
210 N. Michigan   263-3023
3259 N. Ashland   880-0280
Probably the best general selection record stores in the city. Huge selections. The downtown store on Wabash is big, with an especially good selection of classical music and a decent ethnic music section. The store on Ashland also has an excellent general selection and is particularly strong in folk and salsa. There are several other locations in the city and suburbs.

Jazz Record Mart
11 W. Grand   222-1467
A superb collection of jazz and blues, domestic and imports, that draws shoppers from all over the area. A great place to find out what's happening in the jazz and blues worlds in general.

Beverly Rare Records
11612 S. Western   779-0066
A curio shop for record lovers—they've got novelty records that you won't find anywhere else, lots of Sam Cooke, collectors' items, old-time hokey stuff, and original recordings of all kinds. An amazing place. There are two other locations.

Dr. Wax
2529 N. Clark   549-3377
Great selection of soul music and R & B, as well as recently released used records.

Gramaphone
2663 N. Clark   472-3683
A small place with a surprising variety in its selection. A sheet of upcoming releases is always posted near the front door.

Wax Trax Records
2449 N. Lincoln   929-0221
This store is a real scene in itself and knows it. The best place in town to find new-wave, punk-type music. Especially strong in imports. Also has some collectibles from the 60s. Wax Trax has its own record label.

Pravda Records
3728 N. Clark   549-3776
Heavy on Chicago-area bands. Lots of new music and heavy metal.

Rolling Stone Records
7300 W. Irving Park Rd., Norridge   456-0861
This is the place to go for bargains. Best prices on cut-outs and new releases. Good selection.

USED

Used records aren't as cheap as they used to be, but you can still save roughly half the price if you shop at used record stores.

Record Exchange
953 W. Belmont
975-9285
1505 W. Morse
973-0452
609 Dempster, Evanston
475-8848
Good selection of mostly rock, but with a little of everything.

Second Hand Tunes
2550 N. Clark
929-6325
1375 E. 53rd St.
684-3375
818 Dempster, Evanston
491-1690
Rock, jazz, classical, R & B, and show tunes.

The B Side
3774 N. Clark
525-0256
Good selection of most every type
of music.

Vintage Vinyl Records
925 Davis St., Evanston
328-2899
Excellent place for used records.
Great selection but you pay the
price.

International

Most general record stores have ethnic or international sections, of varying quality. Better than these, however, are small shops in ethnic communities that cater to their customers. Try **Italian Records & Video** at 7179 W. Grand (637-5300), **La-Voz-de-America Record Shop** at 4628 N. Broadway (334-1427), **Musica Latina** at 2142 W. Cermak (247-4535), **Polish Record Center of America** at 3069 N. Milwaukee (539-9898), **Quisqueye Transfer Express** at 7608 N. Paulina (262-0073) for French records, and **Slavoff Imports** at 1919 W. Montrose (281-2774) for Balkan music, and **Delta Import Company** at 2242 W. Chicago (235-7788) for Ukrainian records. International music can also be found in ethnic bookstores, which often sell records. (See the Literary Life chapter for some ethnic bookstore listings.)

MUSIC INSTRUCTION

You can get ideas of where to learn how to play an instrument or learn to sing in a few places: musical instrument stores, which often offer instruction on musical instruments or recommendations on where to get it; word of mouth (excellent method); a course at a junior college or university; ads for lessons in the papers or the *Reader*.

If you're more serious, several music conservatories are located in Chicago. See the listings in the Classical Music section. For folk, try the Old Town School of Folk Music or Hogeye in Evanston (see listings in the Folk Music section).

THEATER

By now it's no secret. Chicago has become a major theater town, rivaling (and, in some ways, surpassing) New York City as a center of vital, creative theater work. Greenhorn actors now know of Chicago as a place to learn, grow, and prepare for the "Big Time." And even seasoned actors and directors move here from NYC and LA. Many perfect their craft and move on (or back) to New York or the Coast, but others, like William Petersen (of the Remains Theatre) have remained in Chicago to act in off-Loop shows, while racking up successes in films and on Broadway. So, if you like theater, especially theater of an off-Broadway, off-off-Broadway, repertory, theater-in-the-round, storefront, shoestring, "not all of us are famous, but none of us is bad" kind, then you'll like Chicago theater.

Be forewarned, Chicago has no central theater district to speak of, not even in the Loop. Instead our theaters are spread across the face of Chicago, and you are as likely to see a show in Rogers Park as in Lincoln Park, in Hyde Park as in Evanston.

Also, Chicago theaters vary radically in size. Some theater groups are squeezed into small storefronts that seat at most fifty. Other groups (the larger, more established places) have nice-sized work spaces. The Organic Theater, for example, has a main stage the size of a small aircraft hangar. You'll find the same diversity among theater locations. Although the Goodman is conveniently located in the Loop, and Victory Gardens and The Body Politic are found in the hip, upwardly mobile Lincoln Park area, many of the smaller (and poorer) theaters are located in fringe areas to the west, north, or south of gentrifying areas. For example, The Prop Thtr (on Clybourn near Fullerton Avenue) is just a short walk from the completely gentrified Lincoln Park area to the east, and the Bucktown area to the west which is beginning to be rehabbed, but still is rough and rundown.

THE COMPANIES

Chicago has developed in a very short time a rich tradition in theater. In the sixties, a widely-recognized, largely improvisational comedy style was known as the "Chicago style" of acting. This style, developed by Viola Spolin and Paul Sills and perfected at the Compass Players, at Second City and Story Theatre, eventually won national attention through the work of the original cast of "Saturday Night Live" (many of whom were Second City alums).

Today when anyone refers to the "Chicago Style" of acting, they mean the kind of acting they do at the **Steppenwolf Theatre**. John Malkovich, Laurie Metcalf, and their cohorts do a mean kind of method acting, adding a rock and roll nastiness to traditional Stanislavsky techniques. Imagine Mick Jagger as Hamlet and you will come close to the Steppenwolf style. You'd expect this style to work well with the more cynical and nihilistic contemporary plays, say, anything by Sam Shepard or Lanford Wilson's earlier works, and it does. In fact, Steppenwolf took productions of both Shepard's *True West* and Wilson's *Balm in Gilead* to New York for long runs off-Broadway. But the Steppenwolf style works for the classics, too. In recent years their revivals of Chekhov's *The Cherry Orchard*, Strindberg's *Miss Julie*, and (would you believe it) Kaufman and Hart's *You Can't Take it With You* have been acclaimed, successful, and deservedly so. The Steppenwolf has earned its national reputation.

The **Goodman Theatre**, another nationally known theater, was founded in the twenties as an amateur group associated with the Art Institute of Chicago. Although the theater became a professional company in the nineteen fifties, it wasn't until Gregory Mosher took over direction of the theater in the late seventies that the Goodman metamorphosed from a boring and staid house to a place premiering some of the most challenging work of the decade. Under Mosher's direction, the Goodman became a place in town where talent from New York and Los Angeles worked with Chicago talent to produce shows that were among the best (or were the best) in Chicago. Well, Mosher has left Chicago to become artistic director of the theaters in Lincoln Center in New York and Robert Falls (former director of Wisdom Bridge) has taken the reins as the new artistic director. Falls was the man who brought us the high-tech, new wave, multi-media version of *Hamlet*. And his first season at the Goodman showed the full force of his ambition, imagination, and grandiosity. Under Falls' direction the Goodman will certainly remain the best (or among the best) theaters in Chicago.

Peter Aylward as Hamlet and Del Close as Polonius in the Wisdom Bridge Theatre production of *Hamlet*. Photo by Jennifer Girard.

Another theater going through a transition is **Wisdom Bridge**. After several very successful years under the direction of Robert Falls, they now have to continue without him. Wisdom Bridge gained national attention during Falls' years with a production of Jack Abbott's prison autobiography, *In the Belly of the Beast*. After a very successful run in Wisdom Bridge's space on Howard Street, AT&T underwrote a run of the play at Washington D.C.'s Kennedy Center. Also during Falls' tenure Wisdom Bridge produced a series of Kabuki adaptations of classical texts. *Kabuki MacBeth*, *Kabuki Medea*, and *Kabuki Faust* were all three successful and interesting productions. We hope that Wisdom Bridge's versatility and vitality will continue under new artistic director Richard E. T. White.

Yet another theater, the **Organic Theater**, is weathering the loss of its fearless leader. Under Stuart Gordon's direction the Organic Theater grew from a hole-in-the-wall group (founded in the late sixties) to a very successful theater with its own building and its own style (actually two styles): shows with lots of special effects and shows "dat showed how we live here in da city of She-caw-ga." (Most of the shows weren't art, but they were great box office.) In the seventies and early eighties three shows in particular had very long runs: A science fiction series called *Warp*, a play about Chicago Cubs fans, *Bleacher Bums*, and a slice of life comedy-drama about a hospital emergency room, *E/R*. Since Stuart Gordon moved to Hollywood to make horror movies (*The Reanimator*), the Organic has floundered around, producing several substantial flops. However, all is far from lost. The theater's new artistic director, Thomas Riccio, has turned the Organic Lab into a forum for works in progress, performance art, and experiments in long-form improvisation. Don't pass up the chance to see one of Michael Gellman's *Seed Shows*, shows created by writers and improvisational actors in collaboration. In the meantime, the main stage at the Organic has been used best when used by other theater groups.

Second City, Chicago's second oldest theater company, began in the fifties with the improvisational experiments of Paul Sills, Viola Spolin, and the Compass Players at the Compass in Hyde Park. In 1960 they moved north to a large space in Old Town and renamed the theater The Second City, after A. J. Leibling's snide nickname for Chicago. Since then improvisational comedy has become big business. Second City now has two stages in Chicago (the Main Stage and the ETC Company), two national touring companies, branches in Toronto and Edmonton, and a school of improvisation. An incredible number of very talented actors and comedians have been associated with Second City over the last thirty years: Mike Nichols, Elaine May, Alan Arkin, Barbara Harris, John Belushi, Bill Murray, Shelley Long, Gilda Radner, to name eight. Second City still manages to put together comedy revues with some bite, although they do go for the easy joke, and they lack that angry young beat comic style that made their satire so strong in the sixties. Still, Second City remains one of the best places for comedy in Chicago.

Three other comedy groups worth watching are the **Friends of the Zoo**, the **Practical Theater Company** and the Improv Olympic's **Harold**. Since none of these groups has its own performing space, they must perform in other people's theaters. All three groups have their comic roots in improvisation, although the Friends of the Zoo and the Practical Theater have moved on to scripted material. The Friends of the Zoo perform long, surreal comic sketches with music. Their material is often more interesting than funny, but Mark Nutter *et al.* write the best song lyrics in Chicago, and sometimes interesting is better than funny. The Practical Theater boasts of performing in a new-vaudevillian style, but their shows look a lot like Second City. Still they are as energetic as Second City, and even, from time to time, a tad bit more original. The Improv Olympic is really a poor cousin to the Zoo and Practical, and the actors in the Harold are for the most part amateurs or very green professionals, but the Harold itself is such an interesting improvement on improvisation, and Del Close (former director of Second City, Chicago theater cult figure, and developer of the Harold technique) leads such a great workshop at the Improv Olympic, that the shows at times have an amazing spontaneity and freshness. But be forewarned, a good Harold is wonderful, but a bad Harold is deadly dull.

Victory Gardens and **Body Politic** have been on the Chicago scene for a long time. The two groups are autonomous, with separate governing boards and different artistic directors, but I mention them together because they share the same building on Lincoln Avenue, and because they collaborated on a new playwrights festival in mid-1987. Future incarnations of this festival are not to be missed. Both Victory Gardens and Body Politic have a degree of professional polish that carries them through every production. The Body Politic tends to tackle a somewhat lighter fare—comedies, comic mysteries, British social satires—than Victory Gardens, but only on the rarest of occasions will you find a show without some merit at either of these theaters.

For a long time the **Remains Theatre Ensemble** seemed to be a younger, less successful brother to The Steppenwolf. They had a similar acting style; they showed the same predilection for strange, troubling, vaguely sado-masochistic plays; they even collaborated with Steppenwolf on the landmark Steppenwolf production of Wilson's *Balm in Gilead*. But recently Remains has asserted its own identity, and benefitted from co-founder William Petersen's recent successes in Hollywood. They don't have their own space, but look for them at the Organic Theater's main stage.

Located on the campus of the University of Chicago, **Court Theatre** is one of the few theaters in Chicago to devote itself entirely to producing the classics of world drama. In the past this devotion has been particularly Anglophilic, and productions sometimes looked and sounded like live versions of Masterpiece Theater. But Nicholas Rudell *et al.* have recently expanded their definition of world drama to include plays from non-English speaking countries. Productions at Court may at times be bloodless and academic (the influence of the University of Chicago). But at other times Court gives life to plays other groups would smother with reverence or destroy with ignorance. If you find yourself hankering for Chekhov or Aeschylus or Moliere or Goldsmith or Ibsen or Shaw, check out Court Theatre.

At the opposite end of Chicago, in Evanston, is the **Northlight Theatre**, a consistently able group that produces contemporary plays with an intelligence and energy matched by few theaters in Chicago.

Most of Chicago's theater explosion has been located on the north side among the white middle class; however, Chicago is also graced with three strong black theater companies, all on the south side: **Kuumba Professional Company**, **ETA Creative Arts Foundation**, and **The Chicago Theatre Company**. Of these, Kuumba is the oldest and most consistent. Kuumba's productions are always good, although at times productions may be marred by melodramatic over-acting. A more active theater group is the ETA Creative Arts Foundation, which exclusively produces the work of Afro-American playwrights. ETA Creative Arts Foundation produces a full season of five plays a year. The Chicago Theatre Company seems to like specializing in musicals, some with a slightly barbed social message.

THEATER FESTIVALS

Truly zealous theater lovers should know about the **Chicago International Theater Festival**. In the spring of 1986, the Festival featured twenty-one productions from seventeen theaters from around the world, including companies from Great Britain, Spain, Italy, Israel, and Japan. Also, eleven Chicago theaters represented the hometown at the Festival. Look for the next Festival tentatively planned for spring of 1988.

Another festival worth watching for is the **Off-Off Loop Theatre Festival**. Held every spring and sponsored by the League of Chicago Theatres, the festival highlights the work of ten small but up-and-coming, non-Equity theater companies. Styles and content vary widely from company to company, and during the two-week festival you're likely to see everything from mildly mainstream one-acts to wildly experimental micro-epics—but this is a virtue, not a vice. The city offers no better event for sampling the sheer variety of Chicago's struggling storefront theaters.

If you don't mind a short 3½ hour drive into the heart of Wisconsin, or if you are looking for a great weekend retreat, check out the **American Players Theatre** in Spring Green, Wisconsin. This nationally recognized, Tony-award-nominated theater company performs the best Shakespeare this side of New York City. Also, a little Chekhov, a bit of Ibsen, a dab of Goldsmith and Sheridan. Plays are performed in repertory on an open-air stage from mid-June to September. And if you stay the weekend, it's possible to see two, three, maybe four plays in two days. Spring Green and environs offer many kinds of lodging, from inns and bed-and-breakfasts to motels and campgrounds. For information on lodging in Spring Green call the Spring Green Chamber of Commerce, (608) 588-2402. For a schedule of performances, write or call American Players Theatre at the address listed at the end of this chapter.

THE BARGAIN BASEMENT

One of the truly daunting aspects of Chicago theater is the price of tickets. A show at a big name theater can cost you between $15 and $20, and even inexpensive shows at smaller theaters can run $8 to $10. However, there are a number of alternatives for those of you who have empty pockets like me. First, you can usher. Every off-Loop theater needs volunteer ushers who receive free admission for their trouble. Second, student productions at Northwestern University, DePaul and the University of Chicago often are as good (or almost as good) as any in Chicago (especially Northwestern's). Third, from time to time the Chicago Public Library showcases local productions at the Cultural Center. Not only are these productions free, but the auditorium at the Cultural Center is excellent (which is to say, better than many of the smaller theaters). You can pick up a calendar listing each month's events at any branch of the Chicago Library. Finally, a new kind of theater group has popped up recently, the low-low budget group, without a space of their own, or even an office. These very small theater groups perform in bars (like Sheffield's, Red Lion), art galleries (Chicago Film-makers, ARC Gallery), or use a slightly more established theater's stage, when that larger theater (say, the Organic Lab) is not using it. There is even a theater group that performs in a health club (the Inn Town players). These low-low budget theaters charge as little as a dollar or two for their performances. How do they do it? LOW, LOW OVERHEAD!!

SOURCES OF THEATER INFORMATION

By far the best place for information about theater is the second section of the Chicago *Reader*. The *Reader* has the most comprehensive listing of shows in Chicago. Any little company that sends in a press release will receive some listing in the *Reader*. Additionally, any theater that can afford to advertise will advertise their shows in the *Reader*. Its reviews may also help you weed out the absolutely terrible shows, although the *Reader* critics have a reputation for being difficult to please and you may find you like a show the reviewer absolutely tore to shreds.

The *Chicago Tribune* and the *Chicago Sun-Times* are much softer in their theater criticism but they are wildly inconsistent in their coverage of Chicago theater. Sure, they do a decent job of following the big theaters with the national reputations, but they are often the last to notice a small company on the rise. And if some big post-Broadway touring show like *Cats* comes to town, even the Goodman and Steppenwolf will be ignored. But from time to time the little guys get noticed. Both papers run special sections on Fridays that attempt to give complete listings of everything going on in the "Chicagoland" area. Unfortunately, many of the smaller theaters are left out of this listing.

Chicago magazine falls somewhere between the two dailies and the *Reader*. *Chicago* magazine's listings are more complete than the dailies, but because the magazine is a monthly with a long lead time, information is often old, and theater companies that are not coordinated enough to get their press releases out six weeks ahead of time are not listed.

Finally, for those who like to listen to long recorded messages there is **Curtain Call** (977-1755), a 24-hour theater hotline run by the League of Chicago Theatres. Curtain Call does a good job of mentioning almost every show in Chicago, but listening to the tape from beginning to end may give you a case of telephone ear.

While we're on the topic of the League of Chicago Theatres, the League runs two other services for theater patrons: **Hot Tix** and **Theater Tix**. Hot Tix offers half-price tickets on the day of performance to almost any show you'd want to see (that isn't sold out). Tickets must be paid for in cash, and you must buy them in person at one of the three Hot Tix locations: 24 S. State in Chicago, Park Square Mall in Oak Park, and 1616 Sherman in Evanston. Theater Tix allows you to buy (full price) tickets to any show over the phone using your Visa or MasterCard; the theater will usually hold your tickets at the door instead of mailing them out. The Theater Tix number is 853-0505.

THEATER BOOKSTORES

Of course a city with a reputation for theater would have a good theater bookstore or two. **Scenes** (3168 N. Clark, 525-1007), combining a bookstore with a coffeeshop, has an extensive collection of theater books and serves great coffee. Scenes also hosts readings. **Act I** (2633 N. Halsted, 348-6757) stocks used, remaindered and new theater books, undoubtedly the largest collection in the city. The store also has magazines of interest to theater lovers, including *Variety, Backstage, TDR*, and the hard-to-find *Ross Report* and *Theatrical Index*. And don't forget **Oak Street Book Shop** (54 E. Oak, 642-3070).

THEATER DIRECTORY

(Theaters not to be missed are marked with ★.)

Absolute Theatre
Theatre Bldg., 1225 W. Belmont
327-5252

Alliance Theatre Company
(performance space varies)
943-4442

American Players Theatre
P. O. Box 819
Spring Green, WI 53588
(608) 588-7401

Apollo Theater Center
2540 N. Lincoln
935-6100

★Bailiwick Repertory
3212 N. Broadway
883-1090

Blue Rider Theater
1822 S. Halsted
733-4668

★Body Politic
2261 N. Lincoln
871-3000

Briar Street Theatre
3133 N. Halsted
348-4000

Center Theater
1346 W. Devon
508-0200

Chicago City Theatre Company
3340 N. Clark
880-1002

Chicago Theatre Company
Parkway Theater, 500 E. 67th
493-1305

Commons Theatre
1020 W. Bryn Mawr
769-5009

★Court Theatre
5535 S. Ellis
753-4472

Dreiske Performance Company
Facets Multimedia
1517 W. Fullerton
281-9075

★ETA Creative Arts Foundation
7558 S. South Chicago
752-3955

★Goodman Theatre
200 S. Columbus
443-3800

Huron Theater
(performance space varies)
327-0367

★igLoo
3829 N. Broadway
975-9192

★Immediate Theatre Company
1146 W. Pratt
465-3107

★Improvisation Institute
2939 W. Belmont
588-2668

Inn Town Players
2796 N. Lehmann Ct.
472-2959

*Kuumba Theatre
218 S. Wabash
461-9000

New Tuners Theatre
Theatre Bldg, 1225 W. Belmont
327-5252

*Next Theatre Company
Noyes Cultural Arts Ctr.
927 Noyes, Evanston
475-1875

Night Light
4023 W. Irving Park
777-7373

*Northlight Theatre
Kingsley Theatre
2300 Green Bay, Evanston
869-7278

*Organic Theater Company
3319 N. Clark
327-5588

Palladium Productions
(performance space varies)
282-5613

Passage Theater
5404 N. Clark
975-5939

Pegasus Players
O'Rourke Ctr. for the Performing
Arts
Truman College, 1145 W. Wilson
271-2638

*Prop Thtr
2360 N. Clybourn
935-1155

Raven Theatre Company
6931 N. Clark
338-2177

*Reflections Theatre Ensemble
5404 N. Clark
784-1234

*Remains Theatre
3319 N. Clark
327-5588

Royal-George Theatre
1641 N. Halsted
988-9000

*Second City Theatre and **Second City ETC**
1616 N. Wells
337-3992

*Stage Left Theatre
3244 N. Clark
883-8830

*Steppenwolf Theatre
2851 N. Halsted
472-4141

*Stormfield Theatre
1020 W. Bryn Mawr
878-8458

Theatre Building
1225 W. Belmont
327-5252

Theatre First
Athanaeum Theatre
2936 N. Southport
792-2226

*Victory Gardens
2257 N. Lincoln
871-3000

*Wisdom Bridge
1559 W. Howard
743-6442

Zebra Crossing Theatre
4520 N. Beacon
769-5199

CURTAIN CALL: 977-1755
THEATER TIX: 853-0505

HOT TIX
24 S. State
Hours: Mon 12-6, Tue-Fri 10-6, Sat 10-5
Park Square Mall, Oak Park
Hours: Tue-Sat 10-3
1616 Sherman, Evanston
Hours: Tue-Sat 10-3
Sunday tickets are sold on Saturday at all Hot Tix locations.

—Jack Helbig

DANCE

Chicago cannot boast of as much high-profile activity in dance as San Francisco, Los Angeles, or New York, but a dance scene does exist here, and one that, partly because it is small and not generally famous, holds a lot of opportunity both for spectators and for participants. Over the past twenty years, an indigenous modern dance has grown up here. And, over the past six years, a ballet company—the **Chicago City Ballet**—has been trying to. (CCB is not the first to try, and it is probably not the last. Local ballet has had a hard time finding a niche in Chicago.) The success story of the jazzily eclectic **Hubbard Street Dance Company**—begun in 1977 with four dancers, but now many times larger and touring the world with an ever-growing repertory—poses an inspiration and a challenge to smaller companies who might like to follow in Hubbard's footsteps. Of course, not all really need to. Ethnic dance, for example, commands a usually modest but reliable local audience; for those ethnic companies that are marginally professional or outright amateur, this audience is appropriate. Still, comparatively healthy though dance may be in Chicago, dancers of all kinds naturally hunger for larger local attendance and national recognition. Neither comes easily.

"A nice thing about Chicago is that we have had no gods to imitate," Nana Shineflug has remarked. Shineflug is one of a handful of people (Shirley Mordine and Maggie Kast are others) who, in the late 1960s, laid the foundation of modern dance in Chicago. Currently, Shineflug is artistic director of the **Chicago Moving Company**, a modern dance troupe.

"Basically," Shineflug has recalled of her own beginnings, "we were totally ignorant of quality, style, and training." But, she adds, "We had such enthusiasm. We were in this closet, and enjoying it." Technique has been explored gradually, not worshipped as an end in itself. According to some dancers now, there is still not enough of it in Chicago. But perhaps modern dance, which traditionally requires a degree of maverick individuality in dancers and choreographers to thrive, has actually benefited from Chicago's onetime "closet," if the closet, as some believe, protected dancers from the pressure of New York dance trends and other venal influences.

Says Tara Mitton, once Shineflug's student, and now artistic director of the **Chicago Repertory Dance Ensemble**, Chicago dancers dance "from the inside out, rather than the outside in. We're very different from New York dancers. We've all had a chance to find out who we are," instead of getting lost in a competitive jungle of leotards. Dance in Chicago is not fashionable, and this may be an advantage of sorts to dancers who work here, leaving them freer to do what they want.

And what do Chicago dancers want? They are eclectic, without a doubt. Yet, in Shineflug's words, "It's not abstract, intellectual dancing that goes on here. Most of it has content of some sort. People are striving on a much more personal level."

Chicago dancers may be free to find out who they are, but Chicago audiences haven't found out all there is to know about dancers. Dancer/choreog-

Chicago Repertory Dance Ensemble. Photo by Gary Sigman.

raphers like Shineflug and Mitton attract a loyal following—yet not an enormous one. "People are very busy with being busy," one choreographer has observed of the general, non-dance-going public. "They're conservative . . . they don't want to think." As another dancer puts it, "That they're allowed to use their imaginations to interpret intimidates people," both in Chicago and in general, where dance is concerned. To compound the problem of small audiences, the local media's coverage of dance is spotty at best. The *Sun-Times*, *Tribune*, *Chicago* magazine, and the *Reader* all carry some dance reviews, but dance isn't a high priority for any of them. Often the companies they review are the ones most conspicuously advertised, and these are not necessarily the ones most worth seeing.

Don't follow the path of least resistance when buying your tickets, and do make sure that every once in a while you go to see a company of dance you don't know much about. It can be a pleasantly provocative experience.

According to a 1985 study commissioned by the MacArthur Foundation, better organized, more comprehensive, and better funded marketing strategies on the part of dance companies and dancers are critically needed to stimulate public support and to convince Chicago dance presenters to select local companies for performance engagements on a more regular basis. Also needed are more medium-sized, centrally located theaters suitable for dance; more stable management structures and practices in companies; and, of course, more money, whether generated through earned income or through foundation and corporate support.

Instrumental in fulfilling these needs, stated the study, is the **Chicago Dance Arts Coalition**, Chicago's five-year-old umbrella organization for dance. The CDAC (663-1313) is a good place to go for information about dance in the city.

Some of the performers and companies listed below do not have full-time office staff, and thus have no office phone number. For these companies, the Chicago Dance Arts Coalition (663-1313) is the best source of information.

DANCE PRESENTERS

Jackie Radis is conspicuous as the artistic director of **MoMing Dance & Arts Center**. Radis also directs her own modern dance company, **Radis Dance Strata**. To me, though, Radis is more interesting as a solo performer than as a choreographer or an arts administrator. Her physical presence—she is tall, lithe, and gifted with a dramatic inward gaze—is arresting, and Radis's dramatic introspection onstage can be riveting. Her movements are clear and clean, but their implications can be provocatively ambiguous and unpredictable. Ensemble dances that include her are nearly always dominated by her, intentionally or unintentionally. For performance information, contact MoMing at 472-7662.

Hema Rajagopalan is a South Indian bharatanatyam dancer based in west suburban Lombard, where she teaches bharatanatyam, performs, produces bharatanatyam recitals and evening-length dance dramas with local casts, choreographs, and brings in dancers and musicians from India to perform locally. An accomplished dancer, she is also remarkable for the consistency of her efforts to educate Midwesterners about an ancient, timeless, and fascinating Indian dance tradition.

The **Chicago City Ballet** has its ups and downs, financial and artistic, but its production of *Cinderella* is an unmixed blessing for the city. Usually performed in November, this evening-length narrative ballet premiered in 1981 with the New York City Ballet's Suzanne Farrell dancing the lead role, surrounded by comically evil stepmother and stepsisters, requisite prince, and innumerable enchanted and enchanting forest animals (danced, in part, by students of the School of the Chicago City Ballet). The ballet is luminously beautiful, year after year. Call 943-1315 for information.

Kate Kuper is an indomitable individualist, a theatrically minded modern dancer/choreographer whose work has a ticklish funny bone, in addition to a well-developed, tightly edited gestural language. Her popular early autobiographical work has been followed by dances that are more abstract, and—some of them—composed with props that come to seem as vital as the dancers. Look for Kuper's performances at MoMing Dance Center.

Ensemble Espanol, led by **Libby Komaiko Fleming**, is the centerpiece of an annual three-week Spanish dance festival sponsored by Northeastern Illinois University. Fleming, who has been knighted by the Spanish government for her contribution to Spanish dance in this country, is no mean flamenco dancer herself but, like Hema Rajagopalan, is also a teacher, choreographer, and impresario rolled into one. Fleming and the Ensemble Espanol enrich the variety of dance in Chicago. For performance information, contact the dance department at Northeastern Illinois U., 583-4050, ext. 3011.

The **Chicago Repertory Dance Ensemble** began as a company devoted to modern dance, ballet, and jazz, but has wisely developed into a sophisticated modern dance repertory company without peer locally. Dances by internationally admired choreographers such as Paul Taylor and Lar Lubovitch are among those regularly performed, and the company also encourages its own dancers to choreograph, thereby supporting local choreographers and giving dancers a chance to take creative risks usually not open to them in such a company setting. CRDE dancers, though their ranks turn over regularly, are generally considered some of the finest in the city. Call 440-9494 for information.

Making Dances, a lecture/demonstration program sponsored by MoMing Dance & Arts Center, is based on a simple premise: choreographers can explain what they do to a general audience, and the audience will perhaps understand dance better and want to see more of it. This simple idea works wonderfully. The choreographers so far presented have all been intelligent, articulate, and reasonably accessible. The program is a genuine public service that should be expanded further; I cannot recommend it highly enough. Contact MoMing at 472-7662 for information on upcoming programs in this series.

Joel Hall, the charismatic founder of the **Joel Hall Dancers**, choreographs energetic, multi-racial, multi-ethnic, jazz dances with urban themes that have earned him a nationwide reputation. The company's dances are most noted for their distinctive, highly developed and accessible style. Raised in poverty in the Cabrini-Green public housing project, Hall was fortunate to discover in dance a creative outlet for his energies; dance rescued him. To spread the word, he takes his dances to schools in the roughest neighborhoods of the city. The performances are powerful enough to captivate audiences of tough west side teenagers—an accomplishment in itself. Hall also runs a dance studio at the **New School for Performing Arts**. For more information, call 880-1002.

Postscript: Other dancers and dance companies, too many to count, but well worth seeing, include **Carol Bobrow, Bob Eisen, Jan Bartoszek, Gus Giordano, Chicago Dance Medium, Hubbard Street Dance Company, the Chicago Moving Company, Mordine & Company, Jan Erkert & Dancers, Joseph Holmes Dance Theatre** (carrying on after the death of its founder), **Concert Dance, Muntu Dance Theater**.

In this multi-ethnic city there are also folk dance companies too numerous to list, from Filipino to Jamaican to Ukrainian to Japanese. For information on performances by ethnic dance companies or instruction in folk dance, contact the **Folk Dance Leadership Council** at 328-7793, or to obtain a flyer of upcoming folk dance events, send a stamped, self-addressed envelope to FDLC, 1402 Elinor Pl., Evanston, IL 60201.

DANCE SPACES AND SCHOOLS

Links Hall Studio (3435 N. Sheffield, 281-0824) sponsors dance performances and many other arts events, and **MoMing Dance & Arts Center** (1034 W. Barry, 472-7662) is just a short walk away from Links. Links is a plain studio space, and too raw for some tastes; to me, though, it's a refreshingly unpretentious spot whose ample artistic breathing space (any-thing can go) makes up for its technical limitations. MoMing, on the other hand, is a nationally recognized theater, gallery, and school now in its second decade. (MoMing, translated from Chinese, means "too beautiful to be named.") Along with the Dance Center of Columbia College (4730 N. Sher-idan, 271-7804), MoMing is the most important presenter of modern and experimental dance in Chicago, bringing in luminaries like Lucinda Childs from out of town and also presenting homegrown dancers and companies. MoMing's dark, companionable space has been steadily upgraded over the years, and Columbia's is regarded by many as the best of its kind in the city from a technical vantage point. And there are other modern dance presenters to consider, too: **Northwestern University**'s dance department, the **National College of Education**, the **Dancespace**, and the **Puszh Studio**, to name a few.

Other opportunities to see dance, mostly dance from out of town, abound at the **Auditorium Theater**, the **Civic Center for Performing Arts**, **Centre East in Skokie**, and the **Ravinia Festival** each summer in Highland Park. Ballet, modern, jazz, and more occasionally, ethnic dance are unveiled on these traditionally eclectic stages. Luckily for us, Chicago is a big city in the middle of smaller ones, so it attracts a fair share of national companies on tour. Keep an eye out for visits by the touring Alvin Ailey Dancers, American Ballet Theatre, Twyla Tharp, San Francisco Ballet, Dance Theatre of Harlem, Pilobulus, National Ballet of Canada, and the Joffrey Ballet. Until recently, Merrill Lynch sponsored a dance series at the Goodman Theatre that offered companies long runs by Chicago standards and unpre-dictably wide-ranging programming. In one year, for instance, it was possible to see genuinely original work in ballet (no small feat), tap, and modern dance, performed not just skillfully but with unpremeditated verve. Merrill Lynch let the series expire recently, but the Goodman hopes to revive the program with a new source of funding.

The Lou Conte Dance Studio
218 S. Wabash, Chicago, IL 60604   461-0892
Ballet, jazz, and tap are taught by a faculty of thirteen to a student body of approximately 400. Few students under sixteen are encouraged to enroll. Graded classes are given year round, and fees start at $69 for students taking one class weekly over a 10-week period. Lou Conte is the founder and director of the immensely popular Hubbard Street Dance Company.

The Ruth Page Foundation School of Dance
1016 N. Dearborn, Chicago, IL 60610   337-6543
The Ruth Page School, founded in 1971, offers classes in ballet, jazz, and tap, beginner through advanced. Children's and adults' classes are given year-round, and fees are charged on a weekly basis depending on the number of classes taken (e.g., one class per week for an eight-week period costs $50; two cost $92; three cost $120). Current enrollment is 250, and eight teachers are on staff.

The Dance Center of Columbia College
4730 N. Sheridan, Chicago, IL 60640   271-7804
As well as a B.A. program in dance and a M.A. program in dance movement therapy, Columbia offers a community program open to people and dancers

not enrolled in full time academic study at the college. Besides modern, ballet, modern jazz, tap, and African dance taught at various levels, classes in composition, contemporary choreography, kinesthesiology, and others are offered. Class fees are $6.50/class for nonprofessionals and $4.50/class for professional dancers; it's more economical to sign up for an entire session. Twenty teachers preside, and three to four guest residencies by nationally respected choreographers each year include workshops for students and/or professional dancers.

The Dance School of Jan Erkert & Dancers
1414 E. 59th St., Chicago, IL 60637   753-2274
Jan Erkert is widely admired as a teacher and choreographer of modern dance, and her school's enrollment doubled in the first year and a half of its existence. The school offers modern, ballet, jazz, aerobics, and a choreographic dance workshop. Minimum age of students is fourteen. Average cost per class is $5.50, and classes are taught year-round by Erkert and members of her company, Jan Erkert & Dancers.

School of the Chicago City Ballet
223 W. Erie, Chicago, IL 60610   988-4231
Ballet for the serious student is stressed here and taught as Balanchine taught it. Adult classes are offered in a more casual vein. Classes are taught year-round, with an intensive summer program staff with guest teachers. Average fee is $12/class. Enrollment is about 200. Four teachers are on staff.

MoMing School of Dance
1034 W. Barry, Chicago, IL 60657   472-7662
MoMing offers a young people's program for children aged four to fifteen, which includes a multi-arts camp for four weeks each summer. Adult and professional classes are also offered, of course. Approximately three guest artists conduct workshops each year. Fees average $6.50/class for adults and $5/class for professionals; class cards offer discount rates. Children's fees are charged per season, e.g., $66 for a twelve-week fall period of one class a week. Classes are taught all year round. Children's enrollment is currently 150; other enrollment totals 300. Twelve teachers are on staff. Modern dance instruction is MoMing's specialty, but classes in ballet, jazz, improvisation, and composition are also offered.

Gus Giordano Dance Center
614 Davis St., Evanston, IL 60201   866-9442
For thirty years, classes in jazz ("our main thrust"), tap, ballet, and modern have been offered for beginners through professionals. Eighteen teachers, including Giordano himself, are on staff, and current enrollment is approximately 600. Classes are taught year-round on a semester basis to children and adults; fees are about $7 per class.

Dancespace
410 S. Michigan, Suite 833, Chicago, IL 60605   939-0181
A large, handsome studio distinguishes the school, where classes are taught in contemporary ballet (their specialty), modern, and jazz all year round. Children's, adults', and professional classes are offered. Fees: $7/class for adults, $5/class for professionals, and $5/class for children. Discounted class cards are also available. Nine teachers preside over about 125 students.

Boitsov Classical Ballet
410 S. Michigan, Suite 300, Chicago, IL 60605   663-0844
Run by Elizabeth Boitsov, a Soviet-born dancer trained at the Bolshoi Ballet
Theater School, this school offers instruction in Vaganova technique, a
demanding course of study emphasizing bravura. Children's and adults'
classes are offered year-round, and students perform in occasional full-length
ballets. Fees for students taking one class per week are about $30 per month.
Although the Boitsov does not perform very often, when they do, by all
means see them. Because it has roots in peasant dance, Russian ballet is far
more energetic than its American and European counterparts. The male
roles are especially dynamic.

Ellis-DuBoulay School of Ballet
185 N. Wabash, Chicago, IL 60601   236-4456
Classy downtown ballet studio with a fine reputation. Rigorous instruction
in English Royal Ballet technique can be demoralizing for a beginner-level
adult; this is a serious dance school. Classes for adults and children. Fees
are about $6 per class.

Le Ballet Petit School of Dance
4630 N. Francisco, Chicago, IL 60625   463-3385
A very special school that excels in teaching ballet to children. For over 30
years Madame Kitty LaPointe has offered classical ballet instruction in her
northwest side studio. Ten teachers are on staff; a five week session costs
about $16.

—Molly McQuade

ARCHITECTURE

Justly described as the "birthplace" of modern architecture, Chicago offers a tremendous variety, ranging from monumental public buildings to elegant upper middle-class houses to whole working-class towns such as the one George Pullman built for his factory workers on the city's south side.

The initial impetus for the Chicago architectural renaissance came from the Great Fire of 1871, which virtually leveled the city. Architects and engineers, with large amounts of capital available for construction, had a heyday rebuilding the city. The style in which these early architects and engineers built was the result of a number of factors. First, these men were primarily engineers working as architects; few of them had any but the most limited connections with European architectural traditions. Second, the men for whom they were building were primarily men of commerce interested in simple, efficient designs, men with no stake in recreating in the midwest a Europe that they had never seen and knew little about. Third, a number of important inventions appeared just before the fire that made it possible to construct buildings in fundamentally different ways.

The first of these inventions was the mechanical elevator, which made tall buildings feasible by providing easy access to the upper stories. The second advance was made in foundations—particularly the caisson foundation—which made it possible to construct tall, heavy buildings on Chicago's swampy soil. Finally, iron frames replaced load-bearing masonry walls, which also made it practical to build taller buildings. Until that time, buildings were constructed with brick walls, which limited their height because the walls had to be extremely thick at the base to support the weight. As a result of all these factors, a new architecture was created in Chicago before the turn of the century.

This architecture created new buildings—called skyscrapers—by using an efficient structural system (refined by William LeBaron Jenney) of iron and steel beams in a skeletal building frame. The new frame also allowed windows to be wider, and the "Chicago window" was born: one large fixed pane between two smaller operable windows on either side. A good example of this window can be seen on the sides of the **Carson Pirie Scott Building**.

The aesthetic of these buildings was later labeled "functionalist," which meant that the form of the building should express as clearly as possible its function. In terms of the early office building skyscrapers, this meant that the architect should express the "force and power of altitude." To quote Louis Sullivan, "It must be every inch a proud and soaring thing, rising to sheer exaltation that from bottom to top it is a unit without a single dissenting line." Such an aesthetic produced buildings that were both elegant and simple, in a time when most buildings were neither.

At the time these buildings of the new Chicago School were built, they were almost totally ignored by "serious" architects. But these early Chicago masters—Jenney, Adler, Root, Burnham, and Sullivan—knew their job far better than their "serious" competitors. Well aware of the social implications of architecture, they were convinced that their buildings must be democratic, that they must be built for the people. Buildings, they believed, shouldn't cow people, make them fearful, or put them ill at ease; instead, buildings should enhance the activities that take place inside them and should make people feel comfortable. These high ideals had very practical applications in their work; Adler's principal concern in the **Auditorium Theatre** was how to distribute the highest quality sound to the largest number of people. Louis Sullivan, in the Carson Pirie Scott building, tried to design a building where the masses could shop in comfort, while experiencing the excitement of a bazaar.

But, as Chicago's World Columbian Exposition of 1893 demonstrated, mainstream, respectable, public architecture would continue to be the neoclassical hybrids transplanted to the midwest.

What the neoclassical buildings of the Fair symbolized for the world, and communicated to Americans, was stability, power, grandeur, and wealth—the presence of civilization where most of the world believed there was only wilderness. It is almost unthinkable that America, at the turn of the century, taking its place as a world power and nation of wealth, would have ever considered building its civic buildings, city halls, libraries, and churches in the style of factories, warehouses, and the cheapest speculative office buildings of the day.

The Art Deco movement that flourished in Europe in the twenties and thirties surfaced in Chicago with a few buildings (e.g., the **Board of Trade** and the **LaSalle Bank Building**), but its influence was minor. The next major movement here—the second school of Chicago architecture—was initiated by **Mies van der Rohe**, a German architect and leading Bauhaus figure, who came to the city in 1938. His principles of design, based on years of Bauhaus teaching, were surprisingly similar to those of his predecessors in Chicago—a concern with clarity and order, and a reliance on glass and steel as the primary building materials. There are over forty buildings by Mies in the city, including apartment houses, public buildings and private homes, and his work has been the inspiration for much of the contemporary architecture in Chicago. Mies' work influenced generations of architects in other cities whose designs, which constituted the "Modern" movement, created the boxy, flat-topped contemporary skyscraper.

The impetus to this new generation of architects came from the post World War II building boom, which has its parallel in the building spree that followed the fire of 1871. Once again, huge amounts of capital were made available for building at a time when Mies' dictum "Build, don't talk," made some sense; at a time when once again, cost and expediency were the dominant considerations of the financiers. We should be grateful that the commercial architects of this generation were also men of exceptional ability.

The other primal force in Chicago architecture is, of course, **Frank Lloyd Wright**, who began his career working for Adler and Sullivan, but soon broke with them and set off on his own. Most of Wright's buildings in the Chicago area are private homes, the most important of which are the famous Prairie Houses, which have become landmarks in the history of modern architecture. More about Wright later in this chapter.

In the last twenty years, the demand for space in the Loop set the Chicago School of Architects searching for new answers to the same old questions of how to build taller, more efficient, more economical buildings. One set of answers resulted in the **Hancock Building**, **Sears Tower**, the **Amoco**

Building, and **Water Tower Place**—a generation of architectural beasts, the tallest, most spacious buildings in the world. Engineering virtuosity linked once again with aggressive venture capitalism produced monumental buildings.

Even more recently, however, in response to the repetitive boxes the Modern movement inspired, the "Post-Modern" movement in architecture has led Chicago architects to return to a more ornamental style. The newest buildings in the Loop use more color and curves. The **333 N. Wacker** building is a good example of this. In general, the newest construction tends to be warmer and friendlier, emphasizing plazas and more inviting facades at the street level.

Most guides to architecture stress the schools and the innovations, ignoring the quirky, irreverent efforts of architects and builders. But Chicago is a gold mine for this sort of thing. On innumerable streets in the city you find little gingerbread houses, elaborate iron fences, stunning stained glass windows, intricate granite pillars, inspired Deco decoration, and imaginative stone facades. Unfortunately, these don't fit into easy categories, and so are less talked about by architectural historians and writers. This architecture of "private experience" is all over the place and readily available to anyone willing just to look around with an open, unprejudiced eye.

THE LOOP

The Loop is a knock-out in terms of public architecture. Within a walkable area, you can trace the history of modern architecture and look at an enormous number of great buildings. The area is small enough to cover easily in a morning or afternoon. For those who want an illustrated (and detailed) touring plan of the Loop, we suggest *Chicago on Foot* by Ira Bach and Susan Wolfson. For those who would just as soon wander around, but would like some sort of reference book, we highly recommend *Chicago's Famous Buildings*, also by Ira Bach. This clearly written, easy-to-use book contains several excellent introductions to Chicago architecture, plus photographs and specific information about the most important buildings.

Excellent architectural tours of the Loop and surrounding areas are given by the **Archicenter**, located on the ground floor of the Monadnock Building, at 330 S. Dearborn, 922-3432. Loop tours are given every day by friendly, knowledgeable guides from April through November, rain or shine, at 1 pm, and 2 pm on weekends. The tours last two hours and cost $4. No reservations required. Call 782-1776 for a complete listing of other tours offered (for example, a tour by boat for $10). The Archicenter also has a good selection of books on Chicago architecture for sale.

Our favorite buildings are listed below. Most of the buildings are between Michigan Avenue on the east, Congress Parkway on the south, and Wacker Drive both on the north and west. They are listed alphabetically by location.

South Loop

Auditorium Building (in Roosevelt University)
430 S. Michigan Ave. (Michigan and Congress)
Architect: Adler and Sullivan, 1889; Restoration: Harry Weese, 1967
One of Adler and Sullivan's first commissions, this grand building originally incorporated a beautiful theater, a hotel, and an office building. The theater,

LOOP ARCHITECTURE

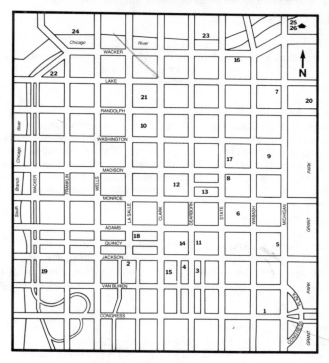

1. **AUDITORIUM BUILDING** (in Roosevelt University)
430 S. Michigan Ave

2. **Board of Trade**
141 W. Jackson

3. **Fischer Building**
343 S. Dearborn

4. **Monadonock Building**
53 W. Jackson

5. **Orchestra Hall Building**
220 S. Michigan

6. **Palmer House**
State and Monroe

7. **Carbide and Carbon Building**
230 N. Michigan

8. **Carson Pirie Scott & Company**
State and Madison

9. **Chicago Public Library Cultural Center**
78 E. Washington

10. **City Hall/County Building**
121 N. LaSalle St.

11. **Federal Center and Plaza**
Dearborn between Adams and Jackson

12. **First National Bank Building and Plaza**
Monroe, Madison, Dearborn, and Clark Sts.

13. **Inland Steel Building**
30 W. Monroe

14. **Marquette Building**
140 S. Dearborn

15. **Metropolitan Detention Center**
Clark and Van Buren

16. **North American Life Insurance Building**
(Jeweler's Building)
35 E. Wacker Dr.

17. **32 N. State St.** (Reliance Building)

18. **The Rookery**
209 S. La Salle

19. **Sears Tower**
233 S. Wacker

20. **Amoco Building and Plaza**
200 E. Randoph

21. **State of Illinois Center**
Clark St. between Randolph and Lake

22. **333 W. Wacker**

23. **Marina Towers**
North bank of Chicago River
Between Dearborn and State

24. **Merchandise Mart**
North bank of Chicago River
between Wells and Orleans

25. **Tribune Tower**
435 N. Michigan Avenue

26. **Wrigley Building**
410 N. Michigan Avenue

which has great acoustics, is well worth seeing, in particular the elaborate interior ornamentation designed by Louis Sullivan.

Board of Options Exchange
400 S. LaSalle St.
Architects: Skidmore, Owings and Merrill, 1983
Across the street to the south of the Board of Trade, the Options Exchange is newly housed in a polished red granite building that combines low rise and high rise in a sleek building design.

Board of Trade
141 W. Jackson
Architects: Holabird and Root, 1930; Addition: Murphy/Jahn, 1982
This towering Art Deco structure, the anchor of the financial district, terminates the LaSalle Street canyon. At the top of the 45 stories stands a 32-foot-high Ceres, the Greek goddess of grain. The trading floor observation area on the 5th floor is open Monday through Friday, 9 am-2 pm; it's worth dropping by to see the craziness of commodities buying and selling (the earlier you go the better the show).

Britannica Centre
310 S. Michigan
Architects: Graham, Anderson, Probst and White, 1926
The "beehive" on the top of this building glows bright blue at night and is a familiar sight to Chicagoans. The beehive, which is made of glass, is supported by statues of four buffalo and houses a bell that sounds every quarter hour.

Dearborn Street Station
S. Dearborn St. at W. Polk St.
Architect: Cyrus L. W. Eidlitz, 1885
Easily recognized by its tall clock tower, Dearborn Street station, one of Chicago's last vintage passenger stations, is a result of the latest wave of adaptive re-use and rehabbing in the city. Walking south on Dearborn Street toward the station, you pass through Printer's Row, once the center of Chicago's commercial printing industry.

Fisher Building
343 S. Dearborn St.
Architects: D.H. Burnham and Co., 1896
A Gothic skyscraper with a glazed terra cotta (a type of fired clay) surface with intricately designed ornamentation.

Manhattan Building
431 S. Dearborn
Architect: William L. Jenney, 1890
The first building where skeleton construction was used for the entire structure. Has a curious mixture of styles, which detracts from its overall appearance.

Metropolitan Detention Center
Clark and Van Buren St.
Architects: Harry Weese and Assoc., 1975
This triangular-shaped, exposed concrete building is the holding tank for people awaiting trials or testifying at trials. The vertical strips you see in

the sides of the building are windows; each cell has one window, which is 5 inches in width (the maximum allowed by the Bureau of Prisons for windows without bars). The building's corners house the stairs and elevators.

Monadnock Building
53 W. Jackson
Architects: Burnham and Root, 1891, for north half, Holabird and Roche, 1893, for south half
The tallest all-brick building in Chicago. To support the structure, the walls had to be more than 6 feet thick at the ground floor, which proved rather convincingly the desirability of using an iron frame to support structures of this size. The facade is dark, but the building has nice lines and attractive windows.

Palmer House
State and Monroe
Architects: J.M. Van Osdel, 1875, Holabird and Roche, 1925
A distinguished hotel with an elegant, opulent lobby. Stop by just to soak up some ambiance.

River City
555 W. Roosevelt Rd.
Architects: Bertrand Goldberg and Assoc., 1985
A huge, controversial concrete housing complex with a lot of hopes attached to it. The futuristic, serpentine design creates curved walls for the apartments inside.

Union Station
210 S. Canal St.
Architects: Graham, Burnham and Co., 1917, Graham, Anderson, Probst and White, 1925
A train station with a grand main waiting room. The waiting room is approximately 112 feet high to the top of its vaulted skylight, with large Corinthian columns and two gilded figures, representing day and night.

Central and North Loop

Amoco Building (formerly the Standard Oil Building)
200 E. Randolph St.
Architects: E.D. Stone and Perkins and Will, 1974
A tall, sleek building of light gray marble with a graceful profile. Somewhat cold at street level. The sunken plaza is little used but has a nice wind-chime sculpture. A building that wears well.

Art Institute of Chicago
Michigan Ave. at Adams St.
Architects: Shepley, Rutan and Coolidge, 1892, Coolidge and Hodgdon, 1924, for McKinlock Court, Holabird and Root, 1956, for North Wing, Shaw, Metz and Assoc., 1962, for Morton Wing, Skidmore, Owings and Merrill, 1976, for East Wing, Vinci/Kenny, 1977, for reconstruction of Stock Exchange, Trading Room
A Beaux-Arts styled building housing Chicago's most extensive art collection. Natural lighting floods the handsome grand staircase; natural lighting is

introduced effectively throughout this building. The Burnham Gallery features architectural exhibits. Also contains the handsome, high-ceilinged reconstruction of the trading room of Adler and Sullivan's Stock Exchange Building, which was demolished in 1972.

Carbide and Carbon Building
230 N. Michigan Ave.
Architects: Burnham Brothers, 1929
Gold-trimmed Art Deco skyscraper that has a main entrance and lobby that are not to be missed. Brass and embossed glass ornament the deco lobby.

Carson, Pirie, Scott and Co. (formerly Schlesinger and Mayer store)
State and Madison St.
Architect: Louis H. Sullivan, 1899, 1903-1904; Renovation: John Vinci
Probably the best known of Louis Sullivan's ornamented works in Chicago and one of the finest buildings of the period. Particularly impressive are large display windows on the first floor, the design of the big windows on the upper stories, and the fine iron ornamentation on the first two floors.

Chicago Public Library Cultural Center
78 E. Washington
Architects: Shepley, Rutan and Coolidge (library), 1897; Renovation: Holabird and Root, 1977
Once the central building for the Chicago Public Library, this Italian Renaissance style building features a breathtaking interior. Note the marble walls, mosaic-tiled floors, and original Tiffany stained-glass dome.

Photo by Glenn Kaupert.

Water Tower, Hancock Building, Water Tower Place. Photo by Glenn Kaupert.

side to see rehabbed buildings in the style known as "Chicago cottage." On the south side, **Hyde Park** and **Kenwood** have some of the best examples of private residential architecture in Chicago, including many houses that were designed by architects from outside the midwest. **Lincoln Park** has some elegant apartment buildings dating from the early part of this century. Wander down streets such as Astor in the **Gold Coast** and Alta Vista Terrace in **Lakeview** to see fine examples of elegant townhouses and row houses.

Prairie Avenue between 18th and 20th Streets is an elegant oasis in a desolate area—evidence of the one-time presence of wealthy homeowners. Now a historic district, the area has some good examples of interesting housing such as the **Glessner House** (118 S. Prairie) by H.H. Richardson and the **Kimball House**—directly across the street—a fine example of the French chateau style.

OAK PARK AND RIVER FOREST FRANK LLOYD WRIGHT ARCHITECTURE

No architectural tour would be complete without visiting Oak Park and River Forest. These suburbs have over 30 buildings—both residential and religious—designed by Frank Lloyd Wright. Built over 80 years ago, these buildings still look fresh. Because the buildings were constructed over a period of 20 years, you can get a good sense of the gradual development of Wright's style, and the evolution of the Prairie House. (The **Robie House** at 5757 S. Woodlawn in Chicago is one of Wright's most successful city homes.)

Try to imagine the world at the turn of the century, when many of these still houses were built. Take a look at photos of houses of the period—compared to most typical residential architecture of that time, Wright's ideas were very different. You can appreciate how strong his personality must have been to bring these designs to life, sometimes at great expense to his clients.

A two-hour walking tour of this lovely area is a wonderful way to spend a Sunday. Start your tour at one of two excellent starting points: the **Visitors Center**, 158 Forest Avenue, which is open daily March through November, 10 am-5 pm; or the **Ginko Tree Bookshop**, located in the **Frank Lloyd Wright Home and Studio**, 951 Chicago Avenue, open daily 10 am-5 pm. Both locations offer maps, guidebooks, and tour tickets. Weekend afternoon tours cost $7 for the complete tour, or $4 for each of the three tour segments. Call 848-1978 for tour times and more information. For those who feel like walking or driving around, the "Architectural Guide Map of Oak Park and River Forest," available for $1.50 from the Visitors Center or the Bookshop, is an excellent resource.

To get to Oak Park by public transportation, take the Lake Street/Dan Ryan el from any station in the Loop. Get off at the Oak Park Avenue or Harlem Avenue stops, and go north to the Visitors Center, 158 Forest Avenue. You can drive from the Loop via the Eisenhower Expressway (I-290) to Harlem Avenue (IL 43); exit north and follow the brown-and-white signs to parking in the Visitor's Center.

—Tem Horwitz, Alan Ness, Jan Rogatz

FILM

Moviemaking came to Chicago in 1896, brought here by a magician, William Selig, who used film equipment that was copied from Edison's design (in clear violation of Edison's patents). He built his new studio, called Selig Polyscope, in a loft in the red light district on 8th Street and prospered by producing short documentaries that were shown as part of vaudeville shows across the country. Later, Selig would be among the first filmmakers to take the radical step from making documentaries to making films that told a story.

Selig quickly outgrew his loft on 8th Street and in 1907 he built a much larger studio at Irving Park Road and Western Avenue. That same year two of Selig's employees—George Spoor and Gilbert "Bronco Billy" Anderson—opened a rival film company called Essanay (S and A), and they too prospered. For a time, a sadly brief time, Chicago was a major filmmaking center, until it was overshadowed by a city with perfect weather. Selig was instrumental in making Los Angeles the film capital of the U.S.

Selig knew how kind the weather was in southern California. No winter to speak of, and hardly a spring or a fall. 360 days a year of pure sunlight—perfectly suited for movies. At first Selig used California as a last resort when he could find no better location, or when Chicago's hostile winter made filming impossible. But the California weather became increasingly important in Selig's work, and in 1909 he became the first filmmaker to move to California when he opened a branch of Polyscope just outside Los Angeles. It didn't take long, however, for other moviemakers to see the wisdom in Selig's move. Essanay opened a Los Angeles branch in 1910. Before World War I began, Los Angeles was already beginning to go Hollywood.

Not so Chicago. Both Selig and Essanay continued to make films in Chicago, and both used their Chicago studios as a base for operations, but when the two companies went under—Selig in 1916 (done in by an over-budget flop called *The Crisis*) and Essanay in 1917—no new film companies replaced them. Everyone ambitious to get into movies was going west.

So Chicago turned from filmmaking to movie watching. We became in the process a major market for film distributors, an economic prowess we retain to this day, although increasingly our movie dollars are being spent at the video store and not at the box office.

Recently, however, Hollywood has rediscovered Chicago. Our prices are right and we have an excellent pool of actors and technical people to choose from, largely because of the strong local theater scene. Every spring and summer, film crews can be seen shooting at locations all over the city. **The Illinois Film Office** (100 W. Randolph, 917-3600) has been instrumental in attracting moviemakers to Chicago.

In any case, Chicago remains a great place for movie going. Any day of the week you can catch premieres, classics, revivals, cult favorites, and even first-run movies.

THEATERS

Most movie theaters advertise in both the *Chicago Tribune* and the *Chicago Sun-Times*, and both papers offer extensive listings of which films are in town in their Friday editions. Still, the *Reader* is the best source for movie information, providing short, pithy synopses of all the movies playing, as well as the most interesting film reviews in the city.

Three movie chains dominate greater Chicago's market: Cineplex-Odeon-Plitt, AMC, and General Cinema. Unfortunately, all three have been busy the past decade building those awful multi-screen complexes with tiny screening rooms, and even smaller movie screens. Of these three, Cineplex-Odeon-Plitt has two theaters in the city that show a consistently high-quality selection of movies: the Biograph (2433 N. Lincoln Ave., 348-4123) and the Fine Arts Theater (418 S. Michigan Ave., 939-3700).

The **Fine Arts Theater** is housed in the Fine Arts Building, which was originally built to house the Studebaker carriage and wagon showroom. The building was renamed the Fine Arts Building when it was converted in 1898 to a fine arts center with two theaters on the first floor and offices, artist's studios, and practice rooms on the upper floors. In 1982, the two theaters on the first floor were converted into a four-screen cinema. The Fine Arts features a very good selection of foreign and domestic independent films, owing to the management's unfailing intuition for choosing the best off-beat films in distribution. Unfortunately the seats in the main theater are uncomfortable, with the leg room of a 1964 VW Beetle. This is, however, the only flaw of the theater complex.

If you know nothing else about Chicago, you probably know that Dillinger was gunned down by the FBI as he was coming out of the **Biograph Theater.** Luckily, the neighborhood around Fullerton and Lincoln has changed a lot since the 1930s. In the 1970s, the Biograph was Chicago's premier art film house, but the quality of its selection has declined a bit in recent years. Still, the theater runs a close second to the Fine Arts. The Biograph tends to show films by more established foreign and American independent directors such as Kurosawa, Rohmer, and Rudolph.

With the exception of the Music Box (more on this theater in a minute), the other movie theaters in Chicago are inconsistent in how they choose their films. To make matter worse, many theaters in town have been designed more for profit than for the comfort of its patrons. For example, the **Water Tower Theater** is not only expensive and crowded, but its small screening rooms have paper-thin walls (distracting when the theater next door is showing the latest Spielberg adventure film).

Thank God for the **Music Box** (3733 N. Southport, 871-6604), with double features that change daily, and an excellent program of second-run, classic American and foreign films as well as week-long premieres and unannounced sneak previews of new releases. Sneak previews are generally shown on Monday or Tuesday evenings and are announced on the theater's phone line 48 hours in advance. The beautiful, old fashioned movie palace is kept in mint condition; among its many pleasures are a huge screen, a large auditorium with stars winking on the ceiling, a fine organist who entertains between shows, and the best selection of food and beverages at a movie house candy counter.

Music Box theater. Photo by Glenn Kaupert.

FILM CENTERS

Film centers are places that take movies seriously. They are usually non-profit organizations that take much greater risks when selecting films, and which also offer workshops, retrospectives on directors and topics, previews of new films, and classes. These centers are also the only places in the city to catch the work of local filmmakers such as Tom Palazzolo, Sharon Cousin, Adele Friedman, Bill Stamets, Colleen Sullivan, Alan Ross, and Angelo Restivo.

Most film centers offer low-cost membership deals whereby you receive discounts to films and other programs at the center (and sometimes at other participating commercial theaters), invitations to members-only previews (usually free), and a subscription to the center's publication. Consider joining a film center if you're hungering to meet other people who like to view and discuss movies. Call the centers for more information on membership prices and privileges.

Facets Multimedia Center (1517 W. Fullerton, 281-4114), with two screening rooms at their Fullerton Avenue location, and another at its Columbia College branch (600 S. Michigan), screens new films and revivals from around the world, as well as retrospectives. Facets is famous for having visiting directors at its screenings. They also have the nation's oldest and most extensive programming of children's films. Facets is home to the Chi-town Puppet Theatre and Facets Performance Ensemble. Other Facets services include the rental and sales of videos (see the Video section below) and one of the best selection of film books and magazines in the city. Check Facets first for your copies of *Cineaste, Jump Cut, Cahiers du Cinema, Wide Angle, The Independent,* and *Film Quarterly.*

For 15 years, the **Film Center at the School of the Art Institute** (Columbus Dr. at Jackson Blvd., 443-3737) has been bringing Chicago retrospectives on major directors, national cinema surveys, lectures by filmmakers and critics as well as new releases of national and international films, and showings of works by local filmmakers. The Film Center has an expanding research library specializing in experimental and independent cinema (especially the work of all-too-often overlooked Chicago artists). Members receive, besides discounts and invitations to previews, the Center's monthly publication, *The Film Center Gazette,* which features coming attractions, a calendar of the month's events, and articles of interest to Chicago's cinemaphiles.

Chicago Filmmakers (1229 W. Belmont, 329-0854) plays an important role in the Chicago film scene as the only film center serving both filmmakers and film lovers. Those interested in independent filmmaking should consider membership in The Co-op, which provides low-cost access to filmmaking equipment (including flat-bed editing tables and a CP-16 movie camera), screening facilities, workshops, classes, and other services essential to independent filmmakers. Membership also entitles you to receive *Point of View,* a bimonthly newsletter providing filmmakers with announcements of competitions, grants, and exhibitions for film and video artists. Those more interested in the viewing than in the making of film should consider becoming a general film member for discounts and invitations to previews, among other things. Once only a forum for experimental filmmaking, Chicago Filmmakers has broadened its programming to include documentary, narrative and animation films, and film series on diverse subjects. In addition, Chicago Filmmakers has become a center for time arts, that mixed medium of film, video, slides, music and slide shows, also called performance art. Filmmakers also hosts evenings of poetry readings, new music, and tres avant garde jazz.

Down Hubbard Street, the **Center for New Television** (11 E. Hubbard, 5th floor, 565-1787) plays a similar role for Chicago video artists, providing access to equipment and sponsoring screenings of local and internationally known videomakers. Membership in the center guarantees low-cost access to production and post-production equipment, as well as a subscription to their newsletter, *Scan*, which lists competitions, exhibitions, and job openings. Members also receive discounts for the workshops and seminars CNTV provides year-round on all aspects of video production, from script writing and video editing to computer animation and video effects. A regional fellowship program at CNTV offers grants for independent film and videomakers in Illinois, Indiana, Michigan, and Ohio.

The **Chicago Access Corporation** (322 S. Green, 738-1400) offers four workshops for people with specific proposals for community and public affairs programming on Chicago cable television. However, waiting lists are long for these courses, and you must have a specific proposal in mind before taking the two technical training workshops. Chicago Access Corporation also sponsors a video competition.

The **Chicago Public Library** sponsors free screenings, not only at the **Cultural Center** (78 E. Washington, 269-2910) but also at many local branches. The library also offers 16-mm and 8-mm films to anyone with a valid library card, and rents video cassettes for a low fee. You can preview films and videos at the Cultural Center, but don't expect to see the entire film at the library, especially when it's busy and many impatient patrons are queued behind you.

The **Experimental Film Coalition** screens experimental and animation films at the **Randolph Street Gallery** (756 N. Milwaukee, 666-7737) about once a month. Randolph Street Gallery is one of the few places (along with Chicago Filmmakers and The Film Center) to regularly screen films by local filmmakers. These screenings provide an interesting survey of who's *in* among the professors of experimental film at the city's art schools.

FILM FESTIVALS

Founded in 1964, the **Chicago International Film Festival** (sponsored by **Cinema Chicago**, 415 N. Dearborn, 644-3400) is the oldest competitive film festival in the United States. Featuring premieres of Hollywood films, never-before-seen documentaries, short subjects, animation, videos, student films, as well as tributes, retrospectives, and celebrities (both film stars and directors make appearances), the festival gives Chicago an annual dose of cinematic sensory overload. Festival audiences seem to be growing each year. The festival is held every year in November.

Women in the Director's Chair (3435 N. Sheffield, Ste. 3, 281-4988) sponsors showings of domestic and foreign films by women directors, and sponsors a yearly festival of films by women. A similar organization, **Women in Film** (30 N. Michigan Ave., 236-3618) screens movies by women directors and sponsors lectures. Women in Film also publicizes grants and job opportunities for aspiring directors, writers, editors, and others working in films.

The **Blacklight Film Festival** features alternative films by local, national, and international black filmmakers. In 1986, for example, Blacklight premiered Spike Lee's *She's Gotta Have It*, and Spike Lee himself was present at the Chicago premiere. Blacklight also focuses on black culture and its influence on other arts, particularly jazz and dance. Usually screened at Chicago Filmmakers, Blacklight does its bit to break Hollywood's white male hegemony. For more information, the office is at 53 W. Jackson; call 922-7771.

The Lesbian and Gay Film Festival, a week-long annual event held in the fall, features films by local, national and international gay and lesbian filmmakers. This festival has grown considerably in importance in the past six years, and can be counted on to attract many of the most talented filmmakers from around the world. Usually, the films are shown at Chicago Filmmakers and the Music Box.

SECOND RUN MOVIE HOUSES

If a VCR is looking more alluring after paying $36.00 (includes popcorn) for you and your five kids to see a movie, then the following second run houses are for you.

Brighton
4223 S. Archer Ave.
523-7599

Bryn Mawr
1125 W. Bryn Mawr
728-0881

Davis
4614 N. Lincoln Ave.
784-0894

400
6746 N. Sheridan Rd.
764-9100

Lake
1020 Lake St., Oak Park
848-9088

Logan
2646 N. Milwaukee Ave.
252-0627

Milford
3319 N. Pulaski Rd.
545-5922

North Shore
7074 N. Clark St.
764-3656

Olympic
6134 W. Cermak Rd., Cicero
652-5919

Pickwick
(An art deco beauty! Also hosts live stage productions.)
5 S. Prospect, Park Ridge
825-5800

Three Penny
2424 N. Lincoln Ave.
281-7200

Village
1548 N. Clark St.
642-2403

Wilmette
1122 Central, Wilmette
251-7411

ETHNIC MOVIE HOUSES

Goethe Institute
401 N. Michigan Ave.
329-0915
Occasionally screens German-language films.

Marshall Theatre
2875 W. Cermak
247-0200
Features films in Spanish.

Mexico Theater
2135 N. Milwaukee Ave.
486-5910
Features films in Spanish.

Milford
3317 N. Pulaski Rd.
545-5922
Occasionally runs Polish-language films.

ECLECTIC MOVIE ALTERNATIVES

Chicago Historical Society
Clark and North Ave.   642-4600
Screens popular as well as historical films and documentaries.

Museum of Science and Industry Omnimax Theater
Henry Crown Space Center
57th St. and Lake Shore Dr.   684-1414
Don't miss the huge five-story screen on which the museum screens films
on aviation, space flight, and other subjects. Every moment is breathtaking.

New World Resource Center
1476 W. Irving Park Rd.   348-3370
Screens political films dealing with the Third World. Also have videos,
American and foreign.

Field Museum of Natural History
Roosevelt Rd. at Lake Shore Dr.   922-9410
Look for the excellent films on anthropology shown here. Also shows films
on natural history.

STUDENT FILM SOCIETIES

Doc Films
University of Chicago
1212 E. 59th St.   702-8574
The oldest continuously running student film society in the country. Doc
programs an interesting mix of classic and foreign films during the week,
and popular, more recent hits on the weekends. Doc people are film fanatics,
so expect to see some of the hardest-to-see films by recognized auteurs. A
cinema paradise.

International House Film Society
University of Chicago
1414 E. 59th St.   753-2274
Another good place to see movies in Hyde Park.

A & O Film Board
Norris Student Center, Northwestern University
1999 N. Sheridan Rd., Evanston   491-3741 or 491-2384
You'd expect a university that has graduated so many talented and successful
actors and filmmakers to have a good film society. And they do. Like DOC
films, the Film Board shows more eclectic films during the week, and big
hits during the weekend.

The other local universities and colleges—DePaul, Loyola, University of
Illinois at Chicago, and Columbia—have film societies that offer screenings
of second-run and classic films, usually at budget prices. Call the schools'
student activities offices for information or look in the listings in the *Reader*.

BOOKSTORES

While Chicago does not have a bookstore devoted specifically to film books
and magazines, most bookstores devote at least some space to film. The best

places for film books are **Barbara's Books** (all three locations are great), **Guild Books**, **The Seminary Co-op Bookstore** (and its branch 57th Street Bookstore) and the **University of Chicago Bookstore**. The **Art Institute of Chicago Museum Store** also has an excellent collection of books, as does **Facets** (see the section above about Facets). If you are more the used book type, check out **Aspidistra**, **O'Gara** and **Wilson's Bookstore**, and **Powell's Bookstore** for great selections of used books. (For more information about these bookstores, see the Literary Life chapter.)

VIDEO

Given the recent explosion of video stores in this city, this list may seem strange. After all, aren't there video stores on every business strip in the city? And don't they all carry the same videos? Well most do, but the following stores are examples of what videos stores could be at their best.

Facets Multimedia Center
1517 W. Fullerton   281-9075
Facets offers the city's most interesting collection of new and classic American and foreign films as well as independent American films to rent or buy. Most of their tapes are not available anywhere else. Call or drop by for their informative catalogue. Rental prices for videos is $5 for non-members and $3 for members, and a $20 yearly membership provides four free video coupons and discounts on rentals. Members can also purchase coupons called Videotix in blocks of 20 for $49, 40 for $89, or 100 for $199. Facets offers another unique service: sales and rentals by mail to anywhere in the country.

Video Adventure
1926 Central, Evanston   475-5280
and
635 Chicago, Evanston   866-8800
The best video store in the north suburbs, and one of the best in the area. Video Adventure has not only the classic and hard-to-find tapes, but also the impossible-to-find tapes by local and national experimental and independent film and video artists. Good selections of foreign films, opera, ballet, and documentaries. A very knowledgeable staff.

Video Beat
911 Main St., Evanston   475-7335
A video store devoted exclusively to music videos, and not just those by popular artists, but also those by less known, more adventurous performers. Selections in mainstream and alternative pop, rock, punk, jazz, heavy metal, classical, and country.

Lightwave Video
956 1/2 W. Webster   348-2906
Chicago's first and only store dealing strictly in the sale of videotapes has an excellent selection of film classics, hard-to-find films, and best-seller video tapes. If you are looking for tapes to buy, this store will be heaven.

International Historic Video
3015 W. 59th St.   436-8051
Specializes in political, historical, foreign as well as Hollywood films. Selection includes German, Polish, Lithuanian, Russian, Czech, and Greek films. Also have contemporary European ballet and opera videos.

TALENT AGENCIES

After 75 years, Hollywood filmmakers are back making movies in Chicago, much to the excitement and occasionally the bewilderment of passersby. If you want to do more than watch films, you should consider trying your hand at work as a stand-in or an extra. To be considered for such work, send an 8 x 10 glossy and a resume, including your physical description, to one of the following agencies:

Durkin Agency
743 N. LaSalle
664-0045

Young-Taylor Agency, Inc.
30 W. Washington
236-8762

—Margaret Maloney

ART

Chicago's visual art scene has witnessed an explosive growth in the last decade. The proliferation of commercial galleries, the greater opportunities for exhibition, the presence of a world-class annual art exposition, and the continued strength and support offered by institutions such as the **Art Institute of Chicago** and the **Museum of Contemporary Art** have all created an art community second in the U.S. only to that of New York.

Franz Schulze, former art critic for the *Sun-Times* and biographer for Mies van der Rohe, points to August 15, 1967, as a key date in the history of art in Chicago. On that day, just after noon, Mayor Richard Daley unveiled the statue that has always since been known as "The Picasso"—and things have never been quite the same. For the first time, the public was confronted with modern art right on the street where they worked, not just tucked away in some museum or gallery. The response was predictable—irate letters to the editors of local newspapers and man-on-the-street television interviews decrying the somewhat incomprehensible image of the head of a woman. One alderman introduced a resolution in the City Council calling for the destruction of the Picasso, suggesting that in its place a monument be raised to Ernie Banks. But the hue and cry did not last long, and today the Picasso is a symbol of Chicago, as much ingrained in our consciousness as the Sears Tower—or Ernie Banks.

Since 1967, a great deal of **public sculpture** has popped up in and around the Loop. In addition to Picasso's sculpture in the Daley Plaza, look for: Alexander Calder's orange steel "Flamingo" dominating the Federal Plaza (1974); Marc Chagall's colorful "Four Seasons" mosaic in First National Plaza (1974); Harry Bertoia's "Sound Sculpture," which produces eerie, beautiful sounds on windy days in the sunken plaza of the Amoco Building (1975); Claes Oldenburg's "Batcolumn" at 600 W. Madison St. (1977); Joan Miro's "Miro's Chicago" (my favorite), across the street from the Daley Plaza (1982); Louise Nevelson's Madison Plaza Sculpture at 200 W. Madison St. (1982); and Jean Dubuffet's controversial "Monument a la Bête Debout" in front of the State of Illinois Center (1984).

But not all art in Chicago is outside. Chicago has developed a highly concentrated gallery district on the near northwest side, bordered by Erie Street on the south, Chicago Avenue on the north, Wells Street on the east, and Hudson Avenue on the west. Local artists refer to this area as "the district," but it's more often called "**River North**." Some insist on calling it "SuHu" after New York's chic art district SoHo, even though most Chicagoans groan when they hear "SuHu" (not another comparison with New York!) Whatever it's called, this area has become Chicago's center of contemporary art.

In these few blocks of rehabbed warehouses some forty commercial galleries ply their trade, rotating exhibitions monthly, and representing hundreds of artists, most of whom are Chicagoans. Some effort has been made to synchronize the exhibition openings, so that one or two Friday evenings each month the streets and galleries are filled with art-world cognoscenti

"Batcolumn," Claes Oldenberg. 600 W. Madison St.

and interested bystanders who are gallery-hopping, ogling nervous artists, and consuming questionable wine.

For one weekend each May, the eyes of the international art world focus on Chicago. **The Chicago International Art Exposition**, also known as ArtExpo, takes over Navy Pier for five days, during which over one hundred galleries from all over the U.S. and from as far away as the U.S.S.R. and New Zealand display their artwork in Navy Pier's beautifully renovated auditorium. ArtExpo is a long weekend of wheeling and dealing, of spotting new art trends and burying old ones, and of reaffirming once again that the business of art is business. It is open to the public, and it is not to be missed.

Likewise not be missed are Chicago's museums. The grande-dame of local culture, the **Art Institute of Chicago**, is the permanent home of Seurat's "Sunday Afternoon on the Island of La Grande Jatte," Van Gogh's "Bedroom at Arles," El Greco's "Assumption of the Virgin," Grant Wood's "American Gothic," and a growing collection of native American and African art. The Art Institute is especially strong in Impressionist and post-Impressionist art, although they are also interested in contemporary art—witness recent acquisitions of work by Anselm Kiefer, Frank Stella, Joseph Beuys, Francesco Clemente, and native son Ed Paschke.

If contemporary art is your main interest, check out the **Museum of Contemporary Art** (founded in 1969), which exhibits current works from around the world. Another important museum is the **Terra Museum of American Art**, which specializes in traditional and contemporary art by American artists.

Many of the more exciting exhibitions of the past few years have taken place at smaller institutions, such as the **David and Alfred Smart Gallery** at the University of Chicago, the **Renaissance Society**, also at the University of Chicago, and the **Chicago Public Library's Cultural Center**. Other museums that occasionally mount interesting exhibitions are the **DuSable Museum** in Washington Park, the **Block Gallery** at Northwestern University, the **Spertus Museum of Judaica** on South Michigan, and the **Ukrainian Institute of Modern Art** on Chicago Avenue.

One interesting phenomenon of the last decade has been the evolution of local alternative galleries. Alternative galleries are not-for-profit spaces founded to house the often unmarketable art that emerged from the highly charged atmosphere of the sixties and seventies, such as performance art, feminist art, political art, and installation art (three-dimensional, environmental sculpture). As these art forms became accepted by mainstream galleries, alternative galleries found themselves without a role to play in the art scene. Some of Chicago's alternative galleries lost some of their direction, and as a result, have become pale imitators of the commercial galleries and museums they were originally founded as alternatives to. Others, like the **Randolph Street Gallery**, somehow found new life and vigor in the eighties, despite the decade's decidedly anti-bohemian stance.

Chicago owes its prominence in the art world to its richest treasure, the artists, many of whom have gained national and even international reputations. Artists such as Roger Brown, Ed Paschke, Phyllis Bramson, Storey Mann, Richard Hunt, Ruth Duckworth, Jim Nutt, Gary Justis, Hollis Sigler, Claire Zeisler, and Martin Puryear often appear in shows of contemporary art here and abroad, as do William Conger, Frank Piatek, Paul LaMantia,

Gladys Nilsson, Don Baum, Karl Wirsum, Vera Klement, Robert Lostutter, Richard Loving, and Susan Sensemann.

Younger Chicago artists to watch include Cameron Zebrun, Wesley Kimler, Richard Willenbrink, Michiko Itatani, Jim Lutes, Dan Devening, Jan Carmichael, Neil Goodman, Ken Warneke, Matt Straub, Hannah Dresner, and Deven Golden.

Although no school of art dominates Chicago today, two schools have imprinted their style on contemporary art here. The work of the "**Monster Roster**" of the 1950s, which included Leon Golub, June Leaf, Cosmo Campoli, Seymour Rosofsky, and Ellen Lanyon, had a melancholic quality perhaps derived from European Surrealism, long an interest of Chicago art collectors.

The "**Imagists**"—also known as the "**Hairy Who**"—followed in the late sixties and early seventies with a funkier, more anti-intellectual approach to art, that openly admitted its roots in the popular culture of comic books, television, movies, and naive art. Members of the Imagists school include Roger Brown, Ed Paschke, Jim Nutt, Gladys Nilsson, Don Baum, Karl Wirsum, Barbara Rossi, Ray Yoshida, Christine Ramberg, and Philip Hanson. The charm and accessibility of the Imagists have secured them an important place in the art history of Chicago, but as important was the serious attention they brought to art in Chicago.

More recently on the scene are **performance artists**, who came along at the same time as the alternative art galleries. Performance artists are going strong, owing to the influence of Chicago's theater scene. Performance artists are painters, filmmakers, video artists, sculptors, and writers who use performance not only as a creative outlet, but also as a way to explore new ideas and stretch the limits of their techniques. The most interesting avant garde theater appears in Chicago in the guise of performance art. Almost every alternative gallery has hosted performance art; the best places for this hybrid of art and theater are the **Randolph Street Gallery, N.A.M.E. Gallery, A.R.C. Gallery, Chicago Filmmakers**, and **MoMing Dance and Arts Center**. Increasingly, the **Organic Lab** also plays host to performance artists. Artists to watch: Michael Meyers, Robert Daulton, James Grigsby, Carmela Rago, Tom Jarimba, Hudson, Beth Berolzheimer, E. W. Ross, Somebody's Daughters, Susan Wexler, Robert Metrick, Lynn Book, Jack Helbig, Jan Fleming, Jeff Abell, Joel Klaff, and Ellen Fisher.

No complete history of Chicago art has yet been written; however, three books well worth reading are Franz Schulze's *Fantastic Images*, Dennis Adrian's *Chicago—Some Other Traditions*, and the multi-authored *Who Chicago*. Each book covers some aspect of Chicago art since 1945.

And what would art be without its critics? Both of Chicago's major newspapers feature art reviews and reports weekly. The *Tribune* has our city's only full-time art critic, Alan Artner, who is well into his second decade of surveying international and national exhibitions as well as the local scene. The *Sun-Times* relies more on free-lance writers, with Sue Taylor's weekly reviews particularly noteworthy. The national monthly art magazines, notably, *Art News*, *Artforum*, and *Art in America*, keep free-lance correspondents in Chicago, and will usually review a local event or two each month. The *New Art Examiner*, founded in Chicago in 1975, is a good place to find reviews and features.

ART GALLERIES

Following is a subjective guide (galleries are listed alphabetically) to some
of Chicago's commercial and alternative galleries. A more complete listing
can be found in the **Gallery Guide**, a free monthly listing of exhibitions,
complete with map, which is available at many galleries. Also, the weekend
sections of the Friday *Chicago Tribune* and *Chicago Sun-Times* print fairly
complete listings of the gallery openings.

These galleries are owned and staffed by friendly, knowledgeable people
who enjoy talking about art. Don't be afraid to ask them questions. Generally,
all galleries rotate exhibitions every four to six weeks, and exhibition openings
on Friday nights in the district are almost always open to the public. Galleries
are open Tuesday through Saturday, 11 am-5 pm. Most are closed Sunday.
But it's always a good idea to call ahead, to check on hours.

If you are in an adventurous mood, the gallery district is a great area for
aimless exploring. With the largest concentration of galleries on the 200 and
300 blocks of West Huron and Superior, you can visit an incredible number
of galleries in a four-block square area. Just look for the long, vertical
banners.

A.R.C. Gallery
356 W. Huron   266-7607
A women's cooperative gallery that regularly exhibits its members' works
as well as those of other, usually local, artists. Home of "Rawspace," an
area for installation art, which is always of interest. The gallery also sponsors
lectures and performance art.

Artemisia Gallery
341 W. Superior St.   751-2016
One of the first women's cooperative galleries in the nation. Features works
by members as well as guest artists. Sponsors lectures and performances.

Arts Club of Chicago
109 E. Ontario St.   787-3997
Open September through May. Founded in 1916, the Arts Club is an interesting and important historic mainstay in the Chicago art community.
Shows avant-garde art and gave Salvador Dali, Marcel Duchamp, and Jackson Pollock their first exhibitions in Chicago, but didn't induct their first
photographer as a member until this decade. The interior, designed by Mies
van der Rohe, is spectacular. Don't miss the Calder mobile.

Axe Street Arena
2778 N. Milwaukee   252-6082
Collective art gallery in Logan Square that features exhibits, music, and
interesting performance art. A little hard to find; look for the sign at the
street level and go up to the fourth floor.

Beacon Street Gallery
4520 N. Beacon   561-3500
Art comes to Uptown! This alternative space, a part of the Uptown Hull
House, concentrates on contemporary and folk art as well as local art of
interest to its community. Offers performances and classes.

Walter Bischoff Gallery
340 W. Huron St.   266-0244
Concentrating on avant-garde German art, this gallery has provoked a good deal of conversation in its few years of existence.

Roy Boyd Gallery
739 N. Wells St.   642-1606
One of Chicago's premier commercial galleries. Some emphasis on local cool abstract painting and sculpture.

Jan Cicero Gallery
221 W. Erie St.   440-1904
Cicero's interest has shifted from abstract to figurative painting. Be sure to go upstairs.

Contemporary Art Workshop
542 W. Grant Pl.   472-4004
Lincoln Park's premier alternative space, this gallery was founded in 1952. Concentrates on two-person exhibitions of local emerging artists. Offers art classes.

Dart Gallery
212 W. Superior St.   787-6366
The owners have a good eye, and some of Chicago's best young artists are represented here.

Marianne Deson Gallery
340 W. Huron St.   787-0005
Always worth a visit; the shows here are consistently challenging and stimulating.

Evanston Art Center
2603 Sheridan Rd., Evanston   475-5300
Located right on the lakeshore, this city-sponsored institution offers rotating exhibitions and art classes.

Fairweather-Hardin Gallery
101 E. Ontario St.   642-0007
Along with the Arts Club and the Joy Horwich Gallery, this is one of the last galleries still on the "Ontario Corridor." Specializes in Chicago and midwestern artists.

Feature
340 W. Huron St.   751-1720
Perhaps Chicago's most consistently avant-garde gallery. Takes a lot of risks, and succeeds more often than not.

Richard Gray Gallery
620 N. Michigan Ave. and 301 W. Superior St.   642-8877
The premier blue-chip gallery in Chicago. Shows a few local artists, but concentrates on twentieth century masters such as Picasso, Lichtenstein, Dine, Dubuffet, and Paladino.

Carl Hammer Gallery
200 W. Superior St.   266-8512
A terrific gallery, focusing on artists usually referred to as self-taught, naive, or outsider. Whatever they are, they're usually fascinating.

Rhona Hoffman Gallery
215 W. Superior St.   951-8828
Concentrates on the finest in contemporary art from New York and Europe.
One of Chicago's most respected galleries.

Hyde Park Art Center
1701 E. 53rd St.   324-5520
Founded in 1939, this is a major alternative space in the city. Has played
an important role in Chicago art. Held first exhibition of the artists later
known as the Imagists. Offers art classes for adults and children.

Phyllis Kind Gallery
313 W. Superior St.   642-6302
Home base for Chicago's Imagists, this is one of the most important galleries
in town. A second gallery has opened in New York. The gallery has imported
some New York artists for exhibitions here, and shown Chicago artists at
the New York gallery. Try to see the back rooms.

Paul Klein Gallery
356 W. Huron St.   787-0400
Large gallery showing local and national artists. Often exhibits wall sculpture.

Lill Street Gallery
430 W. Erie St.   649-1777
Not on Lill Street, but then the Randolph Street Gallery is not on Randolph
Street either. Fine alternative space concentrating on ceramics. Offers classes.

Robbin Lockett Gallery
703 N. Wells St.   649-1230
One of the city's newest galleries, with an independent aesthetic and an eye
for up and coming local and national artists. Worth a visit.

R.H. Love Gallery
108 E. Ohio St.   664-9620
Several galleries exist here under one roof. One focuses on contemporary
art, and another on earlier American art.

Martin D'Arcy Gallery and **Fine Arts Gallery**
Loyola University
6525 N. Sheridan Rd., D'Arcy Gallery: 508-2679   Fine Arts Gallery:
508-2820
Both galleries at the Loyola campus are not to be missed; the Fine Arts
Gallery in the Crown Center shows excellent monthly exhibitions.

Peter Miller Gallery
356 W. Huron St.   951-0252
One of the real risk-takers on the local commercial gallery scene.

N.A.M.E. Gallery
361 W. Superior St.   642-2776
First alternative gallery in Chicago, and the program continues to favor the
avant-garde. Regional and national exhibitions. Frequently shows interesting
performance art.

Isobel Neal Gallery Ltd.
200 W. Superior   944-1570
New gallery devoted to showing black artists exclusively.

Objects Gallery
341 W. Superior St.   664-6622
Interesting, diverse commercial gallery. Some concentration on ceramics.
Frequently displays work with a Central American influence.

Roger Ramsay Gallery
212 W. Superior St.   337-4678
Hard to categorize, other than noting that year in and year out, the high
quality of work shown and the taste with which it is chosen is consistently
excellent. Shares space with **Linda Einfeld Gallery**, which concentrates on
African art.

Randolph Street Gallery
756 N. Milwaukee Ave.   666-7737
Hard to find, but well worth the effort. This alternative gallery has made
the smoothest transition from the highly charged alternative scene of the
1970s to the more sedate 1980s. Some thoughtful exhibitions. Schedules
performance art every weekend.

The Renaissance Society
University of Chicago
5811 S. Ellis Ave.   702-8670
Not a commercial gallery, not an alternative space, and not a museum, this
is nevertheless Chicago's finest exhibition space, with remarkable shows that
balance the best of local art with the very latest in what's going on in New
York and Europe.

Betsy Rosenfield Gallery
212 W. Superior St.   787-8020
A fine gallery that balances coverage of Chicago and national artists.

School of the Art Institute of Chicago Superior Street Gallery
341 W. Superior   944-2306
Art schools that open galleries to feature student artwork is a new trend—
witness that both the School of the Art Institute and Northern Illinois
University have opened galleries in the Superior/Huron district. The School
of the Art Institute has a second gallery at its home base at Columbus Drive
and Jackson Boulevard.

Esther Saks Gallery
311 W. Superior St.   751-0911
Shows work in various media, with a focus on ceramics.

South Side Community Art Center
3831 S. Michigan Ave.   373-1026
Concentrates on work by black artists. Offers a wide range of classes.

State of Illinois Art Gallery
100 W. Randolph St.   917-5322
Located on the second floor of the State of Illinois Center, this gallery often
stages interesting shows of historical and contemporary work in a variety of

media. Focuses exclusively on Illinois artists. A convenient oasis in the north Loop.

Struve Gallery
309 W. Superior St.   787-0563
Focuses on up-and-coming local artists.

University of Illinois at Chicago
Gallery 400
400 S. Peoria St.   996-6114
Montgomery Ward Gallery
750 S. Halsted St.   413-5089
These two galleries on the university campus both have fascinating programs and exhibitions that feature design as well as fine arts.

Van Straaten Gallery
361 W. Superior St.   642-2900
Covering two floors, an excellent gallery in pleasant surroundings where hundreds of prints and drawings can be examined.

Donald Young Gallery
325 W. Huron St.   664-2151
A respected gallery that emphasizes sculpture.

Zaks Gallery
620 N. Michigan Ave.   943-8440
Shows an interesting group of local artists.

Zolla-Lieberman Gallery
356 W. Huron St.   944-1990
One of the pioneers of the River North district, this gallery exhibits a wide variety of artists, many of them local.

If you would like more of a national perspective on the local gallery scene, *American Art Galleries* by Les Krantz (1985) is a good sourcebook. It includes a substantial section on Chicago's galleries, providing historical background on the galleries themselves as well as information on the artists they represent.

—Jim Yood

PHOTOGRAPHY

Chicago is a great place for photography. And Chicago is a great place to learn about photography. IIT, UIC, Columbia College and The Art Institute of Chicago all offer good programs in photography. And, for those more interested in improving their technique than in accumulating college credits, there are numerous photography workshops around the city, too.

PROFESSIONAL EDUCATION

Columbia College
600 S. Michigan Ave., Chicago, IL 60605   663-1600
BA and MA programs teach traditional photographic courses with additional coursework in studio and commercial photography at the undergraduate level. Open admission policy allows both degree-seeking and non-degree students to take any of the courses, provided they have taken necessary prerequisites. Formal lecture series, workshops, and museum exhibition programs supplement the coursework. Columbia College is also home to the Museum of Contemporary Photography.

Illinois Institute of Technology
Institute of Design
3300 S. Federal, Chicago, IL 60616   567-3250
Although IIT's Institute of Design is not as revolutionary or as exciting as during its heyday (from the late 40s through the 60s), the BS and MS programs are designed to tread a thin line between the fine arts and commercial application. Undergraduates should expect a curriculum with rigorous requirements for basic work in the humanities and the physical, biological, and social sciences.

School of the Art Institute of Chicago
Columbus Drive at Jackson, Chicago, IL 60604   443-3700
Renowned tenured and visiting faculty guide students through a self-directed program of full and part-time study. Intensive semester-break sessions, workshops, lectures, School and museum exhibitions complement an extensive academic program. BFA and MFA degree programs are fine arts oriented. Student-at-large courses are also available for those not interested in earning degrees.

University of Chicago
Midway Studios
6016 S. Ingleside, Chicago, IL 60637   753-4821
A small and personal BFA and MFA fine arts program within the most academically rigorous university in the midwest. An excellent program for students seeking to fuse thought with practice. Facilities are not as extensive as at schools strictly geared to teaching art.

University of Illinois at Chicago
601 S. Morgan, P.O. Box 4348
Chicago, IL 60680   996-3337
The BFA and MFA fine arts programs have the distinct advantage of being integrated into the University's science and letters curriculum, providing photography students with a liberal arts education, and allowing students in other diverse fields to study photography.

ALTERNATIVE EDUCATION

In addition to the centers listed below, photography instruction is offered at many city and suburban colleges and junior colleges, including Triton Community College in River Grove and Oakton Community College in Skokie and Des Plaines. All the centers below offer day or evening instruction in beginning, intermediate, and advanced camera operation and darkroom skills.

Jane Addams Hull House
3212 N. Broadway
549-1634

Beverly Art Center
2153 W. 111th
445-3838

Evanston Art Center
2603 Sheridan Rd., Evanston
475-5300

Hyde Park Art Center
1701 E. 53rd
324-5520

Old Town Triangle Arts Center
1763 N. North Park
337-1938

South Side Community Art Center
3831 S. Michigan
373-1026

MUSEUMS AND GALLERIES

Art Institute of Chicago
Photography Galleries
Michigan Ave. at Adams   443-3663
The largest collection in the region sponsors a significant contemporary and historical exhibition program. The print collection is open to the public by appointment. The Photographic Society program hosts receptions, lectures, workshops, and collection tours. The museum bookstore is an excellent source of photographic books and exhibition catalogues.

Chicago Public Library Cultural Center
78 E. Washington   269-2900
Frequently exhibits photographs of historical or cultural significance. Often shows work by local photographers.

Carol Ehlers Fine Arts
883-0888
This is a private, by-appointment-only dealer specializing in the sale of vintage master prints of the twentieth century.

Exchange National Bank of Chicago
120 S. LaSalle   781-8000, ext. 8076
An impressive and thorough corporate photography collection that is open to the public during business hours. A portion of the collection is always

on view in the bank lobby while some of the works are being exhibited elsewhere.

Edwynn Houk Gallery
200 W. Superior   943-0698
An excellent gallery of international importance. The gallery specializes in twentieth century works. The regular exhibition schedule only touches the surface of the gallery's inventory holdings. The gallery produces some of the most exquisite small monographs and catalogs published today.

MoMing Gallery
1034 W. Barry   472-9894
Exhibits photographs by contemporary photographers from Chicago and elsewhere.

Museum of Contemporary Photography
Columbia College
600 S. Michigan   663-1600
An exhibition and study collection program that focuses on photography since the late 1950s. Shows are open to all; the Print Study Room and the permanent collection are open to the public by appointment only.

BOOKSTORES

Art Institute of Chicago Museum Store
Michigan at Adams   443-3600
Extensive collection of books on photography. Museum members receive a discount on book purchases.

Guild Books
2456 N. Lincoln   525-3667
A fine selection of books on photography. Books from small presses as well as from the larger publishing houses.

Kroch's and Brentano's
29 S. Wabash, second floor   332-7500
A quiet backroom filled with photographic books of all kinds—fine art, commercial, how-to, and special editions. Knowledgeable and helpful staff.

57th Street Books
1301 E. 57th St.   684-1300
This may be the finest and most comprehensive bookstore in the city. It has all current major photographic publications and will order books and catalogs from abroad. Shareholding members of this cooperative receive discounts.

Museum of Contemporary Art Bookstore
237 E. Ontario   280-2660
This bookstore is the best source for self-published, small press, and European museum and gallery photography and other art books, catalogs, and

journals. While not as large as the Art Institute of Chicago Bookstore, the MCA bookstore is the best source for obscure publications.

PHOTOGRAPHIC MATERIALS AND PROCESSING

Central Camera
230 S. Wabash
427-5580
This excellent but disheveled enterprise has almost everything photographic and at an excellent price.

Darkroom Aids Co.
3449 N. Lincoln
248-4301
New and used cameras, equipment, and accessories. Trade-ins accepted.

Gamma Photo Labs
314 W. Superior
337-0022
The professional's photo lab. High quality film processing.

Helix
310 S. Racine
421-6000
Excellent source for the best price in cameras but often lacking inventory depth in darkroom materials.

Lion Photo
66 E. Madison
346-2288
Cameras, accessories, and film processing. Also has locations in many suburbs.

Shutan Camera & Video
312 W. Randolph
332-2000
Large inventory of new and used cameras and accessories.

Skrudland's Photo Service
6440 W. Diversey
637-3177
More for the amateur than the professional, but offers good quality developing at reasonable prices. Cameras and accessories, too.

Standard Photo
43 E. Chicago Ave.
440-4920
The store for the professional photographer. Tremendous inventory of every kind of equipment and supply. Rentals of still cameras, VCRs, film projectors, and lighting equipment are available.

Wolk Camera
Two Illinois Center
565-5901
Good selection of cameras and accessories with some excellent buys. Their trade-in allowances are generous.

—Jack Helbig

LITERARY LIFE

Chicago didn't used to be a bookish town. We were a city of hog butchers, hod hoppers, and crooked aldermen. Sure we had a few literary types like Harriet Monroe (poet, founder and first editor of *Poetry* magazine) and Margaret Anderson and Jane Heap (editors of the *Little Review*, first American publishers of James Joyce's *Ulysses*); and Chicago did have a literary renaissance of sorts in the teens and twenties with writers such as Sherwood Anderson, Frank Norris, Edna Ferber, Carl Sandburg, Ben Hecht, Charles MacArthur, and James T. Farrell. But the city as a whole never acquired the literary veneer of a Paris, or a New York City, or even, for that matter, an Oxford, Mississippi.

And Chicago has never been particularly kind to its authors. Most receive less attention than your average TV weatherman, and the few that are noticed must play Nelson Algren's role: the average guy who just happens to be a writer but who could just as easily have been a lathe operator, or a firefighter, or a steel mill worker. Carl Sandburg played that role before Nelson Algren, and Studs Terkel took the part when Algren died. Writers who don't play along are ignored. Like Saul Bellow.

But despite this hostile environment—or maybe because of it—Chicago has been home to and inspiration for many of America's great writers. And just as many other writers owe their careers to the efforts of Chicago's literati. Theodore Dreiser spent tens of thousands of words in *Sister Carrie* detailing the fascinating vulgarity, ugliness, and materialism of Chicago as a boom town. Harriet Monroe used *Poetry* magazine as the official organ of the American Modernist movement and was the first to publish T. S. Eliot, Ezra Pound, Marianne Moore, and William Carlos Williams. And in the late 1950s, the *Chicago Review* showed similar foresight when it published chapters from William S. Burroughs' beat masterpiece, *Naked Lunch*. Not bad for a city known more for Mayor Daley's malapropisms than for its literary heritage.

Over the past twenty-five years Chicago has become increasingly hospitable to the arts in general and writing in particular. The recent boom in theater has been followed by a boom in art galleries and may be followed—knock on wood—by a boom in writing. We have a lot of great bookstores, including a fine collection of smaller local, specialty and used bookstores, many of which are committed to the growing literary community here. Literary magazines are on the rise. We will probably have a central library (in our lifetimes, we hope). Plus we have many fine writers living here. We may become a literary town yet.

BOOKSTORES

Bookstore chains have mushroomed in the Loop of late. Their wide selection and convenience make them attractive to Loop workers and shoppers. Of the major chains in the city, the **Kroch's & Brentano's** at 29 S. Wabash feels the most like a small bookstore. Kroch's began in Chicago and has remained a local chain, with branches throughout the city and suburbs. (See the end of the chapter for a listing of Chicago stores.) The store on Wabash is the flagship store—the largest in the chain—and has an especially strong selection of technical and business publications, as well as a huge selection of hardbacks and paperbacks. The art book section has a superb stock and well-informed clerks, and the magazine and newspaper selection (excellent) includes foreign publications, and literary and scholarly journals.

Two blocks north of Kroch's at 129 N. Wabash is **B. Dalton**, a well-stocked store with three floors of hardbound, paperback, and remaindered (marked-down) books, plus a growing video section. It's a good place to shop for magazines—the selection is huge—and for computer books (the store has one of the largest computer book and software departments in the city). There are several other locations downtown and many others in the city (see end of chapter).

Crown Books at 24 N. Wabash (and elsewhere in the Loop and city—see end of chapter) sells all its titles at 10 percent off the list price. Crown has a good selection of current bestsellers, paperbacks and magazines, as well as a nice selection of inexpensive remaindered books (many of which were recently bestsellers).

Waldenbooks, another chain bookstore, has two branches downtown, one in the Sears Tower and the other in the Amoco (nee Standard Oil) Building, and many more in the shopping malls in and around the city. Waldenbooks stocks the biggest-selling trade and fiction titles, but their real strength is non-fiction, especially self-help, do-it-yourself, cooking, and current events.

A few years ago, some people predicted that the larger chain bookstores would drive the smaller, local bookstores out of the market. But the opposite has happened. The smaller stores survived and even thrived by happily providing services the larger stores were unable (or unwilling) to provide. Like poetry and fiction readings. Like stocking fringe, off-beat, radical, or very small publishers. Luckily for us, Chicago has a number of very fine local independent bookstores.

Guild Books (2456 N. Lincoln) has grown from a small, leftward leaning hole-in-the-wall bookstore, to a large leftward leaning bookstore in a pleasant space with an excellent selection of books and a commitment to Chicago's literary community. Look to the Guild if you are interested in literature, poetry, or politics. Guild Books makes a point of stocking small press books unavailable elsewhere in the city, and also has a large selection of magazines, with an emphasis on literary and art. (Guild also stocks a small but interesting collection of records, including folk, blues, jazz, and women's music.) Several times each month, Guild Books sponsors authors' readings and book signings. Recently, the bookstore increased its size by a third to accommodate these readings. Guild Books has placed itself smack dab in the middle of Chicago's literary reawakening.

Many know about **Stuart Brent's** fine bookstore on Michigan Avenue near the Water Tower (670 N. Michigan), a pleasantly overcrowded place with a good selection of paperback fiction and the wonderful smell of books fresh from the printer. But few people know that Stuart Brent also owns another interesting bookstore in Hyde Park—the bookstore for the University of Chicago. Because the **University of Chicago Bookstore** (970 E. 58th St.) can count on the informed, eclectic, eccentric University of Chicago market for a steady stream of customers, they can afford to maintain one of the most diverse bookstores in the city (maybe even the midwest!). If a subject is taught at the U of C, or even talked about, it is represented in the store. Books on music, history, business, computers, literature, economics, philosophy, poetry, medicine, far eastern studies, middle eastern studies, and law are all stocked. Well worth a trip to Hyde Park.

Perennially bookish Hyde Park is the site of not just one, but two excellent bookstores (plus two fine used bookstores). The **Seminary Coop Bookstore** (5757 S. University) and its branch bookstore, 57th Street Books (1301 E. 57th Street), are worth visiting. Located in the basement of the Chicago Theological Seminary, the Seminary Cooperative Bookstore matches or surpasses the quality of the selection at the University of Chicago Bookstore. In fact, the Seminary Coop Bookstore may have the best selection of academic books—especially in the humanities—in the country.

Furthermore, any books you can't find at the Seminary Co-op are probably on the shelves at the bookstore's branch operation, **57th Street Books**. 57th Street is a less academic, more consumer-oriented store where you can find children's books, science fiction, mysteries, and even calendars among the more scholarly tomes. Both stores have excellent fiction, poetry and drama sections, and both branches are more than willing to special order obscure books in print. Anyone can join the cooperative: members receive a 10 percent discount on all books. Members can also charge their books.

Barbara's Books, with three locations—two in Chicago (1434 N. Wells and 2907 N. Broadway) and one in Oak Park (121 N. Marion) is Chicago's smallest local chain bookstore, although it's a chain in name only. Each branch of Barbara's is a self-contained local store, and each has a staff of friendly, well-read employees who recommend books enthusiastically. Barbara's has a good selection of fiction. The employees work hard to inform customers about fiction books by affixing 3 x 5 cards with mini-reviews of the books onto the bookshelves. Barbara's also publishes a monthly newsletter describing new books and announcing book readings, which are held regularly. Regular customers may want to open a charge account.

The **Unabridged Bookstore** on Broadway (3251 N. Broadway) has an interesting selection of fiction, drama and film, and a good collection of magazines. The gay studies and literature section is one of the most complete in the city. Unabridged's staff is very cooperative and helpful. A great bookstore to order books from.

Women & Children First (1967 N. Halsted) carries books concerning all aspects of women's lives, excellent nonsexist children's books and toys, and a bulletin board full of announcements regarding women's groups, events, and services. They also carry a good selection of records (many made by smaller independent labels) by women artists, including folk, rock, jazz, and blues. The store also hosts readings.

The **Children's Bookstore** (2465 N. Lincoln) has an interesting selection of books, toys, and records for children, and very helpful staff.

Rizzoli International Bookstore and Gallery (Water Tower Place) has the most beautiful (and expensive) collection of art, architecture, and design books in the city. To make matters worse (for those of us who can't afford to buy anything there) Rizzoli's does everything in its power to make it a great place for browsing. Plush carpeting. Classical music. Refined atmosphere. A renowned collection of foreign language books and magazines.

You may tell yourself you're just going to browse through the fiction, bi-ography, history, or drama, while listening to great classical music. But don't be surprised if you buy something.

Platypus Books (606 Dempster, Evanston), is a small, excellent store that is strong on fiction, women's studies, and children's books. Platypus also stocks many interesting books from small presses, and has a small but interesting collection of magazines. It's definitely one of the most pleasant bookstores for browsing.

Another good bookstore in Evanston is **Great Expectations Book Store** (911 Foster, Evanston). This academic bookstore, in pleasant disarray, is great for browsing and the sales people are always helpful. The store excels in fiction, literary criticism, and philosophy.

If you're looking for travel books, don't overlook **Sandmeyer's Bookstore** in the South Loop (714 S. Dearborn), the **Savvy Traveler** (50 E. Washington, second floor), or the **Rand McNally Map Store**. All have great travel book sections. Sandmeyer's has books by and about Chicagoans as well as an extensive and interesting fiction department. The Rand McNally Map Store (23 E. Madison) carries city and national maps, domestic and foreign, as well as some topographic maps. Ironically, the store has a better selection of travel books than maps.

Of course, a city with a growing reputation for theater should have a good theater book store or two. We have three. The **Oak Street Bookshop** (54 E. Oak) is very well known for its drama section, which has books on theater, film, and scripts. The rest of Oak Street's eclectic collection includes art, fiction, and nonfiction hardbacks and paperbacks. **Scenes** (3168 N. Clark) combines a bookstore with a coffeeshop, so that you can buy your book and read it too. The store has one of the largest collections of theater and film books in the city. This lively, pleasant place also hosts readings.

Act I (2633 N. Halsted) is a recent addition, and the collection of used, remaindered, and new books they've crammed into their little storefront make us hope they will thrive and grow. Counting used and remaindered books, they have without a doubt the largest collection of theater books in the city. Act I also stocks magazines of interest to theater lovers, including *Variety, Backstage, TDR*, and the hard-to-find *Ross Report* and *Theatrical Index*.

Chicago isn't only a great place for new books. The city can boast of having some of the most interesting used bookstores in the midwest. If you are a hopeless used book addict, you will want to check out four used bookstores in particular: Powell's Bookstore, O'Gara and Wilson's Book-store, Bookseller's Row, and Aspidistra.

Powell's Bookstore (1501 E. 57th St.) has a great collection of used novels at the most reasonable prices of any used bookstore in the city. It also has a great selection of literature, philosophy, drama, psychology, and history books (with over 200,000 titles, they should have a good selection). If the Hyde Park store does not satisfy you, you can always browse in their ware-house store in the south Loop (1020 S. Wabash, 8th floor).

While you're visiting Powell's, make it a point to walk a few blocks west on 57th Street to **O'Gara and Wilson's Bookstore** (1311 E. 57th St.). O'Gara and Wilson's is similar to Powell's: they have the same huge selection of books (over 200,000 titles), and the same great collection of fiction, history, theology, philosophy, theater, and psychology books. Their prices are slightly higher, however.

Although **Bookseller's Row** (2445 N. Lincoln) has fewer titles than Powell's or O'Gara and Wilson's, the books they do have are in excellent shape, and the store is very well organized. Especially strong in art and literature. Bookseller's Row is one of two great bookstores for browsing in before the picture starts at the nearby Biograph Theater. (The other is Guild Books, just across the street.) **Aspidistra Bookshop** (2630 N. Clark) has a larger selection and lower prices, but it may be hard to find the book you're looking for in the good-natured disorder.

Chicago also has a number of ethnic bookstores serving the sizable ethnic communities here. A few examples are the **Polonia Bookstore and Publishing Company** at 2886 N. Milwaukee (289-2554), **Rosenblum's Hebrew Book Store** at 2906 W. Devon (262-1700), and the **Ukrainian Book Store** at 2315 W. Chicago (276-6373). More ethnic and foreign-language bookstores are listed at the end of this chapter.

LIBRARIES

Chicago's new, central public library is scheduled to open at State Street and Congress Parkway in 1991. At the moment, the central library's collection of books is inconveniently split between the Cultural Center (at Randolph and Michigan) and the Mandel Building (425 N. Michigan Avenue, behind the Tribune Tower). Sometime in 1988, the Mandel collection will move to 400 N. Franklin Street, ten or so blocks west of its present site. Both the Cultural Center and Mandel Building close at 7 pm Monday through Thursday, 6 pm Friday, and 5 pm Saturday—unfortunate hours for anyone working 9 to 5.

The **Cultural Center** (78 E. Washington, 269-2900) was the original Chicago Public Library, now transformed into a beautiful combination art gallery, library, and public assembly hall. The Cultural Center houses arts and literature books, and audiovisual materials. Every month the Center chooses a theme and hosts exhibits, films, lectures, noontime concerts, and poetry and short story readings that reflect that theme. (For recorded program information, dial FINEART.) Unfortunately, the Cultural Center is a great place for everything but reading. The book collection is sparse. The building is short on tables, and the staff sometimes seems too harried to help patrons. Nevertheless, the Center is a beautiful oasis in the Loop, worth a stop if only to see the beautifully restored marble staircases and Tiffany glass, to hear a classical concert at noon in the auditorium, or to see the art exhibits.

 Cultural Center circulation department: 269-2845

 Telephone Information Center: 269-2800–Quick phone reference for questions on just about anything.

 Spanish Information Center: 269-2940–Reference en espanol and gives social service information.

 Programs and exhibit information: 744-6630

 The **Mandel Building** (425 N. Michigan, 269-2900), with plenty of tables and quiet, is a better place to read than the Cultural Center, and it has the lion's share of the central library's holdings. Mandel houses a good business collection, as well as science, social science, education, philosophy, government publications, and general periodicals. The technology section is excellent, and includes low-cost computer search services. The staff are very cooperative about answering questions, both in person and on the phone.

Mandel circulation desk: 269-2970

Computer Assisted Reference Center: 269-2915

Chicago's two regional libraries—the Conrad Sulzer (formerly called Hild) Library for the north side and Carter G. Woodson for the south side—are better alternatives than the downtown libraries for readers. Their hours are more reasonable—both are open until 9 pm Monday through Thursday (closed on Sundays though). The **Sulzer Library** (4455 N. Lincoln, 728-8652; TDD, hearing impaired: 728-2062), housed in an attractive, modern building, has a general collection that is complete and in great condition, as well as the Ravenswood-Lakeview Historical Association collections. Sulzer also offers classes in GED preparation, English as a second language, and hosts puppet shows and theater for children. The library sponsors reading groups for both children and adults. A marvelous modern library, Sulzer is comfortable and a great place for study and reading.

Carter G. Woodson Regional Library (9525 S. Halsted, 881-6900) is also an attractive, well-run library, with large reading rooms, and a huge, well-kept collection. Woodson may also have the politest reference desk in the city. Woodson houses the Vivian G. Harsh Collection of Afro-American History and Literature. Woodson offers classes in GED preparation and English as a Second Language.

There are over 80 branch libraries, located in every neighborhood of Chicago. To find the branch nearest you, look in the white pages under Chicago Public Library—Neighborhood Services, or call your regional library.

If you find the Chicago Public Library collection to be inadequate and their hours inconvenient, you may prefer to study at one of the local university libraries. At public universities, this is not a problem. Some of the private universities (as well as some other private libraries) will require an Infopass, which is a pass you get from your home library to access another library's collection. First, you have to prove that you have exhausted the resources of the public library system. Infopasses are available at branch and regional libraries—call your local branch or regional library for information about the Infopass.

An alternative to the Chicago Public Library is the library at the **University of Illinois at Chicago** (801 S. Morgan, reference desk: 996-2726). This roomy, well-stocked library is a good option for people who do research on Sundays. Anyone may use the library, but you can check out books only if you have graduated from or are a current student at the University of Illinois, or if you are a current student at DePaul, Loyola, Chicago State, Northern Illinois, Northeastern, Illinois Institute of Technology, or Governor's State. The library is good for an urban campus, but don't go there for aesthetics or atmosphere. The library suffers from the same sterile design as the rest of the campus.

Even better libraries can be found at the University of Chicago, Northwestern University, and the Newberry Library. Of these three, you'll find the University of Chicago's **Regenstein Library** (1100 E. 57th Street, 702-

7874) all but impossible to enter, unless you happen to be an alum, an employee of the University, or a currently registered student. This is unfortunate, because the Regenstein Library has one of the largest and most comprehensive collections in the country. Only if you are determined, and willing to struggle with the University's byzantine bureaucracy, do you have any hope of obtaining an Infopass, which will grant you limited access to the collection.

The **Northwestern University Library** (1935 Sheridan Rd., Evanston, 491-7658) is more accessible to the public. The modern tri-towered main library building was designed by the architect of the UIC campus (Walter Netsch), but this is a much nicer building. The general public may use the library anytime except weekday evenings, Saturday afternoons, and all day Sunday.

Also accessible to the public (evenings and weekends included) are the **Loyola University** (6525 N. Sheridan, 274-3000) and **DePaul University** (2323 N. Seminary, 341-8085) libraries. DePaul has a good business library at its downtown campus (25 E. Jackson, 341-8432), especially in accounting. Both Loyola and DePaul participate in the cooperative arrangement among libraries described above.

The **Newberry Library** (60 W. Walton, 943-9090), unaffiliated with any university, is internationally known for its superlative collection, primarily in the humanities. High points of the collection include books on the history and literature of western Europe and the Americas from the late middle ages to the early twentieth century. Newberry is also a great source for books on music theory, printing, typography, calligraphy, and the history of cartography. The extensive manuscript and map collections attract scholars from across the country. Newberry is, however, a closed-stack, noncirculating library. You must register at the front desk and receive an admission card to reading rooms, where you request materials. Only pencils (no pens) are allowed in the reading rooms.

Newberry also sponsors a public program that includes the Lyceum Seminars for adults, an early music concert series, Writer's Corner readings, and special lectures and exhibits. In the event that you wish to join the D.A.R. or are tracing your bloodline, the library has an excellent family history or genealogy collection.

Other libraries worth noting are those at the Chicago Historical Society and the Art Institute of Chicago, as well as the Midwest Women's Center Library, and the Municipal Reference Library.

The **Chicago Historical Society** library (Clark and North Ave., 642-4600) has a huge collection of books, manuscripts, and photos documenting the history of Chicago and the state of Illinois. The library at the **Art Institute** (Michigan Ave. and Adams, 443-3666) has extensive holdings on art, art history, and midwestern architecture; members of the Art Institute and anyone with an Infopass can use the library. The **Midwest Women's Center Library** (53 W. Jackson, 922-8530) is extensive, a godsend to anyone researching legal issues, day care centers, health care services, and any and all services and organizations of interest and importance to women.

An excellent resource for specific information about the city, such as reports written by city agencies, building and tax codes, city ordinances, regulations, and statistics, as well as files of newspaper clippings about Chicago, is the **Municipal Reference Library** in City Hall (121 N. LaSalle),

Room 1002. The library primarily serves City Hall employees but is open to the public. Hours are weekdays, 8:30 am-5:00 pm. 744-4992.

READINGS

The number of places sponsoring readings has grown dramatically in the past few years. Both **Guild Books** and **Barbara's Books** sponsor readings, as does the **Left Bank Bookstall** in Oak Park (104 S. Oak Park Ave.). Two interesting bars also sponsor readings: the **Get Me High Lounge**, and the **Green Mill Lounge**. The Get Me High (1758 N. Honore), an eccentric jazz bar in Bucktown, holds open poetry readings every Monday. The Green Mill Lounge (4802 N. Broadway) holds readings every Sunday. Green Mill is home to the Uptown Poetry Slam, a kind of post-punk poetry reading with a style that fuses art with entertainment, creating a kind of vaudevillian effect.

For those who like their literature straight up, there is the **Poetry Center** at the Art Institute. The Poetry Center sponsors poetry and some prose readings by nationally known authors. In the past, such well-known poets as Tess Gallagher, Robert Merrill, and Lawrence Ferlinghetti have read at the Poetry Center.

For those who prefer the phone to the bookstore, there is **Dial-A-Poem**. Every two weeks a new local poet reads her or his work. That number again is 346-3478.

To keep abreast of poetry and fiction readings, check out the listings in the free weekly *Reader* or stop by Guild Books, Barbara's, or 57th Street Bookstore and pick up a copy of *Open Mike*, a monthly listing of reading events in the Chicago area. The *Chicago Tribune*'s Sunday book section lists literary events within a 200-mile radius of Chicago.

Locations of poetry and fiction readings are listed at the end of this chapter.

GETTING PUBLISHED

This is both the best of times and the worst of times for anyone who wants to get published in Chicago. It's a great time if you are interested in writing nonfiction or journalism; it's not such a great time if you write fiction. And if you write poetry, well, it's a terrible time—more people write poetry than read it, these days. For those interested in nonfiction, you should know the Chicago *Reader* welcomes new writers with open arms, and they are willing to read unsolicited manuscripts. Write or call them for their writers' guidelines.

An excellent reference book containing an exhaustive listing of local publishers, journals, magazines, and papers, as well as good information on the market for free-lancers and other employment opportunities for writers in Chicago is *A Writer's Guide to Chicago-Area Publishers*, edited by Jerold L. Kellman (Writer's Guide Publications, 1985).

Both the *Chicago Tribune* and the *Chicago Sun-Times* publish work by free-lance writers; however, before you begin writing, give the appropriate editor a call to propose your article. The Lerner papers and the little neighborhood weeklies are other good markets for journalistic writing. See the Local Press chapter for their names and address. Writers of fiction and poetry should read the literary magazines published in Chicago, and send their work to those magazines that publish work like their own. Some local literary magazines and publishers are listed at the end of this chapter.

Don't confine yourself to Chicago, however. Better markets for short stories exist in the literary magazines published by university English departments or by high-tech bohemians publishing out of apartments or lofts in New York or San Francisco. The Cultural Center of the Chicago Public Library has an excellent collection of literary magazines published in the U.S.

Photograph courtesy of the University of Chicago.

DIRECTORY

General Bookstores

Barbara's Bookstores
1434 N. Wells
642-5044
2907 N. Broadway
477-0411
121 N. Marion Ct., Oak Park
848-9140

Richard Barnes
821 Foster, Evanston
869-2272

Chandler's
630 Davis, Evanston
475-7200
Good selection includes used
paperbacks and text books, all
located in the basement.

Crown Books
24 N. Wabash
782-7667
201 W. Jackson
341-0505
309 W. Washington
346-8677
1660 N. Wells
642-3950
2711 N. Clark
327-1551
4842 W. Irving Park
736-0886

B Dalton Bookseller
129 N. Wabash
236-7615
175 W. Jackson
922-5219
Xerox Center, Monroe and
Dearborn
580-0015
645 N. Michigan Ave
944-3702
Century City Center, 2828 N.
Clark
549-7277

Woodfield Mall, Schaumburg
882-0660
Hillside Shopping Center, Hillside
449-0228
Forest Park Mall, Forest Park
771-5640
Lincoln Mall, Matteson
481-7272

57th Street Books
1301 E. 57th Street
684-1300

Great Expectations Book Store
911 Foster, Evanston
864-3881

Guild Books
2456 N. Lincoln
525-3667

Kroch's & Brentano's
29 S. Wabash
332-7500
105 W. Jackson
922-8056
516 N. Michigan
321-0989
Water Tower Place, 835 N.
Michigan
943-2452
1711 Sherman, Evanston
328-7220
1028 Lake Street, Oak Park
848-9003
Evergreen Plaza, 95th and
Western, Evergreen Park
424-9550

Left Bank Bookstall
104 S. Oak Park Ave., Oak Park
383-4700

Oak Street Bookshop
54 E. Oak Street
642-3070

Platypus Books
606 Dempster, Evanston
866-8040

**Rizzoli International Bookstore
and Gallery**
Water Tower Place, 835 N.
Michigan
642-3500

Seminary Cooperative Bookstore
5757 S. University
752-4381
Specializes in theology, literary
criticism, history, and philosophy.

Something Else Books
2805 N. Sheffield
549-0495
Specializes in small press and
university press books.

Stuart Brent Books
670 N. Michigan
337-6357

Unabridged Bookstore
3251 N. Broadway
883-9119

Waldenbooks
127 W. Madison
236-8446
Sears Tower, Franklin and Jackson
876-0308
Amoco Building, 200 E. Randolph
565-2489
Rienzi Plaza, Diversey and
Broadway
549-3792
Brickyard Shopping Center, 6465
W. Diversey
745-8660
Ford City Shopping Center, 7601
S. Cicero
581-4833
Northbrook Court, Northbrook
498-3475
Woodfield Mall, Schaumburg
882-6850
Orland Square Mall, Orland Park
349-8823

University Bookstores

DePaul University Bookstore
2334 N. Seminary
341-8423
Primarily arts and sciences.
25 E. Jackson
341-8792
Business and law. Trade and text
books.

Loyola University Bookstore
820 N. Michigan
670-2880
Trade and text books.

Northwestern University
Norris Center Store
1999 Sheridan, Evanston
491-3991
Text books as well as a good
selection of trade books.

University of Chicago Bookstore
970 E. 58th St.
702-8729
Huge selection of text and trade
books.

University of Illinois at Chicago
Chicago Circle Center Bookstore
750 S. Halsted
413-5500
Text books.
Epicenter Bookstore
750 S. Halsted
413-5540
Trade books and magazines.

Used Bookstores

Aspidistra
2630 N. Clark
549-3129

Bookman's Alley
1712 Sherman, Evanston
869-6999
Literally in an alley, behind the old Varsity Theater. Homey atmosphere. Many comfortable rooms filled with used books (some rare) and related artifacts. The music section is marked by a grand piano.

Booknook Parnassus
2000 Maple Ave, Evanston
475-3445
Down the street from Great Expectations.

Bookseller's Row
2445 N. Lincoln
348-1170

J. L. Clark
2463 N. Lincoln
929-5119

O'Gara & Wilson Ltd.
1311 E. 57th St.
363-0993

Powell's Bookstore
1501 E. 57th Street
955-7780

Powell's Book Warehouse
1020 S. Wabash, 4th floor
341-0748

Project 1999 Bookstore, Cafe & Theatre
6544 N. Sheridan Rd.
743-6685
Good selection of twentieth century fiction, plus philosophy, religion, and history. Located on the second floor.

Second Hand Prose
4544 N. Lincoln
728-8923
Good general selection, plus some library discards (including good reference books on occasion). Located in the old Hild Library.

Specialty Bookstores

Besides the stores listed below, note also that museum bookstores (such as those in the Art Institute and the Chicago Historical Society) often carry good selections of specialty books.

Abraham Lincoln Book Shop
18 E. Chestnut
944-3085
American history, books about presidents (esp. Lincoln), and Civil War.

Act I
2633 N. Halsted
348-6757
Theater books: new, used. Also theater magazines.

Archicenter
330 S. Dearborn
782-1776
Fine selection of books about architecture, especially local architecture.

Chicago Historical Bookworks
831 Main, Evanston
869-6410
Extensive collection of books on Chicago and by Chicago authors as well as a good collection of socialist works.

The Children's Bookstore
2465 N. Lincoln
248-2665
Children's books, toys, and
records. Very helpful staff.

N. Fagin Books
185 N. Wabash
236-6540
Especially strong in natural
history.

Hep Cat Comics
3107 N. Lincoln
477-5033
Mainstream and underground
comics.

I Love A Mystery
55 E. Washington
236-1338
Mysteries, mysteries, and nothing
but mysteries.

Larry's Comic Book Store
1219A W. Devon
274-1832
New and back issues.

Logos Book Store
101 N. Oak Park, Oak Park
848-6644
Christian and other books.

Metro Golden Memories
5425 W. Addison
736-4133
Film, TV, and old time radio
books. Also tapes and records of
old radio shows and big bands,
videotapes, posters, and lobby
cards.

Occult Bookstore
3230 N. Clark
281-0599
Books on witchcraft, magic, the
occult, ESP, and parapsychology.

Prairie Avenue Bookshop
711 S. Dearborn
922-8311
Architecture, interior design, and
science.

Rand McNally Map Store
23 E. Madison
673-9100
City and national maps, both
domestic and foreign, topographic
maps, globes, and travel books.

Sandmeyer's Bookstore
714 S. Dearborn
922-2104
Travel books and more. Good
fiction section.

The Savvy Traveller
50 E. Washington, second floor
263-2100
Travel books.

Scenes
3168 N. Clark
525-1007
Theater books and a coffeeshop
too.

Women & Children First
1967 N. Halsted
440-8824
Feminist bookstore with titles
concerning all aspects of women's
lives, excellent nonsexist children's
books and toys, and a bulletin
board full of announcements from
women's groups around the city.
Also carries records by women
artists.

Foreign Language Bookstores

Europa Bookstore
915 Foster, Evanston
866-6329
Large selection of foreign-language
books: French, German, Spanish,
and some Italian. Reference
dictionaries in other languages.
Some periodicals. Another outlet is
located at 3229 N. Clark (929-
1836).

Japan Books & Records
3450 W. Peterson
463-7755
Japanese books and video.

**Polonia Bookstore and Publishing
Company**
2886 N. Milwaukee
489-2554

Rosenblum's Hebrew Book Store
2906 W. Devon
262-1700

Russian Bookstore
6347 N. Sacramento
338-6644

Scholars Bookstore
1379 E. 53rd St.
288-6565
Specializing in Asian studies.
Books in Japanese, Chinese,
Korean, Vietnamese, and other
languages, as well as Asian studies
books in English.

Ukrainian Book Store
2315 W. Chicago
276-6373

Poetry and Fiction Readings

Barbara's Books
1434 N. Wells
642-5044
Readings also held at their N.
Broadway and Oak Park Stores.

Batteries Not Included
2201 N. Clybourn
348-9529

Get Me High Lounge
1758 N. Honore
278-8154

Green Mill Lounge
4802 N. Broadway
878-5552

Guild Books
2456 N. Lincoln
525-3667

Left Bank Bookstall
104 S. Oak Park, Oak Park
383-4700

The Poetry Center
School of the Art Institute
Columbus and Jackson
443-3711

Literary Magazines

ACM (Another Chicago Magazine)
P.O. Box 11223, Chicago, IL 60611
Rising star among Chicago literary magazines. *ACM* also publishes books
under the name Another Chicago Press.

B-City
619 W. Surf, Chicago, IL 60657
Publishes poetry and interviews with poets. Submissions accepted September
1 through December 15. Publishes many rising poets on the local scene.

Black & White
3071 W. Palmer Square, Chicago, IL 60647
As much a forum for experimental artists as for writers of fiction and poetry. Successfully couples the written word with striking photographs and drawings. Good things should come from this cross-pollination of art and literature.

Chicago Review
Faculty Exchange Box C, University of Chicago, Chicago, IL 60637
Well-established literary magazine. Published chapters of Burroughs' *Naked Lunch* in the fifties. Still known for publishing experimental and off-beat literature.

Letter eX
P.O. Box 476917, Chicago, IL 60647
Chicago's only monthly poetry newsletter concentrates on publishing criticism and essays. Open to well-written work by free-lancers.

New American Writing
(formerly called *Oink!*), 1446 W. Jarvis, 3D, Chicago, IL 60626
Interesting, well-designed, nicely printed magazine publishing excellent poetry, fiction, and essays.

Nit & Wit
P.O. Box 627, Geneva, IL 60134
New owners are working hard to make this an interesting literary magazine. Publishes poetry, fiction, and nonfiction.

Oyez Review
Roosevelt University, 430 S. Michigan, Chicago, IL 60605
Publishes poetry, fiction, drama, photographs, and graphics.

Poetry
c/o English Department, University of Illinois at Chicago, P.O. Box 4348, Chicago, IL 60680
Fine poetry since 1912. First literary journal to publish the moderns, including T.S. Eliot, Ezra Pound, Marianne Moore, and William Carlos Williams. Still a great magazine.

Primavera
University of Chicago, 1212 E. 59th St., Chicago, IL 60637
Publishes poetry and fiction by established and unknown women writers. Until recently, only published work by women, but has started to include work by men as well.

Rambunctious Review
1221 W. Pratt, Chicago, IL 60626
Publishes eclectic collection of stories, poems, drawings, and photographs. Very, very open to new writers. Annual poetry and fiction contest.

Review of Contemporary Fiction
1817 79th Ave., Elmwood Park, IL 60635
Each issue devoted to criticism of one or two contemporary novelists.

Rhino
3815 Foster, Evanston, IL 60203
Published once a year in the fall. Includes well-crafted poems and short prose.

Story Quarterly
P.O. Box 1415, Northbrook, IL 60065
In the same class as *Another Chicago Magazine, New American Writing*, and *Whitewalls*. Publishes short fiction, essays, and interviews.

Tomorrow Magazine
212 N. Sangamon, Chicago, IL 60607
Similar to *Black & White*, bridges the gap between artists and writers. Publishes not only fiction and poetry, but also interviews with artists and even art/fringe rock musicians.

TriQuarterly
Northwestern University, 1735 Benson Ave., Evanston, IL 60201
Absolutely first rate, nationally known literary magazine. Publishes fiction, poetry, and essays by Americans and Europeans.

Vice Versa
c/o Jean Lyons
838 E. 57th, Chicago, IL 60637
Publishes cutting edge poetry and short, short fiction.

Whitewalls
P.O. Box 8204, Chicago, IL 60680
Fascinating triquarterly focusing on writings by visual artists, including journals, essays, even fiction and poetry (when accompanied by images). A recent issue published scripts of Chicago performance artists.

Book Publishers

Academy Chicago, Ltd.
425 N. Michigan, Chicago, IL 60601, 644-1723
Publishes mysteries, feminist novels, biographies, and books of local interest. Books are generally well edited and designed.

Another Chicago Press
P.O. Box 11223, Chicago, IL 60611
Publishes poetry, fiction, drama, or translations. The press is a rising star, publishing young Chicago talents such as James MacManus. Also publishes *Another Chicago Magazine*.

Bonus Books Inc.
160 E. Illinois, Chicago, IL 60611, 467-0580
Quite new, aggressive publisher of trade nonfiction.

Chicago Review Press
814 N. Franklin, Chicago, IL 60610, 337-0747
Fast-growing publisher of trade nonfiction, and books of local interest. Also owns Independent Publishers Group, which provides national distribution for a number of small or specialized publishers.

Contemporary Books
180 N. Michigan Ave., Chicago, IL 60601, 782-9181
Publishes popular nonfiction, especially cookbooks, sports books, how-to books, health and fitness, nutrition, humor, and popular culture. Contemporary Books is at least ten times the size of any other local publisher.

Text and Reference Book Publishers

Chicago has a number of textbook and reference book publishers that employ editors and writers. Some of the larger publishers include: Dryden Press, Encyclopaedia Britannica Inc., Dow Jones-Irwin, Longman Financial Services Publishing, McDougal, Littell & Company, National Textbook Company, World Book, Inc., Year Book Medical Publishers Inc., and Scott, Foresman and Company. For a more complete list of text (and periodical) publishers, refer to *A Writer's Guide to Chicago-Area Publishers*, edited by Jerold L. Kellman (1985).

University Presses

Loyola University Press
3441 N. Ashland
Chicago, IL 60657
281-1818

University of Chicago Press
5801 S. Ellis
Chicago, IL 60637
702-7700

Northwestern University Press
Box 1093X
1735 Benson Ave.
Evanston, IL 60201
492-5313

Professional Organizations

Chicago Book Clinic
100 E. Ohio, Suite 630, Chicago, IL 60611, 951-8254
Open to anyone involved or interested in all aspects of publishing. Sponsors educational programs on all facets of bookmaking, including monthly meetings with a wide range of topics. Holds an annual book show for book designers. Every two years, holds PubTech, a publishing trade show with concurrent seminars. Co-sponsors a professional publishing education program.

Chicago Women in Publishing
645 N. Michigan, Suite 1058, Chicago, IL 60611, 951-5277
Primarily for (but not limited to) women working or interested in any area of publishing. Good place for networking. Strong program of educational monthly meetings features speakers and panels. Monthly newsletter and annual directory, and annual Career Carousel.

Independent Writers of Chicago
645 N. Michigan, Suite 1058, Chicago, IL 60611, 951-9114
Organization primarily for but not exclusive to professional free-lance writers. Monthly meetings, educational seminars, monthly newsletter, referral service for free-lance jobs, and annual directory.

P.E.N. Midwest
Contact: Phyllis Moore, University of Illinois at Chicago, College of
Liberal Arts and Sciences, Department of English (M/C 162), Box 4348,
Chicago, IL 60680, 413-2200
For poets, playwrights, editors, essayists, and novelists. Events include
readings by authors and panels. You can be an associate member for $10 a
year, but full members of P.E.N. are voted on by a membership committee
in New York.

—Jack Helbig, Melanie Kubale

MEDIA

Tribune Tower. Photo by Glenn Kaupert.

LOCAL PRESS

Chicago used to be one of the ultimate newspaper towns. In the days when a dozen dailies were published here, Chicago attracted the likes of Ben Hecht, Ring Lardner, and hundreds of other young journalists who wanted to try their luck and learn their trade in the city by the lake. Things have changed, however. We only have two major dailies left, and television is a heavy competitor.

It's happening all across the nation—increasingly, people depend on television for their news. Newspapers are mimicking television to survive, resulting in the *People*-ization of news in print, with more gossip in the hard-news sections, and more "soft" news in general. Perhaps more ominous, papers are being run solely as businesses. In some cities, even papers making a small profit have been retired.

The current state of Chicago's print media reflects these changes. Whereas in the early 1970s, four major dailies competed for the attention of Chicagoans, only two big dailies remain: the **Chicago Tribune** and the **Chicago Sun-Times**. While the major dailies have decreased in number, however, the number of smaller dailies serving specific communities and special interest groups in the city and suburbs have increased. Currently, a dozen dailies are published in the metropolitan area, including the big two.

Despite the nationwide trend toward softer news, the Chicago media maintain a tradition of scrappy competition. This has always been an exciting town for reporters, and the 1980s have been no different. Endless City Council battles, the Greylord investigations of judicial corruption, and the crumbling Democratic Party political machine are only a few of the biggest stories that make this a good place for journalists to be.

In fact, many national news people got their start in Chicago—many of them at the **City News Bureau of Chicago,** the country's first cooperative agency for metropolitan news gathering. Established in the late 1800s, the City News Bureau is a hard-news boot camp and, despite the low pay, every fresh journalism grad's ideal first job out of school. The Bureau's wires are the first source for many of the stories that appear in all of the city's media— print, radio, and TV. Once you get in (it's hard), the Bureau is a tough beat, and there's plenty of competition. But those journalists who survive its rigors are often the future stars of the city's and the nation's newsrooms. A few noted alums of CNB are *Chicago Tribune* columnist Mike Royko, NBC newsman John Chancellor, investigative reporter Pam Zekman (formerly of the *Sun-Times* and currently at channel 2), novelist Kurt Vonnegut, and artist Claes Oldenberg.

DAILIES

Of the city's two biggest dailies, the *Tribune* is the more thoughtful and thorough when covering national and international news. The paper does a good job giving the reader in-depth background for its main news stories. Reporters spend a considerable amount of time unearthing facts before a story comes to print. A wealthy paper with a large staff, the *Trib* is aimed at a middle- to upper-class audience. It is on the dull side and gives short shrift to local stories, especially if they originate on the south or west sides. You'll seldom see an inner-city resident reading this paper. But readers downstate usually turn to the *Tribune* for news about Chicago.

The *Tribune's* strong suit is the long special report. Recently, such reports covered such diverse topics as the economy of the Soviet Union and mass transit in the nation's suburbs. The *Tribune's* coverage of local business news is good. The arts and culture critics in the *Trib* are especially strong, most notably Alan G. Artner on art, Richard Christiansen on theater and opera, Paul Gapp on architecture, Dave Kehr and Gene Siskel on movies, and Larry Kart on everything else.

The *Tribune* carries one of the best columnists in the country, Pulitzer Prize-winning Mike Royko. Royko epitomizes Chicago—his tough, sarcastic, yet tender-hearted style may be all that's left of the Chicago school of journalism. Royko writes some of the best political commentary in the city: he leads public opinion with every column. His book *Boss* was both the first and final word on Hizzoner duh Mare.

Another popular *Tribune* columnist, Bob Greene, on the other hand, writes a softer column. Some of his past columns have focused on such hard-hitting topics as the new Betty Crocker, the return of Clove gum, and his own never-ending surprise at being an adult. Greene devotes an inordinate amount of space to reminding readers he attended a certain North Shore university.

The *Tribune's* parent company, the Tribune Company, is a powerful media force. It also owns WGN ("World's Greatest Newspaper") TV—the national cable channel 9—and radio, as well as other television and radio stations and newspapers around the country, and the Chicago Cubs.

For years the *Trib* could be counted on to endorse the Republican candidates during elections, and to take conservative stands on all the issues. Now, however, the paper has edged its way to a more moderate stance, opposing Ronald Reagan almost as often as it supports Mayor Harold Washington.

The **Sun-Times** offers more consistent and thorough coverage of daily city life than the *Trib*. This may be an example of a paper knowing its audience—the *Sun-Times* far outsells the *Trib* in the city (and conversely, the *Trib* far outsells the *Sun-Times* in the suburbs). Surprisingly, the *Sun-Times* virtually ignores the black and Hispanic communities, even though the *Sun-Times* outsells the *Tribune* in both communities.

The *Sun-Times* often gets the scoop on local stories and has built up quite a reputation for investigative journalism, but occasionally they may have gone too far to get a story. Once the paper conducted an Abscam-like investigation of city inspections by opening a tavern (called ironically, the Mirage) to catch city inspectors in the act of soliciting bribes.

Media merchant Rupert Murdoch's purchase of the *Sun-Times* in 1983 brought *National Enquirer*-style headlines to the city: "Rabbi hit in sex-slavery suit" and "Man drives over own head." After the purchase, some of the *Sun-Times'* finest reporters and columnists, including Mike Royko, defected to the *Tribune*. For a while thereafter, many Chicagoans were certain the *Sun-Times* would go down the tubes. They were wrong. Most of Murdoch's changes were superficial and the paper's coverage of local news remained strong.

Murdoch was forced to sell the *Sun-Times* after he bought local TV station WFLD (channel 32). The new owner, Robert Page, vowed to make the

Sun-Times a more "serious" paper, tone down the sensational headlines, and—more to the point—create an environment in which upscale advertisers are more likely to feel comfortable.

The *Sun-Times'* strengths are its excellent coverage of local news, politics, and sports. Its arts coverage is improving; Roger Ebert continues to write intelligently about movies. The *Sun-Times'* sports writing is especially fresh and gritty—look for features by Ron Rapoport and Kevin Lamb. Even high school athletics are covered thoroughly—no one is ignored.

The *Chicago Daily Defender,* founded in 1905, was at one time the only forum for news about the black community by the black community. The *Defender* was in the past very influential and widely read among blacks in Chicago. In recent years, however, the quality of writing and reporting has deteriorated significantly; yet young black journalists still use the *Defender* as a place to hone their skills. Although circulation for the *Defender* has dipped dramatically in the past 25 years, the black community still looks to the *Defender* as a voice—albeit a conservative one—of the community.

Chicago Tribune, 435 N. Michigan Ave., Chicago, IL 60611   222-3232
Chicago Sun-Times, 401 N. Wabash Ave., Chicago, IL 60611   321-3000
Chicago Daily Defender, 2400 S. Michigan Ave., Chicago, IL 60616
   225-2400

WEEKLIES AND MONTHLIES

The *Reader* is Chicago's liberal, well-written, free weekly. Once produced on publisher and editor Robert Roth's dining-room table, the *Reader* is now one of the most successful free weeklies in the country. But the *Reader* is not a newspaper in the traditional sense—with few exceptions, it doesn't have reporters with designated "beats," nor does it assign stories. In fact, it discourages "hard" news and editorial writing. The paper therefore can't be counted on to report on major news items; rather, it functions more as a writer's forum that frequently tackles controversial issues and topics. The "Hot Type" column provides behind-the-scenes scoops on local media. Good entertainment writing and handsome graphics are other strengths of the *Reader.*

The writing in the *Reader* is usually excellent. Keep an eye out for articles by Michael Miner, Robert McClory, and Marcia Froelke Coburn. The listings in the *Reader* are the your best guide to the week's concerts, club dates, plays, and movies. The housing classifieds are a great place to start looking for an apartment, while the other classifieds are excellent sources of information on lectures and events sponsored by special interest groups, as well as ways to meet unusual people.

You'll find *Readers* on Thursdays throughout the north side in bookstores, bars, record stores, and restaurants. The *Reader* also has a more limited distribution in the Loop, in Hyde Park, and the suburbs of Oak Park and Evanston. Grab a *Reader* quickly when you see a stack of them—the paper has a large and loyal following, and piles of papers disappear quickly.

Crain's Chicago Business is a weekly, and one of the most comprehensive and well-written sources of Chicago's business news, as well as city politics and education. When it first began, *Crain's* often scooped the rest of the press and forced the other papers to address issues they were ignoring. Read *Crain's* to keep up with business as well as other city issues.

The Chicago Reporter is a prize-winning monthly full of solid journalism covering race relations in the city and suburbs. The *Reporter* sometimes scoops the majors and in general covers racial and other issues ignored by the other papers.

Every large city has its glossy monthly magazine, and **Chicago** magazine is ours. Originally a magazine listing the programming for classical music radio station WFMT, *Chicago* evolved into a useful but snooty guide to city and suburban restaurants, cultural events, and programming schedules for WFMT and the PBS television affiliate, WTTW, channel 11. The feature articles are often provocative. Note: *Chicago* magazine's recent sale to the publisher of *Metropolitan Detroit* may change the publication substantially. As of this writing, the changes haven't exactly bowled anyone over. The new management promises a grittier approach—let's hope they do a better job of covering the city beyond the borders of the north lakefront.

An interesting new addition to publications about the city is *Inside Chicago.* This bi-monthly magazine has a hip look (lots of white space and new-style graphics) and tone, as well as more unusual, interesting feature articles, such as the recent "The Prostitute's Priest." Its coverage of city entertainment and restaurants is strong and less staid than *Chicago* magazine's.

Reader
11 E. Illinois St.
Chicago, IL 60611
828-0350

Crain's Chicago Business
740 N. Rush St.
Chicago, IL 60611
649-5200

The Chicago Reporter
18 S. Michigan Ave., #1200
Chicago, IL 60603
236-4830

Chicago
303 E. Wacker Dr.
Chicago, IL 60601
565-5000

Inside Chicago
2501 W. Peterson Ave.
Chicago, IL 60659
784-0800

Chicago Times
180 N. Michigan Ave.
Chicago, IL 60601
372-6612

NEIGHBORHOOD PAPERS

Over the last 10 years, the number of neighbohood papers has grown substantially. Some are very good: the *Back of the Yards Journal* serving the south-side city neighborhood by that name, the *Wednesday Journal of Oak Park and River Forest*, the *Southtown Economist* serving the southwest side and suburbs, and the *Daily Herald* in Arlington Heights. Papers such as the *New City Guide* (south Loop) often lead in the gentrification of neighborhoods, giving a certain legitimacy and voice to areas still trying to establish themselves as "real" neighborhoods.

Generally, neighborhood papers are good sources of information on local hot issues, crime statistics, and great classified ads for apartments and goods. If you've ever dreamed of being a journalist, neighborhood papers are a good place to start. You can buy neighborhood papers (or pick the free ones up) in local grocery stores or newsstands.

Citizens Newspapers
412 E. 87th St., Chicago, IL 60619   487-7700
Publishes papers (e.g., *Chatham Citizen, Southend Citizen*) for south and southeast city neighborhoods and suburbs such as Chatham, Harvey, Markham, and Robbins.

Lerner Newspapers
7519 N. Ashland Ave., Chicago, IL 60620   761-7200
Publishes good-quality community papers for north and northwest city areas and suburbs such as Lakeview, Harlem-Foster, Harlem-Higgins, Norwood Park, Edgewater, Ravenswood, and Lincoln Park.

Nadig Newspapers
4941 N. Milwaukee Ave., Chicago, IL 60630   286-6100
Papers for northwest side and north suburban areas. In the city, coverage includes the areas of Jefferson Park, Edison Park, Mayfair, Albany Park, Edgebrook, Sauganash, Irving Park, and Lincolnwood. Suburban coverage includes Park Ridge, Niles, Skokie, and Des Plaines.

Pioneer Press
1232 Central, Wilmette, IL 60091   251-4300
Papers for northern suburbs such as Glencoe, Glenview, Niles, Evanston, and Wilmette; also Oak Park and Maywood.

Southtown Economist
5959 S. Harlem Ave., Chicago, IL 60638   586-8800
One of the best neighborhood papers, this thick daily serves the southwest side and surrounding suburbs. The same organization publishes the Hyde Park Herald, 5240 S. Harper, 643-8533.

Southwest News Herald
6225 S. Kedzie, Chicago, IL 60629   476-4800
Chicago's largest community newspaper.

Wednesday Journal of Oak Park and River Forest
141 S. Oak Park, Oak Park, IL 60302   524-8300
Good free weekly covering news in Oak Park and River Forest.

Other neighborhood papers of note: the ***Logan Square Free Press*** serving that northwest side neighborhood; the ***Brighton Park-McKinley Park Life*** on the southwest side; and the ***Hegewisch News***, serving that neighborhood on the southeast side of the city.

ETHNIC AND BLACK PAPERS

An incredible number of ethnic papers are published in Chicago, many in the languages of their readers. Some ethnic papers are concerned mostly with the social activities of their alliances and associations, but others devote substantial space to political issues. Sometimes these papers offer the only forum for issues and ideas vitally important to their readers but deemed unimportant by the big papers.

You can buy ethnic papers in the newsstands, grocery stores, and restaurants of the communities they serve, or find them in local libraries. Otherwise, call the main office listed below and ask where they can be bought. The sampling of ethnic and black papers that follows should give you an idea of how much is printed in Chicago.

BLACK

The Chicago Metro News
2600 S. Michigan, #308
Chicago, IL 60616
842-5950
Black-oriented weekly.

Muslim Journal
7801 S. Cottage Grove
Chicago, IL 60619
651-7600
Political weekly.

CROATIAN

Croatian Danica
4851 S. Drexel Blvd.
Chicago, IL 60615
268-2819
Weekly Croatian-language paper.

CZECH

Hlas Naroda
2657-9 S. Lawndale Ave.
Chicago, IL 60623
762-2044
Czech-language weekly with one
English-language page.

Denni Hlasatel
6426 Cermak Rd.
Berwyn, IL 60402
749-1891
Only Czech daily published in the
western hemisphere, coming out of
Berwyn's sizeable Czech
community.

DANISH

Den Danske Pioneer
Bertelsen Publishing Co.
1582 Glen Lake Rd.
Hoffman Estates, IL 60195
882-2552
English and Danish bimonthly.

GERMAN

Abendpost-Sonntagpost
55 E. Jackson
Chicago, IL 60604
368-4800
One of the oldest German- and
English-language papers in the
city.

GREEK

The Greek Star
4710 N. Lincoln Ave.
Chicago, IL 60625
878-7331
English-language paper with some
pages in Greek. Covers local,
national, and international news.

HUNGARIAN

Amerikai-Kanadai Magyar Elet
3636 N. Paris
Chicago, IL 60634
625-8774
Largest Hungarian-language
weekly in the U.S.

INDIAN

India Tribune
3955 W. Lawrence
Chicago, IL 60625
583-6150
English-language weekly carrying
mostly city news.

IRISH

The Irish American News
2500 W. Higgins Rd., Suite 1115
Hoffman Estates, IL 60195
882-4410
Monthly with national syndication.

KOREAN

Hankook Ilbo (Korea Times)
4460 N. Kedzie
Chicago, IL 60630
463-1050
Daily paper in English and
Korean.

LITHUANIAN

Draugas
4545 W. 63rd St.
Chicago, IL 60629
585-9500
Aimed at post-World War II
immigrants, and generally more
conservative in tone. Published by
the Lithuanian Catholic Press.
Largest circulation of any
Lithuanian daily in the U.S.

POLISH

Polish Daily Zgoda
6100 N. Cicero Ave.
Chicago, IL 60646
286-0141
Widely read Polish-language paper
serving Chicago's great Polish
community.

SCANDINAVIAN

Vinland
518 Davis St.
Evanston, IL 60201
492-1828
Bimonthly English-language paper
serving the Scandinavian
community in the midwest.

SERBIAN

Sloboda
3950 W. North Ave.
Chicago, IL 60647
772-7878
Serbian-language paper.

SPANISH-LANGUAGE PAPERS

La Raza
3909 N. Ashland Ave.
Chicago, IL 60613
525-9400
Largest Spanish-language
newspaper in the midwest, this
weekly covers political events in
Central and South American as
well as events in local Hispanic
communities.

El Heraldo
3734 W. 26th St.
Chicago, IL 60623
521-8300
Published in the Czech-turned-
Mexican about-to-gentrify Pilsen
neighborhood, this paper delivers
to most Hispanic areas.

El Manana
2700 S. Harding
Chicago, IL 60623
521-9137
Daily newspaper covering city
news as well as news from Central
and South American, for all
Hispanic groups.

UKRAINIAN

New Star Ukrainian Catholic Weekly
2208 W. Chicago Ave.
Chicago, IL 60622
772-1919
Ukrainian- and English-language
weekly, covering local and national
events of interest to the tightly knit
Ukrainian community in the city
and suburbs.

SPECIALTY PUBLICATIONS

Some high-quality, nationally recognized specialty publications originate in
Chicago. Note especially *Down Beat*, the jazz magazine, and *Ebony* and

Jet, successful magazines written for a black audience and distributed nationally.

You can find some of the following publications at local newsstands, depending on where you live, or at the better bookstores—for example, Guild Books, 2456 N. Lincoln; if not, call the main office at the number listed below.

ART

New Art Examiner
300 W. Grand Ave., #620, Chicago, IL 60610   836-0330
A nationally distributed magazine that began publishing here during the heyday of the Chicago Imagists. Covers painting, sculpture, video art, and performing arts.

BLACK LIFESTYLE

Ebony, EM, Jet
Johnson Publications
820 S. Michigan Ave., Chicago, IL 60605   322-9200
Years ago, John Johnson saw a big void in magazine-format coverage of black life—basically there was none. He began publishing *Ebony* magazine (a glossy magazine emphasizing fashion, entertainment, and news) in 1945; *Jet* magazine (news format with entertainment features) in 1951; and *EM* (a black men's magazine focusing on fashion and features) in the 1970s. All three are distributed nationally. Today, Johnson's daughter, Linda Johnson Rice, oversees his publishing empire.

Dollars & Sense
1610 E. 79th St., Chicago, IL 60649   375-6800
Covers the black business community as well as cultural and political affairs.

CATHOLIC

The Chicago Catholic
155 E. Superior, Chicago, IL 60611   751-8311
Traditional newspaper of the country's largest Catholic diocese.

GAY AND LESBIAN

Windy City Times
Sentury Publications, Inc.
3225 N. Sheffield, Chicago, IL 60657   935-1790
Free weekly that carries good local, national, and international news of interest to gays and lesbians. Complete listings of organizations, bars, and restaurants. Pick it up at bookstores, restaurants, and bars on the north side (especially in the New Town area) and in Hyde Park.

Chicago Outlines
1300 W. Belmont, Chicago, IL 60657   871-7610
Chicago's newest lesbian and gay newspaper. Covers local, regional, and national news and has listings of lesbian and gay organizations, bars, and restaurants. Available free in gay and lesbian bookstores and bars, and other locations around the city.

JOURNALISM

The Quill
840 N. Lake Shore Dr., Suite 801W
Chicago, IL 60611
Professional journal for journalists.

LAW

Chicago Lawyer
20 E. Jackson, Suite 300, Chicago, IL 60604   939-7150
Investigative magazine for the legal profession, well read on LaSalle Street.
Published monthly.

MUSIC

Down Beat
222 W. Adams, Chicago, IL 60606
Started here in 1934, has a national reputation as a jazz magazine. Has
expanded coverage to include other types of music.

Illinois Entertainer
2200 E. Devon, #192, Des Plaines, IL 60018   298-9333
Started in 1974, a free magazine for all-around coverage of Illinois popular
entertainment and performing arts, with an emphasis on local rock. Especially good coverage of local bands. Provides the suburbs with their equivalent of the *Reader's* comprehensive entertainment coverage. Pick it up in
record stores.

POLITICS

In These Times
1300 W. Belmont, Chicago, IL 60657   472-5700
Well-written, independent socialist weekly. Considered the most objective
of this category of publications and well respected by the left.

The Public Eye
343 S. Dearborn, #918, Chicago, IL 60604
Civil rights journal.

NEWSSTANDS

Chicago Main Newsstand
Intersection of Chicago Ave. and
Main St., Evanston
864-2727
A wonderful newsstand, with the
largest selection of local, national,
and international papers in the
area.

Kroch's and Brentano's
29 S. Wabash
332-7500
The Wabash Kroch's store has a
limited selection of out-of-town
and foreign newspapers.

News Two
2939 N. Broadway
281-7696
Good selection of papers, including
some foreign ones.

**Licoln-Halsted-Fullerton
Newsstand**
Intersection of Lincoln-Halsted-
Fullerton. Open 24 hours.

—Margaret Maloney

RADIO

The growth in the number (and influence) of FM stations in Chicago over the last two decades has led to unprecedented competition for listeners. Chicagoans have a choice of radio stations broader now than it has been for years. But don't blink. With the federal government withdrawing from the business of regulating radio, stations now change formats and call-letters with the weather. It's a case of "hear today, gone tomorrow."

ROCK

WXRT (93.1 FM) has won a nationwide reputation as a progressive, adventurous rock radio station. It isn't as eclectic as it was in the early '70s, particularly during the daytime hours. But it still plays a selection of music broader than that of any other station in town. It plays a lot of new music, breaking songs and artists well before they make the playlists elsewhere. And it mixes in some oldies (from the '50s on), blues, jazz, and comedy. It offers several weekly special programs—including a jazz show, a blues show, and a unique oldies show, "Saturday Morning Flashback," which features music, news, and nostalgia from a single year each week. WXRT offers one thing its competitors in this category don't: serious newscasts, morning and afternoon.

Once a month, 'XRT publishes a card listing the artists to be featured each day; it's available at record and book stores.

The music on **WLUP (98.1 FM)** isn't as adventurous as WXRT's, but "The Loop" (as it's known) courts much the same audience. It sticks to the rock of the '60s, '70s, and '80s.

WCKG (105.9 FM) covers a lot of the same musical ground that WLUP covers, but with more emphasis on the album-rock of the '70s and less emphasis on DJ personalities.

For the most aggressive new-music programming in Chicago, check out the non-commercial end of the FM band: Northwestern University's **WNUR (89.3)**. Its format changes through the day—but it's one of the more successful college stations in town. Be warned: Once you leave the north suburbs and the north side of Chicago, reception is spotty.

A small commercial station based in Chicago's north suburbs, **WVVX (103.1 FM)**, also offers a heavy-metal rock show during the evenings. But because the station is time-brokered, its programming changes every few hours.

WZRC, at **106.7 FM,** offers heavy metal 24 hours a day.

POP AND TOP-40, OLD AND NEW

The FM dial is filled with stations offering some combination of these. They go through call-letter combinations like popcorn; more often than not in the '80s, when a company bought a radio station here, the first format it tried would be pop-adult. ("Mom"-adult would be more like it; they seem to target a mainly female audience.)

The music on **WFYR (103.5 FM)** and **WCLR (101.9 FM)** most clearly fits the pop-adult category. Both offer a safe, pre-tested brand of soft rock, new and old—sort of the McDonald's of radio stations. WCLR bills itself as "Lite Rock." That says it all, doesn't it?

They both offer serious newscasts, but WFYR's news programming has shrunken considerably from the mid-70s, when it made a splash as Chicago's first "full-service" FM. Both stations offer non-stop oldies on Saturday nights. WFYR's show is nationally syndicated (it was created here) and includes more from the '50s and early '60s. WCLR's show skews toward the '60s and '70s.

WKQX (101.1 FM) offers a slightly harder brand of rock; **WCZE (820 AM)** and **WLAK (93.9 FM)** play softer pop music, with an emphasis on vocals.

WJMK (104.3 FM) plays nothing but rock oldies. Its line-up includes a couple of DJs who played the songs when they were originally hits on Chicago's AM dial.

WBBM (96.3 FM) is a teen- and pre-teen-oriented station with a "hot hits" format—nothing but the hits, although the definition of "hit" seems to widen and narrow based on what the competition is doing. **WYTZ (94.7 FM)** seems to aim for a slightly older audience; its format includes some songs older than a year or two.

WRXR (95.5 FM) is the newest of the bunch, as far as call-letters go. It's the closest descendant of traditional Top-40 radio in Chicago, offering hits—and nothing but the hits—new and old.

NEWS/TALK

Back before almost every cluster of towns in the nation had at least one radio station, dozens of AM stations around the country were granted exclusive rights to use certain frequencies. The original concept was for those stations—known as "clear-channel stations"—to serve broad regions of the country. More often than not, the result has been stations with appeal so broad they're boring.

Chicago has several clear-channel stations; most of them deal mainly in talk or news.

Traditionally the most-listened-to station in town, **WGN (720 AM)**, offers a mix of talk, sports, news and middle-of-the-road music. As a Tribune Company station, it has a lock on broadcast rights for its sister organization, the Chicago Cubs. It also carries the Bears, forcing it to shuffle any simultaneous Cubs games to another station during the fall. If you're looking for a literate talk-show host, try Milt Rosenberg—when he's not pre-empted by nighttime sports.

WLS (890 AM) for years was the undisputed king of rock radio in Chicago. But with the defection of the rock audience to FM, WLS is shifting toward a talk format featuring rock music—relatively tame rock music. Its news operation once served as a shining example of public service on a music station; now, its reporters are more likely to serve as foils for its "air personalities," as the industry calls them.

As of press time, **WLUP (1000 AM)** had just assumed control of what used to be WCFL. The long-range plan reportedly is to transform it into a hip talk-and-sports station, centered on Steve Dahl and Garry Meier, whose irreverent, scattered, and scatological humor has won them a large and devoted following—and a similarly large league of detractors. They hold some financial interest in the new station. As of this writing, it was mostly just simulcasting the FM station's programs.

WBBM (780 AM) is Chicago's only news station. Despite its mediocre writing and its dull reporters, almost every news room in town keeps a radio tuned to "NewsRadio 78," because it's usually the first to break news in Chicago. It rushes everything on the air, no matter how trivial. It also relies heavily on the resources of its parent organization, CBS. (It's not all-news; the evenings and weekends are filled with sports, vintage radio, and talk shows.)

WMAQ (670 AM) has been a country station for years. As of this writing, it's steering toward a talk-oriented format. It also carries the White Sox games.

WBEZ (91.5 FM) isn't a clear-channel station, but it boasts a news staff larger than that of any other FM station in Chicago. Considering that it also carries National Public Radio's (long-winded but informative) "Morning Edition," "All Things Considered," and "Weekend Edition," WBEZ is a formidable competitor for WBBM-AM during morning and afternoon "drive time." (But its audience is far smaller.)

WBEZ also offers some of the only radio programming in Chicago for children and teen-agers—both produced locally: "Airplay," billed as a sort of "All Things Considered" for kids; and "Zoo Party," broadcast from Chicago's Lincoln Park Zoo.

JAZZ

Chicago radio's one major weakness: No full-time FM jazz station.

WBEE (1570 AM) bills itself as "all-jazz." But FCC rules have restricted it to daytime-only operation. That will probably change; as of this writing, the FCC has just granted WBEE permission to broadcast 24 hours a day. In any event, because its signal originates in the south suburb of Harvey, you can't pick it up easily once you leave the south side.

You'll probably be able to fill the rest of the day with jazz by tuning around the FM dial, but it won't be easy.

Public radio station **WBEZ (91.5 FM)** offers more jazz than you'll find anywhere else on the FM dial—mostly at night—but it competes with lots of special programming, including extensive material from National Public Radio. (WBEZ publishes a monthly program guide, available by mail.) **WXRT** incorporates some jazz into its regular day and programs four hours on Sunday evening, "Jazz Transfusion."

Several high-school and college stations also program some jazz. You'll find them clustered at the low end of the FM dial.

BLACK/SOUL

The radio profession now refers to this as "urban contemporary." Its three major practitioners in Chicago are **WGCI (107.5 FM and 1390 AM), WBMX**

(102.7 FM), and **WJPC (950 AM)**. WGCI generally draws more whites than do the other two stations, partly because it plays more blue-eyed soul ("crossover music," in the jargon of the industry). WBMX seems to offer a slightly grittier, more urban mix of music.

CLASSICAL

WFMT (98.6 FM) and **WNIB (97.1 FM)** offer classical music almost full-time. WNIB plays more instrumental music; WFMT offers more opera. WFMT's announcers drone on more than WNIB's, partly because—unlike 'NIB—WFMT refuses to run pre-recorded commercials. (While we're on the subject, do you really want to know the catalog number of every recording?)

WFMT's schedule (which is detailed in *Chicago* magazine, available at newsstands) also includes a talk show hosted by Pulitzer-Prize-winning author Studs Terkel and, on Saturday nights, the grand-daddy of progressive radio, The Midnight Special—comedy, acoustic folk music, and a variety of work by local performers.

WNIB is a rarity: a commercial station that solicits listener support, in the form of subscriptions to its program guide.

Other Stations

It's a dying art, but **radio drama** can still be heard on **WBEZ**, although most of it originates elsewhere in the public-radio system. And old-time radio fan Chuck Schaden has made a career of re-broadcasting a hodgepodge of shows from radio's golden age, on a hodgepodge of radio stations— **WBBM-AM** and **WNIB**, among others.

WJJD (1160 AM) is the closest you'll come to a full-time **big-band** station . . .but be prepared to sit through some Engelbert Humperdinck, too.

WUSN (99.5 FM) is the only full-time **country** station on the dial in Chicago.

WLOO (100.3 FM). If you use a lower-case "L" to write the call-letters, it looks like W-100; "FM-100"—get it? That's the most interesting thing about this station. Great music to accompany root-canal work.

With most music-lovers defecting to FM and with the average age of the AM listener rising, **religion** represents one of the most profitable formats on the AM dial. Many smaller AM stations program plenty of it.

Of course, the dial is loaded with religious shows on Sunday.

During the week, **WMBI (1110 AM** and **90.1 FM;** the call letters stand for Moody Bible Institute) dominates the field.

Two full-time **Spanish-language** stations serve Chicago: **WIND (560 AM)** and **WOJO (105.1 FM)**. Your correspondent has a hard time describing their programming because his Spanish extends no further than the ability to count to ten.

You'll find plenty of other Spanish (and other foreign-language) programming scattered around the clock and around the dial, mostly on small AM stations that sell time wholesale to ethnic broadcasters who, in turn, retail air time to advertisers.

HAPPY HUNTING!

This survey doesn't come close to being a complete account of stations or formats. With good equipment, you can receive close to a hundred stations in the metropolitan area.

If you're fortunate enough to live in a Chicago suburb with its own radio station (Waukegan, Elgin, Geneva, Aurora, or Joliet, for instance), you may find listening worthwhile. They get only a fraction of the audience the Chicago stations attract; but they're often a faster, more accessible source of news than the small community newspapers that serve the same areas.

If you're arriving here from a smaller town, you may find Chicago's array of radio stations bewildering. It's easy to settle for just one station that seems to meet your needs. But don't. Listening to the radio is one of the easiest, quickest ways to plug into Chicago's culture. And sampling a lot of stations can accelerate the process. Besides, conversation about radio is a great ice-breaker at parties; the more stations you listen to, the better you'll be prepared to participate.

—Bryen Charles

PEOPLE

Photo by Glenn Kaupert.

KIDS

Chicago is loaded with great places to go to and wonderful things for kids to do. Between museums that offer weekend workshops, park programs, library story hours, amusement parks, theater productions, and zoo events, kids can be actively participating in something different every week of the year. It's amazing how many people in Chicago go out of their way to do something special for children. Many programs are free, many others inexpensive. Some require advance registration, but many don't. In any case, whatever your children's interests are, they can be enhanced by the offerings in Chicago.

MUSEUMS

The Museum of Science and Industry (57th and Lake Shore Drive) is a wonderland for kids: they could spend weeks there and not experience everything. With the coal mine, the U-505 submarine, Colleen Moore's Fairy Castle, and Yesterday's Main Street, to name only a few of the exhibits, kids will be delighted and awed by this museum. The Curiosity Place is specifically for children under 7, offering activities in light, motion, force and sound. The Hall of Communications is loaded with buttons to push, phones to use, and games to play. The best thing about this museum is the fact that so much of it involves active participation. You don't just look, you experience.

The Crown Space Center is a must-see for aspiring astronauts. The extensive exhibits on air and space travel captivate adults and children alike. Several spacecraft are on view; displays even include such oddities as the leftover Tang from a space mission. In the same wing is the Omnimax Theater, featuring spectacular films on a 5-story domed screen. Past showings have included a space shuttle flight and a rafting trip through the Grand Canyon. Working parents should note that the Space Center and Omnimax Theater are open late on weekday evenings (except Monday). Call 684-1414 for hours.

The museum also offers classes and workshops on the weekends, focusing on topics like electricity, the body, energy, and sound. Preschoolers can get involved in science too, with classes that offer hands-on activities. Many other programs are available. Call 684-1414 for more information.

The Field Museum of Natural History (South Lake Shore Drive and Roosevelt Road) is also full of exhibits kids will love. There are huge dinosaurs, Egyptian mummies, replicas of old Native American dwellings, and recreations of prehistoric people. The Place of Wonder is the special stop for kids as all the exhibits there are touchable.

On weekends, family workshops are offered covering all kinds of topics. "Come to Your Senses" explores each sense, week by week, through performance, demonstration, and activities. Forms of communication are explored in "Now You See It, Now You Don't", featuring tongue-twisters,

213

limericks, chimes, and a performance by a mime. Many more programs of this kind are available for all aged children, and they're free with museum admission. Call 322-8854 for more information.

The Art Institute of Chicago (Michigan and Adams). The Junior Museum at the Art Institute offers an amazing assortment of activities for children and families, including workshops, demonstrations, and tours. All programs are free (with museum admission) and involve children of all ages.

On Saturdays and Sundays, activities include workshops in costume-making, drawing, mask-making, food art, and face painting, to name a few. There are Assorted Stories by Assorted Tellers in the Little Library on Sundays, and guided gallery walks on Saturdays. Artist demonstrations cover such topics as bookmaking, puppet making, and Japanese calligraphy.

Special games for children 6 years and older are available daily in the Little Library. The games "I Spy" and "Bits and Pieces" send children throughout the museum searching works of art for clues and answers. All finishers receive a prize.

For more information about times and dates call the museum at 443-3680.

The Shedd Aquarium (1200 S. Lake Shore Drive). The Aquarium, also known as "The Ocean by the Lake", is a wonderful place for kids to go just to see the fishy exhibits. Behind the scenes, though, there are also classes and workshops offered every year for children and their families.

In the fall, winter, and spring, classes are on Saturdays and Sundays, and are designed for children ages 3 to 16. All classes include an arts and crafts project, activities, and games, and are both educational and fun. The classes for older children also involve lab work. Topics covered include "Aquatic Mammals: Seals and Walruses;" "Fish Printing;" "Your First Fish;" and "Freshwater Predators." In the summer classes are offered during the week.

On weekends throughout the year family tours are available, taking you behind the scenes at the museum. Each tour follows a single theme, such as exploring the watering system, the feeding system, or the collection procedures at the museum. The Coral Reef exhibit is another special attraction: watch divers feed the fish several times a day.

For more information call 939-2426, extension 377.

O **The Adler Planetarium** (1300 S. Lake Shore Drive). The planetarium also offers classes and shows especially for children.

Sky shows run daily throughout the year in both the Kroc Universe Theater and the Sky Theater, for children 6 years and older. Special sky shows for children under 6 are shown every Saturday morning, and these shows change four or five times a year. In the "Wonderful Rocket" show, Rodney the Rocket leads children on a trip to the planets. In December the "Winter Star" show focuses on the Northern Star and how it guided the three wise men.

Classes at the museum are held Saturday mornings and are designed for specific age groups ranging from 3 to 4 and 10 to 12. Topics covered in the classes answer questions like: Where is the night two weeks long? Are shooting stars really stars? Which planet has a pink sky? Can you spin as fast as Jupiter? Many classes involve arts and crafts projects, and the classes for children 7 and older also involve computers and telescopes.

For more information call the Planetarium at 322-0323.

The Kohl Children's Museum (165 Green Bay Road, Wilmette) calls itself "a place to pretend, invent, touch, explore, discover, learn", and that's exactly what it is. The Museum is one of two in the Chicago area designed especially for children in the new trend of hands-on, active participation for visitors rather than the old exhibit-under-glass type of deal. Mainly for children ages 2 to 10, the museum offers a stimulating and fun environment geared toward learning through doing.

Exhibits at the museum include "Bubblemania"—an excursion into creative bubble-making; "Who Am I?"—dress-up and face painting fun; "Walk Through Jerusalem"—a journey to the old city including costumes, bread-baking, and an underground tunnel; and "Jim Shorts Health Club"—an exercise in fitness and nutrition awareness.

Along with the exhibits, which rotate throughout the year to keep the museum fresh and exciting, there are weekly story times, puppet shows, and special holiday events. **The Learning Store** at the museum offers a large variety of creative, hard-to-find, educational toys.

For more information call 251-7781.

Express-Ways Children's Museum (2045 N. Lincoln Park West) is the other hands-on museum designed especially for children. As at the Kohl Museum, every exhibit involves visitor participation, including arts and crafts, and sights and sounds.

Exhibits include "Touchy Business"—a tactile tunnel; "Good Fib'rations"—more than a dozen activities dealing with fibers and their uses; "Colorforms"—a huge geometric mural in motion; and "Recycled Arts Center"—a model house made from nothing but recycled junk.

Photo by Glenn Kaupert.

On Saturdays and Sundays family workshops deal with such topics as leaf batiks, bulb planting, and recycled art. Special holiday programs are scheduled during the year, as well as annual benefits and festivals.

For more information call 281-3222.

Balzekas Museum of Lithuanian Culture (6500 S. Pulaski Rd.) is a museum not known by many, but one with an excellent program for children. The junior area includes a reproduction of an old farmstead in which children can play; "Castle Quest," focusing on Medieval life in Europe with a do-it-yourself coat of arms activity; a four-foot wooden puzzle of a man in armor; and "Castle Closet," where kids can dress up in outlandish costumes.

Several times a year there are arts and crafts festivals on weekends, such as "Lithuanian Candy Cottage Building," using graham crackers and other goodies to build model cottages.

For more information call 582-6500.

The Chicago Academy of Sciences (2001 N. Clark) has weekend programs for families and children, focusing on animals and nature. Family programs include "Snakes Alive!", an annual event featuring petable snakes and lizards, puppet making, and a performance by the Imagination Theater. "Amazing Experiments" is a weekly excursion into chemistry and physics. Children's programs include "Nature's Stories," a weekly event featuring crafts, games, and songs; "Fabulous Fall Colors," a leaf-gathering affair; and "Date-a-Rock," an exploration of rock formations and the stories they tell.

For children from 8 to 10 there are occasional overnighters at the Academy; one adult must accompany every five children. These events include a crafts project, a presentation, a flashlight tour, and breakfast the next morning.

The new "Touch Tour" is available on weekends and invites visitor participation. A bag full of touchable wonders is a main feature of the tour, as guides interact with their guests.

Call 549-0606 for more information.

FILMS

The best place for children's films is **Facets Multimedia** (1517 W. Fullerton). This alternative movie house shows films your children won't see anywhere else. October through May, every Saturday and Sunday afternoon, films of every description are shown. The program includes live-action and animated features from Europe and all over the world; claymation; old comedy classics like Charlie Chaplin and Laurel And Hardy; and children's classics like *Charlotte's Web* and *From the Mixed-Up Files of Mrs. Basil E. Frankweiler*.

The annual children's film festival is held in October and features approximately 70 full-length and short subject films from all over the world. Children's TV videos from other countries are also shown during this ten-day event—the largest showing of children's films in the country.

Call 281-4114 for more information.

BOOKSTORES

Several bookstores in the area cater specifically to children, stocking extensive collections of children's books and scheduling special events.

The Children's Bookstore (2465 N. Lincoln) has an excellent selection of children's books as well as books about raising children, plus an ongoing schedule of activites. The staff is friendly and will happily make book recommendations. Story hours are held twice weekly for children aged 2 to 5 and 3 to 6. On weekends the Children's Bookstore Storytellers perform, as do other groups including the Child's Play Touring Theater. Most programs are free, but a minimal fee is charged for some events. (248-2665)

Barbara's Bookstore (121 N. Marion Ct., Oak Park) offers story hours on Saturday mornings. Children choose the stories they want to hear and are treated to cookies and juice after the show. Call 848-9140 for information.

Bookworms (1722 Central St., Evanston) offers special workshops for children. Call 328-4660 to be placed on their mailing list.

Women and Children First (1967 N. Halsted St.) also offers activities for young children. Special events are held at the store two or three times a year, featuring a children's concert or magic show. (440-8824)

LIBRARIES

The Chicago Public Library is made up of more than 70 neighborhood branches, each with a section for children. Activities for kids are available at each location—many offer story hours—but the main attraction in town is the **Cultural Center** downtown (78 E. Washington). The Cultural Center offers a variety of exciting programs. "City Child in Summer" is the Cultural Center's summertime way of being good to kids. It's a program of diverse entertainment and unusual learning experiences, offering things children won't see anywhere else. A sample listing would include: the Seoul Youth Dance Ensemble performing traditional dances; Billy Branch and his musicians tracing the history of the blues; movies like *Sounder* and *Fantasia*; North African and Middle Eastern dance; The Illustrated Theater; The Child's Play Touring Theater; juggling; magic; puppets; folksongs. You name it, they've got it, and it's all free and it's all good. During the school year the fun continues, but mainly on weekends.

Summer reading programs offered by CPL (and in most suburban libraries as well) are an excellent way of involving your child in reading. Each program is set up as a game, with prizes at the end, encouraging children to participate. For more information call the Cultural Center at 269-2835, or check the white pages under Chicago Public Library for a listing of the branch library nearest you.

THEATER

Children's theater in Chicago includes many touring companies that play in various locations around town, professional companies with permanent locations, and university groups offering yearly series.

An excellent university group is the **DePaul Theater School Playworks.** Formerly connected with the Goodman Theater, this group now performs at First Chicago Center (Dearborn and Madison, in the First National Bank Building). The group offers three productions a year, ranging from classic fairy tales like *The Nightingale* and *Beauty and the Beast* to new plays by contemporary authors. Performances are Mondays, Wednesdays, and Saturdays and prices are reasonable. Call 732-4470.

Beverly Art Center (2153 W. 111th St.) offers a children's theater series on Saturday afternoons for kids 3 years and older. Shows are performed by touring groups and include old fairy tales, new original works, and puppet shows. One troupe to look for is Child's Play Touring Theatre. This group performs stories and poems written by children. Call 445-3838.

Centre East (7701 Lincoln, Skokie) has frequent programs for children; not on a regular basis, but many times a year. Offerings include dance, music and theater performed by groups from all over the country. Call 673-6300.

Other ideas include **Drury Lane Children's Theater** (2500 W. 95th St., Evergreen Park; 779-4000) which offers four productions a year from October through May; **Second City Children's Theater** (1616 N. Wells; 337-3992); and **North Park College** (5125 N. Spaulding; 583-2700, ext. 4300).

Puppet theaters in the area generally small and very creative. **Animart Puppet Theater** (3901 N. Kedzie; 267-1209) offers programs on the weekends from October to May, featuring puppets and marionettes in a varied repertoire. Audience participation is often encouraged. **The Puppet Parlor** (5301 N. Damen; 989-0308) also has weekend performances for all ages. Shows include classics like *The Sorcerer's Apprentice* and *Aladdin and the Magic Lamp*. Prices at both theaters are reasonable.

PARKS

There are hundreds of neighborhood parks in Chicago; too many to cover in detail. But most have playgrounds for children along with other facilities. The **Chicago Park District** runs programs at the parks covering the whole gamut of activities for kids. They offer baseball, football, dance classes, drama classes, ice-skating, music classes, and swimming, to name only a few. For information about the programs call 294-2493, or check the white pages under Chicago Park District for individual park listings.

Two Chicago parks that deserve special attention are **Indian Boundary** (2500 W. Lunt) and **North Park Village Nature Center** (5801 N. Pulaski). Indian Boundary is a great little park with all kinds of extra attractions. Along with a playground and tennis courts, it has a small zoo, newly renovated, featuring many smaller animals like goats, llamas and raccoons. The park also has a gorgeous duck pond used by various kinds of ducks and geese—they're always entertaining if you have popcorn or peanuts with you. And in the summer, Indian Boundary has an old-style sprinkler for kids to run under. If you don't live in the neighborhood, this park is worth a special trip.

North Park Village Nature Center is not really a park, but a nature preserve. Covering 15 acres, the center offers many family activities. There are bird walks, star watches, and guided family hikes. Workshops are offered in woodworking, solar energy, tinsmithing, and Tai Chi, among other things. The Junior Naturalists (ages 9-11) and the Junior Explorers (ages 6-8) meet after school for outdoor exploration. Special events there include a Halloween Haunted Trail and a Winter Solstice Party. Call 583-8970 for more information.

MUSIC AND MOVEMENT

There's not much in the way of children's concerts in Chicago. Some community orchestras give a children's program once a year, and the Chicago Symphony has programs only for school groups. But here are two ideas you may want to consider: **The Old Town School of Folk Music** (909 W. Armitage), and **Ravinia Festival** (Green Bay and Lake Cook Roads, Highland Park).

The Old Town School used to have an extensive program of concerts for children, but now has only 3 or 4 a year. Mainly on weekend afternoons, these concerts include hootenannies and sing-a-longs by local folk artists as well as more famous performers like Ella Jenkins. Friday and Saturday evening concerts are often family affairs; children are welcomed and frequently encouraged to participate. Call 525-7793 for more information.

Ravinia Festival offers four children's programs during its season from late May to mid September. Performances are on Saturday and include dance and theater, along with classical and folk music. Ella Jenkins is an annual performer there. Other recent artists have been the Joseph Holmes Dance Theater and the Piven Theater Workshop. Prices are reasonable and you can picnic on the lawn while you listen to the music. Call 433-8800 or R-A-V-I-N-I-A.

Also in the area are two programs of music and movement for infants and toddlers and their parents. **The Movement Center** at National College of Education (2840 Sheridan Rd., Evanston) offers four 8-week sessions during the school year, for ages 1 month to 4 years. Kids under age 3 have class with their parents; the 3- and 4-year-olds can come alone. The classes are all group participation, with songs, games, exercises, and dancing. The room is also equipped with climbing and playing apparatus especially for the very young ones, as well as accessories like balls, ribbons, musical instruments, and hoops. I've seen these classes in action and they're a lot of fun. Call 256-2786.

Wiggleworms at the Old Town School of Folk Music is the same type of class but without the apparatus. Classes are for ages 0 to 4 and focus on musical activities like rhythm games, movement exercises, songs and finger plays. Parent participation is required and you're advised to bring a blanket or floor mat. Call 525-7793.

AMUSEMENT PARKS

The biggest is **Great America** (in Gurnee, Illinois); whether it's the best or not is debatable. In general, kids love it. But parents need to consider things like crowds, long lines, high prices and the fact that the park is not really suited for children under 3. In any case, if you go you'll find rides of all kinds, from the huge roller-coaster, The American Eagle, to bumper cars for the little ones. You'll also find music, magic, animal acrobatics, and oversized cartoon characters walking around the park. One price gets you in for a whole day. The staff advises early arrival. Open May to September. Call 249-2020.

Santa's Village (in Dundee) is another mixed bag; many like it and many don't. But there are rides for both older and younger kids; there's a petting

zoo with pony rides; there's live entertainment. Food is plentiful at snack
bars and restaurants. And, yes, Santa is there every day. Open May to
September. Call 426-6751.

Kiddieland (in Melrose Park) is a lot smaller than the other two but has
shorter lines and lower prices. It's a place for rides and snacks, geared for
younger children, especially those under 8. Open April to October. Call
343-1050.

ZOOS

Brookfield and **Lincoln Park Zoos** are both excellent, and both have wonderful programs for kids.

Workshops for kids ages 3 and up cover all kinds of topics. Kids can learn
about different paw prints while making their own souvenir; view a videotape
of an elephant giving birth; learn how keepers handle everything from
aardvarks to zebras; or watch closely as zoo mothers take care of their young.
Most classes involve arts and crafts; some, for younger children, involve
games and stories and puppets.

Both Brookfield and Lincoln Park have children's zoos; places where kids
can touch the animals and observe them close-up, while learning from the
keepers who are always at hand. At Brookfield, in the summer, the "Animals
in Action" show features "stars" of the zoo demonstrating their special skills.
At both zoos, kids can watch cows being milked in the barn.

Special events at Lincoln Park are mainly for members, and include
picnics, concerts, and a children's art show. At Brookfield there's the annual
"Teddy Bear Picnic" (open to the public) held in June, and featuring a teddy
bear parade and contest, bear face painting, paw reading, and live music.
"Boo at the Zoo!" in October is an annual Halloween party, with costume
parade and a children's "Spook House". "Thanksgiving Feast" is the one
day of the year visitors can help feed the animals.

Contact the zoos for more information: Lincoln Park Zoo (2200 N. Cannon
Dr., 294-4660); Brookfield Zoo (First Ave. and 31st St., Brookfield; 485-
0263).

RESTAURANTS

If you're looking for a restaurant you can really take the kids to, try one of
these: **Show Biz Pizza** (955 W. Dundee, Arlington Heights, 577-8801). You
may never want to set foot in the place again, but your kids will love it.
Show Biz is heaven for kids as they can run around and play games without
getting in trouble. There are loads of video games, some computer games,
and a slide and merry-go-round. Mechanical characters are on stage, singing
tunes and entertaining the gang. Try it —for a dining experience you won't
be able to forget.

The **Choo-Choo Restaurant** (600 Lee St., Des Plaines, 298-5949) will
delight younger children. Burgers are delivered by a toy train that runs on
the counter.

SEASONAL AND ANNUAL ACTIVITIES

In the fall, a great family outing is apple picking at orchards not far from Chicago. Through most of September and October, all varieties of apples can be picked by hand for a fixed, per-bushel price. Ladders are provided for reaching up and grabbing an apple. There are many orchards in the area, but my favorite is **Wauconda** (1201 Gossell Rd., Wauconda; 526-8553) which is about an hour's drive from downtown Chicago. Wauconda not only has easy-to-find, well marked orchards, but also an after-picking stop consisting or cheese store, gift store, donut shop, antique shop, and an outdoor beer and brat garden with live music. There's nothing like picking apples on a cold fall day and then warming up with hot donuts and coffee. Other orchards in the area are: **Bell's** (Hwy. 22, 1/4 mile west of U.S. Hwy. 12, near Lake Zurich; 438-2333); and **Edward's** (7061 Centerville Rd., Poplar Grove; (815-765-2234).

Winter in Chicago can be a lot of fun if you like sliding fast down hills; there are several places in the area to go sledding and tobogganing. For both, try **Mount Trashmore** (Oakton and Dodge Streets, Evanston). This hill was made from garbage, then covered with dirt and grass. In the winter it's covered with snow, and offers a small run for little kids, a big hill for older kids, and a toboggan chute for all. Rentals are available, and the hill is free and open to the public.

Schiller Woods (Irving Park and Cumberland) has free sledding for younger kids whenever there is snow on the ground. Bring your own sled, as there are no rentals.

For tobogganing, try **Ryan Woods** (87th and Western), **Jensen Slides** (Devon and Milwaukee), or **Swallow Cliff** (Route 83 west of Mannheim on Route 45, Palos Park). All three charge admission and offer rentals. **Swallow Cliff** is the biggest and fastest of the three.

For more information, call the Cook County Forest Preserve District at 261-8400.

One of the main springtime events in the Chicago area is the **Shriner's Circus at Medinah Temple** (600 N. Wabash). For three weeks every March, this one-ring circus offers the best in circus entertainment, and it's all especially for kids. A special feature of the circus is that it has complete facilities for handicapped children, and the Shriners volunteer to help the disabled kids get in and out. Every year the Shriners go out of their way to make the circus experience the best it can be. Call 266-5000 for more information.

In the summer, a fun afternoon or evening activity is miniature golfing at **Novelty Golf** (3650 W. Devon, Lincolnwood; 679-9434). Offering two 18-hole courses, Novelty is open from March or April (depending on the weather) to October.

SUGGESTED READING

Chicago Parent is a magazine published 10 times a year, offering listings of events, articles on education, medical news for parents, and special features on all kinds of topics. It's distributed free at many locations in the city and nearby suburbs—especially libraries and children's bookstores. Call 508-0973.

Where to Go and What to Do with Kids in Chicago by Andrea Baron and Dyann Rivkin, Price/Stern/Sloan (1973). An excellent book full of activity ideas.

Chicagoland Family Fun Guide by Jerry and Sherry Nelson, Kidslife Books, 1983. This book covers just about everything, and includes money-saving coupons for many events.

—Pamala Goldberg

SENIORS

On a beautiful spring morning in Chicago, a group of people in their sixties, seventies, and eighties gather in Lincoln Park at a grassy area overlooking a lagoon. They greet each other, go through a series of slow and gentle warm-ups, then move in unison in what looks like a cross between slow-motion karate and ballet. "Now," says the instructor, 72-year-old Shizu Lofton, "the white crane spreads its wings and flies forward." Each participant moves forward, weight gradually shifting from left leg to right leg and back, arms floating up and down as though moved by the May breeze.

We are watching a class of **Tai Chi for Elders,** an adaptation of an ancient Chinese approach to staying healthy. The white crane movement improves strength and balance for walking, and is rich in imagery. For throughout Asia, the white crane—a beautiful bird, graceful in flight—has traditionally been a symbol of long life, health, happiness, and peace. This is a class meeting of members of the **White Crane Senior Health Center,** located in the heart of Chicago's Lakeview community, home to the city's largest concentration of older people.

The White Crane Senior Health Center is one of a new breed of centers for older people. The result of a joint effort of a grassroots communization— the **Senior Caucus of Jane Addams Center**—and the Illinois Masonic Medical Center, White Crane offers the services of doctors and nurses specializing in geriatrics, a library and classes for health education, and unique wellness programs including massage therapy, international folk dance, and, of course, Tai Chi for Elders. It's a far cry from Bingo at church, and even farther from the ageist fantasies of so many young people who see aging only in terms of loss, decrepitude, and despair. And it's just one of the many nice surprises for the city's seniors.

Of course, all of Sweet Home Chicago, all its pleasures and resources are for people of all ages, with the extra twist that many museums, theaters, stores, and organizations offer individual and group discounts for seniors. This chapter supplements the rest of the guide with a sampling of the tremendous variety of centers and services developed specifically for those who have been healthy and lucky enough to survive until their sixties, seventies, and beyond.

Note: Phone numbers listed as **TDD** (telecommunications device for the deaf) are equipped with devices to communicate with deaf and hard-of-hearing persons who have specially adapted telephones.

ADVOCACY

Fighting ageism and apathy, here are the groups that stand for "Don't kvetch, organize!"

American Association of Retired Persons
2720 Des Plaines, Suite 113, Des Plaines, IL 60018   298-2852
Regional office of the nation's largest organization for people over 50. Consumer advocacy; literature, slide shows, and speakers on health care rights.

Council for Disability Rights
343 S. Dearborn, Suite 1501, Chicago, IL 60604   922-1092 (TDD)
922-1093 (Voice)
Information and referral, newsletter, and inspiration for activism on health care, transportation, and other issues facing disabled people.

Gray Panthers
343 S. Dearborn, Room 1421, Chicago, IL 60604   663-9093
Local chapter of national group headed by Maggie Kuhn. Fights for national health service as a basic right, intergenerational alliances, and international peace.

Illinois Citizens for Better Care
53 W. Jackson, Suite 1509, Chicago, IL 60604   663-5120
Watchdog group for the rights of nursing home residents. Provides help with nursing home selection, complaints, and rights. Sponsors local groups of laypeople and professionals to improve care in their neighborhoods.

Jane Addams Center–Senior Caucus
3212 N. Broadway, Chicago, IL 60657   549-1631
"Alinsky-style" neighborhood group based in Lakeview, with impressive record of victories on health issues. Initiated White Crane Senior Health Center and negotiated prescription discounts at Osco Drugs. Also active on tenants rights and peace issues.

Legacy: An Association for Lesbian and Gay Seniors
P. O. Box 148444, Chicago, IL 60614   327-2734
A new and much-needed addition to both the senior scene and the lesbian and gay community. Provides speakers, literature, a drop-in center, individual counseling, workshops for health and social service agencies, and an organized voice at rallies and meetings. Equal participation of women and men. Confidentiality assured.

Metropolitan Seniors in Action
220 S. State, Suite 706, Chicago, IL 60604   427-6262
A network of 40 neighborhood-based grassroots groups. Priorities include affordable public transportation, safety, and health care. Publishes a city wide newsletter and sponsors an annual rally for seniors' rights.

EDUCATION AND EMPLOYMENT

Education Network for Older Adults
36 S. Wabash, #624, Chicago, IL 60602   782-8967
Counseling and referrals for seniors who want to continue their education.

Chicago Labor Education Program
University of Illinois at Chicago
815 W. Van Buren, Room 214, Chicago, IL 60607   996-2623
Classes, seminars, and consultation on retirement to meet the needs of labor unions and workers approaching retirement or recently retired.

Jewish Vocational Service
1 S. Franklin, Chicago, IL 60606   346-6700
Counseling and referral; not limited to persons of the Jewish faith.

Operation ABLE
36 S. Wabash, Chicago, IL 60602   782-7700
Chicago's leading program for workers over 50. Job listings and placement
service.

ETHNIC SERVICES

American Indian Center
1630 W. Wilson
Chicago, IL 60640
275-5871
Services for the only true non-
immigrants.

The Ark
2341 W. Devon
Chicago, IL 60659
973-1000
Especially concerned with the
needs of low-income Jewish
elderly.

Asian Human Services
4753 N. Broadway, Room 818
Chicago, IL 60640
728-2235
Multilingual staff.

Association House of Chicago
2150 W. North Ave.
Chicago, IL 60647
276-0084
Multi-purpose center with Spanish-
speaking staff. Several locations in
Westtown and Humboldt Park.

Association for Hispanic Elderly
2600 W. Touhy
Chicago, IL 60645
262-5300
Advocacy services for Hispanics.

**Assyrian Universal Alliance
Foundation**
7055 N. Clark
Chicago, IL 60626
274-9262
English lessons, social services.

**Chinese American Service
League**
310 W. 24th Pl.
Chicago, IL 60616
791-0418
In the heart of Chinatown, one of
the city's most extensive and
respected social service agencies.

Chinese Mutual Aid Association
1000 W. Argyle
Chicago, IL 60640
784-2900
In 'New Chinatown,' home to
Indochinese refugees.

Chicago Urban League
4510 S. Michigan
Chicago, IL 60653
285-5800
The venerable civil rights and
advocacy organization, with
information on special programs
for black seniors.

Copernicus Center
3160 N. Milwaukee
Chicago, IL 60618
744-6681
Part of the city's Department on
Aging and Disability; home to
several Polish-language groups.

Council for Jewish Elderly
1015 W. Howard
Evanston, IL 60202
570-7080
Nationally known organization,
respected for its full array of high
quality cultural, health, and social
services. Offers a variety of
housing options.

Japanese American Service Committee
4427 N. Clark St.
Chicago, IL 60640
275-7212
Founded by and for those who came to Chicago upon release from the infamous World War II internment camps, JASC has grown into a leading high quality, multi-service organization.

Joint Civic Committee of Italian Americans
127 N. Dearborn, 13th floor
Chicago, IL 60602
372-6788
Translation and referral services.

Korean American Community Service
4300 N. California
Chicago, IL 60618
583-5501
Translation and referral services for Korean immigrants.

Mexican Community Committee of South Chicago
2939 E. 91st St.
Chicago, IL 60617
978-6441
Translation and referral services for natives of Mexico.

National Caucus on the Black Aged
2100 S. Indiana
Room 122
Chicago, IL 60616
225-2500
In the next 25 years, Chicago's elderly population will be increasingly black, female, and poor. Here's an organization taking the lead in demanding dignity and innovative services for this group.

Polish Welfare Association
3832 N. Cicero
Chicago, IL 60641
282-8206
Translation, referral, direct services for Polish-speaking people.

Southeast Asia Center
1124 W. Ainslie
Chicago, IL 60640
989-6927
Health center with internist, dentist, and eye doctor.

GOVERNMENT

You pay for it, you're its reason for existing, so use it and expect good service!

Chicago Department on Aging and Disability (D.A.D.)
510 N. Peshtigo Ct., 3rd floor, Chicago, IL 60611
My hat is off to this excellent example of a government agency that truly serves the people. Offers an array of services provided by two downtown offices and five regional centers. When in doubt, call D.A.D.!

City-Wide-Information and Referral
TDD & Voice–744-4016

D.A.D. area multi-purpose centers: Following are places to go for social activities, classes, health education, help in understanding and filling out government forms, and referrals to hundreds of other services, both government and private, for senior citizens.

Central-West
2102 W. Ogden
226-2525

Northeast (Levy)
2019 W. Lawrence
878-3564

Northwest (Copernicus)
3160 N. Milwaukee
744-6681

Southeast (Atlas)
1767 E. 79th St.
731-5523

Southwest
6117 S. Kedzie
476-8700

Other good services of D.A.D.:

Foster Grandparents
744-3221

D.A.D. Library
744-7304

Job Training & Placement Service
744-4407

The above three services are all located at D.A.D.'s main office at 510 N. Peshtigo.

Chicago Police Department, Senior Services Division
1121 S. State, Room 104, Chicago, IL 60605   744-8006
Presentations to seniors groups on crime prevention. A place to get information and register complaints related to safety on the streets and at home.

Lt. Governor's Senior Action Center
100 W. Randolph, Suite 15-200, Chicago, IL 60601   917-3333
Information on seniors' services available in the Chicago area. Offers assistance with various problems of seniors, handicapped, and disabled persons.

Chicago Public Library
Central Library and Administrative Offices
425 N. Michigan, Chicago, IL 60611   269-2900
In addition to the full range of books, films, and cultural programs, the central office and many neighborhood branches offer special services for those with special needs. For example:

Chicago Library Service for the Blind and Physically Handicapped
1055 W. Roosevelt Road
Chicago, IL 60608
738-9200
Talking books, cassettes, and Braille publications for the visually impaired.

Sulzer Regional Library
4455 N. Lincoln
Chicago, IL 60625
728-8652 (Voice) 728-2062 (TDD)
Services for the deaf and hard-of-hearing, including books, films,

videos, and an audio-loop equipped meeting room.

Lakeview Branch Library
644 W. Belmont
Chicago, IL 60657
281-7565
Library materials delivered to the homebound.

Woodson Regional Library
9525 S. Halsted
Chicago, IL 60628
881-6921 (Voice) 881-0121 (TDD)
Same services as Sulzer, but has infra-red system in the auditorium.

Chicago Department of Public Health
Office of Public Information and Communications
50 W. Washington, Chicago, IL 60602   744-4278
Call for referral to neighborhood clinics and special offices for high blood pressure control, cancer control, innoculations, and immunizations. Some offices of special interest:

Lakeview Neighborhood Health Center
2849 N. Clark, Chicago, IL 60657   327-7185
Medical visits and medications provided to seniors on Medicare for $3 co-payment. No one turned away for lack of money or insurance.

North Park Village Senior Citizen Clinic
5801 N. Pulaski, Building A, Chicago, IL 60646   539-9669

Southwest Side Seniors Clinic
5845 S. Cicero, Chicago, IL 60638   582-4038
Health screening, out-patient medical services.

Woodlawn Neighborhood Health Center
6337 S. Woodlawn, Chicago, IL 60637   753-7700
Health screening, out-patient medical services.

Social Security Administration
North of Madison St.: 725-8838
South of Madison St.: 636-8811
The place to call with questions about your social security checks, Medicare Parts A and B, and Supplemental Security Income for the Blind and Disabled.

HEALTH AND MEDICINE

Adult Daycare

Structured, supportive environments for those with physical and medical limitations. This much-needed service provides relief and support to those people who are providing extensive care for their elderly loved ones at home. Individual services vary from center to center.

Council for Jewish Elderly
1015 W. Howard
Evanston, IL 60202
570-7000

Holy Cross Hospital
2701 W. 68th St.
Chicago, IL 60629
471-7300

Hyde Park Neighborhood Club
5480 S. Kenwood
Chicago, IL 60615
643-4062

Japanese American Service Committee
4427 N. Clark
Chicago, IL 60640
275-7212

Warren Barr Pavilion of Illinois Masonic Medical Center
66 W. Oak
Chicago, IL 60610
337-5400

Dealing with Diseases

You have probably donated money to these agencies at some time; don't hesitate to use their services if you are in need.

Arthritis Foundation
79 W. Monroe, Suite 1120
Chicago, IL 60603
782-1367
Features 6-week class on arthritic exercise and pain control.

Chicago Heart Association
20 N. Wacker
Chicago, IL 60606
346-4675

Offers information on heart disease and strokes and referral to services.

American Cancer Society
37 S. Wabash
Chicago, IL 60603
372-0471
In addition to providing speakers and literature, also arranges for loans of hospital beds, wheelchairs, and commodes.

Exercise

Augustana Hospital
Seniors Health Program
2035 N. Lincoln
Chicago, IL 60614
975-5056
Yoga, other classes.

Bernard Horwich Jewish Community Center
3003 W. Touhy
Chicago, IL 60645
761-9100
Many exercise classes, swimming pool.

New City YMCA
1515 N. Halsted
Chicago, IL 60622
266-1242
Many services for the disabled,

arthritis exercise, and swimming pool.

White Crane Tai Chi Club
906 W. Belmont
Chicago, IL 60657
883-7151
Home base for Chicago's own adaptation of gentle Chinese exercise. Good for balance, reducing joint and muscle aches and pains, and achieving peace of mind.

White Crane Tai Chi Club
South side chapter
874-3489
Several south side class locations plus occasional speakers.

Geriatric Assessment

This service provides in-depth evaluation and referral to appropriate services in the Chicago area.

Geriatric Assessment Center of Council for Jewish Elderly
1015 W. Howard, Evanston, IL 60202   570-7056

Hospice

Provides care for dying people at home or in hospitals, featuring pain relief and extensive emotional and social support. See the listings in the Physical Health chapter.

Mental Health and Self-Help

Alzheimer's Disease and Related Disorders Association
845 Chicago Ave., Evanston, IL 60202   864-0045
An outstanding service, featuring a speakers bureau and a network of support
groups for care-givers.

Illinois Masonic Medical Center/Older Adults Support Group
923 W. Wellington, Chicago, IL 60657   883-7065
Support group for men and women age 55 and over.

Ravenswood Hospital Community Mental Health Center
Consultations and Education Department, 4545 N. Damen, Chicago, IL
60625   878-4300, ext. 1455
Chicago's best selection of high-quality support groups, including widows'
group, care-givers' group, and a network of seniors' rap groups.

Self Help for the Hard of Hearing (SHHH)
P. O. Box 10023, Chicago, IL 60610   TDD 248-7154   Voice 275-3878
Services for the hard of hearing and for those who work with them.

Sibling Loss Center
The Southern School, 1456 W. Montrose, Chicago, IL 60613   769-0185
New program offering speakers, workshops, and individual counseling for
people coping with the loss of a sibling or any loved one. Sliding fee scale.

Neighborhood Health Centers

Of the dozens, if not hundreds, in town, here are three of the best:

Bethel Wholistic Health Center
4215 W. Washington, Chicago, IL 60624   826-7474
Primary care physicians, counselors, classes. Part of a progressive, activist
church and social service project; a very positive force on the west side.

Windermere Health Center
5549 S. Cornell, Chicago, IL 60637   702-8840
A new center in Hyde Park's pleasant old Windermere House, staffed with
a variety of specialists from the University of Chicago hospitals.

White Crane Senior Health Center
906 W. Belmont, Chicago, IL 60657   883-7151
Sponsored by Illinois Masonic Medical Center and the Senior Caucus of the
Jane Addams Center. Known citywide and nationwide for its unique seniors-
hospital partnership, its primary care and specialty services tailored to the
medical needs of seniors, and its innovations in support groups such as
W.O.W. (Wise Older Women) and wellness programs, such as massage
services.

Nursing Homes

Don't let your images of snake pits and dumping grounds blind you to the
need for good nursing homes in Chicago. Here are three of the best—one
in the city, and two that are nearby but are connected to Chicago institutions.

For additional information on nursing homes, see Illinois Citizens for Better Care in the Advocacy listings above.

Lieberman Geriatric Health Center of the Council for Jewish Elderly
9700 Gross Point Rd., Skokie, IL 60076   674-7210

Warren Barr Pavilion of Illinois Masonic Medical Center
66 W. Oak, Chicago, IL 60610   337-5400

Westshire Retirement and Healthcare Centre
5825 W. Cermak, Chicago, IL 60650   656-9120
The teaching nursing home of the University of Illinois at Chicago's medical center.

MORE RESOURCES

Metropolitan Chicago Coalition on Aging
53 W. Jackson, Room 918, Chicago, IL 60604   922-5890
Excellent forums for professionals from many disciplines: health care, social service, government, and business. Coordinates the Silver Saver discount program for seniors.

Legal Services
Please refer to the section on Clinics in the Legal Services chapter. Most law clinics have a sliding fee scale based on family income.

Chicago Transit Authority, Travel Information
Merchandise Mart Plaza, 7th floor, Chicago, IL 60654   836-7000
Have a newspaper or book with you when you call. Be prepared to wait on hold for 3 to 20 minutes. Information on reduced fares for seniors, monthly passes, lost and found: 664-7200. To get an application for a Senior Citizen ID, write the CTA at the address above. Special services for severely mobility-limited people: 527-1700

R.S.V.P. (Retired Seniors Volunteer Program)
Hull House Association
118 N. Clinton, Chicago, IL 60606   726-1526
The city's leading program for training and placing seniors in an amazing variety of settings. Individual skills matched to specific service opportunities. Travel expenses and meals usually provided to volunteers.

—Robert Skeist

WOMEN

Times have changed and so has the women's movement. In fact, it's not even called the women's movement anymore. Instead of large advocacy groups trying to raise the public's consciousness, today we have more specialized groups working to improve particular aspects of women's lives. One thing, however, has remained the same—women still have a need for the professional, financial, and legal support provided by organizations such as the ones covered in this chapter.

Professional and business organizations for women have proliferated, reflecting the nationwide obsession with finding jobs and furthering careers. Besides establishing professional contacts, these groups serve another important purpose: they are the only place where many women, especially those in upper management or in fields where they are a minority, can meet with other women in similar work situations. The support and information these groups provide can be indispensable.

Health care and health rights will always be vital to women. Luckily, we have a number of excellent women's health centers and referral services in the city. Abortion is legal in Illinois but a number of clinics have closed.

Women still make lower salaries than men, and only a few women have made it to the top levels of power. A more conservative political climate has made more conservative stands on issues, including women's issues, acceptable. Nevertheless, working women are here to stay, and ambitious women are here to stay, and there is a whole generation of young women who take their equality on all issues for granted. In a way, that's gratifying.

REFERRAL SERVICES AND CENTERS

Midwest Women's Center
53 W. Jackson, Suite 1015, Chicago, IL 60604   922-8530, 663-4163
One of the best sources of information in the city for women and the first place to call when you don't know where to start. Created to further the economic, political, and social empowerment of women in our society, the center provides information, referrals, and training services to women, including employment services for low-income women, apprenticeship and nontraditional job training, and a program for professional women. The center houses an extensive library, open to the public Tuesday through Saturday, with information on services and referrals to legal, day care, health, and other services and organizations.

Directory of Chicago Area Women's Organizations
Leigh Communications, 200 W. Superior, Chicago, IL 60610   951-7600
Useful, comprehensive directory of women's organizations, with listings and descriptions. You can find a copy at the library of the Midwest Women's Center; also on sale at bookstores.

Southwest Women Working Together
3201 W. 63rd St., Chicago, IL 60629   436-0550
Active group on the southwest side providing career counseling, a program for battered women, family workshops, education, health care, placement

program for women over 30 reentering the workforce, and referrals. Offers wide range of services for seniors. Also offers after-school phone friends program for children who are home alone and may need to talk to an adult: 778-KIDS.

Women & Children First (bookstore)
1967 N. Halsted, Chicago, IL 60614   440-8824
Bookstore with titles concerning all aspects of women's lives, women's periodicals, records, nonsexist books for children, toys, and a big bulletin board listing events, services, and organizations for women.

Women's Bar Association
20 N. Clark, Suite 1725, Chicago, IL 60602   346-9224
Referral system available to the general public, but designed especially for women.

Chicago Women's Federal Credit Union
845 Chicago, Suite 216, Evanston, IL 60602   869-8630
Educates women on how to establish credit; helps women who feel they have been discriminated against in this area.

YWCA (Loop center and main office)
37 S. Wabash Ave., Chicago, IL 60605   372-6600
Offers excellent comprehensive services for women, with centers throughout the city. Programs include career counseling, networking breakfasts, financial management seminars, organized sports for women, and help for battered women and rape victims.

PROFESSIONAL ORGANIZATIONS

Women's professional organizations have grown in number over the last 10 years in response to the overall interest in networking, professionalism, and career. Most professions have their own support groups or networks; to find out if there is one for your field, call the librarian at the **Midwest Women's Center** (663-4163), or check the *Directory of Chicago Area Women's Organizations* (described above), or one of the other referral sources listed in this chapter.

**American Women Composers
Midwest chapter**
2143 W. Thomas
Chicago, IL 60622
536-4181
Performs classical music composed by American women, and promotes such music.

Association for Women in Computing
P.O. Box 3568
Oak Park, IL 60303
776-3924
Open to women in computing,

from programmers to directors of data processing.

Association for Women in Science
P.O. Box 13
Lemont, IL 60439.

Black Women's Network
2403 E. 75th St.
Chicago, IL 60649
347-4380
Geared to motivate and encourage financial independence through entrepreneurship.

**Business & Professional
Women's Clubs of Illinois**
528 S. 5th St, #209
Springfield, IL 62701
(217) 528-8985
Local Woodfield chapter: 397-7562
A national organization that claims
to be the oldest national
networking forum for professional
women. Call or write to find the
chapter nearest you.

Chicago Society of Women CPAs
500 N. Michigan Ave.
Chicago, IL 60611
661-1700

Chicago Women in Architecture
c/o A/A, Chicago chapter
53 W. Jackson, #346
Chicago, IL 60604

Chicago Women in Housing
P.O. Box 7420
Chicago, IL 60680-7420
For women in housing
development, construction, and
management. Provides advocacy
and consulting.

**Chicago Women in Publishing
(CWIP)**
645 N. Michigan Ave., Suite 1058
Chicago, IL 60611
951-5277
Active group geared for women in
any publishing field. Monthly
meetings offer strong program of
speakers and topics. CWIP
produces a variety of publications,
including "Equality in Print," a
guide to using nonsexist language.
Offers a job network, resume
counseling, and a free-lance
network that matches up writers
with assignments.

Federally Employed Women
P.O. Box 802046
Chicago, IL 60680
765-4167
Dedicated to promoting
opportunity and equality for
women in federal jobs. Open to
men and women.

**National Network for Women in
Sales**
P.O. Box 578442
Chicago, IL 60657
577-1944

**Network of Women
Entrepreneurs**
560 W. Washington St., Suite 301
37 S. Wabash
Chicago, IL 60606
332-4146
Holds workshops and networking
breakfasts for women
entrepreneurs. Founded on the
belief that women entrepreneurs
feel isolated and need to meet with
one another to share ideas, learn
skills, and develop connections.
Sponsored by the Small Business
Administration.

**Women in Management (Chicago
Loop chapter)**
645 N. Michigan, Suite 1058
Chicago, IL 60611
951-9114
For exchanging ideas and
promoting self-development. Open
to anyone in management or
management training. One of
several chapters in Chicago.

Women in Real Estate
4849 N. Rockwell
Chicago, IL 60625
334-8221

JOB SERVICES/SMALL BUSINESS DEVELOPMENT

Mujeres Latinas En Accion
1823 W. 17th, Chicago, IL 60608   226-1544
Vocational testing, job counseling, and referral primarily for but not limited
to Latino women.

Women's Business Development Center
230 N. Michigan, Suite 1800, Chicago, IL 60601   853-3477
A non-profit business resource center (spun off from the Chicago Labor Institute). Provides free counseling to women in business or to those contemplating starting a business. Successful business owners are the counselors.

Women's Self-Employment Project
500 N. Michigan Ave., Suite 1400, Chicago, IL 60611   661-1700
Unique program helping women to start small businesses by providing peer counseling, expert technical assistance, and small reduced-rate loans.

Please refer to the Employment chapter in this book for more information on starting your own business.

ARTS ORGANIZATIONS

American Women in Radio & TV, Inc., c/o Goodwin & Krab, Inc.
340 W. Huron, Chicago, IL 60610   337-2010
Open to both professionals and students.

Feminist Writers Guild—Chicago
P.O. Box 14095, Chicago, IL 60614
Chicago's chapter of this national organization is particularly active, with regular fiction, poetry, and writing development workshops, plus a fiction book discussion group and frequent readings around the city. Publishes an especially informative newsletter every month with information about Guild-sponsored events, other literary events in the city, and leads on who is looking for manuscripts. You have to join the national group as well as the local chapter.

Women in the Director's Chair
3435 N. Sheffield, #3, Chicago, IL 60657   281-4988
Mounts consistently interesting shows of films by women. Sponsors annual film festival and solicits and screens films directed by women. Also hosts appearances by women directors.

Women in Performing Arts Network
1923 N. Hudson, Chicago, IL 60614
Services includes a resume referral service for actors, directors, and technicians.

HEALTH

American Women's Medical Center
2744 N. Western Ave., Chicago, IL 60647   772-7726
Services include gynecological care, family planning and birth control, abortion services, and pregnancy testing (results provided immediately).

Chicago Women's Health Center
3435 N. Sheffield, Chicago, IL 60657   935-6126
Clinic providing prenatal and gynecological care, as well as community education programs and outpatient services. By appointment only.

Chicago's Picasso, Daley Plaza.

Chicago Women's Physician Network Inc.
1945 W. Wilson, Chicago, IL 60640   275-9545
Group practice consisting of women physicians with various specialties who treat both women and men. Specialists include internists, obstetricians/gynecologists, pediatricians, dermatologists, and general surgeons.

HERS (Health Evaluation & Referral Service)
1954 W. Irving Park Rd., Chicago, IL 60613   248-0166
Unique for its practice of evaluating the places and people it refers people to. Provides referrals to doctors, prenatal education classes, family planning clinics, support groups, abortion clinics, and psychotherapists. Referrals are

based on evaluations by staff and clients; they will share these with you if you ask, as well as information on fees if available. They will also answer questions about pregnancy, childbirth, birth control, and abortion.

Women's Health Resources
904 W. Oakdale, Chicago, IL 60657   883-7052
Excellent center providing health care, education, and treatment for adult women, including a full range of medical services. Health care library available.

POLITICAL GROUPS

Chicago Women's Political Caucus
1143 S. Plymouth Ave., Chicago, IL 60605   987-0038
Promotes opportunities for women in political office and local government.

Cook County Democratic Women
P.O. Box 5019, Chicago, IL 60680   465-5730

Illinois Minority Women's Caucus
c/o Midwest Women's Center—Joyce Short
53 W. Jackson, Chicago, IL 60604   922-8530
Helps women in minorities to develop group consciousness, thus increasing their power in their culture and in the world.

Illinois Women's Agenda
118 N. Clinton, Room 200, Chicago, IL 60606   726-1526
A coalition devoted to meeting the objectives of the National Women's Agenda, which includes goals for employment and job training, safeguarding of reproductive rights, and women's legal rights.

League of Women Voters of Chicago
67 E. Madison St., Chicago, IL 60603   236-0315
Since 1920, has been debating issues and advocating women's rights, affirmative action, welfare, and day care, as well as other global issues.

National Organization of Women (NOW), Chicago chapter
53 W. Jackson, Room 924, Chicago, IL 60604   922-0025
Active political group, advocating for a broad range of women's rights. Engages in electoral work, public speaking, fund raising, and visiting legislators.

Women for Peace
343 S. Dearborn, Chicago, IL 60604   663-1227
Group dedicated to nuclear disarmament.

Women United for a Better Chicago
P.O. Box 578141, Chicago, IL 60657
Dedicated to raising public awareness of local issues and holding city officials accountable for their voting records. They persuaded Mayor Harold Washington to form the Office of Women's Affairs.

JOB DISCRIMINATION

Illinois Department of Human Rights
100 W. Randolph, Suite 10-100, Chicago, IL 60601   917-6200
Publishes "A Guide to the Illinois Human Rights Act," which provides
information on filing a discrimination charge and explains the law in areas
of employment, housing, public accommodations, and financial credit.

Women Employed
5 S. Wabash, Suite 415, Chicago, IL 60603   782-3902
Aids in discrimination problems on jobs, monitors government regulatory
agencies and publishes reports, studies, and brochures on career and work
issues.

DAY CARE/CHILDREN

Day Care Action Council of Illinois—Day Care Connection
4753 N. Broadway, Suite 726, Chicago, IL 60640   561-7900
Referrals and information for child care in the Chicago area.

Hull House Association
118 N. Clinton, Chicago, IL 60606   726-1526
Comprehensive program of services at 32 neighborhood locations. Depending on the center, offers day care for preschool and elementary age children,
and after-school programs. Provides information and referrals to quality day
care centers (call 549-1631). Also trains recreation and day care providers.

Infant Welfare Society of Chicago
1931 N. Halsted St.   751-2800
Provides services for underprivileged children, including medical and dental
care, and therapy and education for emotionally troubled preschool children
and their parents. Also offers gynecological, prenatal, and other services for
adult women. Bilingual staff.

CRISIS INTERVENTION

Chicago Abused Women's Coalition, Greenhouse
P.O. Box 476608, Chicago, IL 60647   278-4110
24-hour hotline: 278-4566
   Oversees **Greenhouse,** a shelter for women and families. If the shelter is
full, they will refer you to other safe houses or concerned groups in the city.

Chicago Women's Therapy Collective
55 E. Washington, Suite 1934, Chicago, IL 60602   372-5560
Provides nonsexist counseling and psychotherapy. Services for women, men,
couples, groups, or families.

Rape Victims Advocates   871-2884
Hotline: 744-8418
If a rape victim goes to one of seven hospitals participating in this program
(Augustana, Grant, Edgewater, Illinois Masonic, Northwestern, Weiss
Memorial, and Norwegian American Hospitals), an advocate will arrive to
help and stay with the victim through examinations and discussions with
attorneys and police. Advocates provide their services 24 hours.

Traveler's Aid Women's Program 435-4500
Referrals and counseling for battered women.

WICCA—Women in Crisis Can Act
2114 W. Belmont, Chicago, IL 60618
528-3303 (Tuesday through Friday, 6 pm-10 pm)
Oldest crisis intervention line in Chicago, for women who want to talk to someone about domestic violence, rape, depression, or alcoholism. Gives information and referrals.

Hotlines

Chicago Abused Women's Coalition
Greenhouse
24-hour hotline: 278-4566
Counseling and referrals.

Metro Help
24-hour hotline: 880-9860
Youth service agency provides referrals and counseling for abused or neglected children and adolescents.

Pregnant teens:
Booth Memorial Hospital
725-7441
Hull House
842-5507 or 842-5508

Domestic Violence Women's Services of Loop center YWCA
372-6600
Provides counseling to victims of sexual assault and domestic violence.

Rape Victims Services for Edgewater-Uptown Community Health Center
24-hour emergency service hotline: 769-0205
Counseling and court advocacy for rape victims.

Rape Victim Emergency Assistance
24-hour hotline: 744-8418

MORE RESOURCES

Chimera, Inc.
10 S. Wabash, #602, Chicago, IL 60603   332-5540
Chimera instructors, all women, teach excellent courses throughout the city on self-defense, how to feel confident walking city streets alone, and how to handle stressful street situations in the city. The courses offer practical, useful techniques. A non-profit organization.

The Women's Gym
1212 W. Belmont, Chicago, IL 60657   549-0700
Clean, attractive space with excellent facilities. Friendly atmosphere, and a nice alternative to more crowded, impersonal clubs. Offers aerobics classes (the floor has 15 inches of foam padding over wood), yoga, karate, massage therapy, free weights and Universal equipment, steam room, sauna, whirlpool, and sundeck. Private weight trainers available by appointment. Babysitting services provided in the mornings, Monday through Thursday.

Chicago Area Women's Sports Association (CAWSA)
P.O. Box 10655, Chicago 60610
472-0154 or 235-1913
Referral service for local women's sports, workshops, and conferences. Provides newsletter.

Women's Studies Program
University of Illinois at Chicago
Box 4348 M/C 360, Chicago, IL 60680   996-2441
Offers undergraduate and graduate programs. Also provides community outreach activities, organizes conferences, and makes speakers and films available to the community.

Northwestern University Library
Women's Collection/Special Collection Department
1935 Sheridan Rd., Evanston, IL 60201   491-3635
Open to the public for research and reference, covers the women's movement since the 1960s. Has the International Women's History Periodical Archive, given to the university by the Women's Historical Research Center at Berkeley, which made this the most comprehensive resource of women-related periodicals in the country.

University of Illinois at Chicago
University Library, Special Collections Department
801 S. Morgan   996-2756 or 996-2742
Open to the public for research, the Midwest Women's Historical Collection concentrates on the nineteenth and twentieth centuries. Contains the personal papers of Emma Goldman and the Jane Addams Memorial Collection. Reference services available to the public by telephone or by letter.

—Melanie Kubale

LESBIANS

Like most major metropolitan areas, Chicago has its share of lesbian bars and events. But what sets this city apart from other cities is the unique flavor of its community, which—like Chicago itself—is divided into a number of smaller communities. Chicago has its Bucktown, Lakeview, and Bridgeport, and the lesbian community has its jocks, political activists, and culture seekers. Of course, these groups often overlap, but within each there is a small-town kind of feel: everyone seems to know everyone else, and they work and play together.

Some might feel that such a variety of groups fragments the community and makes a unified community impossible. To some extent, that's true, but a single community without any subdivisions just wouldn't be practical in a city of this size. There are too many of us and we are too diverse and scattered physically. (And that seems a good sign: that despite homophobia our population has continued to grow and flourish.)

Nevertheless, a real community does exist, and it's evident in times of celebration, sorrow, or mutual need. We unite for the gay pride parade, for example. Or, more significantly, consider the recent battle to get a gay rights ordinance passed here in Chicago. Though we failed to get the ordinance passed this time around, we all came together—gays, lesbians, and our respective subcommunities—for a common cause. As I write, we are continuing to work together for future passage of the ordinance, registering gays and lesbians to vote in record numbers, working toward the reelection of those who supported the ordinance, and campaigning for gay candidates.

Despite the lack of a law guaranteeing equal rights to gay and lesbian residents, life is basically good for us in the city. Discrimination against homosexuals is not unheard of here, of course, but for the most part, we can lead fairly open lives if we so choose—particularly in such areas as Lakeview, Edgewater, New Town, and Rogers Park. We have many bookstores, clothing stores, restaurants, clubs, and support networks that are owned or run by gays and lesbians. We have a **Mayor's Committee on Gay and Lesbian Issues** (made up of some our best and brightest) and active support from many city alderpersons.

I have lived in a number of cities from coast to coast and, all in all, there is nowhere I would rather live than here. Chicago's lesbian community has something for everyone, not to mention all the rest of the city has to offer. In fact, a major question lesbians may ask themselves while choosing whether to live in Chicago is probably not: "Is there a good community?" but rather: "Can I survive the winters?"

Whether you decide to invest in long underwear and stay forever or just for the weekend, Chicago has a lot to offer lesbians. Take in as much as you can!

CULTURE AND REFERRAL SERVICES

Artemis Singers
P.O. Box 578296, Chicago, IL 60657   235-9635
Chicago's talented lesbian choral group. In addition to performing classical choral works by women composers, they also do more modern pieces—complete with choreography.

241

Chicago Outlines
1300 W. Belmont, Chicago, IL 60657   871-7610
Chicago's newest lesbian and gay newspaper, *Outlines* has a weekly women's section—"Nuance"—that features regular columns on women's music, lesbian ethics, and other issues of interest to lesbians. Extended coverage of local, regional, and national news and a complete listing of lesbian and gay organizations, bars, and restaurants. Available free in lesbian and gay bookstores and bars and other locations around the city, and by subscription ($50 a year).

Feminist Writers' Guild
P.O. Box 14095, Chicago, IL 60614
A national organization, not specifically lesbian. Chicago's chapter is particularly active, with regular fiction, poetry, and writing development workshops, plus a fiction book discussion group and frequent readings around the city. Good newsletter packed with information on cultural events of interest to women and writers.

Gerber-Hart Library
3238 N. Sheffield, Chicago, IL 60657   883-3003
Chicago's only independent gay and lesbian library. Their collection includes anything by and about gays and lesbians, including history, novels, poetry, records, tapes, magazines, newspapers (mostly midwestern), directories, posters, and t-shirts. A collection highlight is a complete collection of the 1950s lesbian periodical *The Ladder*. Everyone is welcome to use the facilities. You need to join the library to check things out ($10). Hours: 12-4 pm Saturdays, but this may change, so call. Always looking for volunteers.

Horizons Community Services Inc.
3225 N. Sheffield, Chicago, IL 60657   929-4357
Provides information and referrals on almost any topic of interest to lesbians and gays, including counseling, legal and health matters, and social activities.

Hot Wire Magazine
1417 W. Thome, Chicago, IL 60660   274-8298
The only national periodical covering women's music and culture. Provides good, solid reading, plus lots of photos and illustrations. Packed with information and entertainment. Always looking for hard-working, enthusiastic support staff.

Kinheart Women's Center
2214 Ridge, Evanston, IL 60201   491-1103
A multipurpose women's organization, offering a weekly drop-in time for lesbians every Friday evening from 8-11 pm for discussions and social events, a lesbian mothers support group, and a single lesbians social group. Feminist counseling and coming-out services from professional counselors also available.

Metis Press
P.O. Box 25187, Chicago, IL 60625-0187
Chicago's oldest lesbian feminist press. A publisher of children's books, fiction, and nonfiction, Metis does all its own printing. The quality of production and writing in their books are excellent. Don't miss their bestseller *Bernice*, a fun and funny book.

Mountain Moving Coffeehouse for Women and Children
1655 W. School, Chicago, IL 60657   769-6899
The country's longest-surviving women's coffeehouse. Features a wide variety of programs, including national and local singers, musicians, and other performers, poetry and prose readings, potluck dinners, discussions, slide shows, and movies. Serves excellent baked goods, soft drinks, and teas. Open Saturdays and occasionally on Fridays. Admission on a sliding scale. Always looking for collective members to help run the coffeehouse.

Windy City Times
Sentury Publications, Inc.
3223 N. Sheffield, Chicago, IL 60657   935-1790
Free paper covering local and national news of interest to gays and lesbians. Complete listings of gay and lesbian organizations, bars, and restaurants. Available in all gay and lesbian bookstores and bars, as well as other select locations around the city. Also available by subscription.

Women and Children First Bookstore
1967 N. Halsted, Chicago, IL 60614   440-8824
Known as "THE bookstore." Warm, comfortable environment, friendly, knowledgeable staff, great selection of books by, for, and about women, excellent selection of nonsexist and unconventional children's books. Program nights (readings, discussions, lectures) every other Tuesday evening—donation requested. Also carries records by women artists. Strongly recommended.

RESTAURANTS

The following are a sampling of restaurants that are either run by or cater to lesbians and gays. Consult the *Windy City Times* or *Chicago Outlines* or ask around for other places.

RSVP & Co.
3324 N. Broadway   975-1102
Excellent food. Caters to a lesbian and gay clientele, though others dine there comfortably. Not cheap but well worth the expense. Decor is plain but clean, bright and cheerful.

My Brother's Place
111 W. Hubbard   321-0776
Basically a gay male place, also an intimate, elegant place for lesbians to dine. Prices not cheap but not outrageous.

Two Doors South
3220 N. Clark   935-0133
Elegant dining. Mostly gay men, but lesbians are welcome. Good food and service, varied menu. Moderately priced. An attached store sells cards and gifts.

Ann Sather's
929 W. Belmont   348-2378
Plain and wholesome dinners featuring Swedish cuisine. Many gay patrons. The brunches—especially the cinnamon buns—are what Ann Sather's is

famous for. Be prepared to wait if you show up for Sunday brunch. Reasonable prices.

Melrose Restaurant
3233 N. Broadway   327-2060
Open 24 hours, a pleasant coffee shop serving breakfast in the wee hours. Sidewalk tables are set up in warm weather. Reasonable prices.

Chicago Diner
3411 N. Halsted   935-6696
Wonderful decor, with applicances from the 1940s and 1950s adorning the walls. Large gay clientele. Good assortment of hearty, vegetarian fare. Reasonable prices.

Svea Restaurant
5736 N. Clark   334-9619
A nongay restaurant where you're likely to run into lots of lesbians on a Sunday morning. Most folks come for the Swedish pancakes.

Heartland Cafe
7000 N. Glenwood   465-8005
Large, diverse vegetarian menu. The decor is reminiscent of earthy health food restaurants of 10 years ago. Features an outdoor cafe and an attached health food store. Reasonable prices.

BARS

Augie and CK's
3726 N. Broadway   975-0449
A popular lesbian dance bar. Some gay males come here too. Large dance floor and simple decor. Average prices. DJ and cover charge Fridays and Saturdays. Open till 3 am Fridays, 4 am Saturdays.

The Closet
3325 N. Broadway   477-8533
Mixed gay and lesbian. Small and cozy, a popular place to have a drink after work. Videos at night. Average prices. Big windows let you look out on the crowd walking by on Broadway. Open till 2 am, 3 am Saturdays.

His 'n Hers
5820 N. Broadway   769-1616
Evenly mixed lesbians and gay men. Pool table and outdoor patio, with Sunday afternoon cookouts in summer. Reasonable prices. Open till 2 am Fridays, 3 am Saturdays.

Lost and Found
3058 W. Irving Park Rd.   463-9617
Chicago's oldest lesbian bar. Like many bars of the 1950s, there is no easily visible sign out front (except an Old Style beer sign) and you have to ring a doorbell to get in. A somewhat older, friendly crowd. Pool table, juke box, and a big bar. Average prices. Lesbians only. Open till 2 am Fridays, 3 am Saturdays.

Piggens Pub
674 W. Diversey   929-7876
Basically a men's bar, but more women have been going here of late. A small bar with a friendly atmosphere. Small dance floor. Outside patio during warm weather.

Paris Dance
1122 W. Montrose   769-0602
Definitely a "see and be seen" kind of place. Glitzy, beautiful decor, and an excellent dance floor. Separate room with tables where the music is not as loud for talking and playing video games. Often features special parties and theme nights. Elegant yet fun place. DJ and cover charge on Fridays and Saturdays. Prices tend to be higher than average, but it's worth it. Open till 2 am Fridays, 3 am Saturdays.

The Patch
201 155th St., Calumet City   891-9854
Two pool tables are a big attraction here. Large dance floor with juke box music as well as booths and tables for sitting and talking. Open till 2 am Fridays, 3 am Saturdays.

Razmataz
4174 N. Elston   588-9624
A neighborhood bar with a little class. Nice decor, good-sized dance floor. Pool table, video games, jukebox. Open till 2 am Fridays, 3 am Saturdays.

SPORTS

Metropolitan Sports Association
P.O. Box 10510, Chicago, IL 60610   447-4349
Organizes tournaments for gays and lesbians in everything from bowling to softball, from tennis to volleyball. Most teams have spaces for members of different skill levels; call if you'd like to get on a team. Many sports have both coed as well as gay- or lesbian-only leagues. An excellent, fun, healthy way to meet other people. Membership dues ($12 per year). Call for information on times, dates, and locations of activities.

The Women's Gym
1212 W. Belmont, Chicago, IL 60657   549-0700
Chicago's first full-service fitness facility for women only. Though not lesbian only, lesbians are definitely welcome. Warm, clean, attractive environment—not your typical gym! Facilities include a fully equipped weight room with free weights and Universal equipment, a mirrored room for aerobics, dance, and karate classes, lockers, showers, hairdryers, towel and locker rental, steam room, dry sauna, and whirlpool spa. Massages also available. One-year membership: $325; one-year special daytime membership: $165; single visit: $9; but all memberships go on sale several times a year.

RELIGIOUS ORGANIZATIONS

Dignity
3223 N. Sheffield,Chicago, IL 60657   549-2633
Offers a Catholic mass for gays and lesbians Sundays at 7 pm at St. Sebastian Church on Wellington Avenue, just west of Halsted. Though the congre-

gation is currently mostly gay men, they are interested in getting more lesbians involved. Sponsors yearly retreats. Members of the ministry available to talk about resolving issues of sexuality and religion.

Congregation Or Chadash
656 W. Barry, Chicago, IL 60657   248-9456
Encourages and supports lesbian participation in Shabbat services on the second, fourth, and fifth Friday of each month. Also has complete High Holy Days services and a full schedule of other social, religious, and cultural events, including holiday parties, barbecues, and film showings.

Havurat Achayot
P.O. Box 14066, Chicago, IL 60614   477-5269
A feminist Jewish group. Call for more information.

Metropolitan Community Church
615 W. Wellington Ave., Chicago, IL 60657   477-8708
Of gay and lesbian roots, MCC has services at Good Shepherd Parish (at address shown above) on Sundays at 9 am and 7 pm, as well as at churches in Hinsdale, Evanston, and Hyde Park (call for locations and service times). Depending on the church, there may be a lot of lesbians participating. MCC has an information line and works with the Chicago food drive, providing a food line targeted for gays and lesbians but open to all.

—Yvonne Zipter

GAY MEN

Chicago is a good place to be gay. The 1980s have seen an emerging pride among Chicago gay men—an open pride. The cultural hub of Chicago's gay community is Lakeview East, usually called New Town. Gay-owned and supported shops, restaurants, bars, and other businesses line Halsted, Broadway, and Clark Streets between Diversey and Addison. The area is lively, bustling, and infused with optimism. New Town is not a gay ghetto—it is a dynamic community that reflects the commerce and culture of its diverse population.

A summer afternoon stroll down Broadway Avenue reveals the variety in Chicago's gay marketplace. Walking north from Diversey, stop in Crazy Mary's Cafe or the adjoining Bulldog Road Bar to have one of their famous Bloody Marys. Continuing north on Broadway, you can find gay-themed books prominently displayed in the windows of Unabridged Bookstore. Among the ethnic restaurants, pastry and coffee shops, bars, and other businesses, you'll also find card and gift shops with items marketed to gay consumers. You can finish off the afternoon by brunching and people watching at R.S.V.P. and Company Sidewalk Cafe, or by having a candlelit, quiet dinner at Wickline's on Halsted.

The increasing openness and strength of the community is celebrated every summer in late June during **Gay and Lesbian Pride Week.** Pride Week culminates in a parade: the 17th annual Gay and Lesbian Pride Parade in 1986 brought 60,000 people out for the celebration. The parade featured floats sponsored by many of Chicago's gay-owned businesses and organizations. Among the 130 parade entries were **Mattachine Midwest** celebrating its twentieth anniversary and *Gay Chicago Magazine* celebrating its tenth year as a guide to Chicago's gay businesses and entertainment.

Despite the growing success of events such as Pride Week, gaining increasing visibility remains the biggest political challenge to gays in Chicago. Gays are a sizable minority in the city, according to the Kinsey Reports on Sexuality, which estimate that 10 percent of males and 6 percent of females are primarily homosexual. That translates to a combined gay and lesbian population in Chicago of at least 237,000. Chicago politicians, however, tend to ignore statistics they don't like: one alderman recently stated that there were absolutely no homosexuals in his ward, and furthermore, that they were not welcome there.

To become more visible and to demonstrate the economic strength of the gay and lesbian community in Chicago, a unique campaign was conducted recently by two of the city's tavern owners. Marge Summit of His 'N Hers Bar and Frank Kellas of the Gold Coast called on gays and lesbians to stamp their money, checks, and credit card slips with the words "Gay $." Soon the stamped currency was circulating throughout the city and beyond, and legal battles began with banks that pulled the "defaced" bills to be destroyed.

The gay dollar campaign marked a first step for gaining civil rights protection for gays and lesbians in Chicago—becoming visible. Through this silent protest, gays and lesbians made public their considerable presence in the city marketplace. Businesspeople are discovering that gays have money and will support businesses that support them.

Advertisers, both local and national, have flocked to gay publications in an effort to reach Chicago's gay and lesbian consumers. Advertising from the city's premier department store chain recently reached the pages of the *Windy City Times*, a newsweekly covering local and national news of interest to gays and lesbians. Further proof of the growing economic and political clout of Chicago's gay and lesbian community is evidenced by the recent emergence of another newsweekly, *Chicago Outlines*.

Perhaps the most gratifying evidence of the emerging community is the number of gay men who are helping each other in crisis. When AIDS first appeared in this country, the gay populations of the east and west coasts were hit first and hardest. The virus spread slowly to the midwest, but the early warnings from the coasts provided some time to Chicago's gay community to prepare for the challenge of meeting the crisis.

A local institution that has been instrumental in research, education, and counseling about AIDS and treatment of other sexually transmitted diseases is the **Howard Brown Memorial Clinic**. Howard Brown was the result of two local organizations—**Chicago Gay Medical Students** and **Horizons Community Services**—working together to establish a medical center for gays. The clinic was named in memory of Howard J. Brown, M.D., an Illinois native who served as New York City's first public health services administrator. After publicly announcing his own homosexuality, Brown helped found the National Gay Rights Task Force to promote the causes of gay rights. Since its founding in 1974, Howard Brown has provided confidential diagnosis and treatment for sexually transmitted diseases with respect and concern for each patient, regardless of his or her sexual orientation.

In 1984, the National Institute of Health (NIH) issued contracts in five cities to conduct a study called "The Natural History of Acquired Immune Deficiency Syndrome (AIDS) in Homosexual Men." Howard Brown Memorial Clinic was the only private gay men's health clinic to participate in the study. A subcontract was awarded to Northwestern University to be an additional site for the study. Out of over 4,000 healthy, sexually active gay men who were inducted into the study nationwide, 906 Chicago gay men volunteered at the Howard Brown Clinic, with an additional 197 participating through Northwestern University.

The NIH study volunteers periodically receive complete medical examinations and are questioned about changes in their sexual habits over a period of two and a half years. In the short time the study has been in progress, a great deal has been learned about the spread of the AIDS virus in the gay population. The results will undoubtedly be useful to the other populations— sexually active heterosexuals among them—who are also at risk. Through this and other research, hopefully medical science will find a solution to the AIDS health crisis.

Other gay-supported organizations besides Howard Brown have provided counseling, support groups, housing, education, and other services for gay men. **Horizons Community Services,** an important service center for the community, has a youth group that dispenses important information about safer sex to young gay men. This "post-AIDS" generation of young men are learning to adopt safer sexual practices as a natural part of their coming of age. Many Chicago gays have discovered the life-changing rewards of volunteering to be support managers, providing friendship and a variety of services to people affected by AIDS.

Coming out to parents and family remains the most difficult and perhaps the most important part of the maturing process for gays and lesbians. **The Chicago Chapter of the Federation of Parents and Friends of Lesbians and Gays** has been supportive of the "coming out" process through volunteers such as Gerda Muri. Tagged "Straight Mom" when she first volunteered for Horizons' youth group, Muri became involved in both organizations through acceptance of her own son's gay lifestyle. Her top priority is education.

"I try to tell parents that homosexuality is not a choice. There are gay people from all kinds of family situations. There are healthy gay relationships and there are gays and lesbians who are accepted by their families." An enlightened parent, Muri best expresses her position as a loving mother: "I am not as concerned about why my son is gay as I am concerned that he have a good and happy life."

Not long ago, coming out was too great a risk for most gays. Chicago native Joel Hall, founder of Chicago's world renowned Joel Hall Dancers, first testified in favor of a gay rights ordinance before the city council in the 1970s. Hall recalls, "At the time I was growing up, it was very difficult for gay people to like themselves. We were not liked by anyone. Guys from the suburbs would come around in carloads to beat sissies on the streets. The police were very supportive of the suburban position."

Anti-gay violence still occurs, often sparked by right-wing political extremist groups. Two violent attacks occurred recently in the offices of the *Windy City Times* in less than one year. Often, anti-gay violence goes unreported, but as open gay pride increases, such oppression is no longer accepted passively by Chicago's gay and lesbian community.

In the summer of 1986, a gay rights ordinance designed to include "sexual orientation" as a protected class in civil right discrimination complaints finally came before the city council. The ordinance was to provide relief to gays and lesbians faced with discrimination in employment, housing, and public accommodation. Because Illinois was the first state to legalize consensual sex among adults in private, it seemed logical to extend civil rights to everyone through the city's human rights code.

Many prominent city voices came out in favor of the ordinance, including Joseph Cardinal Bernardin. Mayor Harold Washington actively supported the ordinance as a civil rights issue. Former mayor Jane Byrne (who appeared in the Gay Pride Parade only after she'd left office) was disappointingly silent. The greatest disappointment, however, came on the eve of the city council vote, when Cardinal Bernardin abruptly withdrew his support, saying he opposed the "wording" of the ordinance. The Cardinal refused to compromise. When later that year the content of a papal letter to the Catholic Bishops was made public, it was clear that the Cardinal was influenced by pressure from above. The letter, approved by Pope John Paul II, referred to civil rights protection for gays and lesbians as designed "to protect behavior to which no one has any conceivable right."

Defeat of the gay rights ordinance by a decisive 18-30 margin came on July 29, 1986—a date that Chicago gays and lesbians will not soon forget. The packed crowd of saddened supporters filed out of the council chambers singing "We Shall Overcome." On that day, the political clout of Chicago's once invisible minority began to galvanize. Within weeks, Dr. Ron Sable, co-founder of the Cook County AIDS Clinic, shifted his campaign as the first openly gay candidate for alderman into high gear. Soon a gay voter registration drive started in Chicago's 44th ward. The fight was on.

Unspoken gay repression in our country has been sparked by sensational AIDS headlines and fanned by short-sighted responses from institutions such as the Justice Department and the Supreme Court. Chicago gay men have responded to this backlash by building their own institutions to meet the civic, political, and cultural needs of the city's gay residents. In February of 1987, Mayor Harold Washington announced the first full-time salaried position for a liaison to the community to serve as executive director of the **Mayor's Committee on Gay and Lesbian Issues**. Gay men are becoming more visible members of all of Chicago's business, political, and civic organizations—not just gay organizations—as well as proud citizens of all the city's neighborhoods—not just New Town.

The listing below is selective and not comprehensive. For a more complete listing, consult the directories in the *Windy City Times, Chicago Outlines,* and *Gay Chicago Magazine.*

ARTS ORGANIZATIONS

Chicago Lesbian and Gay Film Festival
Chicago Filmmakers
6 W. Hubbard (but they're planning to move soon; as of this writing, the new location was unknown), Chicago, IL 60610   329-0854
Since 1980, Chicago Filmmmakers has sponsored an annual week-long festival of international films with gay and lesbian themes. The festival, held in early fall, is hosted by the Music Box Theater, located at 3733 N. Southport.

Chicago Gay Men's Chorus
P.O. Box 14146, Chicago, IL 60614   477-9380
This chorus, with over 100 members, leans heavily to pop music. Their performances, which often include numbers in drag, are high-spirited and fun.

Gerber-Hart Library
3238 N. Sheffield, Chicago, IL 60657   883-3003
An independent gay and lesbian library. The collection includes anything by and about gays and lesbians, including history, novels, poetry, records, tapes, magazines, newspapers (mostly from the midwest), directories, posters, and t-shirts. Everyone is welcome. You need to join the library to check things out. Hours are 12-4pm Saturdays, but this may change, so call first.

Lionheart Gay Theater
Box 601, Wilmette, IL 60091
Since 1979, Lionheart has championed gay and lesbian playwrights by introducing forty original plays and giving over seventy-five benefit performances for the gay and lesbian community.

Windy City Gay Chorus
606 W. Barry, Box 216, Chicago, IL 60657   871-SING
Known for their excellent musicianship, this seventy-five member chorus launches Gay Pride Week each summer with a concert at Orchestra Hall. Their concerts play to packed crowds and often include selections by a song-

and-dance troupe called the Windy City Slickers, popular for doing show tunes.

BARS

Stiff competition for business constantly challenges city tavern owners to find new gimmicks for bringing in crowds. Chicago's gay bars include dance, live entertainment, female impersonators, videos, new wave music, leather, after-work bars, juice bars, piano bars—you name it. To find the right bar to suit your taste or mood, pick up a copy of the *Windy City Times, Chicago Outlines,* or *Gay Chicago Magazine* and flip to their directories and maps of Chicago's gay nightlife. Both publications are free and available in bookstores, restaurants, and bars. You can also find a great number of bars in walking distance of each other in New Town (Lakeview East) on Broadway, Clark, Belmont, and Halsted Streets, north of Barry and south of Grace Streets.

COUNSELING AND HEALTH SERVICES

Horizons Community Services Inc.
3225 N. Sheffield, Chicago, IL 60657   929-HELP
This growing social service agency is a clearinghouse for information for gays and lesbians. Need counseling? Legal advice? Looking for a roommate? Just need to hear a friendly voice? Call Horizons' hotline (929-HELP) between 7 pm and 11 pm every night. If they don't have an answer to your question, they will refer you to the organization that can best help. All calls are kept strictly confidential. Horizons also has an education, support, and prevention program for people with concerns or anxiety about AIDS. The program, called PASSAGES ("promoting attitudes that support sexuality through affirmative guidance and effective support") holds sessions that are led by health and mental health professionals in a small group setting.

Howard Brown Memorial Clinic
945 W. George, Chicago, IL 60657   871-5777
AIDS hotline: 871-5696
Confidential diagnosis and treatment of sexually transmitted diseases available Sunday afternoons 2 pm-4:30 pm, and Tuesday through Thursday evenings 7 pm-9:30 pm. For over twelve years, Howard Brown has provided medical services by highly trained staff and volunteers from the gay community.

State of Illinois AIDS hotline
1-800-AID-AIDS
A state-funded information hotline providing telephone counseling services as well as physician and support group referrals. Many callers are heterosexuals seeking safer sex information. Call 10 am-10 pm seven days a week.

Gay and Lesbian Physicians of Chicago
P.O. Box 14864, Chicago, IL 60614   475-0790
For referrals to gay physicians.

Parents and Friends of Lesbians and Gays
P.O. Box 11023, Chicago, IL 60611-0023   472-3079
The Chicago chapter of this national organization meets on the third Sunday of every month. Although members are mostly mothers and fathers of lesbians and gay men, other relatives and friends are also members.

POLITICAL ORGANIZATIONS

Illinois Gay and Lesbian Task Force
615 W. Wellington, Chicago, IL 60657   975-0707
Info line: 975-1212
An organization involved in civil rights issues for gays and lesbians as well as education of the public. Volunteers teach what they call "Gay 101," a class in gay understanding, for the Chicago Police Training Academy and the Cook County Department of Corrections. The Task Force also provides literature and speakers for counselors in the Chicago Public School system. They are very involved with legislative efforts in the city council and state legislature.

Independent Precinct Organization (IVI-IPO), Gay and Lesbian Caucus
Independent Voters of Illinois
220 S. State St., Room 726, Chicago, IL 60604   663-4203
The Caucus seeks to involve gays and lesbians in the mainstream political process. The IVI-IPO employs a full-time lobbyist in Springfield who lobbies for gay and lesbian civil rights.

PUBLICATIONS

Windy City Times
Sentury Publications, Inc.
3223 N. Sheffield, Chicago, IL 60657   935-1790
A free gay and lesbian newsweekly which features local, national, and international news as well as entertainment features. A vital sounding board for gay and lesbian political concerns and an excellent source of information about activities, organizations, and events. Published on Thursdays and available at bookstores, restaurants, and bars, or by subscription.

Gay Chicago Magazine
Ultra Ink, Inc.
3121 N. Broadway, Chicago, IL 60657   327-7271
Once a weekly bar guide, now a more expanded publication with legal and medical columns, entertainment reviews, Tyco's Astrology column, a calendar of events, and classified ads. Available free in bars, bookstores, and restaurants, or by subscription.

Chicago Outlines
1300 W. Belmont, Chicago, IL 60657   871-7610
The city's newest gay and lesbian newspaper. Covers local, regional, and national news and has listings of gay and lesbian organizations, bars, and restaurants. Available free in gay and lesbian bookstores, bars, and other locations, and by subscription.

RELIGIOUS ORGANIZATIONS

Dignity Chicago
P.O. Box 148217, Chicago, IL 60614   549-2633
The Chicago chapter of a national organization that is the largest gay and lesbian religious organization in the country. Although not an official part

of the Chicago Catholic Archdiocese, Dignity maintains communication with the Catholic church. Weekly masses for gays and lesbians are offered Sundays at 7 pm at St. Sebastian Church at 824 W. Wellington; these are followed by a social hour. The office is open for calls from 7 pm-10 pm Monday through Saturday.

Congregation Or Chadash
656 W. Barry, Chicago, IL 60657   248-9456
Congregation Or Chadash is a member of the Union of American Hebrew Congregations and the World Congress of Gay and Lesbian Jewish Organizations. The Congregation meets for Shabbot services on the second, fourth, and fifth Fridays of each month at 8:30 pm. They sponsor many educational events and celebrate all holidays and festivals.

Metropolitan Community Church
615 W. Wellington, Chicago, IL 60657   472-8708
24-hour info line: 327-5168
This church, with a gay and lesbian focus, has three other congregations in the Chicago area besides the Good Shepherd parish at the Wellington address: Hinsdale, Evanston, and Hyde Park. Call the number above for addresses and times of services.

SPORTS

Metropolitan Sports Association
P.O. Box 10510, Chicago, IL 60610   447-4349
MSA sponsors tournaments in a variety of sports including bowling, softball, tennis, and volleyball. MSA, which has over 1,000 members, also hosts registration parties and midwestern regional tournaments.

Frontrunners/Chicago Inc.
P.O. Box 148313, Chicago, IL 60614-8313   871-0914
Whether you are a part-time jogger or a competitive marathoner, this group provides support and activities geared for you, including twice weekly fun runs starting at the totem pole at Addison and Lake Shore Drive in Lincoln Park. Runs are held on Tuesdays at 6:30 pm and Saturdays at 10 am. The club welcomes newcomers.

—J.H. Johnson

SURVIVAL

Photo by Richard Younker.

GETTING AROUND

Chicago is huge and sprawling, and traveling from one end to another (about 25 miles) will take you a long time, no matter if you drive or take public transportation. You can easily live without a car in many parts of the city— the closer to the center you live the better—but if you don't live near an el or major bus route, you'll be frustrated trying to get around. The city is not covered equally by public transit: in general, the north side has better coverage by the faster elevated trains than the south side—especially the southwest side—and that makes a big difference in time.

Everyone complains about the city's public transportation, but our system is excellent for a major American city, especially given how old it is (the first elevated train was built in the 1890s) and how cheap it is. You can get to anywhere you want in Chicago by taking some combination of subway or elevated trains (known collectively as the "el"), bus, or commuter train.

Of course, having a car makes life in Chicago a lot easier. Lake Shore Drive (also called the Outer Drive), which runs along the lake most of the length of the city, is a real pleasure to drive, both for the great sightseeing it provides and because no trucks are allowed!! Although the expressways are always under repair, our traffic jams—even those in the Loop—don't come close to the gargantuan messes in New York or Los Angeles. Parking can be an obnoxious problem, however, in the Loop and near north side.

The easiest and by far the cheapest way to get to O'Hare Airport is by taking the O'Hare/Congress or O'Hare Douglas els. They run frequently and are in service all night long. Getting to Midway Airport involves taking a combination of el and bus by public transit; by car, getting to Midway is easy. More on getting to the airports later.

FINDING ADDRESSES

Chicago has a north side, a south side, and a west side. It also has a near north side, a southeast side, northwest, southwest, and far southwest sides, the boundaries for which are all hazy. The lake is always east. "Going downtown" means going to the Loop, no matter what direction you travel. The Loop officially refers to the blocks downtown circled by the elevated trains—Lake Street on the north, Wabash Avenue on the east, Wells Street on the west, and Van Buren Street on the south—but actually covers a larger area, a couple of blocks further out in all directions.

Finding addresses in Chicago is easy because the streets are laid out in a grid pattern, with the intersection of State and Madison Streets as the zero point. Streets north of Madison and parallel to the lake are prefixed north; those south of Madison are prefixed south. Streets that run east-west are prefixed east or west depending on which side of State Street they are on. Diagonal streets are a bit trickier because their addresses don't always conform to the numbering rules—bring a map when traveling along these streets. Almost every block is numbered in increments of 100. In general, a mile contains 800 address divisions; therefore, 3200 North is four miles north of Madison.

Chicago Street Number Map

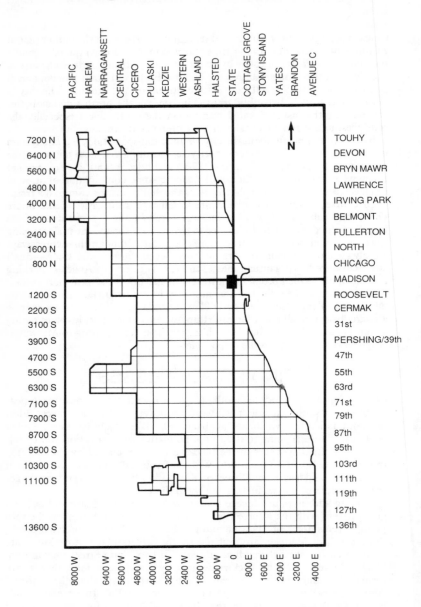

Corresponding street names appear in opposite border.

PUBLIC TRANSPORTATION

The Chicago area's mass transit system is financed and run by the **Regional Transit Authority** (RTA). The RTA, in turn, runs three divisions: the **Chicago Transit Authority** (CTA), which operates the buses and rapid transit trains (the els); **Metra,** which operates or purchases services from railroads for the commuter train system that serves the city and suburbs; and **Pace,** which provides bus services in the suburbs. The newspapers regularly carry stories on RTA and CTA budget fights, reorganizations, and threats to cut service.

Although the CTA does a good job of transporting people and provides excellent coverage of the city, it isn't very user friendly. For example, maps are hard to find. Maps are infrequently posted inside el cars or buses, and maps in el stations are often posted near the fare boxes and not on platforms (the CTA seems to assume that everyone knows how to get where they're going once they get to the platform). It all adds up to an impression that the system is only for insiders. To get a printed map, ask at a major el transfer station, bus garage, or call 836-7000 and ask them to send you one.

Fares for the CTA are $1 for the els and $.90 for buses. Transfers for switching to another el or bus line cost $.25, and you have to buy them when you first enter the system; they're good for 2 hours and can't be used again on the same route they were issued. No round trips allowed on a transfer, no matter how short your jaunt—this is where lack of a zoned system makes for inequities.

Buses require exact fare but accept dollar bills (you won't get change though). You'll have to pay a $.10 differential when transferring from a bus to an el with a bus transfer, or if you're paying with a token. A few express bus lines and one el line—the Evanston Express—require a $.20 surcharge. The CTA also offers monthly ($46) and 14-day ($23) passses. You can buy passes and tokens—cash only—at banks, currency exchanges, Jewel supermarkets, some Dominick's supermarkets, bus garages, and el stations.

To find out about special reduced rates for kids, seniors, and disabled persons, call 836-7000.

The els

There are four el lines. The lines have names that won't always help you understand their routes, so you'll have to memorize which ones go where. All the els, with a few exceptions noted below, operate 24 hours a day. Rush hour service is frequent, and night service is less frequent.

On weekdays during work hours, the els are designated "A" or "B" trains, and each will skip some stops. Route maps indicate which stops are A, B, or A/B stops. Pay your fare at the station or, if the station is closed, then on the train. You won't need a transfer if you can switch at stops designated as transfer points.

A few tips: You won't always be able to rely on the conductor to announce the stops over the PA system, so be alert for your stop. Maps aren't always posted in the el cars, so carry one with you if you're taking an unfamiliar route. If you're on a crowded el (or bus) during rush hour, stand in the aisles between the seats rather than at the doors to avoid being crushed by people exiting.

The **Howard/Englewood** and **Jackson Park/Howard** lines (also called the north/south lines) run north to the northern boundary of the city (Howard Street) and south to 61st Street.

The **Lake/Dan Ryan** runs west from the Loop to Oak Park, and south from the Loop, down the middle of the Dan Ryan Expressway, to 95th Street. If you want to go further south, you have to transfer to a bus.

The **O'Hare/Congress** (also called the west/northwest line) serves the northwest side, running to O'Hare airport, and the west side, running down the middle of the Eisenhower Expressway, to Forest Park.

The **O'Hare/Douglas** travels the same route as the Congress on the northwest side to O'Hare airport, and also serves the west side, ending in Cicero.

The **Ravenswood** starts in the northwest side of the city and zigzags south and east, joining up with the Howard line at the Belmont stop, then circles around the Loop and heads back up north. This is the best el for seeing the sights of the city; the route is described in The Other Top Ten Sights chapter. Limited service on Sundays and at night—check the CTA map or ask about the hours.

The **Skokie Swift** and the **Evanston Shuttle** connect with the Howard el line. The **Evanston Express** provides express service between Howard Street and the Loop on weekdays during rush hours. Neither the Skokie Swift nor the Evanston Express operates on Sundays. The Evanston Express requires you to pay a $.20 surcharge.

24-hour (closed on major holidays, however) **travel information center** to answer questions on routes, schedules, and fares:
From the city: 836-7000
From the suburbs, toll free: 1-800-972-7000
TDD number for the hearing impaired: 836-4949

Regional Transit Authority
1 N. Dearborn, Suite 1100
Chicago, IL 60602
917-0700 (for travel information, call 836-7000)

Chicago Transit Authority
Merchandise Mart, 7th floor
Chicago, IL 60654
General office number for lost and found (open 24 hours); ID cards for seniors, students, and disabled people; and for complaints and commendations: 664-7200 (for travel information, call 836-7000)

Buses

Bus stops are designated by blue and white signs on street corners. Drivers are not supposed to stop between stops, but if they know you or you're the only passenger, they might. Many CTA buses run from 5 am to midnight, Monday through Saturday, and 8 am to midnight on Sunday and holidays. Some lines run all night. (Some people feel safer taking buses rather than els if they have to use public transportation at night.) See the CTA route map for details. Some lines run express from certain neighborhoods to the Loop; these may require a surcharge and may only run certain hours—

consult the CTA map for more information, or call 836-7000. Buses occasionally change routes from year to year; check the latest CTA map for information.

Bus service is more frequent during the day, but how frequent depends on the line. The buses are supposed to adhere to a schedule, which occasionally results in the frustrating phenomenon of having your driver pull the bus over and wait (without explanation) for 5 minutes until they are back on schedule. For information on fare discounts for seniors, students, and disabled people, call 664-7200.

Door-to-door bus service for the disabled is offered, but it's hard to qualify for it. Call 664-7200 for information.

Commuter Trains

Commuter trains, which operate on a zoned system, cost more to ride but they are very comfortable, on time, and clean. Trains make stops in the city on their way to the suburbs (but check schedules for which trains make city stops—not all do). Trains usually stop running shortly after midnight and may only run once an hour or less frequently in the late evenings. Purchase tickets and monthly passes at the stations listed below or at your local station.

Children, students, seniors, and disabled riders are eligible for reduced fares. Call 322-6777 for more information.

At **Union Station,** located at Adams and Canal, you can catch four different rail lines, which serve the areas described below.

The Burlington Northern runs west from Chicago to Aurora.

The Illinois Central Gulf Diesel Line goes southwest between Chicago and Joliet, via Lockport.

The Milwaukee Road: The north line runs north between Chicago and Fox Lake and makes a couple of trips a day to Lake Geneva, Wisconsin. The west line serves northwest Chicago and beyond to Elgin.

The Norfolk and Western runs southwest between Chicago and Orland Park.

At the **Chicago and Northwestern Station,** located at Madison and Canal, you can catch the **Chicago and Northwestern** train, which has three lines.

The North Line runs along the lake between Chicago and Kenosha, Wisconsin. Commuters from Evanston and other north shore suburbs use this railroad.

The Northwest Line runs north and west between Chicago and Harvard, with a branch going to McHenry.

The West Line goes straight west between Chicago and Geneva.

At the **Illinois Central Gulf Station,** located at the Randolph Street Station at Randolph and Michigan, with two other entrances at South Water Street and Van Buren Street, you can catch two lines:

The Illinois Central Gulf Electric Line runs south along the lake, then jogs slightly west to run to University Park (formerly called Park Forest South). Many Hyde Parkers use the IC.

The Chicago, South Shore, and South Bend Line runs south and east between Chicago and South Bend, Indiana. You can take this line to the Indiana Dunes.

At the **La Salle Street Station,** located at 414 S. La Salle, you can catch the **Rock Island Line,** which has a line that runs southwest through the Beverly/Morgan Park neighborhoods of the city and beyond, and a main line that runs southwest to Joliet.

METRA passenger and information services
Weekdays 8 am-5 pm: 322-6777
Evenings and weekends, from the city: 836-7000; from the suburbs, toll free: 1-800-972-7000

TRAVEL BY CAR
Expressways

Chicagoans usually refer to the expressways by name rather than by route numbers. It's a confusing system because sometimes the same route has several names, depending on which section of it you're talking about. You get used to it after a few years.

The north-south expressways are the Dan Ryan and the Kennedy. The Eisenhower runs east-west. Running to the southwest part of the city is the Stevenson. Traffic is usually congested around the "spaghetti bowl" intersection just southwest of the Loop, where the major north-south expressways (I-90/94) meets the east-west expressway (I-290).

Important tip: although the I-90/94 expressways (the Dan Ryan and the Kennedy) run north-south through the city, signs for entrances onto them will be labeled east and west, since that is the overall direction they run across the country. Signs marked east and Indiana will take you south through the city, and those marked west and Wisconsin will take you north.

These are the major expressway names and route numbers.

Stevenson Expressway—I-55, runs southwest from McCormick Place to Springfield and St. Louis. The Stevenson is the city's least crowded expressway.
Dan Ryan Expressway—I-90 and I-94 running south of the spaghetti bowl intersection described above, until 99th St. The exit and entrance ramps on the Dan Ryan are notorious for their poor design: cars leaving the expressway have to directly cut across cars entering, so be careful. The Ryan is always crowded (just where are all those people zooming to at 3 am?) and always challenging; drive alertly at night.
Kennedy Expressway—I-90 and I-94 north of the spaghetti bowl intersection described above, jogging past O'Hare Airport, when it becomes I-90, and continuing to Rockford as the Northwest Tollway (which is still I-90). The Kennedy is usually clogged just west of downtown at the exit for the Eisenhower Expressway.
Eisenhower Expressway—I-290, runs straight west from the Loop. The Eisenhower extension runs further west and north to the Schaumburg area, where you can link up with the Northwest Tollway, I-90.

Edens Expressway—I-94 when it splits off from the Kennedy just before Cicero Avenue at about 4400 North, south of O'Hare. Rush hour traffic is usually clogged at the juncture of the Kennedy and the Edens. The Edens heads north to the northern suburbs, ultimately joining the Tri-State Tollway, I-294.

Tri-State Tollway—I-294, running north-south west of the city, until the Edens joins it, when it becomes I-94.

Calumet Expressway—I-94 running south of the Dan Ryan, when the Ryan splits between I-57, which keeps running south to Champaign/Urbana and ultimately New Orleans, and the Calumet Expressway, which runs south and east to Indiana.

Chicago Skyway—I-90 going southeast when it branches off the Dan Ryan at about 66th Street. Links up with the Indiana toll road.

SHORT-CUTS

In general, use Lake Shore Drive whenever you can. It's a beautiful road, no trucks are allowed so the driving is easier, and traffic is almost always moving at a good clip. Just try to avoid it when sporting events are being held at Soldier Field.

You can hook up with the Dan Ryan (to go south) or the Kennedy (to go north) from Lake Shore Drive. Look for exits just south of McCormick Place (about 1 1/2 miles south of the Loop) for I-55, which feeds immediately into I-94.

LOOP

In the Loop, a fast way to drive north-south, from 500 North to 500 South, is by taking Lower Wacker Drive, the lower level of Wacker Drive. Lower Wacker runs under Michigan Avenue from Grand Avenue (500 North), across the lower level of the Michigan Avenue Bridge, and then under Wacker to the interchanges for the Eisenhower, Dan Ryan, and Kennedy Expressways. Traffic usually moves along quickly. Only certain east-west streets enter onto Lower Wacker, among them Grand, Kinzie, Illinois, Randolph, Monroe, and the Eisenhower Expressway (just east of the main post office).

Columbus Drive, just a few blocks west of Lake Michigan, is a quick way to travel north-south around (east) of the Loop. A new extension of Columbus connects Grand Avenue to Lake Shore Drive.

NORTH SIDE

Some streets are better than others for traversing the length of the city if you can't or don't want to use an expressway. On the north side, try Ashland, Halsted, or Western. Elston is quick for going northwest. Ridge Avenue, which branches off of Broadway at 5600 north, is an alternative to Sheridan Road for getting to Evanston.

SOUTH SIDE

To go north-south on the south side, try Ashland, Halsted, or Western. The Stevenson is the city's least crowded expressway, so if you're traveling southwest, I-55 may be your quickest route. Archer Avenue is an alternative to the expressways for going southwest, and goes through interesting neighborhoods. Far south, Vincennes Avenue is fast for jogging south and west.

PARKING

Parking isn't too bad in most parts of the city, except for the Loop and near north side; however, areas further north are slowly becoming worse. In the Loop, the cheapest parking is at the Grant Street and Monroe Street underground city parking lots run by the Park District. They're cheap and convenient. The private lots are very expensive. Weekends and late at night, it's easier to find street parking in the Loop. Try looking on the southern edge of the Loop first.

In Lincoln Park, and parts of Lakeview, be prepared to circle endlessly, especially on weekend nights.

GETTING TO THE AIRPORTS

Driving to **O'Hare** is a drag, especially during rush hours or at holiday season, because of heavy traffic. To drive to O'Hare from the Loop, take the **Kennedy (I-90/94)** west, stay on the Kennedy when it becomes I-90, and then take the I-190 exit for O'Hare. Once you're there, you must pay to park. If you don't want to park, if you're lucky you'll be able to zoom up and pick up your party if they arrived on time, but the lines of cars waiting at the arrival gates are usually ominous and the police are conscientious about getting waiting cars to move. You might avoid some of this congestion by arranging to meet your arriving party at the departure gates rather than the arrival gates.

An easy, quick, cheap alternative is to take either the **O'Hare/Congress** or **O'Hare/Douglas** el lines to their northwest terminus, which is smack dab in O'Hare Airport. From the Loop, the trip will take about 45 minutes. The trains run frequently, run all night, and are safe. You arrive at a beautiful, modern el stop (designed by architect Helmut Jahn) and you're right next to all the terminals. The only disadvantages are that you have to get to the Congress or Douglas els in the first place, either by getting to the Loop or to one of the stops on the el lines, which may involve more traveling than you want to do. Also, the els don't have luggage racks.

Otherwise, you can spend a bit more money and use the airport express bus service provided by **Continental Air Transport.** The buses are comfortable and offer plenty of room for luggage. Continental buses leave from several hotels in the Loop, once an hour. Continental buses also leave from many locations on the outskirts of the city and from the suburbs. Hours are limited on some runs and certain locations may not offer service on the weekends. Call ahead. Some buses require reservations. Fares vary. Call 454-7800 for fare and boarding information.

Finally, you can take a taxi—ask about the share-a-ride program, which will save you money. Or use of one of many limousine services for a fancier, pricier trip to O'Hare.

For a more complete listing of options for getting to O'Hare, look in the yellow pages under "Airport transportation service."

By car, **Midway Airport** is much easier to get to in terms of traffic than O'Hare. Take the **Stevenson Expressway** to the Cicero exit, and travel south on Cicero almost 2 miles to Midway. Parking at Midway is easy but only a little cheaper than at O'Hare.

Using public transportation to get to Midway is a bit more of a hassle because no el exists to take you there directly. You'll probably have to take a combination of an el and bus to get there, which may take some time. Call 836-7000 for specific information on public transit to Midway.

Otherwise, the same options exist as do for getting to O'Hare. **Continental Air Transport** offers bus service to Midway, but on a more limited basis than their service to O'Hare. Call 454-7800 for schedule and fare information. Or take a taxi or limousine.

Again, look in the yellow pages under "Airport transportation service" for more listings of transportation options to Midway.

OTHER TRANSPORTATION

Amtrak (trains)
210 S. Canal (Union Station)
558-1075
City ticket office: 505 N. Michigan
930-4311

Trailways bus service
119 E. 95th St.
785-9500

Greyhound bus service
74 W. Randolph
781-2900

Drive-away companies offer you the opportunity to drive someone else's car (the other person is usually moving to another location) to another city. You have to buy your own gas but you have the comfort and freedom of driving to your destination. Look in the yellow pages under "Automobile transporters and drive-away companies" for listings of such companies.

EMPLOYMENT

Chicago is a good place for job-hunting, but it helps to be persistent and tenacious. Our economy is broad based and diverse, and we continue to be an important center for manufacturing, financial services, and transportation industries. As in the U.S. in general, the jobs of the future in Chicago will be in service industries such as retail, finance, insurance, real estate, transportation, and public utilities. Less promising fields for the future are education, construction, and manufacturing.

Opportunities for part-time jobs are good here too. Loop businesses employ legions of temporary office workers. Waiting tables, cab driving, and substitute teaching in public and private schools are good alternatives for part-time work.

LANDING A JOB IN CHICAGO

Still a city with big shoulders, Chicago has an incredible number of firms with over 1,000 employees, among them Sears Roebuck, Beatrice, AM International, Amoco, Ameritech, Blue Cross/Blue Shield, Carson Pirie Scott, Commonwealth Edison, Cotter & Company, and Montgomery Ward.

For a listing of Chicago's 1,500 major employers, with addresses and phone numbers, refer to *How to Get a Job in Chicago*, by Tom Camden and Susan Schwartz. This book also provides extensive lists of publications, networks, and professional and trade associations, which will help you make valuable job contacts. Another good reference is *The Greater Chicago Job Bank*, which lists 1,000 major employers, describes their business and the types of positions available, and provides a forecast of the company's future growth. Also important to anyone's job search in Chicago is *Crain's Chicago Business*, a news weekly packed with information about Chicago business trends.

As you begin your job search, use all of your personal contacts to their fullest and invest in several of the excellent books mentioned in this chapter, including the two mentioned above. Begin your job research by assessing your skills and desires. Ask yourself: What do you expect from a job? What is your work experience? What kind of volunteer experiences do you have? An excellent guide is Bolles' *What Color Is Your Parachute?* I cannot recommend enough this journey into self-discovery.

Techniques

CAREER COUNSELING

Sometimes it helps to get professional advice. There are hundreds of career counseling services—some free, some costly. Camden and Schwartz' *How to Get a Job in Chicago* lists many reputable career counselors. It's always best to get a personal referral from a friend or a friend of a friend.

Then do some comparison shopping. Decide how much you're willing to pay, and what services you need (e.g., vocational testing, narrowing career choices, resume writing, interview techniques), then talk to the counselor before making a decision. Check out her credentials. Will she give you references? Check with the Better Business Bureau to see if any complaints have been received. What is the fee and to what does it entitle you? When do you have to pay? Many counselors like to provide a whole package of services, but if you don't need the whole package, don't get it.

If you are a student, use your school's placement service—it's probably free. School career centers offer a full range of services for job seekers. Services may be available to alums too. Many Chicago City-Wide College or junior colleges have career centers with special classes, career and industry information, and job listings.

CHANGING CAREERS

To explore a different line of work, consider continuing education classes offered by most of the universities in the city (see the section on continuing education in the Education chapter of this book). Or do volunteer work. If possible, don't quit your present job while you look for another; it's much easier to find a job while you already have one.

Career consultants may be of help when changing careers. The **Professional Career Counselor's Network (PCCN),** a professional association of career development specialists, can help you select a career consultant. Write PCCN at 36 S. Wabash Ave., Room 1202, Chicago, IL 60603.

PRIVATE EMPLOYMENT AGENCIES

As intermediaries between employers and job seekers, employment agencies usually receive a fee, generally a percentage of the worker's annual salary, often paid by the employer, if the employee completes a stated number of months on the job. Some agencies specialize in a particular field, for example, accounting, health care, or engineering. Most agencies concentrate on placing lower-level jobs.

A reputable agency will try to match an applicant with an appropriate job, but be aware that the agency's bread and butter is commissions, so that the staff's first priority may be to fill a job order, not to place you in your ideal position.

Try to get a referral from a satisfied customer before selecting an agency, or consult Camden and Schwartz' book. All employment agencies must be licensed by the state. If you want to verify that an agency is licensed, call the Department of Labor at 793-2810.

Some things to consider when selecting an employment agency: Does the employer pay the fee? What is the fee and what does it entitle you to? Read the contract before you sign. Caution: the application may be the contract itself. Does the agency actually have the jobs it advertises in the newspaper?

EXECUTIVE SEARCH FIRMS

Executive search firms or head hunters locate persons with specific qualifications to match an employer's request. Generally, they only deal with upper-level management positions; the usual fee for such services is 30 percent of the first year's salary plus expenses, billed to the hiring company. These firms do not work on a contingency basis like employment agencies, but it's difficult to get an interview with an executive search firm because they can't bill the time they spend with you to a client. Furthermore, unsolicited resumes are often thrown away. Ask your personal and professional contacts for a referral to executive search firms. Many executive search firms belong to the Association of Executive Recruiting Consultants.

NETWORKING

Although networking is not as trendy as it used to be, don't discount it as a job-seeking tool. A network can provide advice, support, job leads, and information on career advancement. Professional and business associations, ethnic and other special associations, alumni associations, friends, and relatives all work as formal and informal networks.

Carol Kleiman's *Women's Networks* (1981) is an excellent book on this subject, describing what networks are, how to use them, and how to start them, as well as containing listings by state and by category. Women's networks have been formed for most professions. *Today's Chicago Woman*, a free monthly available in libraries and stores in the Loop, carries a networking column. Camden and Schwartz's *How to Find a Job in Chicago* lists professional associations and even bars where people from different professions gather after hours so you can do some "convivial networking."

RESEARCH

Start any job-hunting research by visiting the Business Information Center of the Chicago Public Library, Mandel Building, 425 N. Michigan Ave., 11th floor, 269-2814. A good comprehensive source of career and company information, the library also holds career-related pamphlets and books.

Begin by reading the description of the company or industry in the following reference books: *Standard and Poor's Register of Corporations, Directors, and Executives*, and *Moody's Complete Corporate Index* (major sources of information on publicly held companies); the *Encyclopaedia of Business Information Sources* (industrial publications); *Metropolitan Chicago Area's Major Employers*; *Directory of Agencies* (social service and non-profit agencies); *Directory of Governments* (departments and offices in local, state, and federal government offices); *Make No Little Plans: Jobs for Metropolitan Chicago* (long-term job trends in the Chicago area); and *Crain's Chicago Business'* regularly published lists of area companies.

Another good source of information is the Computer Assisted Reference Center (call 269-2915) at the Chicago Public Library at 425 N. Michigan, which will give you 5 minutes of inexpensive on-line search time on any company.

The Film/Video Center at the Chicago Public Library's Cultural Center at 78 E. Washington (call 269-2910) has video cassettes you can borrow on job-seeking skills such as resume-writing, interviewing, and goal-setting.

PERSONAL CONTACTS

Don't be shy when you're looking for a job. Use all your personal contacts. Tell everyone you know that you're looking for a job and pick their brains for referrals and advice. Then, set up informal interviews with everyone they refer you to. Remember to ask these people for two or three referrals, for you to follow up on. Even ask people you don't know who you think might be knowledgeable or who have interesting jobs.

NEWSPAPERS

Don't rely on classified advertising. Only 10 percent of professional and technical jobs are found through the want ads. However, want ads can be one source of job leads. Better still, try to find the name and phone number of the person doing the hiring and send your resume and cover letter to them.

Montgomery Ward catalog employees, circa 1940. Photograph courtesy of Montgomery Ward & Co.

On Sundays, the *Chicago Tribune* carries the most extensive employment listings in Chicago. Both the business and job sections of the *Tribune* have good career-related articles and columns. Look for Carol Kleiman's weekly column on careers—it's always a good read. For lists of upcoming meetings, trainings, seminars, and professional association get-togethers, turn to the calendar of events in the *Tribune's* Monday business section. The job listings in the *Chicago Sun-Times* Sunday edition is also a source of job leads.

The *Chicago Reader*, the free weekly, carries want ads; most are for jobs that are part-time, arts-related, or off-beat.

The midwest edition of the *Wall Street Journal* is another source for job listings, although for the most part they only list the higher-level jobs in the Chicago area.

Services and Agencies

Following is a selective list of places and resources to help you in your search for work. At the end is information about unemployment.

GENERAL

Association House
4005 W. North Ave., Chicago, IL 60639
278-6111
Provides job placement services for adults.

Jewish Vocational Services
1 S. Franklin St., Chicago, IL 60606
346-6700
Not limited to people of the Jewish faith. Has several offices in the city, offering a wide range of services, including employment for older people.

Catholic Charities of Chicago
721 N. LaSalle St., Chicago, IL 60610
266-6100
Job clubs meet throughout the year, offering seminars on skills training, interviewing techniques, and writing resumes. Participants can use their phone and typewriters. Job clubs meet for four weeks, three times per week.

Illinois Job Service
6451 S. Central   581-4343
8516 S. Commercial   374-8410
9415 S. Western   881-6830
1751 W. 47th   254-2769
1514-20 W. Division   489-6262
4809 N. Ravenswood   334-6646
This government agency provides a computerized listing of job openings in many fields throughout the state. To get this list, all you need to do is fill out the job service form at your nearest branch office. Let them know if you are a veteran; veterans get special consideration.

Mayor's Office of Employment and Training
510 N. Peshtigo Ct., Suite 2A, Chicago, IL 60611
744-8787
Training and placement for jobs in the private sector. Clients must meet low-income guidelines to qualify for most services. Subcontracts with many community agencies to provide employment services throughout the city. Programs include classroom training, interviewing techniques, resume writing, job placement, and on-the-job training. Operates the Summer Youth Program (call 744-8787), a summer job program for teenagers between 14 and 21 years of age who meet low-income guidelines.

MINORITIES/ETHNIC

Minority Economic Resource Corp.
407 S. Dearborn, Suite 470, Chicago, IL 60640
939-2440
1565 Ellenwood, Des Plaines, IL 60016
297-4705
Helps minorities find jobs in the city and northwest suburbs. Places teens in job readiness and teaching skill programs. Adults are placed immediately if they're job ready and a position is available. Training in word processing, typing, and 10-key calculator.

Chicago Urban League
Employment Counseling and Training Dept.
4500 S. Michigan Ave., Chicago, IL 60653
285-1253
Counseling and job placement for all regardless of race, creed, and religious preference.

American Indian Business Association
4753 N. Broadway, Chicago, IL 60640
784-2434
Provides job readiness training and placement for all who can certify that they have American Indian heritage no matter how far removed. Places trainees in 6-month positions in non-profit agencies, followed by permanent, full-time job placements.

SER (Service Employment and Redevelopment)-Jobs for Progress
1814 S. Leavitt, Chicago, IL 60608
421-7432
2938 E. 91st St., Chicago, IL 60617
221-3252
Coaching in job readiness, referrals. Trains clients for jobs as word processors, administrative clerks, and clerk typists. Placement when client is job ready. Serves predominantly Latinos and blacks but will help anyone. Specializes in helping young people.

South Austin Job Referral Service
5082 W. Jackson Blvd., Chicago, IL 60644
626-1113 or 626-6115
Free job counseling and referral for all residents of the Austin and neighboring communities. Job readiness workshops, job clubs, community job fairs, and GED classes.

Spanish Coalition for Jobs
2011 W. Pershing Rd., Chicago, IL 60609
247-0707
1737 W. 18th St., Chicago, IL 60608
243-3032
Training in word processing, typing, and electronics, followed by placement. Services open to all, including young people (18 and over, but must possess high school or GED diploma). Clients must meet low-income requirements.

VETERANS

Chicago Veteran's Center
1607 W. Howard, Suite 200, Chicago, IL 60626
764-6595
One of four Chicago-area readjustment centers serving all vets, but primarily Vietnam vets. Employment services include job clubs, job-seeking techniques, skills assessment, and job placement. Illinois Job Service counselors available on Tuesdays and Wednesdays.

YOUTH

Association House
2150 W. North Ave., Chicago, IL 60647
276-0084
Job readiness skills training and placement for young people ages 16 to 21.

Chicago Commons
4100 W. Belmont, Chicago, IL 60641
685-1010
Operates five job training programs for 17- to 25-year-olds, aimed at helping high school dropouts, although others may also join the program. Programs

in microcomputers, automatic screw machine set up, plastic injection molding, package machine and mechanics, and industrial mechanical inspection. Has 94 percent placement rate and an excellent reputation.

Jobs for Youth
67 E. Madison, Ste. 1900, Chicago, IL 60603
782-2086
Serves economically disadvantaged youth 16 to 21 years of age, both high school graduates and drop-outs. Programs include pre-employment training (interviewing skills, resume writing), job placement, and GED classes. Has excellent reputation.

Mayor's Office of Employment and Training
See listing under "General" above.

OLDER WORKERS

Operation ABLE
36 S. Wabash Ave., Chicago, IL 60603
782-3335
Network of community-based agencies providing employment services primarily for people over 55 years of age, regardless of income (some programs are open to people under 55). Provides tuition reimbursement for skills training programs in areas including horticulture, security guard work, word processing, bank telling, and clerk-typing. Also provides job search training, job clubs, placement for unskilled job-seekers, and a 3-day intensive workshop, called the Able Worker Institute, on job-seeking for persons with management-level skills.

DISABLED WORKERS

State of Illinois
Department of Rehabilitation Services
9730 S. Western Ave., Suite 804, Chicago, IL 60642
857-2380
Services provided for all persons with physical, emotional, or mental disabilities. Services for the blind provided by the Bureau of Blind Services; call for information. Provides individual vocational rehabilitation, counseling, diagnostic vocational evaluation, instruction and training, and placement. In addition, provides books, materials, and equipment for persons interested in self-employment.

City of Chicago
Department on Aging and Disability
510 N. Peshtigo Ct., Chicago, IL 60611
744-4407
For people over 55 years of age who meet economically disadvantaged income guidelines, they offer classroom training, placement assistance, and job clubs in areas including security guard work, certified nursing assistant, bank telling, home health aids, and word processing. They also offer free employment services for the disabled 18 years and older.

DISPLACED HOMEMAKERS

Displaced homemakers are women reentering or entering the work force for the first time due to changed economic circumstances, for example, after divorce or the death of a spouse.

The State Board of Education provides funds for Displaced Homemaker Services, provided for the most part through community-based organizations and community colleges. Contact the Chicago District, 100 W. Randolph St. (917-2708), for the program nearest you. The following programs both offer workshops on job-seeking skills and emphasizing a positive self-image.

Chicago City-Wide College
Project New Start Displaced
Homemakers Program
226 W. Jackson, 6th floor
Chicago, IL 60606
984-2772

West Suburban YWCA
TARGET Program
26 W. St. Charles Rd.
Lombard, IL 60148
629-0170

EX-OFFENDERS

Safer Foundation
Operation DARE
571 W. Jackson Blvd.
Chicago, IL 60606
922-2200
Job search assistance, referral, placement, and GED classes for ex-offenders.

Service Employees Joint Council (SEJC)
AFL-CIO Ex-offender Placement
Program, Inc.
130 N. Franklin
Chicago, IL 60606
782-9189
Job placement services for ex-offenders.

DISLOCATED WORKERS

Dislocated workers—people who have lost their jobs because of lay-offs or plant relocation—are eligible for programs designed to counsel, retrain, and place them in new jobs. Call the Mayor's Office of Employment and Training, 510 Peshtigo Court (744-8787) to find out about these programs. Union members should note that your union may also provide such services.

Similarly, people who have been laid off because of foreign competition— for example, workers in the steel, textile, and shoe industries—may be eligible for retraining and extended unemployment benefits under the Trade Readjustment Act. Call your local unemployment office for information.

Government Employment

Although jobs in the private sector generally pay better, working for the government offers a sense of involvement that may compensate for slightly lower wages. To find about city government jobs, go to the Department of Personnel on the 11th floor of City Hall (LaSalle and Washington)—bring your resume, proof of Chicago residency, and college transcripts—look at the job postings, and apply for any jobs of interest. Government positions in the city work force are of two types: appointed and therefore subject to changes in administration; and career service, unaffected by changes in administration. In general, upper-level management and policy-making positions are appointed. Career service positions are filled on the basis of education and experience. A similar system is also followed by the state and the federal government.

For government employment opportunities contact the following agencies.

City of Chicago
Department of Personnel
121 N. LaSalle St., 11th floor, Chicago, IL 60602
744-4890
Accept applications for jobs with city departments. To apply, bring a resume, proof of Chicago residency, and a copy of transcripts, if a college grad.

State of Illinois Center
Central Management Services, Bureau of Personnel
100 W. Randolph, 3rd floor, Chicago, IL 60601
917-2390
Job listings in over 1,600 state jobs, but applications accepted only for those jobs posted. You can apply for a job in any county of the state.

Federal Job Information Center, Chicago Area Office
Office of Personnel
175 W. Jackson Blvd., Room 530, Chicago, IL 60604
353-6192
A self-service center where the Federal Job Opportunity list describes open positions in federal government. List also includes where to write to apply for these jobs. Job list may be found at state job service offices, major universities' job placement offices, and personnel offices for large federal agencies.

Temporary or Part-time Employment

If you are in school, raising children, between jobs, or would like to try out a new profession, part-time or temporary work may be for you. Most temporary agencies specialize in temporary work in particular fields. Accountemps, for example, places people with accounting backgrounds. Andy Frain, Inc., specializes in supplying security guard services, mostly for concerts and sports events. Checker Taxi Co. leases taxi cabs. Manpower, Norrel, Olsten, and Kelly Services place temporary office help.

You may be eligible to substitute teach elementary or high school in the Chicago public school system if you have a minimum of a bachelor's degree. Call the Board of Education for information (890-8000). Private schools usually require substitutes to have a bachelor's degree; other criteria vary from school to school. Call the particular school for information. (See the Education chapter for more information on private and public schools.)

Part-time and temporary jobs are listed in both the *Tribune* and *Sun-Times*. The free weekly *Reader* carries want ads for part-time, arts-related, and off-beat jobs. Neighborhood papers are also a good source for ads for local jobs, many of them part-time. (Check your local newsstand or refer to the Local Press chapter for information on neighborhood papers.)

Accountemps
35 E. Wacker
Chicago, IL 60601
263-8367

Andy Frain, Inc.
310 W. Chicago
Chicago, IL 60610
266-6900

Checker Taxi Co.
845 W. Washington
Chicago, IL 60606
421-1300

Kelly Services
55 W. Monroe
Chicago, IL 60603
853-3434

Manpower Temporary Services
55 E. Monroe
Chicago, IL 60603
263-5144

Norrel Temporary Services
108 N. State
Chicago, IL 60602
782-4181

Olsten Temporary Services
123 W. Madison
Chicago, IL 60602
782-1014

Chicago Board of Education
1819 W. Pershing Rd.
Chicago, IL 60609
890-8000

Unemployment

Have you been laid off? You are entitled to unemployment compensation provided your employer has paid the unemployment tax. To find the unemployment office nearest your home, call the Illinois Department of Employment Security (793-5280), or look in the phone book, in the blue pages section of the white pages. When you file for benefits, bring your social security number and two pieces of identification. Benefits should begin arriving in two weeks.

All Illinois residents receiving unemployment benefits must register with the Illinois Job Service. For the office nearest your home, call Illinois Department of Employment Security at 793-5280 or check the listings under the "General" heading earlier in this chapter.

In Illinois, persons receiving unemployment benefits may continue to receive full benefits while enrolled full-time in a state-approved retraining program. Ask at your local unemployment office for a list of these retraining programs.

The city of Chicago offers free credit and mortgage counseling programs to help people cope with financial hardship; these are listed below.

City of Chicago
Dept. of Consumer Services
510 N. Peshtigo Ct., Room 102
Chicago, IL 60611
744-6426
Provides free credit counseling to help people meet bills and manage limited financial resources.

City of Chicago
Dept. of Housing, Mortgage
Default Counseling
318 S. Michigan Ave.
Chicago, IL 60604
922-7922
Operates a mortgage counseling program to help people keep their homes to avoid foreclosures.

Rights on the Job

Equal Employment Opportunity Commission
Public Information and Assistance
536 S. Clark, Room 930, Chicago, IL 60605   353-2713
If you feel you have been discriminated against, contact the Equal Employment Opportunity Commission.

Illinois Department of Human Rights
State of Illinois Center
100 W. Randolph, Suite 10-100, Chicago, IL 60601
917-6200
Also handles discrimination charges, including employment discrimination due to handicap, marital status, and sexual harassment.

Chicago Area Committee on Occupational Safety and Health
506 S. Wabash Ave., Chicago, IL 60605
939-2104
For employee complaints about safety and health.

STARTING YOUR OWN BUSINESS

For those with an entrepreneurial spirit, starting a small business may be the answer. Small businesses, defined as those with fewer than 500 employees, make up 95 percent of all businesses in Illinois, and 75 percent of these businesses have less than 10 employees. Nationally, small businesses employ half the private work force and create 3 out of every 5 jobs. It's a tough game: 50 percent of new businesses fail within the first 5 years, but small businesses are essential to our nation's economic health.

The Small Business Administration (SBA), an agency of the U.S. Labor Department, has survived funding cutbacks and continues to provide excellent and comprehensive services for people starting or already operating a small business. The SBA offers information, classes, and workshops on every imaginable topic, business assistance loans, and services geared toward the needs of women, minorities, and veterans. SBA funds 29 Small Business Development Centers (SBDC) in the city, which provide classes and one-on-one training for entrepreneurs. The SBA also sponsors the Service Core of Retired Executives (SCORE) program, in which retired business people volunteer their expertise to entrepreneurs. Classes often require a nominal fee.

Start your research on starting a small business by calling the Illinois Department of Commerce and Community Affairs Small Business Assistance Bureau hotline at 1-800-252-2923. They will send you helpful information, including their brochure "Starting a Small Business in Illinois."

If you decide to start your own business, remember to meet all your obligations as an employer. You will need to register your organization, get all the required city, state, county, and federal licenses, and an employer's tax number.

Small Business Administration
219 S. Dearborn St., Room 437, Chicago, IL 60604
353-4528

Office of Minority Small Business and Capital Ownership Development
Small Business Administration
219 S. Dearborn St., Room 437, Chicago, IL 60604
353-4528
Program designed to help those socially and economically disadvantaged business people who have traditionally had trouble gaining access to the private marketplace. Blacks, Native Americans, Hispanics, Asian Pacific

Americans, and Asian Indian Americans are all eligible. For all other ethnic groups, the SBA determines eligibility on a case-by-case basis.

Grant Thornton Minority Business Development Center
600 Prudential Plaza, Chicago, IL 60601
856-0200
This company, sponsored by the SBA, provides technical assistance to minority-owned businesses or entrepreneurs just starting out.

Office of Veterans Affairs
Small Business Administration
219 S. Dearborn, Room 437, Chicago, IL 60604
353-4528
Veterans always receive special consideration in SBA programs. There are programs are specifically designed for vets and vets' loans applications are processed before those of nonvets. Contact the Veterans' Affairs Officer at your local SBA office.

Truman College
Veterans Business Resources Center
1145 W. Wilson Ave., 1st floor, Chicago, IL 60640
989-6032
A small business business development center on the north side, sponsored by the SBA.

SCORE Office
Small Business Administration
219 S. Dearborn, Room 437, Chicago, IL 60604
353-7723
SCORE provides free services for persons planning to start or buy a business and for those already in business who need specialized expertise. SCORE volunteers, retired executives in areas such as accounting, marketing, financing, manufacturing, merchandising, engineering, and procurement (securing contracts), provide one-on-one counseling sessions.

The Neighborhood Institute
Career Education and Employment Center
7500 S. Crandon
Chicago, IL 60649
933-0200
The ACCESS program, which primarily services minority women, provides individual counseling and assistance in financial planning, marketing, and other services needed for starting a small business. Free counseling; some programs have nominal fees.

University of Illinois at Chicago
Office for Entrepreneurial Studies (M/C 244)
College of Business Administration
2131 University Hall
P.O. Box 4348
Chicago, IL 60680
996-2670
Offices certificate for undergraduate students and an MBA concentration for graduate students in entrepreneurial studies.

HOME-BASED BUSINESSES (COTTAGE INDUSTRIES)

Home-based businesses, such as word processing, management consulting, sewing, and car repair, are an increasingly popular and convenient way for some people to work. The city requires a business license for most kinds of home-based businesses. Recently, however, legislation has been proposed to legalize some home-based businesses.

Truman College
Center for Home-based Businesses
1145 W. Wilson
Chicago, IL 60640
989-6629
A small business development center specializing in home-based businesses. Conducts classes on how to start your business and make it successful.

National Association for the Cottage Industry
P.O. Box 14850
Chicago, IL 60614
472-8116
Attention: Coralee Smith Kern
Ms. Kern, a leading advocate of cottage industries, works for legislation to legalize home-based businesses in Chicago.

VOLUNTEERING

You don't get paid for volunteering but you certainly do work, and the rewards often make you feel better than work for pay. Moreover, the skills you acquire in volunteer work may help you to land the paying job of your choice later on. You can volunteer almost any service or talent imaginable—everything from helping to put on a fashion show (for a fund-raiser), to translating, to serving on the board of directors of an organization that interests you. You can use the same skills you use at work to help a group that may not be able to afford those skills otherwise, especially given shrinking federal funds for many programs.

If you're interested in volunteering, but you're not sure what you want to do, you might start in your own neighborhood by walking around or looking in the phone book to see what not-for-profit agencies operate in your area. Many organizations are small-scale yet full-service agencies that offer everything from day care and health care services to family counseling. Many of these groups will train you in skills you don't have.

If you want to work for a particular issue or with a specific group of people, there is undoubtedly an organization that services that issue or group. To find such an organization, either call one of the agencies listed below, or approach the group you're interested in yourself.

The list below is by no means comprehensive, but it gives you places to start. Remember also that museums, hospitals, libraries, and the juvenile court (which uses volunteers for court watching, i.e., ensuring that judges are doing their job) always need volunteers.

Lawyers for the Creative Arts
623 S. Wabash, Suite 300-N, Chicago, IL 60605
427-1800
Pro bono legal work for arts organizations. Supplies referrals.

Business Volunteers for the Arts
800 S. Wells, #533, Chicago, IL 60607
431-3368
People with business experience are linked up with arts organizations needing skills such as legal, marketing, public relations, accounting, and fund raising. Also runs training sessions in arts management.

CPAs for the Public Interest
220 S. State, Rm. 1404, Chicago, IL 60604
786-9128
Volunteers—CPAs, corporate accountants, and academicians—provide accounting training (how to design an accounting system, set up a chart of accounts, prepare financial statements, develop a budget, analyze cash flow, etc.) to small non-profit agencies. They train volunteers.

Service Core of Retired Executives (SCORE)
Small Business Administration
219 S. Dearborn, Room 437, Chicago, IL 60604
353-7723
Sponsored by the Small Business Administration. SCORE needs volunteers with business backgrounds to provide one-on-one counseling with small business entrepreneurs in all areas of business management, including accounting, marketing, financing, manufacturing, merchandising, and engineering.

Executive Services Corps of Chicago (ESC)
25 E. Washington, Suite 801, Chicago, IL 60602
580-1840
ESC needs volunteers who are presently or are soon to be retired from a business, management, or professional career to consult with non-profit organizations in areas such as fiscal management, marketing, public relations, personnel, facilities, management, and other services.

Governor's Office of Voluntary Action
100 W. Randolph, 16th floor, Chicago, IL 60601
917-2789
Maintains a statewide resource center on programs for voluntary action and citizen participation in Illinois. Call them for information and ideas for where you could volunteer.

The Volunteer Center
United Way/Crusade of Mercy
125 S. Clark St., Suite 1100, Chicago, IL 60603-4012
580-2700
Recruits, refers, and places volunteers in not-for-profit civic, welfare, and health organizations. Offers consultations to agencies and corporations that want to start volunteer programs. Also does specialized placements of managers and executives on boards of directors of not-for-profit agencies.

Catholic Charities
126 N. Desplaines St., Chicago, IL 60606
236-5172
Huge umbrella organization servicing people of all ethnic and religious backgrounds. Offers information and makes referrals to other programs and

community resources. Among services provided are a refugee resettlement program, schooling and counseling for pregnant girls, adoption services, addiction prevention services, shelters for the homeless, a Latin American youth center, legal services to the poor, and help for the elderly.

Chicago Commons
915 N. Wolcott Ave., Chicago, IL 60622
342-5330
Helps needy people, senior citizens, and recent migrants with comprehensive programs, including emergency aid, job training, counseling, and GED (high-school equivalency) and English-language classes. Outposts all over the city.

Chicago House and Social Service Agency
801 W. Cornelia, Suite N, Chicago, IL 60657
248-5200
Chicago House is a residence program for persons with AIDS or AIDS-related conditions. The House needs volunteers to be "buddies," who provide practical and emotional support for residents (buddies attend one training session), and "groupies," who are assigned to a residence. Groupies are involved in preparing group meals and outings, and clean-up. Chicago House also needs volunteers to do fundraising and clerical work.

Friendship House
1746 W. Division St., Chicago, IL 60622
227-5065
A center for nonviolent social action with programs for raising the public's awareness of social problems and for making lasting change. Most of their clients, according to the House, "fall between the cracks of organized social services."

Hull House Association
118 N. Clinton, Suite 200, Chicago, IL 60606
726-1526
Large settlement house, providing comprehensive services at over 20 neighborhood locations throughout the city. Offers a great variety of services such as day care, family and group counseling, tutoring and adult education classes, employment counseling, arts and crafts, theater, photo and dance classes, shelter and counseling for abused women, and services for the elderly.

Jewish Community Centers of Chicago
1 S. Franklin St., Chicago, IL 60606
346-6700
Comprehensive community centers located mostly at north side locations, but with one center in Hyde Park on the south side. Primarily for Jewish residents, but open to the general public. Services vary according to location, but many include gymnasiums, recreation and education programs, day care and nursery schools, and programs for the elderly.

Lake Michigan Federation
8 S. Michigan, Suite 2010, Chicago, IL 60603
263-5550
An independent civic organization working to protect Lake Michigan and its tributaries. Houses resource centers on pollution and wetlands management technologies.

Literacy Volunteers of Chicago
9 W. Washington, Chicago, IL 60602
236-0341
Matches reading tutors with students, and provides referrals to related agencies. Also offers assistance to businesses or other groups needing adult tutoring programs in reading or English as a second language. Needs translators in all languages.

Little Brothers/Friends of the Elderly
1658 W. Belmont, Chicago, IL 60657
477-7702
Needs volunteers to make friendly visits to senior citizens in their homes, deliver meals, and in general to help in any way they can.

Misericordia/Hearts of Mercy
6300 N. Ridge Ave., Chicago, IL 60660
973-6300
Provides educational and training programs for mentally retarded children. Children and young adults live at Misericordia as well.

Open Lands Project
53 W. Jackson, Suite 550, Chicago, IL 60604
427-4256
Civic organization that negotiates and coordinates public education for expanding public lands acquisition for conservation and recreation purposes. Also works to improve the quality of existing open public space.

Operation ABLE
36 S. Wabash, Room 1133, Chicago, IL 60603
782-3335
Works to help older workers find employment, co-sponsors an annual job fair for older workers, and tries to educate the public and encourage hiring of older workers.

Operation PUSH (People United to Serve Humanity)
930 E. 50th St., Chicago, IL 60615
373-3366
Founded by Reverend Jesse Jackson, PUSH is a large organization with a broad base of popular support, especially with the black community, which it primarily serves (but is not limited to). PUSH offers educational programs and classes, and social activities, as well as serving as a clearinghouse for referrals to other agencies, services, and individuals for legal and other types of help.

Travelers & Immigrants Aid of Chicago
327 S. LaSalle, Suite 1500, Chicago, IL 60604
435-4500
Centers at Union Station, Greyhound Bus Station, and O'Hare Airport provide emergency services as well as information and referral services. Offers many services for women, immigrants, refugees, and the homeless.

United Charities of Chicago
14 E. Jackson, Chicago, IL 60604
461-0800
Centers all over the city for family, individual, and group counseling, family financial services, and services to older adults.

YMCA
755 W. North Ave., Chicago, IL 60610
280-3400
Centers all over the city provide a great variety of services to men, women, and children, including counseling for individuals, families, and groups, day care and day camps, emergency services, employment and training, physical fitness classes and centers, programs for senior citizens, and residences for men and women.

YWCA
37 S. Wabash, 3rd floor, Chicago, IL 60603
372-6600
Centers throughout the city provide comprehensive programs primarily for women and girls, including counseling (for employment, legal issues, domestic violence, rape), hotlines, classes and seminars (on employment, financial issues, and others), child care and day care, employment services, day care for senior citizens, and physical education and athletics.

—Margie Gonwa

EDUCATION

Whether you're investigating a day care center, a high school, or a university, there is no one good place to get reliable information on the quality of schools. You can start with the education department at the Chicago Public Library. They have a good collection of articles on Chicago public and private schools, as well as a file of recent catalogs and literature from the schools themselves. The Public Library also has a useful primer on Chicago schools, *A Parent's Guidebook to Chicago Schools* by Cynthia Giarelli, which outlines how to investigate and choose a good school in the city.

Once you know which schools interest you, a visit to the school will tell you even more about the institution. While you're there, discuss the school with administrators and teachers and then talk to some students, who will give you another point of view to consider. Graffiti, or the lack of, and the state of disrepair of the school's facilities may tell you more than even the students are willing to tell you.

Sit in on a few classes, if you have time, and don't be afraid to question the teacher after class. This suggestion holds as true if you are looking for a good class for your eight-year-old as if you are checking out an MBA program for yourself.

If you are checking out your local Chicago public school, talk to members of the school's Advisory Council, made up of parents, administrators, and business people. Don't write off the Chicago Public School system immediately. Despite how the system is portrayed in the newspapers and on television, there are good schools in the system, and even a few outstanding ones (for example, Lane Tech). But more on this later in the chapter.

What follows is a detailed listing of educational programs in the Chicago area, covered in this order: day care and preschool programs; elementary and high schools; colleges and universities; trade schools; adult, continuing education, and enrichment courses; and cultural exchange organizations.

DAY CARE AND PRESCHOOL PROGRAMS

Illinois Department of Children and Family Services
1026 S. Damen, Chicago, IL 60612   917-2410 or 793-2100
Regulates and licenses day care and night care facilities, and from time to time the staff will recommend specific day care centers. Contact them if you have complaints about a particular day care service. Also publishes a brochure about what to look for when selecting a program. For a copy of their brochure, write to: Office of Communication/Community Relations, Department of Children and Family Services, 406 E. Monroe St., Springfield, IL 62701.

Day Care Action Council
4753 N. Broadway, Chicago, IL 60640   561-7900
A referral and information service that matches the needs of children and parents with day care services. Will give referrals of up to 3 programs. Works both with parents and day care providers to address problems and issues

such as quality, affordability, insurance, licensing, funding, starting a center, and how to make formal complaints.

Evanston Committee for Community Coordinated Child Care
518 Davis, Evanston, IL 60201   475-2661
Child care referrals for Evanston and northern Cook County.

Hyde Park-Kenwood Community Conference
1376 E. 53rd, Chicago, IL 60615   288-8343
Publishes a directory of Hyde Park and Kenwood schools, including day care facilities.

Jane Addams Center
3212 N. Broadway, Chicago, IL 60657   549-1631
Referrals for day care centers and in-home child care.

Another source of information on day care centers is the National Association for the Education of Young Children, 1834 Connecticut Avenue, NW, Washington, DC 20009. Ask for their pamphlet, "How to Choose a Good Early Childhood Program."

ELEMENTARY AND HIGH SCHOOLS

You have basically four choices in Chicago to consider when your children reach school age: public, parochial, established private, and alternative private schools.

Public Schools

Strikes, finances, and segregation issues continue to plague the Chicago public school system; however, with luck and guidance your children can get a good education at some of the public schools. You should work with teachers, principals, and school councils and keep the lines of communication open with your kids. Be prepared to support your children.

Advisory Councils, made up of parents, administrators, and local business people, are mandatory at each school. A Council may review a school's budget; and if its members disapprove, (particularly on items such as appropriations for textbooks and supplies), the School Board must review the budget. Advisory Councils have in some cases requested that a teacher be transferred.

Most children must attend the school in their district; to find your district school, call or write the Chicago Board of Education at the address below. Ask for the phone number of your district office at the same time. The district office should have information about special programs or schools for which your child might be eligible.

Chicago Board of Education
1819 W. Pershing Rd., Chicago, IL 60632   890-3765

Special Programs/Magnet Schools

While responsibility for many of the special programs and innovative or experimental schools is divided up among different offices at the school board, you'll find that a great many of the special programs fall under the jurisdiction of the Board of Ed's Office of Equal Educational Opportunity (890-7790). To get a copy of their booklet, *Options in Education*, call 890-7778. The booklet provides an excellent summary of public school programs that includes magnet schools, voluntary transfer programs, gifted programs offered at high schools (including **Kenwood Academy, Morgan Park, Whitney Young,** and **Lincoln Park**), and special schools that offer a focus on everything from bilingual and other language specialties to music, arts, technical, and vocational programs.

Chicago has a special agricultural high school (**Chicago High School for the Agricultural Sciences**) as well as a school designed to explore the diverse aspects of the city (**Chicago Public High School for Metropolitan Studies**). Several other highly regarded Chicago public high schools (not listed in the *Options in Education* brochure) include: **Lane Tech,** which provides a technical and college prep curriculum; **Prosser,** which provides a vocational education; and Lane's south side counterpart, **Lindbloom.**

Magnet schools are the result of a concept the School Board came up with to deal with a federal directive to desegregate the city's public schools. Instead of ordering students to be bused out of their neighborhoods, the School Board created a variety of innovative educational programs at schools scattered throughout the city. The uniqueness of these special programs attracts students from outside the school district, hopefully creating a more even racial balance without forced busing.

If your child is gifted in science and math, check out the state-run **Illinois Mathematics and Science Academy,** 1500 W. Sullivan Rd., Aurora, IL 60506, (312) 801-6000. The academy accepts incoming 10th graders by application and admission is very selective, limited to 300 students per class. Students live on the premises. Tuition and room and board are free for Illinois residents. Graduates of this strong 3-year college prep curriculum are expected to place out of nearly one year of college.

For further information on the Chicago public schools, or for help on a specific problem, contact the following groups:

Citizen's Schools Committee
36 S. Wabash, Room 1028, Chicago, IL 60602   726-4678
A valuable resource, this all-volunteer organization periodically publishes *Guides to Schools* (covering both elementary and high schools), as well as a newsletter. Their office contains useful reference books, especially the School Board's reference book, *Test Scores and Selected School Characteristics*.

Chicago Panel on Public School Finances
53 W. Jackson, Chicago, IL 60604   939-2202
Composed of 16 civic organizations that investigate issues concerning public school finances. They have published some studies (e.g.,: "Chicagoans View Their Public Schools," and "School Budget Hearing Assessment"), which are available to the public at a nominal cost.

Designs for Change
220 S. State, Suite 1900, Chicago, IL 60604   922-0317
A dedicated, effective not-for-profit research, advocacy, and training organization that works for basic improvements in the day-to-day school ex-

periences of all Chicago public school children, especially those from poor neighborhoods. The group discourages parents from giving up on the public school system, and instead educates them on what is possible through good education and works with them to achieve improvements. Their grassroots campaign, called SCHOOLWATCH, makes helping children considered "at risk" (usually due to poverty or problems at home) a high priority. The organization stresses parental involvement in fighting to improve the quality of education in the schools. They also sponsor programs designed to train parents on public aid for jobs so they can get off the welfare rolls. Designs for Change has initiated lawsuits against the School Board for graduating illiterates from public high schools. Also publishes a checklist parents can use to rate schools and a newsletter.

Other groups involved with education advocacy are:

Chicago Region Parent-Teacher Association (PTA)
53 W. Jackson, Suite 1522, Chicago, IL 60604   786-1476
As a rule, the schools with the most active PTAs tend to be among the best in the city. A PTA functions in much the same way Advisory Councils do, providing input into school budgets and book selection. Call the number listed above to locate your local PTA or find out about setting up a new chapter.

Hyde Park-Kenwood Community Conference
1376 E. 53rd, Chicago, IL 60615   288-8343
A community organization interested not only in education, but also in other issues of interest to the Hyde Park-Kenwood community.

Teachers Advisory Council
161 W. Harrison, Chicago, IL 60605   341-0977
A progressive Chicago teacher organization dedicated to improving the quality of education in the public schools. Its monthly newsletter, *Substance*, edited by maverick George Schmidt, frequently exposes corruption and waste in the Chicago School Board. Covers issues not always reported by the rest of the local media. Subscriptions are not limited to teachers only.

Parochial Schools

Parochial (Catholic) schools are a popular alternative to the public school system, which should surprise no one in a city as Catholic as Chicago. Parochial schools offer high-quality education and charge less tuition than many of the independent schools. But there are other reasons. Many parochial schools have experimental programs with individualized instruction. In some schools, traditional religious education and Church-based authoritarianism is de-emphasized, and non-Catholics are often a substantial minority.

Each Catholic elementary school has its own school board which can respond to the needs of its community and sometimes offer innovative programs, even with limited resources. Such programs include cross-cultural programs, computers, and art and mural painting. All Catholic schools try to involve parents in the school and its administration.

There are approximately 200 Catholic elementary schools in the city, with average enrollments of 300 to 600, and average tuition of $800. There are nearly 40 Catholic high schools in the city, with average enrollments of 400 to 900, and average tuition of $1,800. For further information, write the **Catholic School Board,** 155 E. Superior, Chicago IL 60611, or call 751-5200.

For schools of other denominations, contact:

Lutheran High School Association
333 W. Lake
Addison, IL 60101
628-6289

Jewish Board of Education
5050 Church
Skokie, IL 60076
583-1550

or your local congregation.

Private Schools

Most schools in this category emphasize academics and preparation for the competition to attend "elite" colleges. Quite a few combine a strong college prep emphasis with innovative programs, including excellent open-classroom programs. A low teacher-to-student ratio allows for individualized attention.

Beware! Some schools may have a "pressure cooker" atmosphere emphasizing grades and competition to the detriment of learning, made worse by a limited number of spaces in local private schools. Parents anxious for their child to be admitted to the "right" nursery school (that is, a feeder school for one of the prestigious private schools such as **The Latin School, Francis W. Parker,** or the **University of Chicago Lab Schools**) have even been known to coach their 3-year-old for the nursery school pre-admission interview, hopefully to increase the child's chances of admission.

Tuition fees at private schools are high—fees range from $1,200-7,500 per year. Some schools require an initial cash donation as well. For general information or a list of member schools, contact Anne Tyskling at the **Independent Schools Association of Greater Chicago,** 1234 E. Madison Park, Chicago, IL 60615 (538-4986).

For more information on private schools, refer to the June 1983 issue of *Chicago* magazine, which featured an excellent article about private education in Chicago. An invaluable sidebar to the article lists and describes other very good private schools in the Chicago area. Many of these schools have immediate placement for your child, and are a remarkably good value in terms of tuition in comparison to the "big three"—Lab, Latin and Parker.

The big three schools are expensive and competitive and accept a low percentage of applicants:

The Latin School of Chicago
59 W. North Ave.
Chicago, IL 60610
787-0820
Kindergarten through 12th grade.

Francis W. Parker School
330 W. Webster
Chicago, IL 60614
549-0172
Kindergarten through 12th grade.

University of Chicago Laboratory Schools
1362 E. 59th St.
Chicago, IL 60637
702-9451
Nursery school through 12th grade.

Other schools offer kindergarten through 12th grade programs, good value, and immediate placement:

Morgan Park Academy
2153 W. 111th St.
Chicago, IL 60643
881-6700

Roycemore School
640 Lincoln St.
Evanston, IL 60201
866-6055

Harvard School
4731 S. Ellis
Chicago, IL 60615
624-0394

North Shore Country Day School
310 Green Bay Rd.
Winnetka, IL 60093
446-0674

Chicago City Day School
541 W. Hawthorne
Chicago, IL 60657
327-0900

A very special independent school is **Chicago Academy for the Arts,** located at 718 W. Adams, Chicago, IL 60606. The school's program allows students to study music, dance, theater, and the visual arts in preparation for career in the arts. Students are admitted to this competitive school by application. For information, call 454-9577.

Not all private schools are expensive. Tuition at Marva Collins' **Westside Preparatory School,** 4146 W. Chicago, Chicago, IL 60651, is based on a sliding fee scale. Westside Prep won national attention a few years ago because of the school's success in teaching children to read. For information, call 227-5995.

MONTESSORI SCHOOLS

The Montessori method of teaching emphasizes development of a child's initiative and uses a fairly rigid routine. The schools are most popular for preschool instruction, although they offer classes through the 8th grade. There are Montessori schools located both in the city and in the suburbs. For the location of the school nearest you, call 226-1010.

ALTERNATIVE PRIVATE SCHOOLS

Alternative schools are another type of private or independent school. Frequently (but not always) the schools are geared at teenagers and young adults who found a traditional public school setting difficult. Funding for the schools often comes from government agencies and corporate foundations.

The 40 non-parochial alternative schools in the city have programs for elementary and high school students as well as for adults. Alternative schools generally emphasize greater student freedom and choice and more humane relationships between students and teachers. The schools vary in how much they stress reading and math skills.

Tuition at alternative schools can range from nominal to nearly $4,000 per year. For more information, contact the **Alternative Schools Network,** 1105 W. Lawrence, Chicago, IL 60640 (728-4030). They provide an up-to-date directory and information on existing alternative schools. You can also get advice on the practical problems of starting your own school, including specific legal and city code requirements for Chicago.

COLLEGES AND UNIVERSITIES

When choosing a degree program, you should go through the same steps described at the beginning of this chapter. Visit the school. Ask your friends and the school's alumni about programs and instructors, and job placement. Don't just talk to the college's admissions representative. Even if a college has a good overall reputation, the quality of academic programs can vary from department to department, so find out what you can about particular programs.

For a complete listing of degree programs offered at colleges in Chicago and elsewhere in the United States, see **Peterson's Guide to Undergraduate Study** and **Peterson's Guide to Graduate Study**, both available at public libraries or at larger bookstores.

With few exceptions, all the colleges listed below offer both part-time and full-time study, and some evening courses. Call the schools you're interested in to find out if evening courses are offered. Most colleges offer noncredit courses for people not necessarily interested in earning a degree; these courses are usually provided at a lower cost than regular (degree-credit) courses, and frequently meet on evenings or weekends. See the section in this chapter on Continuing Education.

Junior Colleges

City Colleges of Chicago
30 E. Lake, Chicago, IL 60601   781-9430
Chicago's junior college system consists of eight junior colleges and a technical institute, Dawson Skills Institute. The colleges (called city colleges) offer Associate of Arts and Associate of Science degrees. Many classes are scheduled at times convenient for working people. City colleges offer strong curricula in public service and public safety, English courses for non-native speakers, and literacy courses. City-Wide College shares its home campus with Loop College and offers less traditional courses: some are offered off-campus, either via television, radio, or at remote locations; others are on videotape.

Your instructor at a city college could be a future Nobel Prize winner: the renowned economist, Milton Friedman, began his teaching career at Wright College in the 1940s.

Tuition is currently $26 per credit hour for Chicago residents, plus a $20 registration fee each term. Tuition is generally lower for noncredit courses.

Kennedy-King College
6800 S. Wentworth
Chicago, IL 60621
962-3200

Loop College
30 E. Lake
Chicago, IL 60601
781-9430

Malcolm X College
1900 W. Van Buren
Chicago, IL 60612
942-3000

Truman College
1145 W. Wilson
Chicago, IL 60640
878-1700

Olive-Harvey College
10001 S. Woodlawn
Chicago, IL 60628
568-3700

Wright College
3400 N. Austin
Chicago, IL 60634
777-7900

Dawson Skills Institute
3901 S. State
Chicago, IL 60609
624-3737

Daley College
7500 S. Pulaski
Chicago, IL 60652
735-3000

Chicago City-Wide College
30 E. Lake
Chicago, IL 60601
781-9430

If you can't find the program you need at one of the City Colleges, try one of the nearby suburban junior colleges. If the program of study you need is not available in your district (for Chicagoans, the city is your district), you may be eligible for a tuition chargeback. This means that you pay the in-district tuition rate if you have to attend a junior college outside of your home district. Be sure to apply for a tuition chargeback at your local junior college at least 30 days in advance of registration.

Moraine Valley Community College
10900 S. 88th Ave.
Palos Hills, IL 60465
974-4300
In-district tuition is $24 per credit hour.

Oakton Community College
1600 E. Golf Rd.
Des Plaines, IL 60016 (main campus)
635-1600
also a campus at 7701 Lincoln Ave., Skokie
In-district tuition is $17 per credit hour.

Thornton Community College
15800 S. State
South Holland, IL 60473
596-2000
In-district tuition: $32 per credit hour.

Triton Community College
2000 Fifth Avenue
River Grove, IL 60171
456-0300
In-district tuition is $27 per credit hour.

Colleges and Universities

Chicago State University
9501 S. Martin Luther King Dr., Chicago, IL 60628   995-2000
Bachelor's degrees and some master's degrees offered. Some Saturday classes. Stronger programs are in elementary and physical education. Tuition for Illinois residents is $640 per semester for full-time study.

Columbia College
600 S. Michigan, Chicago, IL 60605   663-1600
Emphasis on the arts, media and communications, along with comprehensive programs in liberal arts and sciences. Open admissions policy has resulted in a diverse student body. Popular programs include radio, television, and photography. Full-time undergraduate tuition is $2,294 per semester.

DePaul University
25 E. Jackson, Chicago, IL 60604 (main campus)   341-8300
2323 N. Seminary (Lincoln Park campus)
Strong programs in music, theater, computer science, business (especially accounting), and law. Enrollment at this Catholic university has increased since its basketball team became a regular in national collegiate tournaments. Undergraduate tuition is $131 per credit hour; theater and music schools are higher.

Illinois Institute of Technology
3300 S. Federal, Chicago, IL 60616   567-3000
Technically oriented institution known for its programs in engineering, architecture, design, business, and law (Chicago-Kent College of Law is located downtown at 77 S. Wacker). Much of the architecture of the main campus on the south side was designed or influenced by Mies van der Rohe, who was dean of the architecture school for many years. Recently acquired a campus in west suburban Downers Grove. Tuition is $290 per credit hour.

Kendall College
2408 Orrington, Evanston, IL 60202   866-1300
Small liberal arts and business college also offers the only culinary and hospitality degree in the midwest. Limited evening classes. Tuition is $180 per credit hour; full-time tuition is $5,100 per year.

Loyola University
6526 N. Sheridan, Chicago, IL 60626 (main campus)   274-3000
820 N. Michigan (Water Tower campus)
A Jesuit institution with an emphasis on liberal arts and business curricula. Undergraduate students can choose between the downtown and Rogers Park campuses. Graduate business and law schools are located at the Water Tower campus. Bachelor's degree programs in premedicine, nursing, and political science are highly regarded. Graduate programs in law, dentistry, medicine, and industrial relations have fine reputations. Full-time tuition is $6,470 for an academic year.

Mundelein College
6363 N. Sheridan, Chicago, IL 60660   262-8100
A women's Catholic liberal arts college. Special programs for women returning to school after a long absence. Also offers Weekend College, a degree program that can be completed exclusively on weekends. Tuition is $639 per course.

National College of Education
2840 Sheridan Rd., Evanston, IL 60201   256-5150
Undergraduate and graduate degrees offered in education and administration. Also campuses in the Loop and west suburban Lombard. Tuition is $120 per quarter hour.

Northeastern Illinois University
5500 N. St. Louis, Chicago, IL 60625   583-4050
State-supported institution located on the far northwest side of the city. Known for its programs in education. Also offers a unique graduate program in exercise physiology. In-state tuition is $570 per trimester for full-time study.

Northwestern University
180 Hinman, Evanston, IL 60201
491-3741 (main campus), 908-8649 (Chicago campus)
Major private university with an excellent national reputation. Many well-regarded schools and programs, including the Medill School of Journalism, the schools of Speech and Music, the Technological Institute, and the Kellogg Graduate School of Management. The Evanston campus is beautifully situated on Lake Michigan. The Chicago campus, located at Chicago Avenue and the lake, houses the professional medical, dental, and law schools, and the evening programs. Full-time undergraduate tuition is $11,600 per year.

Roosevelt University
430 S. Michigan, Chicago, IL 60605 (main campus)   341-3500
2121 S. Goebbert Rd., Arlington Heights, 437-9200
Roosevelt was a pioneer in having an open admissions policy, enrolling students without regard to sex, race, age, or economic class. The university is especially committed to serving the needs of students who work full-time. The main campus is located in the magnificent Adler & Sullivan Auditorium building. Good programs in music, business, public administration, and journalism. Undergraduate tuition is $194 per credit hour.

Rosary College
7900 W. Division, River Forest, IL 60305   366-2490
Small liberal arts college located in near west suburban River Forest offering instruction in liberal arts, education, business, and the area's only program in library science. Degrees offered include foods and nutrition, gerontology, and special education. Tuition is $210 per credit hour.

St. Xavier College
3700 W. 103rd St., Chicago, IL 60655   779-3300
Located on the city's southwest side. Popular programs include nursing, criminal justice, and business. Weekend College program can be completed by attending only on Fridays, Saturdays, and Sundays. Undergraduate tuition is $204 per semester hour.

School of the Art Institute of Chicago
Columbus and Jackson, Chicago, IL 60604   443-3700
Nationally known school of art provides professional studio-oriented art education for students interested in painting, design, filmmaking, video, and time arts. On the cutting edge of such new art forms as holography, computer-generated art, and video production. Courses in art history, criticism, and liberal arts complement the undergraduate program. Undergraduate and graduate tuition is $3900 per semester for full-time study; $780 for a 3-hour class.

Spertus College of Judaica
618 S. Michigan, Chicago, IL 60605   922-9012
In cooperation with eight area colleges and universities, Spertus offers degrees in liberal arts and Judaic studies. Extensive, active teaching museum and research library are open to the public. Tuition is $285 for one undergraduate course, $330 for one graduate course.

University of Chicago
5801 S. Ellis, Chicago, IL 60637   702-1234
Located in Hyde Park, the U of C is generally regarded as one of the top universities in the country. The undergraduate program is small and intense; graduate and professional study and research are emphasized. All undergraduates must take a 1-year sequence of core courses in the humanities and sciences. Boasts excellent humanities and social science programs, especially in economics, sociology, English, foreign languages, and history. Strong programs in the natural and physical sciences. Divinity School is unsurpassed. Outstanding professional programs in medicine, law, business, and social work. Undergraduate tuition is $12,120.

University of Illinois at Chicago
601 S. Morgan, P.O. Box 4348, Chicago, IL 60680   996-4350
Formed by the 1982 merger of the Medical Center and Chicago Circle campuses of the U of I, UIC is the largest institution of higher learning in the Chicago area. While most students are commuters, the university is beginning to make more residences available on campus, including a new dormitory at Harrison and Halsted. The highly regarded medical and dental schools are part of the metropolitan area's largest hospital complex. Almost any major you can think of is offered at the undergraduate level; graduate study is offered in many fields. Strong offerings in the fields of architecture, engineering, biology, business, and education. Full-time undergraduate tuition ranges from $715 to $797 per quarter.

Commercial, Trade, and Correspondence Schools

While a great many commercial, trade, and correspondence schools (truck driving and beauty culture are examples) are legitimate, and an acceptable (if expensive) way to learn a trade, there are enough "bad apples" that a note of caution is in order. Find out all you can about a school before you enroll.

Follow the same steps you'd follow for finding any good school. Interview current students and some of the graduates who are the school's success stories. Be sure to talk to a sample of the "end users"—those prospective employers who would hire you if you had this new skill. Get their recommendations on the top programs or the best preparation for a beginner who wants to work in the field.

Contact the **Illinois Department of Registration and Education,** 100 W. Randolph, Chicago, IL 60601, 917-4500. They oversee the licensing of 30 professions, and should be aware of potentially bogus programs, or less than scrupulous advertising claims. To find out if a school is approved for veterans, contact the **Veterans Administration's Approving Section,** 353-0687. They can tell you if a school is approved for veterans and will send out a list of approved schools. The list can be taken as (at least) an indicator of credibility.

Before you sign any school contract, make sure you understand all the implications—including your right to cancel, and any amounts of money you might have to forfeit. If a school is legitimate, it is likely to have classes starting on a regular basis. Don't rush into signing anything.

Finally, don't forget to investigate other alternatives: you might be able to take similar courses in the trade you want to study at colleges that offer evening and noncredit courses. These programs áre usually less expensive than trade schools. See the following section on Adult and Continuing Education.

CONTINUING EDUCATION

If you're interested only in learning and obtaining a degree isn't important to you, consider adult or continuing education courses. Continuing education courses are offered at most colleges and universities, and frequently at high schools, YMCA's and YWCA's. The Latin School and Francis Parker School publish catalogs of their noncredit courses. Usually continuing education classes are much cheaper than regular degree-credit courses at a college. Call your local college, "Y", or high school to see if courses in the subject in which you're interested are offered.

Specialty education businesses are an education alternative that has developed to meet the needs of an information-hungry society. The classes taught at these proprietary schools vary greatly in quality and few are cheap. Many are taught by people who know a topic well but have never taught a course before. Courses are typically short in duration—okay if you're in a hurry, but can you really learn much in three hours? Some of the classes are marketed as places to meet other people.

Discovery Center
2930 N. Lincoln, Chicago, IL 60657   348-8120
Monthly catalogs of course offerings are easily available downtown and in the trendier neighborhoods. More multiple-session courses than its competitor, the Learning Annex. Topics range from the practical to the bizarre: aerobics, investments, exotic tours of the city, and the ever-popular flirting course.

The Learning Annex
8 E. Delaware, Chicago, IL 60611   280-7575
Like Discovery Center, this national chain blankets the city with its monthly catalog of courses remarkably similar to DC's. There's less pretense that people are taking the courses to learn something.

CULTURAL EXCHANGE ORGANIZATIONS

Chicago Council on Foreign Relations
116 S. Michigan, Chicago, IL 60603   726-3860
The largest independent nonprofit international affairs organization in the country. Sponsors lectures by major policy makers and foreign relations experts from the United States and around the world.

Alliance Francaise
810 N. Dearborn, Chicago, IL 60610   337-1070
Promotes French culture through an extensive program of language and literature classes, social events, and films.

Goethe Institute
401 N. Michigan, Chicago, IL 60611   329-0915
Encourages the appreciation of German culture through lectures and classes on German language and arts.

Japan America Society of Chicago
40 N. Dearborn, Suite 910, Chicago, IL 60602   263-3049
Promotes awareness of Japanese culture through lectures and social activities. Many members are corporate executives with business interests in Japan.

For cultural organizations of other countries, contact the local consulate listed in the Yellow Pages.

If you're a student or faculty member from another country and want to meet people from your homeland, or if you just want to meet people from other cultures, these international organizations will be of interest to you. Most are open to students and faculty of the educational community of the entire metropolitan area. Affiliation with a university is not always required: the most important prerequisite is a desire to interact with people from other cultures.

International House
1414 E. 59th, Chicago, IL 60637   753-2270 or 753-2280
Both a residential unit and an important center of international student social and educational activities for students from the entire Chicago area. Social dances, folk dancing, and an international film series are scheduled regularly. Established in the 1930s as a semi-autonomous unit of the University of Chicago, International House has space to house about 500 people. Residents (half are Americans and half are foreigners) are primarily graduate students. Housing fees for the academic year average $2,500 plus board. Single rooms are available at $20 per night. During the school year, you usually have to make reservations in advance. The building houses a cafeteria, snack shop, and gift shop.

Crossroads Student Center
5621 S. Blackstone, Chicago, IL 60637   684-6060
Another cultural center in Hyde Park for foreign students. Crossroads is primarily a social center, with no housing space. English (three levels), French, and Spanish classes are offered. Some child care is available. A variety of seminars and discussion groups are offered periodically on the weekends.

Institute of International Education
401 N. Wabash, Suite 534, Chicago, IL 60611   644-1400
Offers information about scholarship opportunities for foreign students, and will assist international students with many kinds of problems. Open Monday through Friday from 9 am to 5 pm.

International Visitors Center of Chicago
520 N. Michigan, Chicago, IL 60611   645-1836
Sponsors a variety of events throughout the year for international students, including city tours and social activities.

—Bobbye Middendorf

PHYSICAL HEALTH

People have more control over their health than they realize. If more of us followed these simple rules, we could avoid many, if not most, of our health problems:

Eat a low-fat, high-fiber diet—lean meats, polyunsaturated oils, fresh fruits and vegetables, and whole grains.

Stay away from alcohol, caffeine, salt, and sweeteners.

Exercise at least three times a week for twenty minutes. I recommend walking, bicycling, and swimming.

Use sunscreen lotion, number 15 or higher, if you're going to be spending time out-of-doors. Stay out of the 10 am-3 pm sun and stay away from tanning parlors.

Stretch and relax daily for about 20 minutes to relieve stress. Yoga, meditation, various stretching exercises, and walking along the lake all qualify. Do something you like for yourself.

Don't smoke!

Women, get pap smears whether you are having problems or not. After three normal yearly paps, one every two to three years is probably OK.

Get a tetanus shot every ten years. You would be surprised how important tetanus shots are for all sorts of injuries, more than just rusty nails. When was your last tetanus shot?

If you are worried about a medical problem, have it checked out. If you like, bring a friend or interested party with you. They can listen, ask questions you forgot, and support you. Bring your health insurance cards or a form of payment with you; charge cards are OK for payment in hospitals. If surgery or a substantial amount of money is involved, get a second opinion. And don't be afraid to ask questions if you do not understand what the person is saying!

Our Bodies, Ourselves, by the Boston Women's Health Collective, is a good self-help health exam book.

The Blue Book, a human care services book, lists all the social services in Chicago. It's available at libraries, social service deparments, or from the United Way/Crusade of Mercy, Publications Department, 125 S. Clark, Chicago, IL 60603, for $25.

The *Directory of Self Help Mutual Aid Groups* is a comprehensive book listing support groups and services in the city and suburbs. It lists and describes hundreds of groups that provide support for patients and their families. The book is available at most social services departments, or by mail for $10 from the Self-Help Center, 1600 Dodge Ave., Evanston, IL. Call 328-0470.

HOSPITALS AND EMERGENCY CARE

All hospitals are equipped with emergency rooms, prepared to handle most emergencies—or at least prepare patients for further treatment. However,

emergency rooms are less well equipped to handle general health care problems. You can find better and cheaper places to have your sore throat looked
at, or to get that tetanus shot.

If you have an emergency, and can't get to the hospital quickly or safely,
call **911**. They will send paramedics. (We all know or have heard of cases
where 911 was slow to answer. If you can't get through, call the operator
and ask to be connected to the nearest fire station.) Paramedics have to take
the injured person to the nearest hospital. If you want to be taken to another
hospital further away, call a private ambulance agency instead; they will
take you anywhere you request.

By law, if your life is threatened, any hospital has to admit you. If you
don't have health insurance, they will probably send you to **Cook County
Hospital** for additional treatment—Cook County Hospital as a public hospital has to accept everybody. Cook County is big and the staff overworked.
But it does have an excellent emergency room and a renowned burn unit.

University and teaching hospitals are larger medical centers with plenty
of backup that will accept complicated cases. Community hospitals will often
refer very complex cases to university hospitals.

In general, hospitals provide many social as well as medical services. They
usually have social workers who can help you work out a payment system
for your medical bills, and help set up services such as sending visiting
nurses to your home, if needed.

REFERRAL, ADVOCACY, AND EDUCATIONAL SERVICES

AIDS Assistance Association
3240 N. Racine, Chicago, IL 60657   529-2437
A volunteer agency that provides emergency and basic needs for people with
AIDS or ARC (AIDS-related complex). Offers temporary shelter, food, and
clothing. Also linked with other agencies.

American Cancer Society
37 S. Wabash, 4th floor, Chicago, IL 60603   372-0471
Provides high-quality educational materials in addition to hospital beds and
home health care aids such as bedside commodes, walkers, or wheelchairs
for people with cancer. Transportation for the homebound is also available,
as well as referrals.

Chicago Area Committee on Occupational Safety and Health
33 E. Congress, Suite 723, Chicago, IL 60605   939-2104
Lawyers and activists working to improve health and safety conditions on
the job.

Chicago Dental Society
30 N. Michigan Ave., Room 1301, Chicago, IL 60602   726-4076
24 hour emergency referral service: 726-4321
Will refer you to three dentists in your area of the city.

Chicago House and Social Service Agency, Inc.
801 W. Cornelia, Suite N, Chicago, IL 60657   248-5200
Residences for persons with AIDS and AIDS-related conditions.

Chicago Medical Society
515 N. Dearborn, Chicago, IL 60610   670-2550
Will refer you to three physicians. Offers additional information about fees, the hospital the physician is connected with, public aid acceptance, and languages the physician speaks.

All hospitals also have their own referral list of MDs.

Community Information and Referral Service
125 S. Clark St., Suite 1326, Chicago, IL 60603   580-2850
A central source of information for health and human services, including referrals to day care centers and health clinics.

Gay and Lesbian Physicians of Chicago
P.O. Box 14864, Chicago, IL 60614   475-0790
For referrals to gay physicians.

Gray Panthers
343 S. Dearborn, Chicago, IL 60604   663-9093
Advocacy organization, composed of mostly older, many middle-aged, and some younger persons, working primarily for accessible, affordable health care and housing.

HERS (Health Evaluation Referral Service)
1954 W. Irving Park Rd., Chicago, IL 60613   248-0166
One of the best information resources. A referral service of women, by women, for women, in existence for more than 10 years. Will provide you with evaluations made by clients of physicians and agencies. Also does advocacy and public policy work, as well as educational workshops.

Illinois Citizens for Better Care
53 W. Jackson, Chicago, IL 60604   663-5120
A nursing home watchdog organization involved in advocacy, research, and education to improve the lives of nursing home residents. They are helpful in providing information on how to find and choose a nursing home.

Metro-Help
2210 N. Halsted, Chicago, IL 60614   929-5150
A hotline and a central clearinghouse for health service referrals for young people and others. Services available 24 hours.

Midwest Association for Sickle Cell Anemia
65 E. South Water St., Room 2200, Chicago, IL 60601   663-5700
Provides referrals for treatment and testing, speakers, vocational rehabilitation counseling, emergency transportation for those with sickle cell anemia, scholarships, and more.

National Abortion Rights Action League (NARAL)
100 E. Ohio, Chicago, IL 60611   644-0972
Primarily an advocacy and legislative action group. Also does lobbying. Educational and lobbying skills workshops for members; speakers are available as well.

Physicans for Social Responsibility (PSR)
220 S. State St., Suite 1330, Chicago, IL 60604   663-1777
PSR's national counterpart won the 1985 Nobel Peace Prize. PSR is an educational and legislative group working to inform the public of the medical

effects of nuclear war: no one "wins." Will provide speakers and audiovisual materials. Holds workshops that are often open to the public.

For referrals to acupuncturists, chiropractors, naprapaths and other alternative therapists, look in the Yellow Pages.

CLINICS

During the 60s, alternative clinics sprang up all over. But those days have passed, and clinics are fewer in number. The ones listed below still do a good job providing necessary services at lower costs.

Chicago Board of Health
50 W. Washington, Chicago, IL 60602   744-8500
Provides free testing, counseling, and clinics for just about everything, including diabetes, venereal diseases, tuberculosis, heart diseases, immunizations, infant and maternal care, and health maintenance. Chicago Board of Health clinics are all over the city; call to find out where the one in your district is.

Chicago Women's Health Center
3435 N. Sheffield, Chicago, IL 60657   935-6126
In existence for more than 10 years, the center offers gynecological exams, screening for venereal diseases, birth control and pregnancy counseling, and prenatal care, done by trained lay women and medical professionals. Fees are based on a sliding scale.

Family Practice Unlimited
6122 N. Lincoln Ave., Chicago, IL 60659   539-0808
A 10-year practice that has five physicians on staff for home births, hospital deliveries, and a birthing center. Their offices are scattered throughout the city. This is the only group I know of with MD-supervised home deliveries. First consultation is free.

Howard Brown Memorial Clinic
945 W. George, Chicago, IL 60657   871-5777, AIDS hotline: 1-800-AID-AIDS
Serving the gay male and general community and offering varied resources such as a sexually transmitted disease clinic with confidential HIV testing (by appointment only; fee required), bereavement support groups, a speakers bureau, and a full range of care in conjunction with other organizations for persons with AIDS or ARC (AIDS-related complex). Also conducts educational and research projects.

Planned Parenthood
17 N. State, Chicago, IL 60602   781-9550
An international organization that offers complete birth control services, gynecological exams, pregnancy testing and counseling, and abortion services in their locations on the north and south sides, and two Loop locations.

Women's Health Resources
904 W. Oakdale, Chicago, IL 60657   883-7052
Recently covered in *MS*. magazine as a model for women's health centers. The clinic offers a full range of services, including internal medicine, Ob-

Gyn, psychological, nutrition, and educational programming. Also has a resource library.

Dental Clinics

Loyola College of Dental Surgery
2160 S. First Ave., Maywood, IL   531-4200
Call to make your initial appointment.

Northwestern University Dental Clinic
240 E. Huron St., Chicago, IL 60611   908-5950
For your first appointment, you'll need to drop in to the clinic at 8 am or 1 pm Monday through Friday. $5 fee for registration and first examination.

University of Illinois College of Dentistry Clinic
801 S. Paulina, Chicago, IL 60612   996-7555
Call to make your first appointment.

Dental clinics associated with university dental schools will provide economical, high-quality dental work at much lower prices than private practitioners. Students do the work under the supervision of their instructors, who are dentists. The clinics provide all types of dental and orthodontial services. One disadvantage is the amount of time it takes to get your work done; usually it takes longer, sometimes quite a bit longer, than it would take a private dentist. Registration, the first visit, and assignment to a dental student may take as long as one month.

HOME HEALTH CARE SERVICES

Visiting Nurses Association
322 S. Green St., Chicago, IL 60607-3599   738-8622
Offers almost any home health care service, provided by nurses, nurses' aids, physical therapists, and other professionals. Health insurance will often cover these services.

Chicago Easter Seal Society
220 S. State St., Chicago, IL 60604   939-5115
In addition to the many services and referrals they offer for handicapped children, they can also arrange for home dental work for disabled children.

HOSPICES

Hospices provide supportive home care for terminally ill persons and their families. They try to relieve pain as well as provide emotional support. There are many hospices throughout the city. Call the social service department in the hospital nearest you to find out what is available in your area. Services are usually free, though donations are helpful. A few are listed below. See also the Seniors chapter in this book.

Horizon Hospice
2800 N. Sheridan
Chicago, IL 60657
871-3658

Meridian Hospice
5445 S. Ingleside
Chicago, IL 60615
955-5529

Illinois Masonic Medical Center
Home Health and Hospice
836 W. Wellington
Chicago, IL 60657
883-7048

—Julia Bell, M.D.

MENTAL HEALTH

Even if you've had a stable childhood, you can't always be prepared for everything life dishes out. Therapy can help you cope with life's challenges.

WHAT TO LOOK FOR

In seeking outpatient therapy services, you should consider the therapist's approach, the cost, and your personal reaction to the therapist. It's perfectly acceptable to meet with several therapists before choosing the one you'd like to work with. Questions about their training, experience, and which type of therapy they practice are all advisable.

In Illinois, anyone can bill herself as a therapist, although many therapists here are pushing for a licensing program. Remember that psychiatrists, psychologists, and social workers must have appropriate credentials (i.e., academic degrees from accredited programs) to use these titles.

Most therapists are eclectic; they use a combination of approaches but usually have a bent toward a particular type of therapy. Some of the major types of therapy follow.

Psychodynamic. This approach asserts that symptoms (such as anxiety and depression) are alleviated through understanding a past psychological conflict, which permits resolution in the present. The therapist is comparatively nondirective and follows the client's lead, while offering periodic interpretations. The psychodynamic approach is most often used for longstanding problems.

Behavioral. Behavioral therapy assumes that symptoms are learned behavior and therefore can be unlearned, or new, more adaptive behaviors substituted. The therapist acts more like a doctor or a teacher, diagnosing the problem and prescribing some action as a remedy. This approach is most often used to control specific problems such as weight loss, quitting smoking, and phobias.

Gestalt. As in the behavioral approach, the Gestalt therapist will focus on the here and now; the difference lies in the emphasis on feelings rather than strictly on behavior. Gestalt's goal is to increase the client's awareness of feelings and to integrate them into conscious experience and action. The therapist acts as a guide to awareness, often providing exercises that promote awareness. Often used for growth and self-enhancement.

Humanistic. Humanistic therapy is characterized by the therapist's active listening to and unconditional acceptance of the client. According to this method, the therapist's genuine concern and acceptance will help you resolve your difficulties while more fully actualizing your potential.

Psychoanalysis. Developed by Sigmund Freud, psychoanalysis is based on the assumption that the more you understand your past, the easier it is for you to make changes in the present. Particularly useful for longstanding conflicts, psychoanalysis often requires a committment by the client to undergo therapy for several times a week over several years. Strictly speaking, psychoanalysis is only practiced by psychoanalysts; however, other types of therapists may also use psychoanalytic or Freudian ideas in their practice.

These types of therapy may be practiced by various professionals: psychiatrists, psychologists, social workers, and others. Again, your comfort with the therapist should be primary in your choice.

Psychiatry is practiced by physicians who have had a residency in psychiatry. Only psychiatrists can prescribe medication to treat clients in therapy. Psychiatrists also vary in what approach or approaches they use in therapy and to what degree they advocate prescribing medication.

Psychodynamic psychotherapy, which is practiced by many therapists in the Chicago area, is a blend of approaches, but emphasizes examination of a person's past to make changes in the present (called an insight-oriented approach).

Fees for therapy vary, with psychiatrists, psychologists, and analysts topping the scale at $50 to $120 per session in private practice. Social workers and other professionals less able to collect insurance payments charge from $30 to $70 per session. Clinics often have a sliding scale.

You can go through therapy alone, with another person as a couple, with your family, or as a member of a group.

Remember, however, what therapy can't do. Therapy will not be a cure-all—frustration and disappointment are parts of life. Therapy will not make you perfect; rather, it can help you to cope with life's ups and downs and become more self accepting.

SELF-HELP GROUPS

Self-help groups, consisting of a group of people with a common problem supporting and helping each other, are an alternative to the more traditional types of therapy. Many groups are free of charge and permit open-ended involvement. Often meetings are not attended by a professional. Groups exist for just about every need, from heart surgery patients to men's support groups.

The clearinghouse for information about self-help groups in the Chicago area is the Self-Help Center in Evanston (phone: 328-0470). You can send for their comprehensive *Directory of Self Help Mutual Aid Groups* ($10), which lists and describes self-help groups for every purpose under the sun—support groups for everything from victims of brain tumors and cancer to victims of acne, to infertility, workaholic, singles, and parents' groups.

Some of the more familiar groups are:

Alcoholics Anonymous
346-1475
Support and education for people who want to stop drinking.

Al Anon
890-1141
Support and education for family and friends of alcoholics.

Anorexia Nervosa and Associated Disorders
869-0539
Support and education for individuals suffering from eating disorders (help also available for their families).

Cocaine Anonymous
278-7444
For people recovering from cocaine addiction.

Vet Center
155 S. Oak Park Ave.
Oak Park, IL
383-3225
Counseling and self-help groups for veterans and their families and loved ones. Good center for referrals to other veterans' groups.

Narcotics Anonymous
848-4000
Support for individuals recovering
from drugs or alcohol.

**National Depressive and Manic
Depressive Association**
Merchandise Mart
Box 3395, Dept. NI
Chicago, IL 60654
Support group for manic
depressives.

Recovery, Inc.
337-5661
Help for people trying to control
nervous symptoms and fears.

Smoke Enders
386-7873
Support for people trying to quit
cigarette smoking.

Weight Watchers
573-8700
Group support for people who
want to control their eating habits.
Many locations throughout the city
and suburbs.

CRISIS SITUATIONS

If you're desperate and need immediate help, you have two choices: call a
hotline number or go to a hospital emergency room.

24-HOUR HOTLINES

Ravenswood Hospital
769-6200
Crisis intervention hotline staffed
by hospital personnel. Provide
referrals. Good follow-up services
available at the hospital if you live
nearby.

Contact
644-4357
All-purpose crisis line.

Talkline
228-6400
All-purpose crisis line, particularly
targeted to northwest Chicago and
suburbs.

Mt. Sinai Hospital Care Unit
650-6509
Counselors will listen and provide

referrals for people with substance
abuse problems.

**Chicago Abused Women
Coalition**
278-4566
For women who are victims of
domestic violence.

Child Abuse Hotline
1-800-25-ABUSE (24-hour
number)
Chicago-area number: 25-ABUSE

**DuPage Women Against Rape
Rape Hotline**
971-3927
Counseling and referrals for
victims of rape.

**Rape Victims Emergency
Assistance**
744-8418

OTHER HOTLINES

Mujeras Latinas en Accion
226-1544
For Latino women, this hotline is
part of an organization of Latino
women who also do advocacy.

AIDS Hotline
1-800-243-2437 (11 am-9pm only)
Information on AIDS and referrals
to services.

HOSPITAL EMERGENCY ROOMS

If you are feeling desperate or afraid you may hurt yourself or someone else, or if you have been raped or a victim of domestic or other violence, go to a hospital emergency room. We consider the emergency rooms at the following hospitals among the best: Ravenswood, Northwestern, and Michael Reese. The following hospitals have a service called Rape Victim Advocates to help victims: Northwestern, Weiss, Augustana, Grant, Illinois Masonic, Edgewater, and Norwegian American. Rape Victim Advocates are on call 24 hours; an advocate will come to the hospital and stay with the victim through physical examinations and discussions with attorneys and police (daytime phone for Rape Victims Advocates is 649-1855).

REFERRAL SERVICES

In a noncrisis situation, if you're seeking information about mental health services or a specific referral, the following can direct you or provide service.

Community Information & Referral Service
125 S. Clark, Suite 1326, Chicago, IL 60603
580-2850
Direct referrals to health and human services agencies. Deals with problems ranging from aging and health to child care, substance abuse, and emergency food and shelter.

HERS (Health Evaluation & Referral Service)
1954 W. Irving Park Rd., Chicago, IL 60613
248-0166
Unique for its practice of evaluating the places and people it refers callers to. Service providers are evaluated by staff, board members, volunteers, and the consumers. Provides information on women's health issues. Offers referrals to feminist therapists, self-help support groups, family planning clinics, physicians, VD clinics, abortion clinics, workshops on pregnancy and childbirth, and seminars on pregnancy over 30 years of age.

Loop YWCA Women's Services Project
37 S. Wabash, Chicago, IL 60603
372-6600
Counseling for rape, battery, adolescent victims of abuse including sexual abuse, and employment-related problems. Frequently offers support groups for adult and adolescent women.

REFERRALS TO PRIVATE PRACTITIONERS

National Association of Social Workers (NASW)
30 N. Michigan, Chicago, IL 60602
236-8308
State and national directories of certified clinical social workers in private practice.

HERS (Health Evaluation & Referral Service)
1954 W. Irving Park Rd., Chicago, IL 60613
248-0166
See description above. Offers information on areas of expertise and fees of therapists.

Jung Institute
550 Callan Ave., Evanston, IL 60202
475-4848
Referrals to Jungian therapists. Jungians emphasize the unconscious and reflection on the past, and aim more for insight about internal processes than overt changes.

Gestalt Institute
P.O. Box 14248, Chicago, IL 60614
944-5556
Offers information on Gestalt theory, which emphasizes the present rather than the past, and referrals, which are usually to graduates of the Institute.

The following referral sources also offer outpatient clinical services.

Adler Institute, Dreikurs Center
618 S. Michigan, Chicago, IL 60605
294-7100
Staffed by Institute students, who have degrees in psychology, psychiatry, or social work, and prefer to be interactive and egalitarian with patients and emphasize social goals and lifestyles. Referrals are often to graduates of the Institute. Sliding fee scale.

Center for Family Studies/Family Institute of Chicago
666 N. Lakeshore Dr., Chicago, IL 60611
908-7285
Treatment combines aspects of different family systems theory bases. Therapists often work in teams and tend to be directive. Referrals are to graduates of the Institute's training programs—psychiatrists, psychologists, or social workers.

Horizons Community Services, Inc.
3225 N. Sheffield, Chicago, IL 60657
929-4357
Support groups and counseling for gays and lesbians as well as for relatives and loved ones. Advocacy and referrals to private practitioners and other resources.

Institute for Psychoanalysis
180 N. Michigan Ave., Chicago, IL 60601
726-6300
Psychodynamically oriented psychotherapy and psychoanalysis conducted by students of the institute's four-year training program. Human development theories are incorporated into traditional psychoanalytic theories. Treatment is often long term, aiming to resolve underlying causes of present-day problems. Referrals to private practitioners. Sliding scale fees.

OUT-PATIENT CLINICS
WITH SLIDING SCALES

DePaul Counseling Service
2219 N. Kenmore, Chicago, IL 60614
341-8292
Good-quality, short-term treatment for residents in the service area. Specializes in treatment of children and young adults.

Howard Brown Memorial Clinic
945 W. George, Chicago, IL 60657
871-5777
Primarily a VD clinic, also offers counseling to people suffering from AIDS or ARC, as well as to loved ones.

Katherine Wright Psychiatric Clinic
923 W. Wellington, Chicago, IL 60657
883-7065
Reputable, psychodynamically oriented clinic affiliated with Illinois Masonic Medical Center. Offers counseling for individuals, groups, families and couples, and treatment of children, adolescents, and adults. Has a couples resource center.

Michael Reese Hospital
Wexler Psychiatry Clinic
2960 S. Lake Park Ave., Chicago, IL 60616
791-3800
Treatment for children, adolescents, adults, and families. Special services include treatment of eating disorders and sexual dysfunctions.

Ravenswood Hospital Community Mental Health Center
4545 N. Damen, Chicago, IL 60625
878-4300
Comprehensive program including inpatient, outpatient, community education, and support groups serving all ages. Will accept clients from outside their service area, depending on availability.

University of Chicago Medical Center
Billings Hospital, Department of Psychiatry
5841 S. Maryland, Chicago, IL 60637
For information, referral and intake: 702-6199
Offers both inpatient and outpatient programs. Among outpatient services, known for their: anxiety-depression clinic, which can prescribe medication; sexual and marital therapy clinic, which tends to be behavioral; intensive sequence, which offers 2 to 3 visits per week; and behavior-medicine clinic, for stress management treatment, biofeedback, relaxation, weight training, and smoking cessation.

University of Illinois, Outpatient Psychiatry
840 S. Wood, Chicago, IL 60612
996-3586
Offers program for sufferers of chronic depressive or manic-depressive disorders who are better suited for treatment with medication.

Catholic Charities
126 N. Desplaines
Chicago, IL 60606
236-5172
Offers counseling and a variety of services. Makes referrals. Many centers throughout the city.

Chicago Board of Health
Bureau of Mental Health
50 W. Washington
Chicago, IL 60602
744-8033
Refers clients to their local county mental health center; centers are

scattered throughout the city. Call
to find the center in your area.
Quality of service varies from
center to center, so ask around.
Psychiatric backup is on the
premises. Therapists are assigned
to clients. Sliding scale fees.

Lutheran Social Services
4840 W. Byron
Chicago, IL 60641
282-7800

6229 N. Northwest Highway
Chicago, IL 60631
774-7555
10340 S. Western
Chicago, IL 60643
239-4550
Offers counseling and a variety of
services. Makes referrals. Good
reputation.

SUBSTANCE ABUSE TREATMENT

If an addiction has gotten too severe for you to control without the help of
a protective environment, you should consider enrolling into a formal treatment program.

To check the credentials of a particular program, call or write:

Joint Committee on Hospital Accreditation
875 N. Michigan, Chicago, IL 60611
642-6061

You have the right to ask a potential service provider about his or her
credentials, as well as the size and competence of the staff, whether 24-hour
coverage is offered, safety of the environment, whether individualized treatment planning is offered and if you are involved in the planning, your rights
and responsibilites in the program, and expected duration of treatment.

We consider the following programs, most of which offer comprehensive
services—including inpatient, outpatient, and follow-up—to be effective.

Jackson Park Hospital
7531 S. Stony Island, Chicago, IL 60649
947-2330
Comprehensive treatment, mostly inpatient, some outpatient, for both teenagers and adults.

Martha Washington Hospital
4055 N. Western, Chicago, IL 60618
583-9000
Comprehensive psychodynamic treatment, with a reputation for thorough-
ness and professionalism.

Martha Washington Loop clinic (has evening hours)
121 S. Riverside, Ste. 1652, Chicago, IL 60606
930-9648
Cocaine hotline: 287-2653

Lutheran Center for Substance Abuse
1700 Luther Lane, Park Ridge, IL
696-6050
Good track record.

The Better Way
11030 S. Longwood Dr., Chicago, IL 60643
881-1900

Grant Hospital
550 W. Webster, Chicago, IL 60614
883-2000
Comprehensive treatment with a medical bias, that is, alcoholism is considered a disease. Services include detoxification and abuse therapy, and individual and group counseling. Inpatient fees at prevailing rates; outpatient fees at a sliding scale.

Chicago Lakeshore Hospital
4840 N. Marine Dr., Chicago, IL 60640
878-9700
Psychodynamically oriented treatment includes detoxification, 28-day inpatient medical-psychodynamic treatment. Individual, group, and family counseling. Fees are at a flat rate; health insurance accepted.

If you have any questions about your rights as a patient or feel that your rights have been violated by a therapist or treatment center, call the **Legal Assistance Foundation, Mental Health Project** (341-1070). Fees are on a sliding scale.

BIBLIOGRAPHY

To better understand what therapy is like, what the different approaches are, and to gain some perspective on problems common to us all, we recommend the following books.

Family Crucible, Augustus Napier and Carl Whitaker, M.D., Bantam, 1978. About a real family in therapy together. A good book for learning about family therapy, written from the therapist's point of view.

Gestalt Therapy Verbatim, Fritz Perls, M.D., Bantam, 1959. Written by the founder of Gestalt therapy, the book consists of verbatim accounts of Gestalt therapy sessions.

Introduction to Psychoanalysis, Charles Brenner, M.D., Doubleday, 1974. A good introduction to psychoanalysis.

On Becoming A Person, Carl Rogers, Houghton Mifflin, 1961. The introduction to this book, written by the founder of client-centered therapy, explains why Rogers thinks that humanistic therapy works.

Passages, Gail Sheehy, Bantam, 1976. An examination of stages in adult life, with numerous interviews of average adults. Unusual because most books concentrate on the early stages of life rather than the later stages.

Peoplemaking, Virginia Satir, Science and Behavior Books, 1972. Written by a family therapist with an interest in how families communicate.

The Road Less Traveled, M. Scott Peck, M.D., Simon and Schuster, 1978. About the importance of spiritual values in human growth and development, written by a psychiatrist with a humanist approach. Easy to read, with little jargon.

—Linda Harper, Margaret Grau

LEGAL SERVICES

Back when the Daley Machine was the most powerful political organization in the country, it was more important to find a lawyer with the right political clout than to find one who knew something about law. But recent events have changed all that. For the time being, the Regular Democrats have been routed. Blacks, Hispanics, and women have begun to come into their own in the legal profession. Operation Greylord has documented long rumored corruption in the Circuit Courts, and many corrupt judges and crooked lawyers have been jailed. Today, instead of looking for a well-connected attorney, you would do well to find a competent one.

WHEN TO HIRE A LAWYER

You know you really need a lawyer when

You have been charged with a crime.

You are being sued over a civil matter.

You are drafting your will—to ensure that all statutory requirements have been satisfied.

You have been arrested for DUI (driving under the influence of alcohol or drugs).

You are buying or selling real estate. An attorney can make certain that the title is good, and that all documents have been checked and are in order.

You are getting a divorce and have children (or property).

Your driving record is poor and you have gotten another speeding ticket.

You have been fired without just cause.

You may not really need a lawyer when

You are sued for a small amount of money.
You are getting a divorce and you have no children (or property).
You sue someone for a modest amount of money (and want to avoid legal fees). In this case you may want to take your case to *pro se* court. *Pro se* court, a division of the Cook County Circuit Court, handles small claims (up to $1000) for people not represented by lawyers. You can represent yourself in other courts, too, but you're more likely to be mired in procedural muck. (Defendants may have attorneys in *pro se* if they wish.)

Don't consider hiring a lawyer if you want simply to vindicate a principle. This can be very expensive, and you may not make your point anyway.

HOW TO FIND A LAWYER

There are various ways to find a lawyer. Talk to friends and relatives to see whether they know of a lawyer who handled a similar matter. In addition, bar associations often make referrals—but they usually won't give you an evaluation of the lawyer's ability. Attorneys are now allowed to advertise the fields in which they practice, their experience, and the fees they charge. As with all advertising, however, buyer beware.

Before you hire a lawyer, be sure to find out the cost of the legal services. It's difficult to list even ballpark estimates of legal fees because they vary so widely. However, here are a few rough estimates of fees: simple divorce with few property issues, $300-500; residential real estate closing, $250-500; DUI defense, $1500 and up. The fee will depend on the complexity and nature of the case. Fees can be a fixed rate for a case, an hourly rate, a contingent fee (the attorney gets paid if you win the case—primarily used in personal injury cases), or a combination of these. Some attorneys will give you a free initial consultation, others will charge for this service. Find out before you make an appointment. If you lack the money to hire a lawyer, there are some organizations (see below) that may provide legal services at a reduced cost or at no cost.

If you want some basic legal information before seeing a lawyer, you might try **Dial-Law,** free tape-recorded messages on about 75 general interest legal questions. Dial Law is sponsored jointly by the Chicago Public Library and the Chicago Bar Association. Areas covered and sample topics include: real estate law (home mortgages); landlord-tenant law (eviction; security deposits); immigration law (permanent visas and work permits); criminal law (traffic violations; spouse abuse); family law (divorce; adoption); employment rights; and many others. To hear the messages and get a complete list of topics, call 644-0800 during the following hours: Monday through Thursday 9 am–7 pm; Friday 9 am–6 pm; Saturday 9 am–5 pm.

Another source of general legal information is Call A Lawyer, sponsored by the Chicago Bar Association. On the third Saturday of each month, volunteer attorneys answer questions on civil and criminal matters over the phone. Call 332-1111 from 9 am until noon on the third Saturday of the month.

COURTS AND GOVERNMENT BUILDINGS

Richard J. Daley Civic Center
Clark and Randolph Streets
State civil cases are heard here. Leave your knives and guns at home or risk activating the lobby metal detectors.

City Hall/County Building
LaSalle and Randolph Streets
Connected by underground tunnel to Daley Center. Located here are the Mayor's Office, City Council chambers (scene of the infamous "Council Wars"), and various county and city agencies.

State of Illinois Center
100 W. Randolph
This Helmut Jahn atrium is an amusing place to visit. Perhaps the first state building to combine a shopping mall with offices for state agencies.

Dirksen Federal Building
219 S. Dearborn
The Dirksen Building and the adjacent Kluczyinski Building together make
up Chicago's Federal Center. Federal cases are held in the Dirksen building.
Usually a newsworthy trial is occurring somewhere in the building. Again,
beware walking in with guns or knives on your person. Federal agencies are
housed in both the Dirksen and Kluczynski buildings.

Criminal Courts Building
26th and S. California
Most criminal felony trials are held here. If you want a heavy dose of reality,
this is the place to go. Adjacent is the Cook County Jail.

Traffic Court Building
321 N. LaSalle
If you get a traffic ticket in Chicago and want to contest it, you will need
to visit here. Always crowded with lost people trying to find their courtrooms
and overeager attorneys looking for clients.

BAR ASSOCIATIONS

Each organization listed has a referral system and can assist you in finding
an attorney.

Chicago Bar Association
29 S. LaSalle, Chicago, IL 60603   332-1111
Most lawyers in Chicago belong to this association. They have an extensive
referral system—$10 for an initial evaluation; after that, the fee is set by
the attorney.

Chicago Council of Lawyers
220 S. State, Suite 800, Chicago, IL 60604   427-0710
The second largest and most activist of the major bar associations in Chicago.
Offers the most critical recommendations of judges up for retention.

Decalogue Society of Lawyers
179 W. Washington, Chicago, IL 60602   263-6493
Bar association of Jewish attorneys dedicated to fighting anti-Semitism.

National Lawyers Guild
343 S. Dearborn, Chicago, IL 60604   939-2492
The Legal Left. Members have worked for prison, labor, civil rights and
immigration movements. Participated in the Chicago 7 and Fred Hampton
defenses.

Women's Bar Association
20 N. Clark, Suite 1725, Chicago, IL 60602   346-9224
Referral system available to the general public, but designed especially for
women.

CIVIL RIGHTS ORGANIZATIONS

Illinois Department of Human Rights
100 W. Randolph, Chicago, IL 60601   917-6200
This state agency is the starting point for discrimination claims.

Equal Employment Opportunity Commission
536 S. Clark, Chicago, IL 60605   353-2713
Federal agency that polices job discrimination.

American Civil Liberties Union
220 S. State
Chicago, IL 60604   427-7330
This organization chooses its cases carefully and generally limits itself to cases involving important issues of civil liberties and constitutional rights.

Chicago Lawyers Committee for Civil Rights Under the Law
220 S. State, Chicago, IL 60604   939-5797
Free legal services in civil rights. It is less interested in constitutional law principles, and more interested in representing community groups.

CONSUMER PROTECTION AGENCIES

Attorney General of Illinois, Consumer Fraud Division
100 W. Randolph, Chicago, IL 60601   917-3580

City of Chicago, Consumer Protection Division
1000 E. Ohio, Chicago, IL 60611   744-8538

OTHER LEGAL ORGANIZATIONS

Attorney Registration and Disciplinary Commission (ARDC)
203 N. Wabash, Suite 1900, Chicago, IL 60601   346-0690
If you want to complain about an attorney's services or conduct, this is the place to go.

Business and Professional People for the Public Interest
109 N. Dearborn, Chicago, IL 60602   641-5570
Has sponsored environmental and corporate public interest suits. Best known for its litigation that desegregated public housing in Chicago.

Lawyers Committee for Better Housing
6925 N. Ashland, Chicago, IL 60626   274-1111
Does exactly what its name says. (See also the section later in this chapter on housing law.)

Lawyers for the Creative Arts
623 S. Wabash, suite 201, Chicago, IL 60605   427-1800
Legal referrals for people in the arts. Free assistance for indigent artists.

Leadership Council of Metropolitan Open Communities
401 S. State, Chicago, IL 60604
341-1470 for general legal action programs
341-1543 for housing discrimination

FREE LEGAL HELP

Legal Assistance Foundation of Chicago
343 S. Dearborn, room 700, Chicago, IL 60604   341-1070
Civil legal services available to people who can't afford private lawyers.

Downtown office offers divorce assistance, Children's Rights Project, Women's Law Project (battered women, child support cases), and legal assistance for migrant workers.
Neighborhood offices:

911 S. Kedzie
638-2343

852 W. 63rd
651-3100

4655 S. Michigan
538-0733

1212 N. Ashland
489-6800

1661 S. Blue Island
421-1900

4753 N. Broadway
769-1015

Also, the Legal Center for Immigrants program operates out of the Blue Island office, 226-0173. For divorce assistance, call 341-1046.

Legal Aid Bureau
14 E. Jackson, Chicago, IL 60604   922-5625
Privately funded legal aid for needy people. Civil cases only.

Cook County Legal Assistance Foundation
1146 Westgate, Oak Park, IL 60302   524-2600
Civil legal aid for the suburbs. The organization also has offices in Harvey and Evanston.

Chicago Volunteer Legal Services Foundation
203 N. Wabash, Chicago, IL 60601   332-1624
Free legal aid by volunteer lawyers. The organization maintains offices throughout the city, but they are open only for a few hours, generally in the evening. The organization also sponsors the Cook County Jail Project, which provides civil legal aid to those in jail.

Illinois Guardianship and Advocacy Committee
527 S. Wells, suite 300, Chicago, IL 60607   793-5900
Protects the rights of the mentally ill and developmentally disabled.

Jewish Volunteer Legal Services Clinic
c/o American Jewish Congress
22 W. Monroe, Suite 2102, Chicago, IL 60603   332-7355
A variety of free legal services are available for those with demonstrated financial need.

Legal Clinic for the Disabled
Rehabilitation Institute of Chicago
345 E. Superior, Room 1129, Chicago, IL 60611   908-4463
Free civil legal services to low-income, disabled Cook County residents. Offers referrals to area attorneys doing pro bono work for the disabled.

Public Defender of Cook County
118 N. Clark, Chicago, IL 60602   443-6350
Free criminal defense for indigent people. Usually the staff is made up of recent law school grads, but some people make a career out of it. Public defenders are assigned to various courtrooms throughout the city and suburbs. Call to get the location of the office nearest you.

Neighborhood offices:

13th & Michigan
341-2730

Juvenile Court
1100 S. Hamilton
738-7047

Criminal Court
26th and S. California
890-3217

State's Attorney's W-D (Wives and Dependents) Unit
Child Support Enforcement Unit
32 W. Randolph, Chicago, IL 60601   793-3120
Unit will represent free of charge any parent seeking to have a father (or mother) declared as such and will seek to institute child support payments. There is no indigency requirement.

MEDIATION

Neighborhood Justice Center of Chicago
53 W. Jackson, suite 1511, Chicago, IL 60604
939-7383
Provides mediation services as an alternative to traditional court litigation.

LAW SCHOOL LEGAL CLINICS

Legal clinics are usually staffed by second- and third-year law students under the supervision of faculty members. With the exception of Chicago-Kent, these clinics provide limited services and serve only those with financial need. The Chicago-Kent clinic has no restrictions on who may use its services, and its services are similar to (and fees generally lower than) other law firms.

DePaul University Law Clinic
23 E. Jackson, Suite 950
Chicago, IL 60604
341-8294

IIT Chicago-Kent College of Law
Law Offices
77 S. Wacker
Chicago, IL 60606
567-5050

Loyola University Law Clinic
721 N. LaSalle
Chicago, IL 60610
266-0573
Special projects on unemployment compensation and Medicare.

Northwestern University School of Law
Legal Assistance Clinic
357 E. Chicago
Chicago, IL 60611
908-8576

University of Chicago
Mandel Legal Aid Clinic
6020 S. University
Chicago, IL 60637
702-9611
Affiliated with the Legal Aid Bureau.

TENANTS' RIGHTS ORDINANCE

Tenants' rights in Chicago were strengthened considerably by the recent passage of a citywide tenants' rights ordinance. The ordinance affects those tenants residing in all rental units with written or oral leases, except owner-occupied buildings containing 6 or fewer units. The new ordinance (a summary of which landlords must attach to all leases—old, pre-ordinance ones as well as new leases) establishes a balance between the rights of tenants and landlords, and defines in detail the obligations each has toward the other. One of the most important new rights for tenants in the ordinance concerns their options if the landlord doesn't keep the property in repair, that is, in compliance with the Chicago Building Code. If a necessary repair is not made, the tenant has several options:

Request in writing that the landlord make repairs within 30 days or the tenant can terminate the lease.

Request in writing that the landlord make repairs within 14 days or the tenant can reduce his or her rent check by an amount that reasonably reflects the reduced value of the unit.

Request in writing that the landlord make repairs within 14 days or the tenant may have repairs made and deduct up to $200 or one-fourth of the monthly rent, whichever is more. The repairs must be "done in a work-manlike manner" and in compliance with legal and building regulations. The tenant must supply the landlord with a receipt for the repairs and deduct no more from the rent than the cost of the repairs.

File suit against the landlord to recover damages and obtain injunctive relief.

The tenant MAY NOT exercise any of the above remedies if damage is the fault of the tenant, tenant's family, or guests.

The ordinance also addresses other areas such as: tenant responsibilities, landlord responsibilities, loss of essential service (gas, electricity, water, heat, hot water, plumbing), security deposits, subleases, lockouts, and eviction. You can pick up a summary of the ordinance at the Chicago Department of Housing at 318 S. Michigan (call 922-7925 for more information), or you can buy a copy of the ordinance from the Office of the City Clerk, Room 107, City Hall, 121 N. LaSalle, Chicago, IL 60602. A copy is also available at the Municipal Reference Library in Room 1002 of City Hall.

Tenants' Rights and Landlords' Responsibilities

Landlords are responsible for supplying adequate heat from September 15 to June 1, hot water, ventilation, plumbing, security, extermination of pests, general maintenance, and a number of other services. (To obtain a complete listing of landlord responsibilities, get a copy of the Tenant-Landlord Handbook described below.) If these responsibilities are not being met, you should first call the owner, janitor, or management company. If nothing happens in a reasonable amount of time, send your landlord notice that you will start reducing your rent, or exercise one of the other options available to you and listed in the tenants' rights ordinance (see description above). At the same time, contact your local tenant union, community organization, or one of the legal and other resources listed in this chapter.

If matters are really serious, you can call to request that a city building inspector come out and inspect the problem. You have a couple of options: You can call the 24-hour number for the Mayor's Office of Inquiry and

Information at 744-5000. Or you can call the Department of Inspectional Services at 744-3420 and ask for an inspection.

Still another alternative for handling tenant-landlord problems is suing your landlord in *pro se* court.

WHERE TO GET HELP

Get a copy of the summary of the tenants' rights ordinance from the Chicago Department of Housing, 318 S. Michigan (call 922-7922). Another excellent resource is the Tenant-Landlord Handbook published by the Legal Assistance Foundation (341-1070). The Chicago Urban League publishes an excellent free handbook for tenants and community groups on how to deal with housing problems at the city inspector and Housing Court levels called "Housing Court Handbook." Call the Chicago Urban League at 285-5800 to get the booklet. Still another good resource is a book entitled *Chicago Tenants' Handbook* by Ed Sacks.

TENANTS' ORGANIZATIONS

Chicago is unique for the number of tenants' organizations we have. Tenants' organizations organize tenants, give advice to tenants with problems, work alongside lawyers to help resolve problems, and will sometimes accompany tenants to court. They will refer you to lawyers they trust and to other organizations that can help you. If you don't know if your area has a tenants' group, call the Metropolitan Tenants Organization at 549-1631 and ask them for advice and referrals.

Some of the larger tenants' and community organizations are listed below.

Rogers Park Tenants Committee
1545 W. Morse
Chicago, IL 60626
973-7888

Uptown Tenants Union
5121 N. Clark
Chicago, IL 60640
769-3232

Lakeview Tenants Organization
3212 N. Broadway
Chicago, IL 60657
549-1631

Kenwood/Oakland Community Organization
1236-38 E. 46th St.
Chicago, IL 60653
548-7500

Action Coalition of Englewood
6220 S. Sangamon
Chicago, IL 60621
471-0080

South Austin Coalition Community Council
5112 W. Washington
Chicago, IL 60644
287-0206

Woodlawn East Community and Neighbors (WECAN)
1541 E. 65th St.
Chicago, IL 60637
288-3000

Metropolitan Tenants Organization
3212 N. Broadway
Chicago, IL 60657
549-1631
A coalition of tenants' organizations, MTO works on citywide legislation and coordinated the recent effort to get the tenants' ordinance passed. They give advice over the phone, make referrals, and work on Housing Court reform issues. They also give educational workshops for local groups about the tenants' rights ordinance.

OTHER GROUPS THAT HELP

Check with the organizations listed above for groups that offer legal help for housing problems. In addition, consult:

Lawyer's Committee for Better Housing
6925 N. Ashland, Chicago, IL 60626
274-1111
Primarily serves the Rogers Park, Edgewater, and Uptown communities. Provides legal advice to both tenants and landlords on building conditions. They don't represent people in court, but will offer advice on tenant-landlord problems, and will intervene to a degree.

Legal Assistance Foundation
343 S. Dearborn, Chicago, IL 60604
341-1070
Low-priced legal help for lower-income residents, including assistance with tenant-landlord problems. Distributes a Tenant-Landlord Handbook ($6 by mail). See listing earlier in this chapter for addresses of neighborhood locations.

Neighborhood Housing Services of Chicago, Inc.
123 N. Jefferson, Chicago, IL 60606
454-0290
An organization helping lower-income residents rehab older buildings. Among services offered is helping clients obtain loans. Also has seven other neighborhood offices.

Chicago Council of Lawyers
220 S. State, Suite 800, Chicago, IL 60604
427-0710
A public interest bar association. The housing committee has produced a tenant-landlord handbook and a standard lease fair to both landlords and tenants, and is currently working to update both items. The committee has also done influential studies of eviction and the housing courts, and made recommendations based on the results.

CITY OFFICES

Chicago Department of Housing
318 S. Michigan
Chicago, IL 60604
922-7922

Chicago Department of Inspectional Services
To request an inspection: 744-3420

Mayor's Office of Inquiry and Information
24-hour number: 744-5000

To find out who your alderman is and how to contact him or her, call 269-7900.

Also, look in the blue pages in the white pages phone book under City of Chicago, Consumer Services, Streets and Sanitation, and the Health Department for more city numbers to call for help.

—Ron Schwartz

RELIGION

Many Chicago churches are healthy, flourishing, and involved. Many congregations are growing as we discover that church can provide us with a sense of community, fulfill our longing for spiritual growth, support us during personal crisis, and provide a good structure for helping us to teach our children values. However, it's important to know that other congregations are struggling. Churches are especially important in this multiethnic city, because many churches help ethnic groups maintain their heritage. Occasionally one church is shared by two or more congregations who speak different languages.

Activities of Chicago churches range in scope from social services such as outreach programs to issues of world-wide consequence, such as nuclear-free zones. Local churches sponsor a wealth of activities for individuals and families, including social, educational, recreational, and self-help and counseling programs. Community activities of churches in Chicago range from evangelism to the sponsorship of food pantries, shelters for the homeless, nursing homes, hospitals, and political action organizations. Religious bodies often participate in national and international debates as well--over defense spending, abortion, the teaching of evolution, civil rights, and many other issues.

In selecting a church, you may want to visit several to find one compatible with your beliefs and concerns. But be patient: the excitement of worship doesn't usually come at the first or second visit. It takes a bit longer to get to know a congregation.

FINDING A CONGREGATION

Most people feel that they have to go to the local neighborhood church. Although this would help keep your transportation costs down, it's not a logical way to choose a church. Instead, first determine your motivations and needs. Then shop around. The Chicago area contains over 4,000 local congregations. Below are brief descriptions of a few local churches of various denominations that may interest you. I have also included a listing of the major denominational offices that can refer you to other churches. Chicago has churches serving all the ethnic groups represented here--if you want to find one, call the appropriate major denominational office with your request. I don't mean to endorse any churches with this list, but rather provide you with a sampling.

St. Paul's United Church of Christ
2335 N. Orchard St., 348-3829
A medium-sized congregation with a wide range of programs, located just east of Children's Memorial Hospital. In addition to its noteworthy programs for children, St. Paul's has an excellent music program. Occasionally, it mounts a religious drama in cooperation with Organic Theatre. They also have a concert series.

Photo by Glenn Kaupert.

St. Thomas of Canterbury Catholic Church
4827 N. Kenmore Ave., 271-8655
Located in Uptown, this Catholic parish has a wide variety of helping programs for the community, ranging from a food pantry to a local school. The
parish ministers to the needs of white, black, hispanic, Vietnamese, as well
as other groups. For using a variety of ethnic music in its worship services,
this parish is second to none.

Trinity United Church of Christ
532 W. 95th St., 962-5650
One of the largest and fastest growing churches in the United States, Trinity
is a black church that appeals to the rising liberal black middle class. With

an incredible variety of programs, from music to social action to education in black history, this congregation is an exciting place.

Emanuel Congregation
5959 N. Sheridan Rd., 561-5173
A Jewish Reformed Congregation with a long history of activity in Chicago. Located on the north side lakefront, Emanuel Congregation offers a traditional Jewish religious school, Sunday school, and adult education, as well as an exciting variety of musical programs.

St. Luke Evangelical Lutheran Church (AELC)
1500 W. Belmont, 472-3383
This congregation has a school for children through the eighth grade. Their worship is traditional, with an excellent professional music program that offers both classical and traditional religious music. St. Luke's also offers a series of art shows through its Community Art Gallery, featuring painting, sculpture, and water colors.

University Church (United Church of Christ/Disciples of Christ)
5655 S. University Avenue, 363-8142
Remember the "Days of Rage" in the 60s? Some of those people first met at a coffee house at the Blue Gargoyle of University Church. University Church is a racially integrated congregation offering a repertoire of spiritual and classical religious music during its services. They also have a liturgical dance group. In 1985, University Church voted to become a sanctuary congregation and has since housed a refugee family from Guatemala. The church is also a nuclear weapon free zone; members are active in that movement as well. The Blue Gargoyle Coffee Shop offers a variety of programs for neighborhood youth, including tutoring and job training. University Church is adjacent to the University of Chicago; the church also houses the United Campus Christian Ministry.

Wellington Avenue United Church of Christ
615 W. Wellington, 935-0642
Wellington Avenue is another congregation that is both a sanctuary congregation and a nuclear weapon free zone. Like University Church, it is active in a variety of social justice issues.

Good Shepherd Parish Metropolitan Community Church
615 W. Wellington, 472-8708
The Good Shepherd Parish, with Wellington Avenue United Church of Christ, offers a special ministry and fellowship to the gay community. The church shares spaces with Wellington Avenue United Church of Christ. The Chicago area has several Metropolitan Community Churches, but this congregation is the most active.

North Shore Baptist Church
5244 N. Lakewood, 728-4200
A large American Baptist church offering a full range of traditional church programs. Its music program and its Sunday school program for children and youth are excellent.

Uptown Baptist Church
1011 W. Wilson Ave., 784-2922
This Southern Baptist congregation is probably one of the most socially active churches in that fellowship. Worship services and programs are offered

in English, Spanish, Vietnamese, Cambodian, Lao, Hmong, and Russian. The church runs a food pantry, houses an emergency shelter program, and offers alcoholism counseling.

Fourth Presbyterian Church
126 E. Chestnut, 787-4570
Located between Rush Street and Water Tower Place, this congregation is well located for its special singles ministry. Several worship services are offered on Sundays. Fourth Presbyterian also has several active singles and married groups for all ages, as well as a counseling center, senior center, and day care center.

LaSalle Street Church (non-denominational)
1136 N. LaSalle, 787-3756
In addition to its exciting worship services, LaSalle Street offers a wide variety of special ministries, among them, ministries for single adults, unwed mothers, senior citizens, a chaplaincy program for international college students, tutoring, and CYCLE, a special program for young people at Cabrini Green.

First Baptist Congregational Church
1613 W. Washington, 243-8047
A large black congregation affiliated with the National Baptist Convention USA, and the United Church of Christ. The church offers several weekly worship services, weekday prayer services, and special primary and children's church worship services. It has several gospel choirs, including a children's choir and a young adult choir. One of its special outreach programs is at a local housing project, Henry Horner Homes.

Saint Luke's (San Lucas) United Church of Christ
2914 W. North Ave., 227-5747
This predominantly Puerto Rican congregation offers a variety of special programs to its community. It is active in the WestTown Coalition, an activist community organization. It offers special programs for unwed mothers, as well as a day care program. It also has a special youth orchestra, and offers music lessons--an exciting alternative to less creative youth activities in the area.

Lincoln Park Presbyterian Church
600 W. Fullerton, 248-8288
A small, active congregation that prides itself on being an extended family of faith, with a wide diversity of people in its membership. It supports an active young adult ministry, as well as a traditional church school. Located in a beautifully restored classical building, this congregation is proud of its music program and its participatory worship style. The church shares space with many local community groups, and is home to the Midwest Academy, a community organizing center, and Family Focus, a parent-child drop-in center.

Holy Name Cathedral
735 N. State, 787-8040
Nothing is as grand and magnificent as worship and music in the setting of a Catholic cathedral. Much classical religious music can only be fully appreciated in such a setting. Holy Name is the cathedral for the Chicago

archdiocese, the largest Catholic archdiocese in the United States and one of the largest in the world. Holy Name offers mass 5-6 times every day, and coordinates a wealth of other church programs.

Chicago Temple—First United Methodist Church
77 W. Washington, 236-4548

Listed in the Guinness Book of World Records as the tallest church in the world, the Chicago Temple houses the corporate offices for the Northern Illinois Association of the United Methodist Church. The church offers a traditional range of Sunday worship, children, youth, and adult education, and special music. During the week, a Wednesday worship is offered at noon for Loop-area workers. Occasionally, organ concerts are given during the noon hour.

St. Clement's Catholic Church
642 W. Deming, 281-0371

A Lincoln Park church and school (pre-school to eighth grade) with a full range of programs for north side Catholics, including singles groups and special educational programs. Many music programs are offered, including a traditional, full production of Handel's "Messiah" during the Christmas season.

People's Church
941 W. Lawrence, 784-6633

Dr. Preston Bradley, who founded this congregation, was a famous radio preacher of an earlier generation. His influence is still felt today at this church. This is a renewed congregation, now affiliated with the Unitarian Universalists Association and the United Church of Christ. People's Church sponsors a wide range of special programs and events including folk concerts, political rallies, continuing education for adults, and shelter for the homeless during winter.

First Unitarian Church
5650 S. Woodlawn, 324-4100

Located in Hyde Park, this congregation sponsors the Chicago Children's Choir, a group that performs with the Chicago Symphony Orchestra, as well as other musical groups. The Church also sponsors Depot, a family counseling program; the Samaritans, a suicide prevention group; as well as pre-school, aerobics, and traditional religious education programs for children, youth, and adults.

57th Street Friends Meeting House
5615 S. Woodlawn, 288-3066

Relaxed, friendly Quaker meeting house founded in the 1930s.

MAJOR DENOMINATIONAL OFFICES

The thirty or so offices listed below can refer you to the nearly 3,000 congregations in the Chicago area affiliated with the major religious denominations. There are well over 1,000 other local congregations, some with denominational offices, many totally independent. I have listed only a few of the larger Protestant, Catholic, and Jewish offices. All addresses are in Chicago unless otherwise noted.

African Methodist Episcopal Church, 4448 S. Michigan, 60653, 373-6587
African Methodist Episcopal Zion Church, 7158 S. Indiana, 60619, 723-8624
American Baptist Church, 59 E. Van Buren, #2517, 60605, 341-1266
American Friends Service Committee (Quakers), 59 E. Van Buren, Ste. 1400, 60605, 427-2533
American Jewish Congress, 22 W. Monroe, Suite 2102, 60603, 332-7355.
American Lutheran Church, 1908 Weeg Way, Park Ridge, 60068, 823-4536
Christian Board of Rabbis (Conservative, Reformed, Traditional, and Reconstructionist), 1 S. Franklin, 60606, 444-2896
Chicago Rabbinical Council (Orthodox) 3525 W. Peterson, 60659, 588-1600
Christian Church (Disciples of Christ), 634 N. Austin, Oak Park, 60304, 383-3113
Christian Science Church, 72 W. Adams, 60603, 782-8181
Church of the Brethren, 1451 Dundee Ave., Elgin, 60120, 742-5100
Church of Jesus Christ of Latter Day Saints (Mormons), 1319 Butterfield Rd., Downers Grove, 60515, 969-2145
Episcopal Church, 65 E. Huron, 60611, 787-6410
Evangelical Covenant Church, 5101 N. Francisco, 60625, 784-3000
Evangelical Free Church, 5249 N. Ashland, 60640, 561-7544
Greek Orthodox Church, 40 E. Burton Pl., 60610, 337-4130
International Council of Community Churches, 900 Ridge, Homewood, 60430, 798-2264
Lutheran Church in America, 18 S. Michigan, Room 800, 60603, 346-9229
Lutheran Church-Missouri Synod, 2301 S. Wolf Rd., Hillside, 60162, 449-3020
Mennonite Church, 18 W. 757 22nd St., Lombard, 60148, 629-3060
Orthodox Church in America, 8200 S. County Line Rd., Hinsdale, 60521, 325-6608
Presbyterian Church, USA, 100 S. Morgan, 60612, 243-8300
Reformed Church in America, 17060 S. Park, South Holland, 60473, 333-0402
Roman Catholic Church, 155 E. Superior, 60611, 751-8200
Southern Baptist Convention, 329 Madison, Oak Park, 60302, 848-9120
Unitarian Universalist Association, 141 S. Oak Park Ave., Oak Park, 60302, 383-4344
United Church of Christ, 18 S. Michigan, #1210, 60603, 372-5918
United Methodist Church, 77 W. Washington, Room 1806, 60602, 346-8752
Universal Fellowship of Metropolitan Community Churches, Good Shepherd Parish, 615 W. Wellington, 60657, 472-8708

The Chicago area is also the home to other local congregations outside of the Jewish-Christian tradition. A few offices are listed below, but there are many more.

Baha'i Chicago Center, 1233 Central, Evanston, 60201, 869-9039. Visit the beautiful Baha'i Temple overlooking Lake Michigan in north suburban Wilmette (Sheridan Rd. at Linden).
Islamic Center of Chicago, 4380 N. Elston, 60641, 725-9047
Midwest Buddhist Temple, 435 W. Menomonee, 60614, 943-7801
Muslim Center, 24 N. Pulaski, 60624, 533-9558.

Vivekananda Vendata Society, 5423 S. Hyde Park Blvd., 60615, 363-0027
Zen Buddhist Temple, 608 W. Dempster, Evanston, 60201, 272-2070

In late 1987, a complete listing of all 4,000 Chicago area local congregations--Catholic, Protestant, Jewish, Moslem, and other--will be published by the Church Federation of Chicago (101 E. Wacker, 565-1100).

SPECIAL MINISTRIES

Agape House
University of Illinois at Chicago
1046 W. Polk, Chicago, IL 60607   666-2676
Interdenominational Protestant student center near the University of Illinois campus. Social organizations for students and faculty.

Catholic Youth Organization
1122 S. Wabash, Chicago, IL 60605   939-7273
Athletic and social activities for Catholic teenagers.

Friendship International
1011 W. Wilson, Chicago, IL 60640   784-2922; evenings and weekends call 561-3168
Christian organization aimed at international students, especially those from Africa. Sponsored by the Uptown Baptist Church.

Hillel Foundation of B'nai Brith
Northwestern University
1935 Sherman Ave., Evanston, IL 60201   328-0650
Serving Jewish college students, graduate students, and others. An alternative Jewish religious organization with most types of Jewish religious services. Lectures, Hebrew classes, social activities, and special events during the holidays. To locate organizations at other campuses in the area, call Hillel's downtown office at 346-6700.

Hillel Foundation of B'nai Brith
University of Chicago
5715 S. Woodlawn, Chicago, IL 60637   752-1127

Hillel Foundation of B'nai Brith
University of Illinois at Chicago
750 S. Halsted, Chicago, IL 60607   996-3385

International Evangelical Free Church
1743 W. Harrison, Room 722, Chicago, IL 60612   226-8026
Special ministry for international students.

John Paul II Catholic Student Center
University of Illinois at Chicago
700 S. Morgan, Chicago, IL 60607   226-1880
Student Center for the entire Archdiocese of Chicago. Religious services, educational and social programs, and outreach activities are provided. A weekly cheap lunch (about $1) attracts many students.

Lutheran Student Movement
35 E. Wacker, Chicago, IL 60601   332-1387
National office provides information about campus ministries at college campuses in the Chicago area.

Night Ministry
835 W. Addison, Chicago, IL 60613   935-3366
Pastoral counseling and crisis intervention open to all. Call even if you just want to talk.

People United to Serve Humanity (PUSH)
930 E. 50th, Chicago, IL 60615   373-3366
Wide-reaching religious and service organization founded by Rev. Jesse L. Jackson. Unique Saturday morning service is radio broadcast.

BOOKSTORES

Chicago Baptist Institute Bookstore
5120 S. Martin Luther King Dr.
268-2253

Chicago Hebrew Bookstore
2942 W. Devon
973-6636

Cokesbury Book Store
1661 N. Northwest Hwy.
Park Ridge
299-4411
Good selection of books on Christian philosophy and literature.

Covenant Press
3200 W. Foster
478-4676
Bookstore affiliated with the Swedish Covenant Church.

Fortress Church Supply Store
1100 E. 55th
752-1766
Specializes in Christian literature.

Logos Book Store
101 N. Oak Park Ave. (Oak Park)
848-6644
Large selection of religious books supplemented by books on psychology and sociology.

Moody Bible Institute Book Store
150 W. Chicago
329-4352

Mustard Seed Christian Bookstore
1139 W. Sheridan
973-7055

Rosenblum Hebrew Bookstore
2906 W. Devon
262-1700
The area's largest selection of books on Judaism and Judaica.

St. Paul Catholic Book and Audio Visual Center
172 N. Michighan
346-4228
Catholic religious literature available in every medium.

Seminary Cooperative Bookstore
5757 S. University
752-4381
The most comprehensive selection of religious titles in the midwest. If they don't have it, the other seminaries' bookstores (located nearby) probably will.

—Dale Richesin

RECREATION

SPORTS

You can watch or participate in just about any sport imaginable in Chicago. Chicagoans worship sports, despite what people's bellies might indicate. We have a long tradition of sporting events: in 1927, the first ski meet held in an outdoor stadium took place in—of all places—Soldier Field. A mountain, some 13 stories high, was built for the gentleman's sport of ski jumping.

Chicago has its own version of softball (16-inch, no gloves, please), the most golf courses of any metropolitan area in the country, and a lengthy and tragic sports history. This city has a lot to offer. If you just want to watch, then learn Cubspeak and the Bear's bark; both are mandatory for spectators. If, however, you'd rather participate, and your interests lie between archery and windsurfing, you'll find it in Chicago.

SPECTATOR SPORTS

In 1963, the **Bears** won the NFL title and **Loyola** won the NCAA basketball championship. Things were looking up for Chicago, but the moment didn't last. It was 1981 before we won another championship. That was when the **Sting** (the soccer team) won top prize, but no parades were held because—at least in the minds of the local media—soccer is not a "real" sport. In 1983, the **White Sox** won their division by an overwhelming margin. Citizens frolicked in the streets, but not for long, because Baltimore quickly disposed of the Sox in the playoffs.

In 1984, the **Cubs**, who almost won their division in 1969 until a black cat crossed the field, finished in first place. The Cubbies proceeded to demolish the San Diego Padres in the first two games of the playoffs. Salvation was on our doorsteps and self-confidence returned. Icons were quickly made of all club members, including the trainer. Harry Caray (Cub announcer and mayor of Rush Street) even became eloquent. Then the Cubs lost the next three games.

While Cubspeak was garnering most of the attention, a strange development was taking place along the lakefront. A man named Ditka, a cowboy from Texas, was on a divine mission. George Halas, founder of the NFL and owner of the Bears, was on his deathbed. He named this man Ditka as head coach. The God of football had spoken. Move over Moses; Ditka brought with him only two commandments. Team and attitude. But what did they mean? Curiosity was aroused.

Before 1985, the **Bears** played well, especially on defense. Walter Payton was the offense. The Bears seemed to lack that essence, whatever it is, that makes champions. Numerous "if only" theories circulated throughout bars as to why they could not go all the way. If only Jim McMahon, savior apparent, could stay healthy, if only Willie Gault (a speedster receiver) could catch, if only the Bears were in another city. Yet, in the 1985-86 season, strange phenomena were witnessed. The Bears started to dismantle every team they played. In the playoffs, they shut out all opposition. It was time for the Super Bowl, and they won. Euphoria! The city council voted unanimously for a parade. Agreement in the city council? Stranger things have not happened. On the day of the parade, a crowd of mob proportions braved subzero weather to cheer the team.

Sports in Chicago are played not only on the field but also in political arenas. For a while, the Cubs, Sox, and Bears were all talking about moving to the northwest suburbs. (The prevailing theory was that people "out there" are polite, don't drink, and will purchase $200 worth of hot dogs at each game.) As of this writing, however, it looks as though the teams may stay in the city—a big relief to loyal city fans—but no one is sure where.

Professional Teams

BASEBALL

Chicago Cubs
Wrigley Field
1060 W. Addison St.   878-CUBS
Howard el line, Addison B stop
The game is one reason to watch a baseball game; I think, however, that the crowd is a better show. For a mere four bucks, you can soak up some sun, and watch the people show in the bleachers at Wrigley Field. But watch out for balls aimed at your head when the Cubbies are on the field. The oldest park in the big leagues.

Chicago White Sox
Comiskey Park
West of Dan Ryan Expressway at 35th St.   924-1000
Dan Ryan el line, 35th St. A/B stop
Home of the late Mayor Daley, the old political machine, Connie's pizza, and a truly unique Chicago dialect is Bridgeport, the neighborhood adjacent to Comiskey Park, home of the White Sox. Jerry and Eddie (owners of the Sox) have attempted to mold these proud people into surburbanites by installing a large security force to ensure the fans do not act like fans. Catch a game; relive your memories.

BASKETBALL

Chicago Bulls
Chicago Stadium
1800 W. Madison St.   943-5800
From the Loop take the Madison St. bus #20 to the front door of the Stadium.
The Bulls always seem to make the last slot for the playoffs so that they can never get that top draft pick. But Michael Jordan is worth the price of admission. The surrounding area is not a place to stroll in after the game.

HOCKEY

Chicago Blackhawks
Chicago Stadium
1800 W. Madison St.   733-5300
From the Loop take the Madison St. bus #20 to the front door of the Stadium.
The first Blackhawk coach, Muldoon, was hired and fired during the 1926-27 season. Out of spite, he reached into his Haitian bag of tricks and produced "Muldoon's curse": May the Hawks never finish in first place. It worked; the Hawks did not slither into first place until 1969. Now the Hawks field a good team, supported by fans who are devoted and like to be loud. Fun atmosphere.

SOCCER

Chicago Sting
245-KICK
Lee Stern, owner of the Sting, has really tried to promote soccer. The Sting only play indoors now, and if you have never seen the indoor game, check it out—it's exciting. Call the Sting's office to find out where and what league they're playing in at the time.

FOOTBALL

Chicago Bears
Soldier Field
425 E. McFetridge Dr. (12th St. and the lake)   663-5100
or your local saloon's wide screen TV.
And, finally, our beloved Bears. Chicago/World's Champions. Opposites do occasionally attract. Learn how to drink beer and bark.

Collegiate Sports

FOOTBALL
Sad but true, the only Division I football team in the area is at **Northwestern University**. They defend their record in the name of academic excellence. You can see their football at Dyche Stadium in Evanston. 491-7070 for information.

BASKETBALL
In basketball, Ray Meyer (candidate for nicest guy of the century) coached **DePaul** for eons. He never won the big one, but was always close. Taken over by son Joey, DePaul has slipped a bit, but still plays exciting urban street ball at the Rosemont Horizon, 6920 Mannheim Rd., in suburban Rosemont. 341-8010 for information.

Loyola won the NCAA in 1963, and always fields a good, and occasionally excellent, team. Games are at the UIC (University of Illinois at Chicago) Pavilion, 1150 W. Harrison. 274-1211 for information.

Chicago State is a true democratic institution. They let anyone play ball, and can give any powerhouse a run for their money. They also have an excellent summer league, in which many pros participate. 95th and King Dr., 995-2295 for information.

Northwestern usually has better luck with this game. They play in McGaw Hall's Walsh-Ryan Arena in Evanston. 491-7070 for information.

OTHER COLLEGIATE SPORTS
In high school, our basketball coach claimed there exists a direct correlation between physical coordination and reading ability. **Northwestern's** women's teams uphold their half of this potential axiom with excellent basketball, volleyball, and softball teams. 491-3204 for information.

University of Illinois at Chicago (UIC) has a good hockey team that plays in a nice stadium (the UIC Pavilion). They also have good women's volleyball and gymnastic teams. Take a look if you want to beat the crowds. 996-2498 for information.

Monsters of the Midway, Big Ten champions, first Heismann Trophy winner? Believe it or not, that's the **University of Chicago**. This is the school that not long ago elected a refrigerator for their homecoming queen—not your typical rah-rah place. They're Division III now, but they left the Big Ten with a provision that they could re-enter anytime, replacing Michigan State. I say let's start a campaign to have U of C reinstated in the Big Ten. Northwestern could use a manageable cross-town rival. Call 702-7681 for information.

If you're into fencing, lacrosse, or Bulgarian dirt diving, there are numerous other smaller colleges and universities with all sorts of teams throughout the city. Go to the yellow pages, look under schools, and give them a call.

Other Spectator Sports

HORSE RACING
Arlington Park Race Track caught fire in 1985. The fire destroyed everything but the track. Gamblers wept while their spouses thought of buying such

luxuries as food. Now it seems they will rebuild the track at the same site. The other tracks are:

Balmoral
Rt. 1 and Elms Court Lane
Crete
568-5700

Hawthorn
3501 S. Laramie
Cicero
780-3700

Maywood (trotters and pacers)
North Ave. and River Road
Maywood
626-4816

Sportsman's
3301 S. Laramie (next to
Hawthorn)
Cicero
242-1121

And just in case:
Gamblers Anonymous
30 W. Washington
Chicago, IL 60602
346-1588

POLO
Try polo when your Bentley is in the shop. International competition and Prince Chuck (when he's in town) play at:

Oak Brook Polo Club
2700 York Rd.
Oak Brook
571-7656
Wednesday and Friday matches start at 4 pm and are free. Weekends, the matches start at 3 pm and the prices are $5 and up. The polo season runs from May through October.

SPORTS CAR RACING
For stock car races on a clay track, the place is:

Sante Fe Speedway
9100 S. Wolf Rd.
Hinsdale
839-1050

If you prefer spectator racing, or late model, hobby stock, and mini stock racing on a blacktop surface, try:

Raceway Park
130th St. and Ashland Ave.
Calumet Park
385-4035

Other notable events are **America's Marathon**, held in the early autumn, which attracts a world-class field; the **Golden Gloves** boxing tournament, held in the winter; the **MacMurray Basketball Tournament**, which is the ultimate street basketball championship, held in the summer at 53rd and Kenwood; and the **Mackinac sailboat race**, which starts off Belmont Harbor in Chicago and ends at Mackinac Island in Michigan and is the oldest sanctioned race in America.

Check the Friday or Weekend sections of the *Tribune* or *Sun-Times* newspapers for news of other sports events.

PARTICIPANT SPORTS

Whether you want to slenderize or simply have some fun, you'll find an activity below. Besides these activities, check the "Go" section in the *Chicago Tribune* Friday section for varied listings of sports activities, as well as *Windy City Sports*, a free fitness and recreation guide with a good calendar of races and other events, available around town. Refer also to the Outdoors chapter of this book for more ideas of where to bike, hike, ski, or canoe in the Chicago area.

Facilities

CHICAGO PARK DISTRICT

The Chicago Park District offers extensive facilities and activities, including some things you might not expect: for example, archery, model yacht basins, and roque (a form of croquet) courts. Classes are offered for many activities. The Park District also has golf courses, an indoor ice rink, and yacht harbors. Unfortunately, facilities are often underused. To find out what programs are available in your area, walk to the park office closest to you (or look up their number in the white pages under Chicago Park District) and ask what's offered there. Be persistent. I'll bet you'd be surprised to find out what you've been missing.

Chicago Park District
(main office)
425 E. McFetridge Dr.
Chicago, IL 60605
294-2200

Instructional classes in all areas, as well as the best facilities, are at:
McFetridge Sports Complex
(not to be confused with the office on McFetridge Dr.)
3485 N. California
478-0210
McFetridge also has the best indoor ice skating in town.

Other parks that offer good facilities are:
Lincoln Park (complete with zoo)
Fullerton Ave. west of Lake Shore Dr.
294-4750

Portage Park
4100 N. Long Ave.
545-4337

Marquette Park
6700 S. Kedzie
776-9879

Washington Park
5531 S. Martin Luther King Dr.
684-6530

See the Outdoors chapter for more information on city parks.

FOREST PRESERVES

For cross-country skiing, golfing, ice fishing, ice skating, picnicking, sledding, snowmobiling, or a simple romp through the woods, try the forest preserves. Lots of land, woods, and not many people.

Forest Preserve District of Cook County
(main office)
536 N. Harlem Ave., River Forest, IL 60305   261-8400 or 366-9420
The Forest Preserve has six main locations in and around Chicago, so check

the white pages for the one nearest to you. See also the Outdoors chapter for more information.

Activities

ARCHERY
The **Park District** (294-2200) has six ranges at locations throughout the city. Call for addresses and hours. To find 20 indoor ranges and professional instruction try: **Archery Sales and Service**, 3542 W. Lawrence, 588-2077.

BACKGAMMON
You can roll the die with the **Backgammon Club of Chicago**, 951-1055

BADMINTON
For information on where to play and tournaments call or write

Badminton Association of Chicago
5106 N. Cicero
Chicago, IL 60630
736-1072

Midwest Badminton Association
contact: Kevin Hussey
313 Rimini Ct., #3A
Palatine, IL 60067
358-6057

BALLOONING
Northeastern Illinois Balloon Association, 948-0506.

BASEBALL
The **Park District** (294-2200) has over 500 diamonds. There is an abundance of leagues for children within the Park District system; the leagues charge a nominal fee. Go to the park nearest you and inquire.

BASKETBALL
The **Park District** (294-2200) and **YMCA** (280-3400) host many basketball leagues. Community churches often support leagues as well. Of special note is the **MacMurray Basketball Tournament**, held on a playground on the south side at 53rd and S. Kenwood, which offers the ultimate in street ball. Held in the summer. Any team can enter, so if you are Michael Jordan minus ten years, give it a try.

BEACHES
The **Park District** (294-2200) has 31 beaches all along the lakefront. They do not allow alcohol, rafts, or scuba gear. Officially open from June 15 to September 15--this is the only time when lifeguards are present (from 9 am to 9 pm). At other times, swim at your own risk.

For a nominal fee, you can venture to the North Shore to **Wilmette Beach** in Gillson Park.

For natural beauty, you can trek further north to **Illinois Beach State Park** in Zion. If Indiana is closer, try the **Indiana Dunes** in Tremont, Indiana. Both can be reached by train (see the Outdoors chapter for more information).

BICYCLING
You can buy ($5) or order by mail (check or money order for $6.41) detailed maps of bicycle trails in Chicago and the surrounding suburbs from offices of the Northeastern Illinois Planning Commission. Write or drop in on them at: **Bikeways**, Northeastern Illinois Planning Commission, 400 W. Madison, Room 200, Chicago, IL 60606 (454-0400). For maps of bike trails in the

forest preserves, call the forest preserve offices for **Cook County** (261-8400) and **Kane County** (232-5980).

The **Park District** (294-2200) has 21 official bicycle paths, but they are usually dangerously crowded. You're better off just peddling along the lakefront; if you want to bike downtown, do it on the weekend, when it's pleasantly less crowded. In all cases, be careful of local drivers, and use all your hand signals. It's rough on the streets. Bicycles may be rented in Lincoln Park, at Fullerton Avenue west of Lake Shore Drive.

For information on competitive cycling, pleasure rides, or bicycle touring, check with **American Youth Hostels** (327-8114), which sponsors many well-run, inexpensive trips, or the Friday and Weekend sections of the papers. Or ask at a bike shop.

There are plenty of local cycling clubs. For information about them and about locally organized rides, you might try perusing the bulletin boards at your local bike shop or asking the employees and customers there if they can help you out. Some good bike shops to try are:

Belmont Cycles
1444 W. Belmont
281-2623

Cyclery North
6637 N. Clark
743-4446

Beverly Cyclery
9121 S. Western
238-5704

Cycle Smithy
2468 1/2 N. Clark
281-0444

Buckingham Bike Shop
3332 N. Broadway
975-0050

Turin Bicycle Co-op
1027 Davis, Evanston
864-7660

A regional bicycling advocacy group claiming many local cycling clubs as members is: **Chicagoland Bicycling Federation** Box 1454, Evanston, IL 60204

BILLIARDS
For tournament information contact the **Illinois Billiards Club**, 2435 W. 71st St., 737-6655.

BOWLING
You're in luck here. Chicago is a Fred Flintstone paradise for this sport. Look in the yellow pages for the alley nearest you, and inquire about league play. If you're downtown, try: **Marina City Bowling Lanes**, 300 N. State St., 527-0747.

If you have a strong dislike for machines and would rather have your pins reset by people, try the intimate atmosphere--there are only four lanes--at **Southport Lanes**, 3325 N. Southport, 472-1601.

And if you're a late-night kind of person, the **Waveland Bowl** is open all night: Waveland Bowl, 3700 N. Western, 472-5900.

BOXING

Lincoln Park Boxing Program
2045 N. Lincoln Park West
294-4751

For boxing classes at all levels try:

**Degerberg Academy of Martial
Arts and Physical Fitness**
4717 N. Lincoln
728-5300

For a good time, catch the **Golden Gloves Tournament** in the winter. Anyone can enter this amateur tournament (look for announcements in the papers). In fact, a friend, Les "42nd Street" Firestein, once competed even though he was legally blind without his glasses. Give it a go.

BRIDGE
Contract bridge is regular bridge where your hand is determined by the luck of the deal. In duplicate bridge, all tables are given identical hands to play. Trump up the party at:

**Chicago Contract Bridge
Association**
5756 N. Lincoln
271-0133

Midwest Bridge Unit
1420 E. 87th
933-9475

Duplicate bridge games are held every night and Sunday afternoons at the **Bridge Studio**, 655 W. Irving Park, 348-9421.

CANOEING
Check with **American Youth Hostels** (327-8114) about organized trips. For the real low down on canoeing and rentals, or on the annual canoe race down the Des Plaines River, talk to Ralph Frese, the owner at **Chicagoland Canoe Base**, 4019 N. Narragansett, 777-1489.

CAVING
Caving is a fascinating experience. To get involved with a local group, try the **Windy City Grotto of the National Steleological Society**, contact: Ralph Earlandson, 5457 S. Ingleside, Chicago, IL 60615, 752-8669.

Windy City Grotto emphasizes safety and conservation on their caving trips, which are usually to sites within 200 to 300 miles of Chicago, but occasionally further out. They usually have one trip a month.

CHESS
For tournament information try the

Midwest Chess Federation
P.O. Box 305
Western Springs, IL 60558
246-6665

Illinois Chess Association
1521 Circle Court
Waukegan, IL 60085

Closer to home is the

Chicago Chess Center
2923 N. Southport
Chicago, IL 60657
929-7010
They hold tournaments every two or three months. They also have more casual chess in the basement in the evenings.

For public play, try the chess pavillion at North Avenue and the lake. Major tournaments are listed in *Chess Life* magazine.

CRICKET
The Park District (294-2200) has a pitch (field) in Washington Park, at 55th Street and South Cottage Grove. Also try the

Golden Gloves boxing tournament. Photo by Glenn Kaupert.

U.S. Cricket Association   or   **Evanston and Skokie Cricket Club**
12515 S. Union   7358 N. Clark
Chicago, IL 60628   Chicago, IL 60626
821-6613   761-6668

CROQUET

The Park District (294-2200) has three courts, or go to the local drug store and buy a set.

DANCING

For information about serious or recreational dancing lessons, performances, and dance benefits, or simply to get involved, try the **Chicago Dance Coalition**, 410 S. Michigan, Suite 520, Chicago, IL 60605, 663-1313.

They also publish a calendar of dance events.

DARTS

Dart clubs are fascinating establishments, stocked with beverages that make you feel very confident while playing. For information on clubs and tournaments, try **Windy City Darters**, 4749 N. Kenneth, 286-3848.

FENCING

Fencing instruction is offered at the **Great Lakes Fencing Association**, 1929 N. Cleveland, Chicago, IL 60614, 280-4582.

FISHING

You need a license to fish in Illinois. Licenses may be obtained at either City Hall (121 N. LaSalle) or the State of Illinois Center (100 W. Randolph). Some currency exchanges and tackle shops also sell them.

If you desire a party without a pole, try smelt fishing. Usually in late spring, the smelt are running. Buy a net (about $25), a case of beer, and have fun.

For true fishermen, check the *Chicago Tribune* for listings of locations.

FOOTBALL

The Park District (294-2200) can refer you to numerous touch football leagues.

GOLF

Chicago has 60 public and private courses from which to choose. If you want to play inexpensive urban golf (seniors and juniors get discounts), try the Park District, which has five 9-hole courses:

Robert A. Black course
2045 W. Pratt

Waveland
N. Lake Shore Dr. and Addison

Marquette Park
67th and S. California

South Shore Course
71st St. and S. Lake Shore Dr.

Columbus Park
5700 W. Jackson

The Park District also has an 18-hole course at:
Jackson Park
63rd St. and S. Lake Shore Dr.

Fees are $3.50 on weekdays, and $4 on weekends and holidays. Jackson Park is $5 and $5.50 for weekdays and weekends, respectively. Seniors and juniors get discounts. Cheap and you get what you pay for. The Forest Preserve (261-8400) also has four courses.

Some country clubs welcome nonmembers; others don't. If you want tournament play, the **Illinois Open** is held in the beginning of the summer, and the **Chicago District Amateur** is held in mid-July. Locations vary.

For viewing, the **Western Open** in early July attracts top professionals. It is held at the Butler National Golf Course, 2616 S. York Road, Oak Brook, 990-3333.

HORSEBACK RIDING

Both group and private lessons, as well as boarding for horses, are offered year-round at an indoor arena at: **Coach Horse Equestrian Center**, 1410 N. Orleans, 266-7878.

Otherwise, check the yellow pages for suburban stables. Call the Cook County Forest Preserve (261-8400) or your local county forest preserve for information about local bridle paths.

ICE FISHING

Warming up for the Polar Bear Club? Regardless, ice fishing is legal only in designated areas of the Forest Preserve (261-8400). Ice must be at least 4 inches thick.

ICE SKATING

The Park District's **McFetridge Sports Complex** at 3845 N. California (478-0210) has open indoor skating. Price is $1.50/hour, and skates are available.

You can ice skate outdoors at the outdoor rink at the north end of Grant Park at the **Daley Centennial Plaza** just south of the Amoco Building (formerly the Standard Oil Building), where the rink is frozen by machines and so is usually skatable. When weather permits and the ice is thick, try Lincoln Park on the north side of the city, Marquette Park on the south side, and various other parks. Call the Park District for more information (294-2200).

LA BOCCI (BOCCI BALL)
You don't have to be 70 years old or able to curse in French or Italian to enjoy this game. Try it, you'll like it. The Park District (294-2200) has twelve courts. Call for locations.

LAWN BOWLING
Before Bedrock was built, Fred Flintstone's ancestors played this game, which is a version of bowling played on a lawn with a small wooden ball. You can yabba, dabba, or doo at the **Lakeside Lawn Bowling Club**, 5800 S. Lake Shore Dr., 684-9799.

ORIENTEERING
This sport involves giving you a map, a compass, and a destination. Then you're on your own. For more information, contact the: **Chicago Orienteering Club**, R.R. 5, Lemont, IL 60439, 739-6230.

RACQUETBALL
The Park District (294-2200) has 23 racquetball/handball courts. Also try the McFetridge Sports Complex at 3845 N. California (478-0210). Otherwise, try your local YMCA or health club.

ROQUE
Roque is a version of croquet played on a hard surface court with raised border. The Park District (294-2200) has one court.

RUGBY
If you enjoy roughhousing, drinking beer, and singing risque songs, this is the sport for you. The main clubs are:

Chicago Griffins Rugby Football Club
588-0350

Lions Club
168 N. Michigan
621-1137

Chicago Women's Rugby Club
For more information look in the Friday or Weekend sections of the papers or *Windy City Sports*

Lakeshore Women's Rugby Club
For more information look in the Friday or Weekend sections of the papers or *Windy City Sports*

Lincoln Park Rugby Club
2019 N. Fremont
528-8844

RUNNING
See Track and Field below and the Fitness chapter.

SKEET SHOOTING
For a semi-private club, where you bring your own gun and buy the shells there (but you have to have an Illinois Firearm Owner's Identification Card), try the **Lincoln Park Gun Club**, Diversey and Lake Shore Dr., 549-6490.

SAILING
If you want some basic instruction in sailing, or safety tips, go to the Coast Guard (353-1228 for information). The Park District (294-2200) also offers

classes that fill up very quickly, so sign up as early as possible. If you can spend a bit of cash, try the **Chicago Sailing School** (also the **Lake Michigan Sailing Racing Federation**), 2000 N. Racine, Chicago, IL 60614, 871-2628. Northwestern University also offers sailing classes.

The Park District has eight facilities for boats, located on the lake at Belmont (3200 North), Burnham (1500 South), 59th Street Harbor, Diversey (2600 North), Jackson (6500 South), Monroe (100 South), and Montrose (4400 North). A special loading dock for the handicapped is located at Belmont Harbor. The Park District offers over 7,000 docks and slips (you have to take a rowboat to get to your boat). Getting a spot for your boat is still fairly difficult; however, recently prices have increased enough to drive many boaters away to the suburbs and even other states.

SKIING

Cross country   The flatlands of the midwest are ideal for cross-country skiing. You can ski at Chicago parks when snow cover is deep enough. Try some of the bigger parks such as Lincoln Park, Marquette Park, and Jackson and Washington Parks. The Forest Preserve (261-8400) has five mapped trials; call for information. Skiing is permitted on most Forest Preserve property except nature centers and golf courses (where snowmobiling is ok!?). Equipment may be rented at two Forest Preserve locations from 8 am to 4 pm on days when weather and snow conditions permit skiing: **Jensen Sports Area**, Devon and Milwaukee, and **Swallow Cliff**, Rt. 83, west of Mannheim Rd. (Rt.45), Palos Park.

Also try **MC Mages** (620 N. LaSalle, 337-6151) and **Erewhon** sports shops (414 N. Orleans, 644-4411), both downtown, for equipment rentals.

American Youth Hostels (327-8114) does a good job organizing both cross-country and downhill skiing trips, to locations ranging from Wisconsin to Colorado to Austria.

Downhill   Watch Wide World of Sports. Otherwise, you have to trek up to Wisconsin, to such areas as Alpine Valley (northwest of the city, just across the border) or Mount Majestic (near Lake Geneva, Wisconsin, and built on an old garbage dump). Many area ski clubs sponsor trips to midwestern ski resorts (again, check with **AYH** at 327-8114 about their trips). Check the Weekend or Friday sections of the papers. For a list of clubs, contact the **Chicago Metropolitan Ski Council**, P.O. Box 7926, Chicago, IL 60680, 346-1268.

SKY DIVING

You'll have to drive a bit to get to the open cornfields to find:

Hinckley Parachute Center
Hinckley
377-9219 or
(815) 286-9230

Skydive Sandwich Skyline Center
Sandwich
(815) 786-8200

Kankakee Skydiving Center
Kankakee
(815) 426-6614

SOCCER

You can catch some excellent games with ethnic players at lots of parks, among them Lincoln Park and Jackson Park. For information on teams and leagues, try the

Illinois Soccer Association
3334 W. Montrose
Chicago, IL 60618
463-0653

National Soccer League
4534 N. Lincoln
Chicago, IL 60625
275-2850

The National Soccer League is mostly composed of ethnic teams, but will accept good players who can mumble a few words of the native tongue. (By the way, the word "soccer" came from the British abbreviation, Assoc. Football, which was eventually shortened to soccer).

SOFTBALL

Softball is probably the most popular participant sport in Chicago, home of the 16-inch version (no gloves) of the game. An abundance of leagues exist throughout the city. Some leagues are tough to get into, and the Grant Park league is the best known. To get involved, go to your local park for information, and organize yourself or your team early. Then go to your local pub, get the owner drunk, and convince him to support your team (financially), solely for his benefit. Some top-flight teams and tournaments are played at **Hart Park**, 12301 S. Western, Blue Island, 385-5667.

SWIMMING

The Park District (294-2200) has 31 natatoriums (indoor pools), and 57 outdoor pools, open in the summer. The natatoriums offer swimming classes for all ages. Two natatoriums with two of the best swim teams in the Park District are located at:

Portage Park
4104 N. Central Ave.
777-3660

Ridge Park
9625 S. Longwood Dr.
238-1655

The Park District can also give you information on competitive swimming. Try the YMCA for classes also.

TENNIS

The **Park District** (294-2200) has over 700 courts. Most are free (a few charge fees), concrete, many are lit at night, and playing time is usually determined by gentlemanly conduct (theoretically), although some courts require reservations. The twelve courts at the Daley Centennial Plaza (in Grant Park south of the Amoco Building) require reservations and a fee (call 294-4792 a day ahead). The courts at Waveland and Lake Shore Drive (in Lincoln Park) also charge a fee. The only clay courts operated by the Park District, at Diversey Avenue just west of Lake Shore Drive, also require a fee.

The Park District also offers lessons and sponsors tournaments. Their Junior League program for young people at participating parks (e.g., Riis, Mather, McFetridge, McKinley, and Marquette Parks) is an excellent program consisting of coaching, lessons, and tournaments.

Another organization that sponsors leagues and tournaments at all levels and is the district branch of the USTA (United States Tennis Association) is the **Chicago District Tennis Association**, 982 Bryan, Elmhurst, IL 60126, 834-3727.

Some excellent tournaments are held at **Mid-Town Tennis Club**, 2020 W. Fullerton, 235-2300.

TOBOGGANING

Ever top dizzying speeds of a mile a minute? Well you can try at one of the five Forest Preserves (261-8400) that have toboggan slides, located at

Bemis Woods
Ogden Ave. west of Wolf Rd.
Western Springs

Dan Ryan Woods
87th St. and Western

Deer Grove--Grove #5
Quentins Rd. north of Dundee Rd.
Palatine

Jensen Slides
Devon and Milwaukee Avenues

Swallow Cliff
Rt. 83 west of Mannheim Rd. (Rt.
45) Palos Park

All are open 10 am-10 pm when conditions are good (below 20 F, with 4 inches of snow). Toboggans may be rented at all locations.

TRACK AND FIELD

If you want to run for pleasure, check the Weekend or Friday sections of the papers: they list races and clubs. The **Chicago Area Runners Association** (CARA), which sponsors many local races, is a good resource of information about running clubs and races (664-0823). The majority of races in the city are run in Lincoln Park. For more serious competition, you can get registered by the Amateur Athletic Union for races: **Amateur Athletic Union**, Box 183, Clarendon Hills, IL 60514, 789-9097.

America's Marathon, which attracts world-class marathoners, is held in early fall. The international prep championships are held in the spring in Naperville. And, if you are really nuts, the Park District (294-2200) holds a triathalon in the summer.

Please refer to the Fitness chapter of this book for more information about running.

VOLLEYBALL

Chicago has always been a volleyball town. Catholic girls' schools here consistently produce players of national caliber (Mother McAuley High School on the south side is a good example), and Northwestern University, DePaul, and the University of Illinois at Chicago always field good women's teams. Good USVBA men's teams come out of Chicago too. For recreational players, leagues abound in churches, parks, and other clubs for all levels of play.

The **United States Volleyball Association** (USVBA) often schedules tournaments in the Chicago area. If you can't play, go as a spectator--the play is always good.

To learn more about the game from competent instructors, try attending a special **volleyball clinic** held Monday nights 6:30 pm-9:30 pm in the gymnasium of the Latin School at the corner of North and Clark Streets. The clinic is open to players of all levels; a nominal fee is required. For more information about the clinic and about summer outdoor tournaments at North Avenue beach, call 472-4286.

Two excellent stores specializing in volleyball equipment are:

AA Sports
3556 N. Southport
472-8171

VBC
3542 N. Southport
472-4195

WALKING

Now this is a rational sport. Every Sunday at 2 pm, the **Lakeshore Walking Club** (869-5745) has 3.5- and 7.5-mile walks starting from Dempster and the lake in Evanston. Be sure to call ahead; occasionally, the club has other activities planned.

WINDSURFING
Official windsurfing beaches are at Montrose (4400 North) and Rainbow Beach (7900 South). Another popular spot is the beach just south of Northwestern University's Evanston campus.

The Park District (294-2200) holds yearly championships. If you want the inside dope, go to the **Windward Sports Windsurfing Shop**, 3317 N. Clark, 472-6868.

YACHTING
For racing information, contact:

Jackson Park Yacht Club or **Columbia Yacht Club**
6400 S. Promontory Dr.   111 N. Lake Shore Dr.
288-9714   938-3625

The biggest race in the area is the 333-mile **Mackinac**, which starts off Belmont Harbor.

If a yacht is a bit out of your price range the Park District has two basins for model yachts (294-2200). Bon voyage!

NON-PROFIT SPORTING ORGANIZATIONS

American Youth Hostels (AYH)
3712 N. Clark
Chicago, IL 60613
327-8114
A great worldwide organization for bicycling, skiing, camping, hiking trips, as well as cheap communal accommodations. The local chapter is very active. Call about the hours before you drop in.

Boy Scouts of America
730 W. Lake
Chicago, IL 60606
559-0990
Hiking, camping, and canoeing are the mainstays, and camps are dotted throughout the midwest.

Foundation for Student Athletes
1851 E. 79th
Chicago, IL 60649
731-0430

Girl Scouts of America
55 E. Jackson
Chicago, IL 60604
435-5500

Among other things, offers camps, outdoor activities, and sports for young girls. A good organization. Volunteer to be a troop leader.

Young Men's Christian Association (YMCA)
755 W. North Ave.
Chicago, IL 60610
280-3400

Young Women's Christian Association (YWCA)
37 S. Wabash
Chicago, IL 60603
372-6600
Both the YMCA and the YWCA are good organizations, steeped in tradition and humanistic values. A wide range of activities and classes are offered, all appealing to those who want good value for their dollar. Some YMCA facilities resemble those of health clubs, at a much lower price.

—Andrew Szpur

OUTDOORS

It's true—Chicago doesn't have much of a following with the rock climbing, backpacking, and whitewater rafting population of this world. Our city will never be the backdrop for a cover of *Outside* magazine, unless they're writing about great flat places. But there's more to do here outdoors than you think. Our part of the midwest has quiet natural wonders of a smaller scale, yet they're still delightful and have their own beauty.

The city was built on marshlands and prairie, and pockets of midwestern grasses and bogs are preserved in nature centers. Chicago is magnificently situated on Lake Michigan, and most of the 26-mile shoreline is landscaped park land open to the public. An extensive park system provides open green spaces to relieve the concrete environment, and the city is ringed with an impressive system of forest preserves. Close to the city, we have good rivers for canoeing, huge sand dunes, and plenty of trails for hiking, biking, horseback riding, and cross-country skiing. Chicago is full of unexpected natural sights if you're willing to look. Following is a list of arboretums, gardens, nature centers, trails, zoos, and other places of interest that might stir your imagination. Go before the concrete jungle drives you mad.

ARBORETUMS AND GARDENS

Cantigny
Winfield and Roosevelt Rds., Wheaton, 668-5161
The 500-acre estate of the late Robert T. McCormick, former editor and publisher of the *Chicago Tribune*. The grounds include ten acres of gardens that are rated among the finest in America. The garden is divided into separate "alive rooms," that is, self-contained units. Plants have been selected from all over the world to create a dramatic and colorful effect. A bed of 4,000 begonias await you at the end of a tour of the estate. The Chicago Peace Rose was developed here, and, ironically, McCormick's former mansion now houses a war museum. Free.

Chicago Botanic Garden
Just east of intersection US 41 and Lake Cook Rd., along Lake Cook Rd., Glencoe, 835-5440
Built on 300 acres of landfill on what was once marshland, but you'd never know it. Among the many attractions are Sansho-En, a Japanese garden planted on tiny islands. Also, a special "Trees of Illinois" section, in which you can discover some of the state's 110 species. Currently restoring a section of prairie. Free; small fee for tram tour.

Fabyan Forest Preserve
On IL 25, one mile south of intersection of IL 38 and IL 25, near Geneva, 232-1242
Lies on both sides of the Fox River. Once an estate of Colonel Fabyan, includes a Frank Lloyd Wright house that contains a museum exhibiting the eclectic interests of the Colonel. Beautiful Japanese garden, which is opened by special arrangement only. An authentic Dutch windmill that is

now on the National Register of Historic Places. Accessible from the Illinois Prairie Path bike trail (below). Free.

Ladd Arboretum
2024 McCormick Blvd., Evanston, 864-5181
Includes an outdoor tree museum, an open meadow, prairie flowers, and a bird sancturary. Contains the Ecology Center, home of the Evanston Environmental Association, which advocates and demonstrates the viability of alternative energy sources (e.g., solar and wind power). Library and bookstore. Free.

Morton Arboretum
Just north of intersection of IL 53 and Interstate 5, on IL 53, Lisle, 968-0074
Located 25 miles west of the city, this is a 1,500-acre outdoor museum and education center devoted to plant life of all kinds. Founded in 1922 by Jay Morton of Morton Salt fame. His father was an avid conservationist and originator of Arbor Day. In May, lilacs and crabapples blossom as warblers pass through on their migratory path. Excellent bird watching, and extensive plant and animal life. Hiking and nature trails. You are asked to observe nature passively and refrain from picnicking, sports, bicycling, and collecting plants. Great cross-country ski trails open to members of the arboretum only. Nominal parking fee per car; no additional admission charge. Open 9-5 year round.

NATURE CENTERS AND PRESERVES

Braidwood Dunes and Savanna
One mile southeast of Braidwood, Contact: Will County Forest Preserve District, Cherry Hill Rd. and Rt. 52, R.R. 4, Joliet, IL 60433, (815) 727-8700
205 acres of the largest intact remnant of the inland sand dunes of the Kankakee River Valley. With dunes some 20 feet high and an open savanna of black oaks. You'll find plants uncommon to this area, as well as marshes, snakes, lizards, and an abundance of birdlife. The place to go if you want solitude and a variety of unusual wildlife. To enter, you have to cross private land. Contact the Will County Forest Preserve for permission to enter. You must be accompanied by a naturalist.

Crabtree Nature Center
On Palatine Rd., just west of US 14, Barrington, 381-6592
1,100 acres of hills, woods, and marsh, intended solely for nature study and education. Contains an impressive natural history museum. The preserve attracts thousands of birds during migration--this is a good spot from which to observe waterfowl during spring migration.

Fermilab Prairie
On Kirk Rd, Batavia, 840-3351
640 acres of prairie located within the loop of the Fermilab electron accelerator. This provides for an ideal environment for prairie restoration because the site is set ablaze every year: fire is essential to a prairie for maintaining its ecosystem. Buffalo, ducks, and swans on the grounds.

Goose Lake Prairie State Park
5010 N. Jugtown Rd., Morris, (815) 942-2899
The largest expanse of protected prairie in Illinois. The park has a 1.5-mile
nature trail with signs identifying the unique varieties of prairie plants grown
here. An interpretive center offers lectures, shows, and hikes. Nearly 7 miles
of trails for cross-country skiing.

Grosse Point Lighthouse Park
2600 Sheridan Rd., Evanston, Tours c/o Evanston Environmental Assoc.,
864-5181
The nature center houses a museum with maritime exhibits. A greenhouse
and gardens will familiarize you with native and foreign plantlife. For an
interesting view of the city, venture to the top of the 113-foot lighthouse if
your lungs permit.

The Grove
1421 Milwaukee Ave., Glenview, 299-6096
Robert Kennicott, founder of the Chicago Academy of Sciences, grew up
in the Grove, where the study and appreciation of wildlife still persists.
Aside from the interpretive center, where you can learn about native plantlife,
the Grove is known for its activities: a pioneer arts and crafts workshop, a
writer's workshop, an annual folk fest, and various children's programs.

Illinois Beach State Park
Just south of Illinois-Wisconsin border, on Lake Michigan, near Zion,
662-4811
5,400 acres with a 900-acre natural preserve. The preserve contains many
species of plant and animal life endangered in Illinois, as well as the mean-
dering Dead River, prairie, marshes, and forests. Beautiful swimming beach,
camping, and cross-country skiing in the winter.

Indiana Dunes
Chesterton, Indiana. Take I-90 east to exit for Chesterton Rt 49, (Rt 49
and US Hwy 12), (219) 926-4520
Less than an hour's drive from the Loop, also accessible by the South Shore
commuter train. 2,200 acres of sand dunes and wooded areas ideal for hiking.
Weekdays are especially nice because it's uncrowded. Fee of $1.50 per car
to enter. Campgrounds available for $4.50 a night.

Illinois Prairie Path
45-mile footpath beginning in downtown Elmhurst, near the train station.
Once a railroad line running from Chicago to Aurora and Elgin, now a 30-
mile, hard-packed gravel path passing through marshes, woodlands, and
ponds. Used by hikers, bicyclists, horseback riders, and joggers. Begins in
downtown Elmhurst and splits into two paths at Wheaton; one path goes
southwest toward Aurora, the other northwest to Elgin. The northwest path
cuts through the Pratt-Wayne Forest Preserve, a wonderful place for bird
watching and enjoying unspoiled, varied terrain. Land developers and ecol-
ogists frequently battle over developments in the western suburbs that would
use parts of the path and destroy its continuity. For more information about
the path or to join the association that supports it, write or call: **Illinois
Prairie Path**, Box 1086, 616 Delles Rd., Wheaton, IL 60187, 665-5310.

RECREATION

Kankakee River State Park
North and west of Kankakee on IL 102, (815) 933-1383
An hour's drive south of the city, and well worth the effort if you want to relax. Over 3,700 acres of land make up this peaceful retreat, running 11 miles along the Kankakee River. Enjoy dunes, a canyon formed by Rock Creek, woods, and a visitors' center. Hiking and biking trails. The Kankakee River is great to canoe—you can rent canoes at the concession stand in the park (call 815-937-0048 for reservations).

Little Red Schoolhouse
In the Palos and Sag Valley Forest Preserve, north of IL 83 on Willow, Springs Rd., Willow Springs, 839-6897
(See also description under Cook County Forest Preserves below.) The surrounding area was formed by retreating glaciers, and has an abundance of hills. Several wildlife sanctuaries are located on the preserves, and falcons inhabit the area. The star attraction, at least for children, is the Little Red Schoolhouse (really a former schoolhouse until 1948), which regularly rotates its indoor and outdoor exhibits.

Nelson Lake Marsh
On Nelson Lake Rd. just south of Batavia Rd., near Batavia, 232-1242
Largest natural preserve in Kane County. Low marshland surrounded on three sides by rolling land. The wetland supports a great variety of waterfowl, including some endangered species.

North Park Village Nature Center
5801 N. Pulaski, 583-8970
This nature center is conveniently tucked away in a neighborhood on the city's northwest side. Covering 15 acres, the center offers many family activities. Bird walks, star watches, and guided hikes are regular features, as well as workshops in woodworking, solar energy, tinsmithing, and Tai Chi. Many activities for young people, including a winter solstice party.

River Trail Nature Center
In Des Plaines Forest Preserve, at Milwaukee Ave. on the west side of the Des Plaines River, in the northwest suburbs, 824-1900
A bevy of natural gardens: a wild birdseed garden, a moss garden, a herb garden, and a native Indian herb garden. Beehives too. Trails for hiking, bicycling, and horseback riding. Good fishing. Free.

Ryerson Conservation Area
South of IL 22 on Riverwoods Rd., near Lincolnshire and Riverwoods, 948-7750
Nature center and library sponsor activities such as night walks and maple syrup making (the area is an excellent example of old-growth sugar maple forest). Rare wildlife, such as bald eagles and red foxes, can be sighted occasionally. Popular with children is the working farm on the land. You can hike on 10 miles of hiking trails, or cross country ski in the winter.

Thorn Creek Nature Preserve
247 Monee Rd., Park Forest, 747-6320
Located in the southern suburbs. Formed by glaciers, the preserve has creeks, ponds, prairies, and springs. You can find fossils and many primitive

varieties of plantlife. Animal life includes deer and muskrats. Nature center is housed in a primitive church over 100 years old. Hiking and nature trails.

Volo Bog State Natural Area
North of Sullivan Lake Rd. on Brandenburg Rd., Ingleside, (815) 344-1294
Volo bog is a national natural landmark, and the last open-water bog in Illinois. You can see all stages of natural bog development. The soil is fragile, and contains rare plantlife. The area is primarily for nature study, and nature walks are conducted by the staff.

ZOOS

Brookfield Zoo
8400 W. 31st St., Brookfield, 485-2200
Big (200 acres), open zoo that houses over 2,000 animals in natural (sort of) settings. For a first-time orientation, take the zoo safari coach (runs from spring to early fall) around the periphery to get an idea of its size and see areas you might not otherwise take in. The tropical rain forest (Tropic World) is the largest indoor zoo exhibit in the world, and includes the expected (monkeys and gorillas) and the unexpected (a pygmy hippo). A must see. Daily dolphin shows. Admission charge. Open 10-5 year round.

Indian Boundary Park Zoo
2555 W. Estes Ave., 775-4060
Little known, this 13-acre park is a hidden treasure in the city. The zoo has a small but representative selection of animals. Take the kids here to avoid overwhelming crowds. Feeding time is 1 pm every day but Sunday. The park also contains tennis courts and a children's playground.

Lincoln Park Zoo
Fullerton and Cannon Drive, 294-4660
Lincoln Park Zoo, established in 1868, claims to be the most visited zoo in the world. Everyone's favorite spot seems to be the Great Ape House. Patrons can watch through glass walls as families of gorillas eat their fruits and vegetables and occasionally throw them at observers (something to do with invasion of privacy). The zoo also has a farm where children can venture and pet their favorite barnyard buddy. For its size, the zoo is quite extensive. Admission is free.

CAMPING

For information on places to camp as well as state parks, call or write the Illinois Office of Tourism. They can send you a free brochure.

Illinois Office of Tourism
310 S. Michigan
Chicago, IL 60604
793-2094

There is also another office in the Sears Tower, Chicago level.
Wisconsin has excellent campgrounds and state parks within a few hours' drive of Chicago. Call or write the **Wisconsin Department of Tourism,** 75 E. Wacker, Chicago, IL 60601, 332-7274.

PARKS

You may not think of city parks as part of an outdoors experience, but think again: our parks contain bird sanctuaries, flower gardens, conservatories, zoos, and lagoons for boating.

Though urban planners of the nineteenth century may not have kept the city's motto, "Urbs in Horto" (City in a Garden) in mind at all times, they did allocate most of the city's lakefront property solely for parks. Wealthy merchant A. Montgomery Ward fought the city and Illinois Central Railroad for years to prevent commercial development on the lakefront. Renowned planners such as Frederick Law Olmsted were instrumental in building parks with grandstands, refectories, boating ponds, and promenades, such as those in Washington and Jackson Parks.

The **Chicago Park District** manages city parks and spends about $200 million a year doing it: it is the best funded park district in the country. The District must balance the demands of both naturalists and developers. Organizations such as the citizens' group **Friends of the Parks** have criticized the Park District for having a long-standing pro-development stance, and for maintaining some parks at the expense of others. City parks have been steadily losing ground to pavement; a significant number of new parking lots are located on former park land.

Recently, however, things have been looking up. The Park District has made significant efforts to restore some city parks. The patronage system of hiring employees, long used by the Park District, has been challenged and District management is being reorganized and encouraged to stress community involvement.

Chicago Park District
Public Information Office
425 E. McFetridge Dr.
Chicago, IL 60605
294-2493

Friends of the Parks Inc.
53 W. Jackson Blvd.
Chicago, IL 60604
922-3307

Lakefront Parks

Lake Michigan gives our lakefront parks miles of beaches and our city much of its character. You can travel much of the length of the shoreline on the bike path that runs through these parks; it's possible to travel by bike or on foot from the 5800 north block all the way down to 6700 south. On gorgeous summer days, try biking early in the morning or late in the afternoon—the path gets dangerously crowded on nice days.

LINCOLN PARK
Stretching from North Avenue at Clark Street at its southern edge to Foster Avenue on the north, Lincoln Park is Chicago's largest park—5 miles long and 1/2 mile wide at its widest point. It borders some of the wealthiest and trendiest of Chicago's neighborhoods. On a sunny weekend afternoon, the park is jammed with picnickers, softball players, and joggers. Some may complain about the crowds in Lincoln Park, but it's the numbers and variety of people that make the park so enjoyable, not to mention safe. It's nice to see a park so well used.

Lincoln Park is a great place to bird watch, not only because it's situated along a major flyway, but also because so much of the park comprises natural bird habitats: lagoons, the lake, open lawns, and small wooded areas. The park also has a five-room conservatory lush with ferns, palm trees, and rare orchids. Just south of the conservatory is a formal outdoor garden planted with vivid floral displays in the warm months.

The park also has a good zoo, described earlier. You can jog on the park's beautiful path along the lakefront, rent a bike at the stand on Fullerton Avenue (and cycle along the path), or rent rowboats at the lagoon. The park also has a golf course and driving range.

GRANT PARK

Located just east of the Loop, at Michigan Avenue at Randolph and stretching south, Grant Park, with acres of grass and beautiful flower gardens, helps relieve the uninterrupted concrete and congestion of downtown. The park attracts a lot of tourists (and a lot of street people), and is a fine place to take a stroll. The park is home to many softball leagues. Sailboats dot the lake during the season, and you can see some of the fanciest, most luxurious boats in the area at the marina on the east edge of the park.

One of the park's big draws is Buckingham Fountain, an enormous outdoor fountain modeled after one on the grounds of the Versailles palace in France. The fountain's gaudy, colorful, and crowd-pleasing light and water show appears nightly at 9 pm from Memorial Day through Labor Day. Equally popular among tourists and residents, the shows draw a good-sized crowd every night to admire the fire-engine red, lime green, and brilliant blue columns of water shooting from the fountain. Rose gardens are planted near the fountain, including a garden where new varieties are tested for the midwest before they're offered on the market.

In summer, free classical music concerts, frequently featuring guest conductors and showcasing young soloists, are held at the Petrillo Music Shell at Columbus Drive and Jackson Boulevard. A recent season included both a Beethoven series and the premiere of a new composer that combined a 200-piece orchestra with a rock band. One of the best outdoor experiences the city can offer is a Grant Park concert on a balmy summer night with the Michigan Avenue skyline lit up in front of you and the lake breeze wafting behind you.

JACKSON AND WASHINGTON PARKS

Jackson and Washington Parks are located next to each other on the south side--Jackson located at 56th Street and the lake, east of the University of Chicago in Hyde Park; Washington Park is just west of Jackson. The two parks are connected by a magnificent expanse of lawn called the Midway Plaisance (at Stony Island and 59th St.). The Plaisance, ringed by the gothic buildings of the University of Chicago, makes excellent use of the flat terrain and illustrates how grand open space can be. (In winter, it's flooded for ice skating.)

Both Jackson and Washington Park have a rich architectural heritage and used to be gorgeous; today, they are unraveling a bit. During good weather days, these parks are crowded with barbecues, picnics, and soccer and cricket games. Don't hang around them at night, however.

The 1893 World Columbian Exposition, which was held on the park land, was designed by urban planner Frederick Law Olmsted, who created acres

of landscaped gardens and lagoons in Jackson Park. Vast neoclassical buildings were built to ring one of the lagoons; among these buildings was what
is now the Museum of Science and Industry at 57th Street and Lake Shore
Drive.

Another remnant of the Exposition in the park is Wooded Island, now a
popular place for bird watching, as well as the site of the Japanese Garden,
a small-scale representation of the traditional Japanese garden originally built
for the Exposition as a gift from the Japanese government. The garden,
restored by the Park District in 1981, is serene and lovely. To get there,
walk from the south end of the Museum of Science and Industry, cross the
bridge over the lagoon, and follow the path until you see signs for the garden.

You can golf at an 18-hole golf course at Jackson Park. In winter, these
parks are nice for cross-country skiing and ice skating.

SOUTH SHORE COMMUNITY CENTER
Located on the south side, right on the Lake at 7059 South Lake Shore
Drive, the South Shore Community Center, formerly a country club, was
for many years an elite center of the area's social activity, when South Shore
was the most affluent neighborhood on the south side. As the neighborhood
declined economically, the club declined too, eventually closing in 1974.
The club buildings were almost torn down, but were rescued by the Chicago
Park District, which purchased the club and restored it. The South Shore
neighborhood is also showing signs of revitalization, largely due to the efforts
of the South Shore Bank.

The clubhouse, which is open to the public, no longer has the opulent
furniture it used to, but is still an elegant building that features rooms with
floor-to-ceiling windows and lovely unobstructed views of the lake. During
the summer, music festivals are occasionally held on the grounds. You can
golf on the 9-hole course on the grounds. The city's mounted police train
their horses at the stables located here. For more information call 753-0640.

Neighborhood Parks

COLUMBUS PARK
Located at Austin Boulevard and the Eisenhower Expressway, at the western
edge of the city and the eastern edge of suburban Oak Park. Worth a visit
to see the beautiful old refectory building, which was once used for dances
(entrance on Jackson Boulevard), to see its wide stone terraces facing the
park lagoon and its big leaded glass windows. Other popular attractions at
the park are a golf course, archery range, and field house. While you're
there, I recommend touring the neighborhoods surrounding the park to see
the old Victorian homes.

DOUGLAS PARK
Located west of the Loop on Ogden Avenue, just southwest of Randolph
Street. Douglas Park is big, covering 174 acres of lawns, formal gardens,
and lagoons. On warm weather weekends, it's crowded with people playing
soccer and softball, and picnicking.

GARFIELD PARK
Located on the west side at Central Park Boulevard and Lake Street. Garfield
Park was a jewel of a park in its day, with its lagoons, gold-domed boating

pavilion, field houses, and lovely walking paths. The well-kept beauty has deteriorated, but there are still a few compelling reasons to visit the park.

One reason is to see the huge (4 1/2 acres), remarkable Garfield Park Conservatory, at 300 North Central Park Avenue. Much larger than the Lincoln Park Conservatory, the greenhouse contains over 5,000 varieties of flowers, trees, cactuses, and other plants. One interesting section of the conservatory is devoted to plants with commercial uses. Admission is free. Hours: 9 am-5 pm every day. Phone 533-1281 for more information.

MARQUETTE PARK

Located on the southwest side at 6700 South Kedzie Avenue. A big, sprawling, well-used park, with one of the midwest's largest rose gardens. Over eighty varieties of roses are grown on over one acre of land from early summer through October. Other floral displays include 15,000 tulips, which bloom in early spring, and a trial garden used mostly for experimenting with new annuals and perennials. The trial garden also contains a cactus garden, a rock garden, and a herb garden.

Among other activities, the park offers an archery range, a bike path, a 9-hole golf course, and cross-country skiing in the winter. The lagoon attracts lots of fishermen.

Beaches

Beaches and the lake are an integral part of outdoor life in Chicago. We are blessed with a shoreline that is open, free, and clear. All the beaches are free and easy to get to, and all are well used.

Unfortunately, we have a serious erosion problem, and rising water levels are destroying many beaches and buildings. The problem is worse on Lake Michigan's eastern shores.

Lake Michigan water at the city's shore is reasonably clean, considering the number of people and boats in the water and on the beaches. Considerable effort has been made in recent years to purify Lake Michigan, resulting in a marked improvement in the quality of the water. (A good thing, because the city and some of the suburbs rely on lake water for their drinking water.) In the past, the lake was polluted to such a degree that its natural cleansing process was not working. Alewives (salt-water fish that used to regularly come through the St. Lawrence Seaway and wash up on Chicago's shores, producing a less than pleasing aroma) have been all but eliminated. Even though the beaches are still closed a few days a year because of pollution, the problem is not as severe as it once was. Cleaning the lake is a mammoth and time-consuming task, and the effort should be appreciated.

Chicago's beaches, like its parks, are managed by the Chicago Park District. For information about beaches, call the Park District at 294-2333. Beaches open on Memorial Day and close mid-September. Hours: 9 am to 9 pm. All Chicago beaches are free. Suburban beaches are much smaller and sometimes difficult to find, and some have an admission charge or won't admit you unless you're a resident of the town.

A few of the city beaches are highlighted below, listed from north to south. Those beaches located adjacent to Lake Shore Drive may look impossible to reach at some points. Do not fear: there are underground walkways leading to the beaches at Chicago Avenue, Oak Street, and Addison Street.

Lunt Avenue (Leone) Beach
Lunt Avenue and the lake
More secluded, because unlike other beaches, it doesn't lie next to Lake Shore Drive and is therefore further from traffic; also, it doesn't adjoin other beaches. Popular, with a real mix of ages and nationalities. Especially nice at night, when it's quiet and relaxing.

Fullerton Avenue Beach
Fullerton Ave. and the lake
Popular beach, lots of crowds. A good place to watch people is from a seat on the cement wall next to the bike path, just south of Fullerton Avenue. Less crowded on the cement further north toward Diversey Avenue. Even further north, just south of Belmont Avenue, is the beach spot for gay men.

North Avenue Beach
North Ave. and the lake, just east of Lincoln Park
Bigger than Oak Street Beach; showers and a changing area are provided. Friendly crowds, good mix of people.

Oak Street Beach
Oak St. east of Lake Shore Dr.
Not much of a beach in size, but this is where the beautiful people go. Teeny boppers meet on the sand, and older trendies congregate on the cement further north. Good beach volleyball tournaments.

Promontory Point ("The Point")
55th St. and the lake
Relaxed, uncrowded spot in Hyde Park for hanging out and talking. No beach, only grass.

Rainbow Beach
76th St. and the lake
Big, clean beach adjoined to a large park.

Calumet Beach
99th to 103rd St. and the lake
Since the steel mills south of the beach were closed, the water has become cleaner and the air fresher. Crowded with families and soccer players. Ethnic crowds of all types.

COOK COUNTY FOREST PRESERVES

One of the city's pleasures is the system of forest preserves that encircle it. Many of these areas even have hills! Cook County forest preserves can give you a sense of the wilderness without traveling too far. Our system of preserves owes much to Daniel Burnham, whose plans for the city at the turn of the century included preserving some of the natural forests in the county. Many preserves have trails for hiking, biking, horseback riding, and cross-country skiing. Visitors are forbidden to collect specimens or abuse the land contained in the 65,000-acre system.

Cook County Forest Preserve District, main headquarters
536 N. Harlem Ave.
River Forest, IL 60305
261-8400

Some of the more interesting Cook County preserves are listed below. Most are outside the city, but not far.

NORTH

Skokie Forest Preserve (usually referred to as the Skokie Lagoons)
Get maps at Skokie Division Headquarters, Cook County Forest Preserve District, Willow Rd. and Edens Expressway, Northfield, IL 60093, 446-5652
Favored canoeing spot because of the 190 acres of interconnected lagoons. Because you can complete a 6-mile circuit in your canoe, there's no need to arrange a shuttle service. No rentals; bring your own boat. Plenty of bicycle, bridle, and foot paths as well. Great place for bird watching. Botanic garden.

Indian Boundary Forest Preserve
Get maps from Indian Boundary Division Headquarters, Cook County Forest Preserve District, 8800 W. Belmont, Chicago, IL 60634, 625-0606
Located along the banks of the Des Plaines River, and on the site of former Indian villages. Indian cemetery still remains. 11-mile hiking trail, biking trails, and nature center. Fishing in the river, Axehead Lake, ponds, and lagoons.

SOUTH

Palos & Sag Valley Forest Preserve Divisions
Get maps from Palos Division Headquarter, Cook County Forest Preserve District, 9900 S. Willow Springs (104th Ave.), Willow Springs, IL 60480, 839-5617
These two preserves, formed by the retreat of a great glacier, are probably the best of the Cook County preserves. Certainly the largest, at over 10,000 acres. These preserves have it all: the best toboggan run in the area; plenty of hills; miles of trails for hiking, horseback riding, and nature study; lakes; good bird watching at the sloughs; four nature preserves filled with plants and wildlife of all kinds; swamps; and the only quaking bog in Cook County. Boating (including motorized) allowed on the lakes. Excellent fishing. Good cross-country skiing in the winter.

ORGANIZATIONS

Enjoying nature sometimes gives us the urge to help preserve it. Following are some organizations working for that cause; all welcome members and volunteers.

Citizens Against Nuclear Power
220 S. State
Chicago, IL 60604
786-9041

Citizens for a Better Environment
33 E. Congress Parkway
Chicago, IL 60605
939-1530

Greenpeace
921 W. Van Buren
Chicago, IL 60612
666-3305

Nature Conservancy
Illinois Field Office
79 W. Monroe, Suite 708
Chicago, IL 60603
346-8166

Open Lands Project
53 W. Jackson
Chicago, IL 60604
427-4256

Sierra Club, Great Lakes Chapter
506 S. Wabash
Chicago, IL 60605
431-0158
National organization concerned with nature and its interrelationship with man. Strives to protect and conserve our national resources. Sponsors trips of ecological and sporting nature, and does some political work. Check the Friday or Weekend section of either daily paper for information about activities.

—Barbara Macikas

FITNESS

Fitness is serious business these days. On a sunny morning along the lake, you can see virtually every form of physical exercise being practiced, from jogging and biking to team sports, yoga and tai chi. This chapter gives a rundown of our most popular options for fitness.

RUNNING

Chicago is a real running town. For places to run in the city, there's nothing like the 17 1/2-mile jogging course that follows the lakefront, starting at Bryn Mawr Avenue on the north side and ending at 71st Street on the south side. You don't need to worry about cars, just enjoy the beautiful scenery and let the lake breezes keep you cool. You'll never be alone on this route (watch out for cyclists) and there are plenty of water fountains along the way. The lakefront is by far the most popular running route in the city, and Lincoln Park is the most popular site for races.

For the latest information on road races and places to run, ask the **Chicago Area Runners Association (CARA)**. CARA is a non-profit association of runners and running clubs that also sponsors races and running clinics. The CARA office is located at 708 N. Dearborn (call 664-0823), and is open Monday through Friday, 10 am-5 pm. Annual membership is $18; benefits include a subscription to *Finish Line* magazine, schedules of races, calendars, and discounts on race fees and at running shoe stores.

If you're looking for a place to get a good speed workout, stop by the outdoor track at the **University of Illinois at Chicago** (just west of the intersection of Roosevelt and Halsted Streets) on any Wednesday at 6 pm. From April until October, runners of all speeds and capabilities meet for a 60-minute speed workout, led by Tom Brunick. The workouts are tough but fun and provide good training for races. A minimal fee goes toward the track rental cost. Call CARA (664-0823) for more information.

You might also investigate the possibility of working out on tracks at local parks and high schools. Ask at high schools in your area or call the Park District (294-2200) for information.

A good source of camaraderie is a running club, of which there are many in Chicago. You can share tips and trade horror stories about your latest injury, or find a fellow 8- or 9-minute miler to train with. Some active clubs are: the **Lincoln Park Pacers** and the **Riis Park Striders** on the north side, and the **Rainbow Road Runners** and the **Stony Island Runners** on the south side. **Frontrunners,** Chicago's gay and lesbian running club, runs weekends in Lincoln Park. Call CARA (664-0823) for information about these and other clubs.

Shoes

Do some research before you buy your running shoes--a good pair of shoes may mean the difference between getting injured or not. Remember to look for good arch support, good padding (1 inch under the heel), and firm support at the heel.

Some places to buy shoes:

MC Mages Sports
620 N. LaSalle
337-6151
Periodically have big sales; check the papers for their ads.

Athlete's Foot
2828 N. Clark
327-7333
2140 N. Halsted
477-1200
Sales personnel are trained in the various components of tennis, basketball, and running shoes. The company has a national wear test center in Naperville where new brands of running shoes are tested by runners.

Sportmart
3134 N. Clark
871-8500
Good selection and low prices.

Murphy's Fit
2843 N. Clark
327-3020
513 Dempster
Evanston
869-4101
Good selection.

Sport Stop
119 N. Marion St.
Oak Park Mall
524-2122
Knowledgeable employees willing to spend time with you while you're choosing your shoes.

Vertel's Chicago
1818 N. Wells
664-4903
Many shoe styles to choose from. They have registration forms for upcoming races and events.

Races

Chicago-area runners are lucky. Besides having that gorgeous lakefront as their training ground, they've also got plenty of well-organized and scenic road races throughout the year.

Chicago is the site of what has become, over the past 10 years, the finest marathon not only in this country, but perhaps the world—**America's Marathon/Chicago**. Held in late fall in the past (but as of this writing, the timing may change), this marathon gets bigger each year. The flat course winds through some of Chicago's most interesting neighborhoods: the Loop, Chinatown, Greektown, and Pilsen, just to name a few.

Some of the finest marathoners in the world have run in the Chicago marathon. Over 12,000 runners usually participate. They come from all over the country, as well as from nearly 60 foreign countries. The race always attracts thousands of supporters lining the route, cheering on even the last-finishing runners.

The Scholl College of Podiatric Medicine occasionally offers running clinics (sponsored by PUMA). The clinics, staffed by students and doctors from the school's sports medicine clinic, offer advice on preventing injuries, stretching, how to pick running shoes, and other topics. The clinics are also held at some of the major local road races. Call 280-2913 for information. CARA also offers running clinics for beginning runners and racers; call 664-0823.

WALKING

It was bound to happen—walking has been elevated to cult fitness status. Walking as a way to keep in shape makes good sense. It conditions muscles (half of our 650 muscles are involved in walking), relieves stress, and improves circulation and cardiovascular efficiency. Besides, it's free.

One local group of walkers, the **Chicago Walkers Club,** meets for a workout at 9 am every Sunday morning near the Lincoln Park Zoo entrance, 2200 N. Cannon Drive. The club is open to walkers of all ages and levels of ability. Hardcore walkers can get advice and training trips from the racewalking professionals in the club. You can write the club at Chicago Walkers Club, 762 Bluff, #101, Carol Stream, IL 60188.

If you go a little overboard in your enthusiasm for walking, and wind up with blisters, bunions, or bad callouses, you might want to make an appointment with a podiatrist. Podiatry has gotten a bum rap in the past, but when it comes to foot problems, it pays to go to a specialist. A good place to try is **Dr. William M. Scholl College of Podiatric Medicine,** 1001 N. Dearborn, 280-2935.

Walking is treated less as a sport and more as a way to enjoy nature by the **Prairie Club.** Contact Clara Glabe, 7350 N. Odell, Chicago, IL 60648 631-5717. The club is a 75-year-old organization dedicated to the enjoyment of hiking and the conservation of nature. Every Saturday and Sunday morning throughout the year (except July, August, and December), the club takes a hike. Hikes range from 5 to 26 miles. Look in the "Go" guide of the Fridays section of the *Tribune* for listings of hikes and other events.

Every Sunday afternoon at 2 pm, the **Lake Shore Walking Club** has 3.5- and 7.5-mile walks starting from Dempster and the lake, in Evanston. Be sure to call first before showing up, however; occasionally, the club has other activities planned. Call 869-5745 for information.

HEALTH CLUBS AND GYMS

What do you get when you join a health club? Companionship, amenities (showers, saunas, whirlpools, massages, juice bars, and sometimes parking garages and nurseries), protection from the elements, and a membership fee. Fees vary, but at some of the more expensive clubs, expect to pay an initial membership fee in the $400-$600 range, as well as monthly fees that could run you another $600 over one year's time.

Before you sign a conract for membership at a club, consider the following: Does the club have all the equipment you want? Is the swimming pool at least 50 feet in length? (Any shorter and all you do is turn around.) Are there extra charges for classes and court time? Is the floor for aerobics classes carpeted and cushioned (unless they're low-impact aerobics)? To get a good feel for what to expect as a member, visit the club at the time of day that you plan to use it.

Besides health clubs, gyms are also listed below.

Downtown Sports Club
441 N. Wabash Ave.   644-4884
Relaxed, informal atmosphere. You pay for the location, but you get all the facilities and amenities you could want, including a banked indoor running track; 130 aerobic classes offered per week; Nautilus, Universal, Eagle, Muscle Dynamics, and Hydra Fitness weight training equipment; indoor tennis courts; racquetball and squash courts (the club has a squash club and traveling squash team), plus pool, sauna, whirlpool, nursery, restaurant, and lounge. One-time initiation fee plus monthly dues. Court fees are extra.

Lakeshore Athletic Center
1320 W. Fullerton   477-9888
A big club with excellent facilities, open for extended hours (5:30 am-midnight Monday through Friday and 6 am-11 pm Saturday and Sunday). A good place for tennis, with four courts on the club's roof and nine more indoors. Also offers: a 1/4-mile indoor running track, volleyball and basketball teams for club members, an extensive class schedule (including 6-week prenatal and postpartum exercise classes, yoga, and floor exercise classes), and unusual programs such as swimstroke analysis, powerwalking (taught by a three-time national champion), and eating for endurance sports. Members receive a newsletter. Athletic memberships that don't include tennis as well as individual tennis memberships that include all classes and court privileges are available.

East Bank Club
500 N. Kingsbury St.   527-5800
Posh facilities but boy, do you pay for it. Has a 7,200 square foot golf center with driving stations, putting green, and sand trap, as well as 10 cushioned indoor tennis courts, swimming pool, running track, exercise studios, weight rooms, and dining and catering facilities. Lots of trendy people.

Charlie Fitness Club & Hotel
112 S. Michigan Ave.   726-0510
Beautiful building at a nice location, and the exercise facilities are open 24 hours a day. The owners converted this 20-story Michigan Avenue building into a hotel and fitness center. Club features a swimming pool, racquetball courts, squash, a dance studio, free weights, a 1/16-mile track, sauna, steamrooms, and a co-ed whirlpool. For those who like to combine glitz with sweat, the club also has a 4-story nightclub with glass elevator and winding staircase.

Lehmann Sports Club
2700 N. Lehmann Court   871-8300
Features 8 courts for racquetball and handball enthusiasts. Also offers basketball, volleyball, full Nautilus fitness center, free-weight room, Universal gym, 1/18-mile track, sauna, steam room, whirlpool, restaurant, and bar. Classes include aerobics, dance, and self-defense.

University of Illinois at Chicago
Circle Center Recreation
750 S. Halsted   413-5150
The public is invited to use the University's excellent facilities by purchasing any of several passes, all offered at very reasonable prices. Facilities include a 25-yard, 6-lane swimming pool; weight room with free weights, Paramount, and Universal machines; 5 racquetball courts; sauna; exercise room; and lockers and towels. You can buy passes for one day, one quarter (good for 10 weeks), and one year.

Powerhouse of Chicago
3727 N. Broadway   975-9497
A full-service health club, but better known as a major weightlifting facility. Has the largest free weight workout facility in the city. 7 tons of free weights, and many other weight machines, including Nautilus. Trainers will meet

Jesse White tumbling team.

one-on-one with members to work out a personalized program. Also offers 9 different types of aerobics/exercise classes, emphasizing medium- to low-impact aerobics. Annual memberships as well as one-day passes are offered.

The Women's Gym
1212 W. Belmont   549-0700
A clean, attractive space with excellent facilities. Friendly atmosphere, and a nice alternative to more crowded, impersonal clubs. Offers aerobics classes (the floor has 15 inches of foam padding over wood), yoga, karate, massage therapy, free weights and Universal equipment (instruction available for beginner and intermediate weightlifters and one-on-one instruction for body

builders and powerlifters), steam room, sauna, whilrpool, and sundeck. Private weight trainers are available by appointment. Babysitting service Monday through Thursday mornings.

Jam-Nastics Exercise Center
2700 N. Halsted   477-8400
Jamnastics classes are total body workouts set to upbeat music. Specialty in pre- and postnatal exercise for mothers and gymnastics for children. Other classes offered in toning, aerobics, and stretching. Weight room. First class is free.

The Body Shop
3246 N. Halsted   248-7717
Nautilus fitness center for men. Nautilus instructor on hand to help members plan their workouts. Private instruction on free weights also available. Aerobics classes.

Women's Workout World
2540 W. Lawrence, at Lincoln Square   334-7341
108 W. Germania Pl., at intersection of North and Clark St.   664-2106
3125 N. Central   725-3055
15 locations in all. City locations are on the north side; south-side locations are in the suburbs. Attractive for its reasonable membership fees, and abundance of class offerings. Limited weights.

YMCAs
There are 25 YMCA facilities in Chicago. Fees and quality of facilities vary from place to place; some (not all) centers have residence areas. All but four centers have pools, and all but five have weight-training circuits. In general, annual membership at a Y facility will cost you less than membership at a commercial health club, sometimes much less.

Some YMCAs are listed below; for information on others, call the main office at 280-3400.

Lawson YMCA
30 W. Chicago Ave.   944-6211
Located just north of the Loop, this Y's facilities include: a swimming pool, handball/racquetball courts, squash courts, free weights, Nautilus and Universal machines, sauna, steamroom, and massage. Also offers programs in yoga, judo, martial arts, weight management, adult fitness and conditioning, volleyball, and aerobics.

New City Y
1515 N. Halsted   266-1242
A popular place in an attractive building. Outdoor track (1/3 mile) and indoor track (1/18 mile). Facilities include: swimming pool, whirlpools, fitness evaluation and a personalized fitness program, and instruction on Universal weights. Programs offered in aerobics, assorted dance classes, aikido, fencing, volleyball, scuba instruction, judo, yoga, weight management, and adult fitness and conditioning.

Lincoln-Belmont
3333 N. Marshfield Ave.   248-3333
Has an indoor track, handball/racquetball courts, swimming pool, free weights, Universal weights, men's and women's fitness centers, sauna, whirlpool,

massage, and sunroom. Programs offered in yoga, weight training, and adult fitness and conditioning.

111th Street YMCA
4 E. 111th St.   785-9210
Facilities include: gym, handball/racquetball courts, indoor track, swimming pool, free weights, Universal weights, sauna, and whirlpool. Programs offered in tennis, judo, martial arts, and adult fitness and conditioning.

Jazzercise
747-7119
Jazzercise combines simple jazz dance movements with basic principles of exercise physiology. It's inexpensive and a good workout. If you've never taken an aerobic dance class of any kind before, this might be the best place to start. The novice won't die, but will get a good workout. Jazzercise is taught at over 150 Chicago-area locations--in schools, church halls, and the like. Bring an exercise mat to do your floor work on if you don't like cold, hard church floors.

Chicago Health and Racquetball Club
6451 N. Ridge Blvd.   743-7602
4950 W. Fullerton   237-1146
300 N. State   321-9600
230 W. Monroe   263-4500
2038 W. 95th St.   881-0800
These clubs provide a serviceable place to work out, with good weight training equipment, exercise classes, swimming pool, and indoor running track.

Combined Fitness Centers
1235 N. LaSalle St.   787-8400
188 W. Randolph St.   269-5820
1301 E. 47th St.   548-1300
You can try out these centers for a free complimentary workout. They have Nautilus, free weights, exercise cycles, aerobics, and tanning beds. No swimming pool.

EXERCISE STUDIOS

Exercise studios are facilities geared more toward offering high-quality classes only. They're also easy places for out-of-towners and visitors to drop in for a day or two of classes.

Body Elite
445 W. Erie   664-5710
Classes here are tough, emphasizing proper form and offering a rigorous combination of calisthenics, weight training, and aerobics. The chief instructor and co-owner, Fima Feigin, is a a former coach of the 1968 Soviet Olympic fencing team, and taught physical education at the Red Star Military Academy in Leningrad. You'll work hard but it's worth the effort. Annual membership plus fees for classes required.

The Workout, Ltd.
22 E. Elm   280-9166
After 6 years in the business, this place has generated quite a reputation, partly because the studio has been used as photographic background for spreads in *Harper's Bazaar* and *New Body* magazines, and more importantly, because the classes are good. They draw a mixture of housewives, young professionals, and out-of-towners looking for a workout. Three types of classes are offered: body conditioning, weight training, and circuit training. All classes are by appointment only and you only pay for those you attend.

MARTIAL ARTS

Martial arts have been growing rapidly in popularity in Chicago, which has become one of the nation's leading centers of martial arts activity. These Chinese, Japanese, and Korean art forms all combine—with different degrees of emphasis—meditation, breath control, mental concentration, and the execution of a sequence of body movements. There are similarities among all the martial arts, but the primary difference distinguishing them is that some are more oriented to self-defense, while others are more passive and meditative.

The main martial arts, in order of most active to passive, are: **Karate,** which incorporates more aggressive practices and stresses efficiently struck blows; **Tae Kwon Do,** a Korean version of Karate that uses the feet and legs more than Karate; **Kung Fu,** an active, highly disciplined martial art, which you probably know best from the wonderful television series that ran opposite the Waltons; **Judo** and **Juijitsu,** which are Japanese arts similar to wrestling and considered to be more sports than self-defense; **Aikido,** a noncompetitive martial art emphasizing the training process and mental concentration; and **Tai Chi Chuan,** which is based on the principles of the I Ching (Chinese Book of Changes) and the philosophy of Tao, and is a system based on fluidity, flexibility, relaxation, and balance, all enabling you to release energy through strengthened bones and lengthened sinews rather than through tensed muscles. Of these categories, Judo is probably the most popular in Chicago.

Before you choose which form to study, you should do some research on the martial art of your choice because they are not only exercises, but also philosophies of life. In Karate, for example, many instructors use Zen, which teaches you how to lose your ego, enabling you to relax and strip away any emotions that might bias a rational decision. Most importantly, remember to ask around about your instructor. The quality of the education and instruction you will receive depends heavily on his or her quality and enthusiasm.

Lessons are usually not expensive (about $40-50 per month for lessons three times a week), and practice facilities should be free and open during convenient hours. Look in the yellow pages under martial arts for the large listing of the various schools. Remember that YMCAs often offer classes, usually at lower prices. Or consider the examples below as places to start.

Aikido Association of America
1016 W. Belmont   525-3141

American Jiu-Jitsu Institute
316 S. Wabash   922-8322
A large facility offering classes for all levels of skill and all ages. A diverse crowd is taught by Shunnichi Namba, an excellent instructor.

Cloud Hands
814 N. Franklin   944-0589
Instructors Tem Horwitz and Susan Kimmelman teach the classical Yang form of the art and their classes are very relaxing. They stress the meditative and centering qualities of Tai Chi.

Degerberg Academy of Martial Arts and Physical Fitness
4717 N. Lincoln   728-5300
Classes for all levels and ages in a great variety of martial arts as well as boxing and wrestling.

Irving Park YMCA
4251 W. Irving Park   777-7500
Judo lessons taught by Henry Okamura, a 7th degree black belt, in classes filled with people of all ages.

Japanese Karate Association International
5643 W. Irving Park Rd.   283-8200
Run by Mahmoud Bouyani. Shotokan Karate is taught here. This association is one of the original schools of Japan and is a well-respected organization. Classes for all skill levels.

Shaolin Kung Fu Temple
1639 W. Belmont   348-3322

Tai Chi Tao Center
433 South Blvd., Oak Park   386-0266
Provides individual training programs.

Many Judo and Karate tournaments are held periodically at Glenbard East High School in the western suburbs. Observe the fine techniques the competitors use.

FITNESS ALTERNATIVES

DANCE

Lou Conte Dance Studio
218 S. Wabash   461-0892
The official school of the Hubbard Street Dance Company. Offers classes in basic jazz, ballet, and tap dancing. No previous training required.

MoMing Dance and Arts Center
1034 W. Barry   472-7662
MoMing, translated from Cantonese, means "too beautiful to be named." MoMing's philosophy is that of mind and body working together; they stress the importance of direction and intelligent instruction. MoMing's forte is modern dance, but also offers classes in jazz, ballet, and dance improvisation, for all levels of ability. All classes are performed to live musical accompaniment--piano, drums, or guitar. Classes in jazz, ballet, tap, and creative movement are also offered for children 4-15 years of age.

Folk Dancing at the Old Town School of Folk Music

909 W. Armitage

525-7793

Folk dancing is great exercise, not to mention the cultural benefits you get as well as new steps to do at weddings. A group called the Chicago Barn Dance Company meets here every Monday night. The public is welcome to come for a low fee. Another international folk dance group meets Wednesday night; also open to the public for a low fee.

YOGA

Temple of Kriya Yoga

2414 N. Kedzie   342-4600

Yoga is not just learning to breathe properly and to stretch for flexibility. Its ultimate aim is to direct our thoughts so that we can study problems carefully and then make decisions clearly. Yoga relaxes the mind and body, allowing us to achieve integration, a feeling of oneness, which is really the natural state we all should be in. More advanced study also requires control and strength. The Temple of Kriya Yoga offers classes for beginners and advanced students Wednesday evenings for a modest fee.

OUTDOOR PARCOURSE

Lincoln Park, cinder running path south of Diversey to Montrose

This is a series of fitness stations (consisting of apparatus and a board with instructions and a diagram showing you what to do). Each station gives you the chance to do something different: test your balance, do some chin-ups or sit-ups, or stretch out some tight tendons.

HOME FITNESS

So you don't have any money in your budget for a health club, running makes you nauseous, and you lack the necessary coordination for dancing. Take heart—fitness is as close as your stairwell.

Though easily taken for granted, stair climbing is good exercise. It's a great calorie burner, though it's not the best aerobic exercise (unless you can set aside the time to really attack a particular stairwell). If you run out of stairs in your own home, you might try attacking the formidable stairways at Soldier Field Stadium at 12th Street and Lake Shore Drive. Unless an event is being held there, the public can use the stairs 9 am-4:30 pm Monday through Sunday.

Jumping rope is another excellent aerobic exercise you can do at home. Wear athletic shoes when jumping and try to jump on a cushioned surface. For a good workout, you have to jump quickly—a fast 70-100 steps per minute. Don't start at such a rate; rather, start slow and work your way up. Your goal should be a session of 10-15 minutes, three times per week.

SPORTS MEDICINE

Many hospitals now have sports medicine clinics, and a number of small independent clinics have sprung up throughout the city. Call one of the major hospital complexes (e.g., Presbyterian-St. Luke's, University of Illinois Medical Center) for information about their sports medicine programs, or look in the listings in the yellow pages.

—Margaret Brady

ABOUT THE AUTHORS

Born in Urbana and raised in Danville, Decatur, Elgin, and Northbrook, Illinois, **Sherry Kent** has called the city of Chicago (mostly the north side) home since 1979. Inspired by the songs of Steve Goodman, she came here in search of folk music, the blues, theater, and the city's rampant ethnicity, which offered her a chance (she thought) to shed her WASPy roots. Although she's never lived in Paris, France, she has lived in Paris, Illinois.

Mary Szpur, a former Ukrainian debutante, is a fiercely loyal Chicagoan who has lived here (mostly on the south side) for most of her life, except for sojourns in Urbana and Paris (France). She has worked as an editor, planning consultant, and an appraiser. More interesting, however, have been her stints as a leader of bicycling trips to eastern Europe, which were highlighted by being detained for stumbling inadvertently into a military installation in Czechoslovakia and witnessing gypsy fights in Romania.

The authors would like to thank the contributing writers and artists, as well as numerous friends and friends of friends for their help, especially: Jack Helbig for invaluable editorial help as well as comic relief, Stan Kent for his computer terminals and steadfast technical support under stress, Tom Palazzollo, Bonnie Jo Campbell, C.M., L.B., Tatiana Szpur for her good food, Robert Czeschin, Smiley, Orest Szpur, Ellen Wood, Jeff Hackett, Laurie Druse, Stuart Deutsch, George Schmidt, Charles Gene McDaniel, Tim Carpenter, Stu Kent, Stuart Pellish, Carol Reeder, Mike Miller, Dick Simpson, Daphne Burgess Brown, Chuck Thurow, Neil Parker, Victoria Benham, Alan Cohen, Matt Rhoades, Don Kingman, Pat Tegler, Aidan O'Connor, Bill Anderson, Steve Lafrenière, and Tem Horwitz.

CONTRIBUTORS

Julia Bell is a physician who worked in Chicago as an alternative high school teacher ten years ago. When she left, she swore she'd never return. Well, she came back to finish her residency training, which took her to three different Chicago hospitals over two years. She learned a lot about Chicago, medicine, and herself, and furthered her interests in public health, home health care, hospices, and the counseling needs of the ill and their families. Now she's moving on again. Bye.

Margaret Brady is. . .a poet, a writer, a runner. Like many people, she has a fear of fat. She hates her thighs. Maybe that's why she thought she could tackle a chapter on fitness. When she's not running, she's earning a living in public relations for Palos Community Hospital. She used to write features for the south suburban newspaper, *The Star*. Allen Ginsberg once said, "Don't hide the madness." She tries not to.

Chris Carr is an editor and writer with an abiding interest in the local music and entertainment scene.

Under his real name, **Bryen Charles** works on-air for a Chicago radio station. He loves music, but has a small record collection. . .because he prefers listening to radio.

Philip Charles was born on the south side, moved to the north side, and now lives on the west side of Chicago.

Pamala Goldberg recently graduated from National College of Education, and is now working in the book publishing department of the American Library Association. Her long years of experience as a nonparent provided crucial background data for her chapter on kids.

Margie Gonwa, a successful Chicago job-hunter, made a happy career change, though she feels the term "career evolution" more accurately describes her progression from a Northwestern BA in psychology and four years in youth social services, to an MBA from the University of Illinois at Chicago and a job with the Research and Development Division of Chicago's Department of Economic Development. There, she dreams up creative and innovative ways to retain and attract industrial jobs in Chicago. Margie is currently planning a year-long trip to Europe and points in the exotic Far East.

John J. Gorski has been a self-employed photographer in the Chicago area since 1975. He provides all types of professional photographic services.

Margaret Grau is a clinical social worker. Over the past 10 years she has worked as a psychotherapist, consultant, and facilitator of personal growth seminars. She currently practices in the Loop, working with adolescents, adults, couples, and families.

While Mayor Daley was spitting on dishonest Chicago reporters, **Marj Halperin** was honing her journalistic skills within spitting distance of Chicago (she can spit very far). In 1978, Halperin moved to Chicago as City Hall reporter for WXRT radio. Unlike Mayor Bilandic, Halperin survived the Blizzard of '79, and continued covering Chicago politics under two more mayors and one more radio station (WKQX-FM, a.k.a. "Q-101"). Now a freelancer, Halperin's work appears regularly in the *Chicago Sun-Times*, *Crain's Chicago Business*, and several national publications, as well as on NBC radio news and National Public Radio's "All Things Considered" and "Morning Edition" programs.

Linda Harper works as a family therapist in a community-based outpatient setting. She is particularly interested in family education and short-term, specialized programs for families in crisis or transition.

Chris Heim has so far survived a "normal" upbringing on the northwest side, an "abnormal" education in Hyde Park, and the deprivation of never having lived in Wrigleyville. Having emerged intact after 12 years in radio, she is now engaged in more pacific activities as a public relations consultant and freelance writer—*vox audita perit litera scripta manet*—all of which is merely an excuse to sustain a lifelong addiction to Chicago music, theater, and restaurants.

Jack Helbig is a freelance writer living in Chicago. Jack's fiction has been published in *The Chicago Literary Review*, the *Rave Review*, and *The Virginia Literary Review*, and, recently, his short story, "Dry Ice," was accepted by *Tomorrow* magazine. Also a performance artist, he has performed at The School of the Art Institute, CrossCurrents, Chicago Filmmakers, and the Randolph Street Gallery. Jack is currently working on a novel about Chicago called The Loves and Likes of Chandler McTeague. Look for him in Tom Palazzollo's new film, the as yet untitled sequel to *Caligari's Cure*.

J. H. Johnson is a theater producer, freelance writer, and columnist for the *Windy City Times*, where his weekly "Outspeak" column has featured interviews with newsmakers including Pulitzer Prize-winning playwright James Kirkwood, actress Betty White, TV journalist Linda Ellerbee, author

Quentin Crisp, and Yoko Ono. Johnson was formerly assistant for the *Chicago Tribune's* "Inc." column.

Glenn Kaupert is a lifetime Chicagoan and artist working for the *Chicago Tribune* for the last 10 years. In addition to his photography, he is an airbrush illustrator and photo retoucher.

Melanie Kubale is a researcher, a part-time writer, and a full-time woman.

Nancy Liskar would like to thank her parents for listening to "The Midnight Special" on WFMT when she was young and impressionable. As a member of the Jewish POCET steering committee, she helps produce the biannual Greater Chicago Jewish Folk Arts Festival. In addition to her interest in folk music, she is a violinist with the Northbrook Symphony Orchestra and senior publications editor at Northwestern University. Her contribution to *Sweet Home Chicago* is dedicated to the memory of Steve Goodman and Stan Rogers.

Barbara Macikas was born in Chicago and has considered moving away but hasn't found anyplace she likes better. She is an animal lover and a runner and her personal hero is Walter Payton.

Margaret Maloney. . .her life is full of *contes de la cigogne*.

Molly McQuade is a Chicago-educated writer and editor whose work has appeared in newspapers, magazines, books, and journals. Her writing has received two Illinois Arts Council Literary Awards, and was included in the P.E.N. Syndicated Fiction Project, cosponsored by the National Endowment for the Arts; it has also been nominated for several Pushcart Prizes.

Bobbye Middendorf is a writer, collagist, and bricoleur. She practices the arts of publishing and publicity on the side, and to pay the bills. She lives in one of Chicago's changing neighborhoods, near St. Mary of the Angels.

Alan Ness has a B.A. from Hampshire College, and a Bachelor of Architecture degree from the Boston Architectural Center. He has worked with John Macsai and Associates in the Loop. He is a member of the Dharmadhatu buddhist meditation group and has studied the architecture of meditation.

L. Dale Richesin is a Chicago area pastor, writer, and Cubs fan. He is the pastor of First Christian Church, located in Maywood. He has written several articles and edited many works, including *The Challenge of Liberation Theology: A First World Response* (published by Orbis Books), as well as the forthcoming Church Federation Church Directory.

Jan Rogatz, a partner in the Chicago-based firm of Johnson/Rogatz Associates, received a bachelor's degree in economics from the University of Illinois-Champaign and a master's degree in architecture from the University of Illinois-Chicago. Aside from devoting her life to architecture, Jan hopes to design a restroom paper towel dispenser which will prevent, instead of foster, water running down one's arms.

Wendy Schulenberg is a landscape architect for a major architectural firm and a sometime graphic artist. She's the only lifelong south sider she knows of who has never attended the St. Patrick's Day Parade. She toils long hours over a drafting board but prefers to spend her time on the tennis court or the golf course or searching for a bridge game.

Ron Schwartz is a clinical attorney at the law offices of Chicago-Kent College of Law, a clinical education program. He is a lifelong resident of a northwest suburb of Chicago.

Robert Skeist has lived in Chicago since 1966 and has worked with seniors groups throughout the city since 1977. He is a Registered Nurse with a Masters of Science degree in Human Services Administration. Rob knows the work of many of the groups mentioned in the Seniors chapter from personal contact and experience. For additional information, he gives special thanks to Marty Pick of the Chicago Department on Aging and Disability. Rob is Director of the White Crane Senior Health Center, a national speaker and consultant on health care and aging, and author of the Chicago Review Press book *To Your Good Health: A Practical Guide for Older Americans, Their Families and Friends*. He credits his Grandma Annie, 94 years old, for his commitment to the dignity and well-being of his elders.

Steve Spiegel is the proprietor of Mostly Chamber Music, a mail order classical sheet music business he operates out of his home. He is also a professional violinist, performing with other chamber musicians at weddings and parties.

Sir Andrew Peter Szpur might be famous in the future for something, but who knows for what, and does it really matter? He hopes to return to reality soon, when a public disclaimer for all previous actions shall be issued.

James Yood is Chicago and Midwest Editor of the *New Art Examiner*, and an art historian on the faculty of Loyola University.

Yvonne Zipter has lived in Chicago for about five years now. A copy editor for the Journals Division of the University of Chicago Press, she also does a column in *Chicago Outlines*, is the author of a collection of poetry (Refining the Art of Conversation—as yet unpublished), is working on a book about softball dykes for Firebrand Books in Ithaca, New York, and a young adult novel (The Unfolding of Rin), and plays softball, football, and volleyball.

INDEX